AQA Media Studies for A-level Revised Edition

Stephanie Hendry
Elspeth Stevenson

Approval message from AQA

This textbook has been approved by AQA for use with our qualification. This means that we have checked that it broadly covers the specification and we are satisfied with the overall quality. Full details of our approval process can be found on our website.

We approve textbooks because we know how important it is for teachers and students to have the right resources to support their teaching and learning. However, the publisher is ultimately responsible for the editorial control and quality of this book.

Please note that when teaching the *AQA Media Studies for A-level* course, you must refer to AQA's specification as your definitive source of information. While this book has been written to match the specification, it cannot provide complete coverage of every aspect of the course.

A wide range of other useful resources can be found on the relevant subject pages of our website: www.aqa.org.uk.

HODDER Education

Although every effort has been made to ensure that website addresses are correct at time of going to press, Hodder Education cannot be held responsible for the content of any website mentioned in this book. It is sometimes possible to find a relocated web page by typing in the address of the home page for a website in the URL window of your browser.

Hachette UK's policy is to use papers that are natural, renewable and recyclable products and made from wood grown in well-managed forests and other controlled sources. The logging and manufacturing processes are expected to conform to the environmental regulations of the country of origin.

To order, please visit www.hoddereducation.com or contact Customer Service at education@hachette.co.uk / +44 (0)1235 827827.

ISBN: 978 1 3983 8801 7

© Stephanie Hendry and Elspeth Stevenson 2024

First published in 2024 by Hodder Education,
An Hachette UK Company
Carmelite House
50 Victoria Embankment
London EC4Y 0DZ

www.hoddereducation.com

Impression number   10 9 8 7 6 5 4 3 2 1
Year   2028 2027 2026 2025 2024

All rights reserved. Apart from any use permitted under UK copyright law, no part of this publication may be reproduced or transmitted in any form or by any means, electronic or mechanical, including photocopying and recording, or held within any information storage and retrieval system, without permission in writing from the publisher or under licence from the Copyright Licensing Agency Limited. Further details of such licences (for reprographic reproduction) may be obtained from the Copyright Licensing Agency Limited, www.cla.co.uk

Cover photo © Pawel Horazy – stock.adobe.com
Typeset by Integra Software Services Pvt. Ltd
Produced by DZS Grafik, Printed in Slovenia

A catalogue record for this title is available from the British Library.

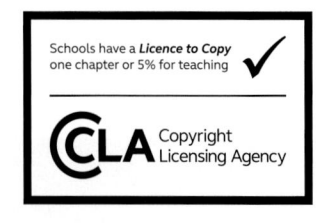

Contents

	How to use this book	v
Chapter 1	**Reading print media**	**2**
	1.1 Decoding print media texts using basic semiotics	2
	1.2 The technical codes and features used in print media texts	9
	1.3 Narrative organisation in print media texts	15
	1.4 Genre and print media texts	18
Chapter 2	**Reading audio-visual media**	**24**
	2.1 Technical codes and features used in moving image texts	24
	2.2 Applying semiotics to audio-visual media	26
	2.3 Narrative organisation in audio-visual and audio texts	35
	2.4 Genre and audio-visual and audio media	41
Chapter 3	**Reading digital media**	**49**
	3.1 Technical codes and features used in online texts	49
	3.2 Narrative organisation in digital media texts	54
	3.3 Computer games	59
	3.4 Intertextuality in digital media texts and computer games	65
Chapter 4	**Media language**	**68**
	4.1 What we have learned so far about media language	68
	4.2 How media language constructs and incorporates values and ideologies through ideological reading	77
	4.3 Structuralism and post-structuralism	78
	4.4 Postmodernism	82
Chapter 5	**Media representations**	**90**
	5.1 General theories of representation	91
	5.2 Constructing 'reality' through representation – Stuart Hall's encoding and decoding	98
	5.3 The relationship between representations and reality	101
	5.4 Stereotyping and counter-representations	106
	5.5 The ideological nature of common media representations and how we respond to them	110
	5.6 Theories of identity and the role of the mass media	111
	5.7 How industry contexts impact on representations	114
	5.8 Discourses around representation and ideology: gender studies and the mass media	114
	5.9 Ethnicity and postcolonial theory	125
	5.10 The social, historical and cultural dimensions of media representations	131
Chapter 6	**Media audiences**	**134**
	6.1 How the media industry targets audiences	135
	6.2 The impact of new technologies on patterns of media consumption	142
	6.3 Theories of media effects	145
	6.4 Cultivation theory	153

6.5	Reception theory	156
6.6	Fandom and the media	159
6.7	'End of audience' theory	167

Chapter 7 Media industries — 173

7.1	The ever-changing nature of the media	173
7.2	Distribution and circulation: what they are and why they vary across media	183
7.3	Issues of ownership and control	186
7.4	How the commercial or not-for-profit nature of media organisations shapes the content they produce	190
7.5	Regulation of media consumption in the UK	193
7.6	New technologies and media regulation	196
7.7	The rise of digital producers and distributors	199
7.8	Netflix: disrupting the TV industry	202
7.9	Marvel and diversification	207
7.10	News and social media	209

Chapter 8 Developing media studies skills — 215

8.1	Introduction	215
8.2	Analysis of media products and audience response	216
8.3	The social, cultural, political and economic role of the media	226
8.4	Essay writing	230

Chapter 9 Making media — 238

9.1	Producing different types of media	238
9.2	Print production	240
9.3	Producing and working with still images	246
9.4	Moving image production	252
9.5	Audio production	260
9.6	Approaches to e-media production	262

Chapter 10 The NEA — 273

10.1	Introduction to the NEA	273
10.2	Working on the NEA	276
10.3	A sample NEA brief	284

Chapter 11 The examinations — 290

11.1	Introduction to the A level examinations	290
11.2	Paper 1: Media One	292
11.3	Paper 2: Media Two	302

Glossary of key terms	**312**
Index	**329**
Acknowledgements	**334**

How to use this book

This book has been created to support your study of the theoretical framework of AQA A Level Media Studies. It explores all the key theories and debates highlighted in the specification associated with media language, representations, audience and industries.

This new edition of the book puts all the theory you will need in one place. It can be used in lessons to ensure a thorough introduction to each area. You can also use this book to support your studies at home for independent learning, and for revision as you approach your final exams.

Also included is guidance on how to approach the Non-examined Assessment (NEA), developing your skills in Media Studies, and preparing for examination.

How the chapters relate to the specification

■ Chapter 1

This chapter introduces you to the techniques used to study print media products. It also offers some introduction to narrative and genre theories and how we can apply these to print media, as well as introducing the concept of intertextuality in print media.

This section is of particular use in studying the advertising and magazine Close Study Products on your course. Some of the techniques used to explore print media product are also transferable skills you will use when studying your online, social and participatory CSPs.

■ Chapter 2

In this chapter you will be exploring the technical codes of audiovisual media. You will further develop your understanding of narrative, genre and intertextuality.

This part of the book effectively supports your study of television and advertising. It can also be used to support your learning and analysis of video content in online, social and participatory CSPs, and computer games.

■ Chapter 3

This chapter explores what makes digital media products distinctive in their use of media language, and helps you to understand how the technical codes and theories you have encountered in earlier chapters may be successfully applied to CSPs such as websites, computer games and social media content.

■ Chapter 4

By this time, you will have a good understanding of how to analyse the technical codes of a range of media products, as well as how to apply theoretical approaches to narrative and genre. This chapter develops your understanding of media language and contextualises it within movements in critical thinking known as structuralism, poststructuralism and postmodernism.

■ Chapter 5

Media language is used to construct meanings for audiences – to represent events, places, issues, ideas and groups. In this chapter we will consider how representations are constructed using a range of critical approaches and key thinkers.

This chapter is useful for all the CSPs that require the study of media language and close textual analysis to support your learning.

■ Chapter 6

In this chapter, we will explore how the media targets and attempts to reach audiences and how audiences respond to and interpret media products. We will also consider how audiences participate in mass media.

This chapter is particularly important for the full CSPs that require study of the whole theoretical framework, as well as for newspapers and radio CSPs.

■ Chapter 7

Here we focus on media industries, and the ways in which they produce, distribute and circulate media products. We will consider the relationship between audiences and producers, the economic issues that motivate industries and the way industries respond to changes in the media landscape.

This knowledge will be most applicable to your study of radio, newspapers, film industries and the full CSPs.

■ Chapter 8

This section of the book advises on how to develop the media skills you have acquired so far. It explores the types of activities you can undertake to develop both production and critical thinking skills as you progress throughout the course.

■ Chapter 9

The practicalities of media production are covered here, and some general information on the principles of producing work across print, e-media and audiovisual production. We will be considering how we can successfully replicate the codes and conventions and common media forms using media technologies.

■ Chapter 10

In this chapter you will be given an introduction to the NEA and how to select the brief that's best for you. You will think about how best to release your product through media technologies and how to write your Statement of Intent to accompany it.

■ Chapter 11

Here we provide an overview of the examinations you will take at the end of the course – their structure, content and assessment objectives. You will also consider how to build your skills in comparing CSPs. We will also explore how to demonstrate your knowledge of the theoretical framework through focused use and selection of examples from your CSPs.

Features in the book

■ Apply it

These sections in each chapter allow you to consider ideas in light of your own media knowledge and experience, and to test out newly acquired learning.

■ Key terms

These are highlighted throughout on first use and include all essential vocabulary from the specification. To find out the meaning of word and see it used in a sentence, look for the key terms boxes on each page.

■ Stretch and challenge

One of these features is included per chapter to help you to look beyond your initial learning to further ideas and concepts.

The authors of the book would like to wish you all the best on your journey through your A Level Media Studies course and in developing your academic understanding of this aspect of popular culture, and what it can tell us about the world we live in today.

■ Quick questions

These questions will help you extend your application of the ideas being discussed. (Suggested answers to quick questions are available at: **www.hoddereducation.com/AQAMediaStudiesRevised**.)

How to use this book

Chapter 1: Reading print media

Enabling ideas

The following 'enabling ideas' from the specification are introduced in this chapter:

3.4.1.1 Semiotics
- sign
- signifier
- signified
- dominant signifier
- icon (iconic)
- index (indexical)
- code
- symbol
- anchorage
- ideology.

Barthes' ideas and theories on semiotics:
- signification
- denotation
- connotation
- myth.

3.4.1.2 Narratology

Todorov's ideas and theories on narratology:
- narrative structure
- equilibrium
- disruption
- new equilibrium.

Narratology:
- narrative codes.

Note: Throughout the chapter we will be considering how audiences respond to and interpret these aspects of media language, since without the audience to interpret meaning there is none.

🔗 You can read more about structuralism and post-structuralism in Chapter 4, which also explains their relationship as critical approaches with another enabling idea, postmodernism.

→ What you will learn in this chapter

Chapter 1: Reading print media covers:
- how print media language can communicate multiple meanings and combine to influence meaning
- the common codes and conventions of print media forms and products
- the contribution of narrative to meaning in print media texts
- the codes and conventions of print media genres
- what we mean by intertextuality in print media.

1.1 Decoding print media texts using basic semiotics

Understanding how the combination of elements of media language influence meaning is a crucial part of learning to 'read' the media. We will be building this knowledge and understanding based on the examples of the forms of unseen or Close Study Product Media you will encounter on the course over the next three chapters. First, we will be considering print media.

One of the key approaches you will be using throughout the course is **semiotic analysis**. Semiotics is the study of signs in a culture. These might be any aspect of print, audio-visual or digital media, including images, sounds and language. Semiotics is a complex field, and at A-level you will not be expected to have an exhaustive knowledge of the subject, but you will need to have a working knowledge of some of the basics. Some of the principles of semiotics you will use repeatedly; others you will use less frequently.

> **TIP** ✓
>
> When you use semiotic analysis to help you *decode* a text, you should use it alongside other elements of the theoretical framework and terminology associated with each field. Some of the introduction you will find here is applicable across all the media forms that you will be studying; other aspects are specific to print media. In Chapters 2 and 3 we will consider how you can modify the approach in this first chapter to suit different mass media forms. As you begin each of those chapters, it is suggested you re-read this section to help you internalise the approach.

■ The origins of semiotic theory

Semiotic theory is the study of signs in our culture and how they communicate meaning. Semiotics is related to **linguistics** and is part of two wider fields in **critical theory** known as **structuralism** and **post-structuralism**.

> **Key terms**
>
> **critical theory** an approach to the study of culture that considers how various forces are at work in its production
> *Critical theorists focused on gender have tended to focus on representations of women in popular culture.*
>
> **linguistics** the study of structural aspects of language, with many sub-specialisms
> *A linguistic analysis of the lexical codes allows us to read the headline as being in favour of the government's move.*
>
> **post-structuralism** later work on structuralism that both extends its ideas and critiques its approach
> *This emphasis on the multiple meanings of the car as a sign is post-structuralist.*
>
> **semiology** Saussure's term for the study of signs, which he regarded as being similar to a science
> *A semiological reading can be determined by breaking down the complex sign into its component signifers + signifieds.*
>
> **structuralism** a way of analysing culture that prioritises its form/structure over function according to codified systems
> *A structuralist reading of the text would highlight the repetition of the conventions of adverts for grooming products.*

Before we learn more about some of the key terms we will use in semiotic analysis of products, it is worth exploring where these enabling ideas come from. Ferdinand de Saussure was a Swiss linguist and is considered by most to be one of the founders of semiotics, although the ideas that informed his work have much earlier roots. Saussure is not a named key thinker on the course, but you will be using his terminology regularly in your analyses of your Close Study Products. Saussure viewed semiotics as a scientific discipline, although it is not usually regarded in this way by modern theorists. Because of this, his thinking applied to reading signs is sometimes referred to as **semiology**, although it is fine to use the term semiotics.

Saussure believed that linguistics provided a good model for application to wider cultural phenomena. Written or spoken language is the primary form of communication between humans, but it is not the only form. The mass media are forms of communication that deploy traditional language structures, but also are full of other codes. Semiotics allows us to access these other codes and to understand the sense that audiences make of them.

At its simplest, Saussure's model of the sign and signification process can be illustrated as follows: *sign = signifier + signified*

It is usually drawn as shown on the right.

It would work as follows, where the word 'tree' conjures in the reader's mind the tree as a real-world object:

A signifier cannot exist without a signified – the two parts of the sign work in tandem. The mental concept (the signified) is almost simultaneously triggered the moment a signifier (the symbol or real-world object) is perceived. This element of Saussure's work remains at the heart of how we use semiotics in media studies. The sign itself can be thought of as the overall effect of the signifier and signified combined.

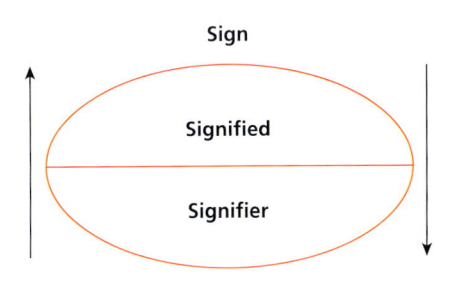

1.1 Decoding print media texts using basic semiotics

Signs can be simple or complex. Some print advertising uses simpler signs – which can be very effective. Most media texts you analyse can be regarded as complex signs, comprised of many signifiers plus signified which combine into a larger overall signification of the sign.

EXAMPLE: The open or closed shop

In his book *Semiotics: The Basics*, Daniel Chandler gives the example of an 'OPEN' sign encountered by someone at a shop door. Because the word 'open' (the signifier) has a context – being on the shop door – the signified is that the shop is open for business. Similarly, a 'closed' sign would signify the opposite.

Apply it

Depending on how confident you feel with this idea, either:

- think of five examples of simple sign construction using Chandler's example of an open sign on a shop door

or

- use the internet to search the phrase 'Examples of semiotic analysis' to find some simple examples of the signification process and how it makes simple signs.

Key term

arbitrary relationship a relationship between signifier and signified that is not obvious (e.g. the word 'cat' written using the Roman alphabet and our mental image of the animal)
The shaka is an arbitrary sign unless the cultural meaning of its association with surf culture and friendly intent is understood.

For the signification process to work in a culture, users have to agree on the signified. The relationship between the signifier and signified is not always obvious unless you have prior knowledge of the role of the signifier in a culture, and this is sometimes referred to as an **arbitrary relationship**. A good example of this is European languages that use the Roman alphabet, which only makes sense to its users because they all agree what the letters and words mean – there is no literal relationship between the shape of the letters that form the words and the meaning of the word. In European culture, we inherit the arbitrary meanings when we learn language from our parents and those around us. However, some other languages use lettering systems that do bear some resemblance to their meaning in the real world – for instance, the origins of the Chinese characters for tree, water and moon are in pictographic representations of these objects. In most cultures, children inherit the arbitrary meanings of signs when learning language from their parents and those around them.

At the same time, we inherit the agreed meaning of a sign. Signs in popular culture are more complex than the meanings of words and, because of this, not all users may agree completely on their meaning. Their intended meaning, though, is usually understood by most, with only subtle variations in the decoding process.

Apply it

Research a text from a culture you are not familiar with. Depending on your background, for example, you could choose a trailer or digital advert for a South Korean television show from any network, such as K-Dramas on Netflix. Which aspects of the text can you understand within your own cultural frame of reference? Which are more difficult to understand?

EXAMPLE: Advertising in different cultures and the signification process

Seeing how a familiar product is advertised in another culture can be very interesting. Some elements of the branding are likely to remain recognisable, whereas others will be better matched to regional signifying practices. This could include changes in language used, photography, gender representations and other factors. This article from *Insider* website demonstrates the sheer variety of different images used by Coca-Cola, a truly globalised brand, around the world:

https://tinyurl.com/4eah4a66

🔗 To further your understanding of how and why audiences may read media products differently, see Chapter 6: Media audiences, reception theory.

CHAPTER 1 READING PRINT MEDIA

Like Saussure, US-born scientist and philosopher Charles Peirce is credited with making some of the most significant contributions to the field of early semiotics, although his ideas differ slightly from Saussure's.

The categories he defined were:

- **Arbitrary signs**, or **symbolic signs**, where there is no physical relationship between the signifier and its concept. Language, which we discussed earlier while looking at Saussure, falls into this category.
- **Iconic signs** look like their signified, making the relationship between the two very straightforward and obvious.
- **Indexical signs**, where there is a causal relationship between the signifier and signified.

EXAMPLE: Peirce's three signs

Daniel Chandler gives some excellent examples of all three of these categories of signs in *Semiotics: The Basics*.

- Symbolic signs – numbers, Morse code, traffic lights
- Iconic signs or icon – portraits, a scale model, sound effects
- Indexical signs or index – footprints, a skin rash, a weathervane

△ A symbolic sign (left) and an indexical sign (right)

We mentioned earlier that media texts are complex signs. One of **Roland Barthes'** contributions to the field of semiotics was to study more closely the relationship between **denotation** and **connotation** in the signification process. Barthes believed there was a layered process taking place, which he referred to as the **order of signification**. This begins with denotation, which is often thought of as the literal meaning of the sign, although many semioticians argue that this is more complex.

Connotation is the meaning arising from the sign. According to Barthes, a simple unit of signifier + signified can result in just identification – the recognition of an agreed meaning of a sign. We saw this earlier with the example of the word 'tree' and the concept it signifies. This is the **first order of signification**. The **second order of signification** is layered so that a signified becomes a new signifier – an intricate process, but one that describes very well the processes we all undertake when reading a sign as complex as a media text. Several layers of signification may all be operating at once, which gives rise to much more complex meanings than simply understanding the meaning of a word.

Quick questions

1. Give an example of a sign where the relationship between signifier and signified is arbitrary.
2. What factors can affect how well you understand a sign in a culture?
3. Explain the relationship between signifier and signified in a sign.

🔗 For more on Barthes see section 1.3: Narrative organisation in print media texts.

KEY THINKER

Roland Barthes (1915–80) was a French theorist whose work on myth extended his exploration of semiotics and structuralism. He is known for his influence on literary criticism and study of Western popular culture.

Key terms

first order of signification the recognition of the agreed meaning of a sign
Using the first order of signification, the uniform tells us he is a military man.

second order of signification a layered and more subtle interpretation of a complex sign
The non-verbal codes of the soldier and debris and dirt on his uniform suggest compassion but also battle-weariness.

1.1 Decoding print media texts using basic semiotics

EXAMPLE: Barthes' magazine front cover

Barthes created a now-famous example of a magazine front cover, *Paris Match*, to illustrate his ideas. Barthes encountered this text on a routine trip to the barber, but his thinking about it became a well-known model of how to apply his ideas about the orders of signification.

The magazine cover depicted a young black soldier saluting the French flag – you can readily find this image through an image search for 'Barthes Paris Match'.

In his example, Barthes decoded the image from Paris Match in the following way:

Signifier 1: The colours and shades of ink in a specific order.

Signified 1: A young black male wearing a hat.

Sign 1 is therefore: A young black male salutes a French flag.

Signified 2: Frenchness and the military.

Sign 2/myth: French colonisation is acceptable because the people colonised accept French military authority and the flag.

Another of Barthes' contributions to the field was the concept of myth, which remains very important in any study of culture. The way in which Barthes uses the term is distinct from the meaning of myth as something which is 'false' – a cultural myth is neither true nor false. It is a group of shared cultural connotations that reflect a **dominant ideology**. Cultural myths are one way in which we share ideas about ourselves and make sense of our society. They are part of a higher level of signification. Myths help to make the way things are in societies seem natural, so can be viewed as an important contributor to ideology. Barthes understood clearly that myths could be and often were created in society to political ends. He believed that ideology could be thought of as the third order of signification. Likewise, many myths about consumerism serve to generate economic revenue for big businesses. It is important to understand that Barthes uses the term myth not to mean something that is false – a myth can be true or false – rather that it is a way of rationalising daily life around us, and of connecting with our culture at almost every level.

Key term

third order of signification the relationship between the first and second orders of signification and myths and ideology
The positioning of the soldier in the aftermath of the attack signifies an ideological reading about the role of British forces in the conflict as peacekeepers.

Apply it

Choose three print advertisements for contrasting products. Can you identify any myths in our culture that they appear to draw on to promote the products? Consider how denotation and connotation draw on myths, and how each advert perpetuates these. For each advert, try to use around 50 words to sum up your ideas. This will help you to express your ideas clearly and succinctly.

EXAMPLE: Omo soap powder

In his book, *Mythologies*, Barthes looks at the advertising of a soap powder brand, *Omo*. Specifically, he considers how the separation of dirt from cleanliness draws on ideas about perfection, and the ideas of depth (efficacy) and foaminess (luxury). These combine powerfully to create a persuasive message for the audience, interacting with myths about cleanliness – that the advertised product will lead to a greater standard of overall whiteness or cleanliness. This would have been powerful for the female target audience at the time, part of whose identity was often formulated on their outward ability to perform domestic roles with ease and effectiveness. This helped to create a 'false desire' for the product, which the women are persuaded will help them to achieve this.

CHAPTER 1 READING PRINT MEDIA

Enabling ideas

Semiotic theory and their applications in print media analysis

As we discussed earlier, semiotics is a complex academic field and a sub-discipline of cultural analysis. There are many terms associated with its use, but the ones listed below are the ones you are likely to find yourself using most frequently.

Enabling idea	Explanation and application in print media
anchorage	Like an anchor keeps a ship in place, anchorage fixes meaning. In print media texts, anchorage consists of lexical codes that firmly establish the connection between an image and the reason it has been used. They may appear as slogans, copy, headlines or captions accompanying an image. This can add value to the use of the image and maximise its impact. *'The anchorage "best dressed" fixes the meaning that it is the clothing we should pay attention to in the image.'*
arbitrary or symbolic sign	A sign that does not have an obvious connection with what it represents, but the meaning of which is agreed on by users of a particular code. Saussure referred to these types of sign as **symbolic**. Many road signs can be regarded as symbolic if you need to have read the *Highway Code* to understand what they mean. *'The logo itself is an arbitrary sign since there is no iconic reference to the product itself.'*
code	A system used to create meaning. Most forms of meaning production have specific codes: frameworks that are used to encode meaning. It is vital that codes are shared and their meanings agreed upon across a culture or they cannot be decoded. Where these are limited to a specific mode of expression in media productions or forms, they are referred to collectively as technical codes. The various kinds of code used in print media analysis are described in more detail in section 1.2: The technical codes and features used in print media texts. *'The use of high-street fashion dress codes for the group signifies their youth.'*
connotation	The meaning evoked by a sign – what it makes us think. It can be thought of as the end result of reading a sign, the mental image we have of its meaning. *'The use of the lion motif within the brand connotes strength, regal qualities and power.'*
decoding	When audiences interpret a text in order to make meaning. *'The audience will decode this image and lexical coding using their knowledge of mental health issues.'*
denotation	May be understood as the literal meaning of a component of a code. You can also use the term as a verb, saying that an element of an image denotes – but be careful. The term is easily confused with **connotes**, which you would more commonly be using in meaningful semiotic analysis rather than description. *'The trees denote plant life.'*
dominant ideology	In Marxist critical thinking, this is the values, opinions and attitudes of the majority in a society which may also serve the interests of those in power. It is useful to be able to identify dominant ideologies when reading media texts because they help us consider the role their meanings may play in people's lives and how they relate to them. *'The image of the woman challenges dominant ideologies about motherhood and perfection.'*
encoding	The process of creating intended meanings within a text. *'Derogatory attitudes to fans are encoded through use of the term "potty".'*

1.1 Decoding print media texts using basic semiotics

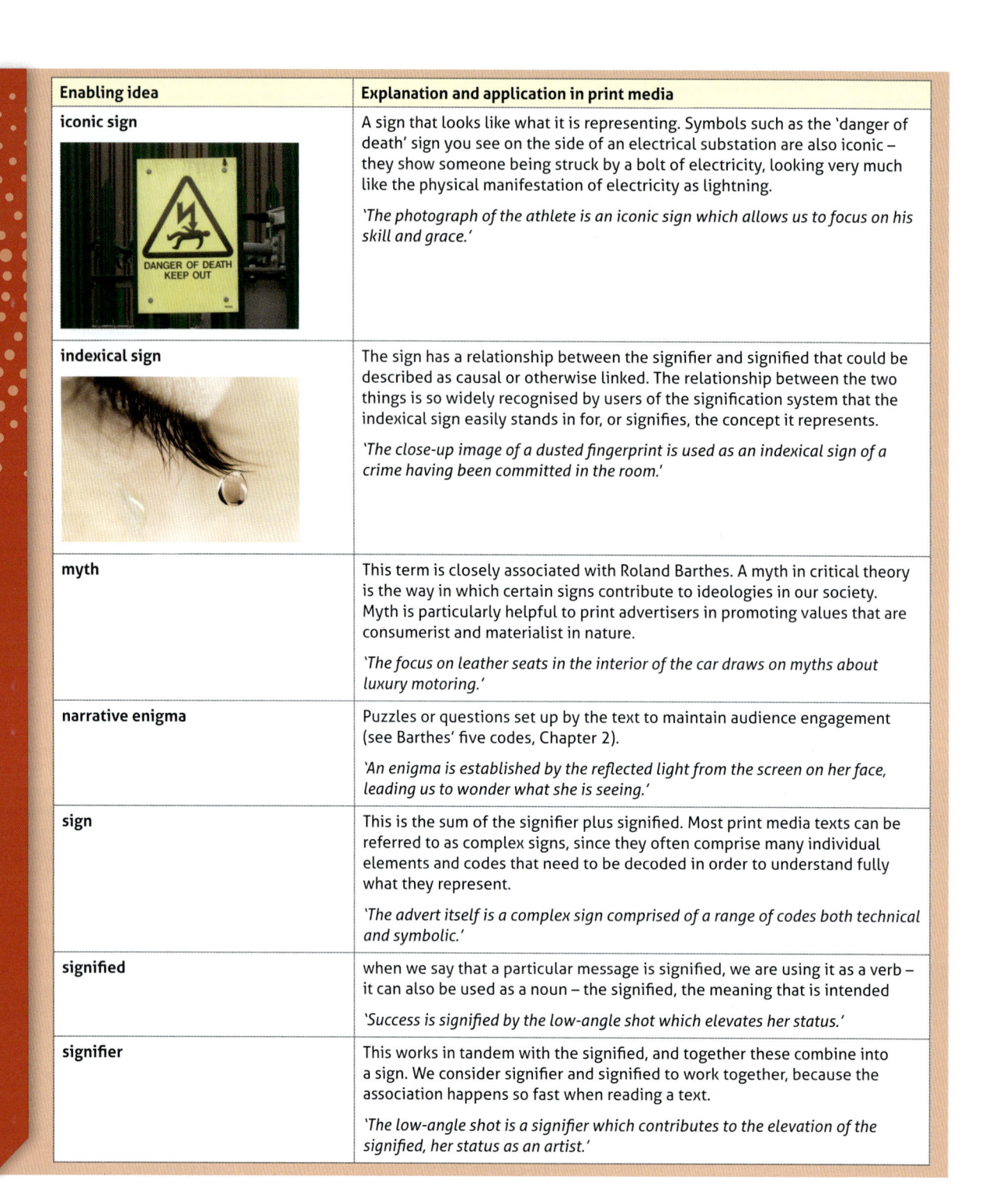

Enabling idea	Explanation and application in print media
iconic sign	A sign that looks like what it is representing. Symbols such as the 'danger of death' sign you see on the side of an electrical substation are also iconic – they show someone being struck by a bolt of electricity, looking very much like the physical manifestation of electricity as lightning. *'The photograph of the athlete is an iconic sign which allows us to focus on his skill and grace.'*
indexical sign	The sign has a relationship between the signifier and signified that could be described as causal or otherwise linked. The relationship between the two things is so widely recognised by users of the signification system that the indexical sign easily stands in for, or signifies, the concept it represents. *'The close-up image of a dusted fingerprint is used as an indexical sign of a crime having been committed in the room.'*
myth	This term is closely associated with Roland Barthes. A myth in critical theory is the way in which certain signs contribute to ideologies in our society. Myth is particularly helpful to print advertisers in promoting values that are consumerist and materialist in nature. *'The focus on leather seats in the interior of the car draws on myths about luxury motoring.'*
narrative enigma	Puzzles or questions set up by the text to maintain audience engagement (see Barthes' five codes, Chapter 2). *'An enigma is established by the reflected light from the screen on her face, leading us to wonder what she is seeing.'*
sign	This is the sum of the signifier plus signified. Most print media texts can be referred to as complex signs, since they often comprise many individual elements and codes that need to be decoded in order to understand fully what they represent. *'The advert itself is a complex sign comprised of a range of codes both technical and symbolic.'*
signified	when we say that a particular message is signified, we are using it as a verb – it can also be used as a noun – the signified, the meaning that is intended *'Success is signified by the low-angle shot which elevates her status.'*
signifier	This works in tandem with the signified, and together these combine into a sign. We consider signifier and signified to work together, because the association happens so fast when reading a text. *'The low-angle shot is a signifier which contributes to the elevation of the signified, her status as an artist.'*

Apply it

Choose two print media texts. Write a paragraph of semiotic analysis based on each text. Try to use at least five terms from the list in the table above in each paragraph, looking back at the examples given to check you have used each word in context correctly. Highlight the terms you used to help reinforce their use in your memory.

Quick questions

1. Give one example each of an iconic, indexical and symbolic sign.
2. What different forms might anchorage take in a print media product?
3. Explain the concept of myth in no more than 15 words.
4. Explain the difference between denotation and connotation.

In Chapter 2: Reading audio-visual media, we will encounter two further important enabling ideas relating to semiotics – paradigm and syntagm.

CHAPTER 1 READING PRINT MEDIA

1.2 The technical codes and features used in print media texts

In the previous section, we talked about codes as a group of conventions that are used to organise and create meaning. As well as semiotic terms, there are some other codes and features that are likely to be frequently used when analysing print media texts. Other terms, some of which have their origins in the industry, are specific to one or two media forms.

In this section, we will explore the relevant codes and more general features first. Some of these codes will appear again in Chapter 2, but in a slightly different context as their usage varies depending on the media form. In this chapter, we will also look at the features peculiar to each main print form you will study on the course: magazines and print advertisements.

■ Dress code

Dress code forms an essential part of the signification process in any print media text. The clothing worn by anyone can be used to signify meanings about their social status, lifestyle, age and many other factors. We need to look closely at the details of how the clothing is being worn, any accessories or details, the colours, whether they coordinate, therefore connoting more simple ideas, or clash and so suggest contradictory meanings and conflict. We should also consider to what extent they help meet audience expectations.

■ Colour codes

Colour codes may be inherent in the environment in which a photograph is taken, particularly if it is photo-journalism. Colours may still be subject to manipulation such as colour correction or saturation of the whole or part of an image in post-production. The extent to which this is acceptable is a grey area of **ethics** in photo-journalism and documentary photography. In the case of photo-journalism, colour codes are part of the factors considered in the editorial process, along with framing and cropping. For magazine shoots or print advertising, colour codes are often derived from a limited palette that strongly signifies a mood, theme or atmosphere.

■ Framing or cropping

Where everything about the subject is within the control of the producers, such as on a magazine or studio/location shoot for a print advert, framing is used to carefully construct meaning. Everything that appears in the frame is styled to contribute to the meaning of the sign. In the case of photo-journalism, photographs are not only selected for the best match of meaning to accompany the article, but also frequently are cropped as a further way of anchoring meaning. Cropping a photograph has the power to significantly change the way in which it is read and, like processing of colour, can be controversial.

■ Props, décor and location

Similar issues arise with analysing props, décor and location as when you are studying framing and cropping. Remember to consider every tiny detail of image content, and treat it as though it has significance initially, even if you later discard any elements that seem incidental to the dominant reading or don't contribute much overall to your analysis.

△ The visual expression, eye-line and posture in this photo are all non-verbal codes that this girl is probably upset

Non-verbal codes

Gestural codes, facial expression, eye-line and posture are all significant **non-verbal codes** in print media images. In combination these can have a subtle or powerful effect. Make sure you look at the whole-body language, rather than just focusing on one aspect of meaning. Consider any apparent communication implied between multiple subjects in the frame as well as the **direct/indirect address** of the audience.

Key terms

cropping	the removal of sections of an image to emphasise its subject or remove clutter or unwanted signs
	The image of the politician on stage has been cropped to show them alone.
décor	selection of the appearance of interior locations
	The décor is shabby, signifying poverty.
direct/indirect address	the way in which a text addresses its audience; for example, where a subject is gazing into the lens of the camera, this could be said to be a direct mode of address
	The actor's mode of address is direct, using an eye-level shot so we feel they are knowable.
framing	careful selection of what will appear in a final shot
	The paparazzi shot is framed to emphasise her reaction to the encounter above others.
location	choice of place for an exterior shoot
	The choice of location of a farmyard signifies that he is at home in any environment and has a highly adaptable personality.
non-verbal codes	in human subjects, this is facial expression, posture, body language and some aspects of appearance and personal expression such as tattoos and hair
	'The portrait of the singer with an angry expression and close-up photography that emphasises his body modifications combine to signify the metal genre.'
props	items that are consciously added to a shoot because they contribute to meaning
	Eighteenth-century furniture is used to lend a nostalgic, whimsical feel to the photoshoot.

■ Camera positioning and proxemics/para-proxemics

The positioning of the subject within the frame is vital in communicating meaning, as is the hierarchy of positioning of multiple people within the frame. Studying these relative positions and their meanings is known as **proxemics**. Another consideration that affects the mode of address is sometimes known as **camera proxemics** or **para-proxemics**. This is the technique whereby the shot selected affects the perceived distance between the subject and the audience, created by their proximity to the camera and how much of their body is shown. This creates an imagined relationship between the subject and the audience.

CHAPTER 1 READING PRINT MEDIA

■ Typographical codes

The font style chosen for various elements of the design are **typographical codes**, which can signify **house style** in a magazine – in fact, many magazines use **proprietary fonts** that contribute to **brand recognition**.

■ Lexical codes

Lexical codes work in combination with other codes, contributing to the anchoring of meaning in **captions** and headlines in magazines and newspapers, and consistently being selected from a vast array of different choices available to producers to try and ensure a preferred reading. It isn't within the scope of the course to conduct a linguistic analysis of a whole article, and neither do you have time – but there are clear cases where selecting for comment some of the wording used, and identifying how it contributes to meaning, is going to form an essential part of a balanced analysis. Other examples of lexical codes might include the **copy** written about the product in a print advertisement or a slogan for a brand.

■ Graphical elements

Graphical elements is a broad term that encompasses many different features and techniques. Whenever you notice a design feature, computer-generated, that does not fit comfortably into any other category, you are considering a graphical element. These may be used in a minimal way, or they may dominate a print media text. They may be used on their own as a main feature, or to add to photographs – they can be used alongside typography and add to its effect (logos are a great example of this in action) or constitute a whole, computer-generated scene or image. Many of the other aspects of technical code listed above are applied to graphical elements to signify the appropriate meaning.

> **To see the terminology of print media analysis in action turn to Chapter 8: Developing media studies skills, which models how to approach close analysis of products.**

Apply it

Collect one example from each of the two main print media forms you study on the course: a magazine feature and a print advertisement. Make notes on the contribution of all the features described on these pages.

Write a 500-word case study of each example, exploring how it uses the technical codes and features of print media language.

Quick questions

1. What is the difference between proxemic and camera or para-proxemics in describing relationships in print media products?
2. Give three examples of non-verbal codes.

Key terms

brand recognition	when an audience becomes familiar with a brand
	The pack shot contributes to brand recognition.
camera proxemics	sometimes known as para-proxemics, this is the distance/relationship between subject and audience
	Distance is implied in the relationship using para-proxemics.
caption	written anchorage accompanying an image and fixing its meaning
	The caption for the image constructs him as a victim.
copy	the term used for body text in a newspaper, print advertisement or magazine
	The copy is situated in the left side third, drawing the eye.

1.2 The technical codes and features used in print media texts

graphical elements	any graphics generated that do not consist of pure typography or photography	
	The graphical elements include oceanic elements of illustration to signify his connection with the sea.	
house style	the way in which codes combine in print media to produce a familiar and recognisable brand	
	The typographical codes and graphical features throughout the magazine form a consistent house style.	
lexical codes	words selected to generate specific effect	
	The choice of 'adventurous' and 'death-defying' in the lexical coding of the headline for the article emphasise his masculinity.	
proprietary fonts	fonts that are developed exclusively for a particular publication	
	The magazine uses a proprietary font for its headlines, which is a distinctive part of its branding and house style.	
proxemics	power relationships signified by relative positioning within the frame	
	The positioning of mother sightly in front of daughter signifies her protective role.	
typographical codes	selection of font and graphical choices	
	The typographical codes signify the brand values of the magazine and its arthouse aesthetic.	

■ Magazines

Generic variation, particularly evident in house style, is considerable across magazines. Despite this, you will find that there are certain consistent design elements that recur. Your analysis will be stronger if you understand what these features are before you begin to account for their specific meanings.

Front covers of magazines will include a **masthead**. This is the name of the magazine and may also be associated with a **strapline**. Straplines sometimes make claims about the merits of the magazine or simply give more information about its contents. Usually, at least some of the most appealing content in that issue will be picked out in the form of **coverlines**, which entice the audience by letting them see the scope of articles included – particularly the lead article. Coverlines frequently use a personal mode of address and help to signify the genre codes. The middle area of the left-hand third of the cover is known as the **sweet spot**, where the eye tends to rest. It is sometimes used to engage the audience by positioning either a prominent coverline such as a feature article, an important element of an image, or a **puff** – a feature that may be a promotion or other item that adds perceived value to the purchase. Commonly, the whole of the **left side third** is considered prime space when attracting the consumer's attention.

Menu strips are another common feature. They are usually found at the bottom of the page, although variations in house style and edition may see them moved to the top (sometimes referred to as the skyline) or, less commonly, positioned as a side bar. Menu strips may have different functions, but their most common use is to promote familiarity by displaying regular content. A large proportion of the cover will be image or images. This may consist of one large **primary image**. It is equally possible that you may have a range of images with a sense of hierarchy in size and positioning, or one primary image with further **secondary images**.

Key terms

coverline	feature and secondary articles promoted on the front of a magazine
	The coverlines all connote positive messages about the audience's capacity for self-improvement.
left side third	area of a magazine cover where key content is usually positioned
	The majority of the coverlines are positioned in the left side third to emphasise value for money.
masthead	the name of a magazine
	The masthead has a distinctive typographical style connoting technology.
primary image	the image that predominates visually where more than one has been used
	The primary image has been selected to send a powerful message about the environment.
puff	a call-out feature, often circular in shape, that draws attention to a price or promotion on a front cover
	The puff bleeds over the masthead to draw attention to the publication's supposed value for money.
secondary image	an image that appears to be hierarchically less important when more than one is used
	The secondary image focuses on the social aspects of the activity.
strapline	sometimes accompanies the masthead on a magazine – a promotional slogan
	The strapline states that the magazine is the most 'original' of its genre.
sweet spot	position to the centre left of a single page of print media, where the eye naturally falls
	The coverline is positioned in the sweet spot to draw attention to the feature article.

EXAMPLE: Variations in how technical codes are used across contrasting magazine covers

Despite wide variance in subject matter and target audience, these covers deploy the same technical codes adapted to suit their house style – each is still instantly recognisable as a magazine.

1.2 The technical codes and features used in print media texts

Key terms

advertorial an extended print advertisement that may resemble editorial in its use of codes, but will be clearly labelled 'advertisement' under UK media law.
The magazine includes a number of paid partnerships in the form of advertorials for health products.

body text the majority of article text, usually at the smallest size, appearing in a magazine or newspaper
There is a high proportion of body text to image in the article, signifying the audience is prepared to read to acquire the specialist knowledge it provides.

composite image presentation of images using a montage effect
The poster uses a composite image to signify character hierarchies.

drop cap an enlarged first letter – an attention-grabbing aesthetic device
The use of a drop cap adds prominence to the opening section of body text and adds to its visual appeal as an entry point to the article.

entry point a visually appealing and prominent spread in a magazine
There is a use of aesthetically-pleasing and dramatic landscape photography at the entry point.

mode of address how the text 'speaks' to the audience – can be formal or informal – created by use of codes
The mode of address is personal and the lexical coding addresses the reader directly as 'you'.

pull quote excerpt from interview enlarged as a device to hook the reader in and for visual contrast with body text
Pull quotes are used to construct an emphasis on the emotional response of the celebrity to the event.

slug a line in larger print introducing a feature that acts as a hook
The slug draws the reader in by describing more lurid aspects of the singer's lifestyle.

studio shoot a highly contrived photographic set-up, usually in an interior location
The use of a studio shoot projects an image of perfection and highlights the importance of personality in the article.

Inside the magazine, there are other aspects of technical codes that you will see repeated. Headlines draw our attention to the feature and allow us to decide quickly whether or not the magazine is likely to interest us. These are often accompanied by a **slug**. Slugs appear in a larger typeface than the main **body text** and provide more information for the reader and draw them into the article as a narrative strategy. Columns are included, and their width and number for a particular type forms a crucial part of the house style. **Pull quotes** may also be used if the article is an interview, or any other subtitling techniques. These function to visually break up the text, providing relief for the eye and contributing to the ease with which the material is absorbed. **Drop caps**, an example of typographical code where the first letter at the beginning of an article is enlarged for stylistic effect, can also appear at the start of an article; again, these function partly as an aesthetic device, and partly to signal clearly to the reader where to begin.

Magazines are necessarily visually rich and appealing. Depending on the genre, some prioritise visual content over written. Feature articles are sometimes referred to as **entry points** in the magazine – these are the articles that are most likely to draw your eye as you flip through the magazine. Unlike the capturing of real events that we expect to see in newspapers, these are often highly stylised **studio shoots**. Digital manipulation of these images is common, with a great deal of retouching and other post-production work being undertaken to get exactly the right look for the magazine brand and article. In interviews, it is common to see the subject gazing into the lens, creating a direct **mode of address**.

Apply it

Collect two different examples of double-page spreads from three different magazine genres. What do you notice about the ways in which they deploy the technical codes of print media? What similarities do they have and what differences? How have text and image been combined to appeal to the target audience? Write a 500–1000-word exploration of your three chosen texts.

■ Print advertising

Print advertising is necessarily high impact, with extreme care given to every production decision to maximise response. At the stage of awareness, the consumer's eye needs to stop and be cast over the brand or product name. The advertisers then hope to encourage a more intense lingering over the page or place, which is interest. When that interest turns into a desire to find out more about the product or service, the signification processes at work in the advert are successful.

Composite images, rarely seen in magazines or newspapers, do appear in adverts. There is huge variation in the ways that print adverts are used. **Advertorials**, which appear in the body of a magazine (or newspaper), tend to replicate to some degree the house style of the destination publication. By law, advertorials must be labelled as such to make clear that the 'article' is promoting a product rather than serving as a source of information.

Most adverts make some use of lexical coding. Usually, we would expect to see the product name, perhaps a slogan, or information about where we might buy the product, or social media and web links as a minimum. Some adverts may include supplemental information about the qualities of the products, or to make clear their **brand values**. Advertising copywriting is a specialist field, and huge importance is placed on every element of lexical coding included.

Most print advertising sells its products on some kind of image. The image usually features the product, although there are exceptions to this. Some of the styles of print advertisement you might see are:

- **Conceptual** – the product is depicted through an idea or feeling conveyed visually, sometimes in a hyperbolic way. On occasion, the product itself may appear to be almost incidental.
- **Informative/demonstration** – the product may be shown in action.
- **Pseudo-scientific or technical** – often combining graphics to construct the product as one that makes the most of advanced technologies.
- **Narrative** – the advert tells a story of some kind.

Many advertisements use a combination of these techniques in a single-page space. Composite images are particularly common in film posters, where they are a common convention and, in fact, one of the most obvious signifiers of film promotion as a form.

EXAMPLE: Conceptual advertising

In 2016, Miele ran a series of adverts with the slogan 'monster suction' (view it here: https://tinyurl.com/mpbzm3yt). It used a simple hyperbolic concept to unify its campaign and convey its main proposition, which is the power and effectiveness of the product. It relies on a simple but effective visual joke, which appeared sometimes with the slogan 'monster suction' and sometimes without.

Semiotic approaches to image analysis are therefore really important when decoding visual images but need to be consistently used alongside narrative codes and generic expectations of the product or advertising style. **Logos** also contribute strongly to brand recognition and are usually placed prominently to reinforce consumer associations between the product and the brand.

Quick questions

1. Why do advertorials need to be labelled when conventional print advertisements don't?
2. Explain the distinction between typographic and lexical codes when looking at how words are presented in a print media product.
3. Explain the function of three technical codes consistently used on magazine covers.

1.3 Narrative organisation in print media texts

■ Approaches to reading narratives in print media

In media studies, we use narrative theories to explore how texts organise information in a way that tells a meaningful story which the audience can correlate with their own experience.

TIP ✓
Don't forget to analyse logos, which are often neglected by students new to print advertising analysis.

TIP ✓
You will need to reflect the importance of the lexical coding by giving it due attention in any analysis of adverts you conduct.

△ The poster for the 2016 film *Hidden Figures* is a good example of the use of composite images

Key terms

brand value the image a company intends to convey of its product or service
The centring of the advert on the home and family leisure time promotes its brand values as wholesome.

logo a design, sometimes consisting of typography and a symbol, that identifies a brand
The logo is an arbitrary sign but highly recognisable to a youth audience and is therefore prominently positioned.

Apply it

Think of five brands that are instantly recognisable to your age group. Research the logo for each and consider how the logo communicates brand values.

> See Chapter 2: Reading audio-visual media and Chapter 3: Reading digital media for an introduction to further narrative terms and approaches.

TIP ✓

It's important that you don't try to apply narrative theories in a slavish way at the expense of your own observations about the form, structure and progression of the text.

Key terms

attempt to repair in Todorov's theory of narrative, attempts made by the protagonist or other characters to bring about a new equilibrium
The couple entering marriage guidance counselling is clearly sequenced following recognition as an attempt to repair the broken relationship which is ultimately unsuccessful, leading to the new equilibrium of their divorce.

disruption in Todorov's theory of narrative, an event that disturbs the equilibrium
The equilibrium is disrupted by the arrival of the athlete's new coach who has new training methods.

equilibrium in Todorov's theory of narrative, the stable situation or balance at the beginning of a narrative, and the new state achieved by the end
An equilibrium where the runner is training hard but not winning competitions is established in the slug.

recognition in Todorov's theory of narrative, the realisation that a disruption to the equilibrium has occurred
Recognition occurs when the girl in the advertisement realises she has hair breakage.

■ Todorov's narrative theory

KEY THINKER

Tzvetan Todorov (1939–2017) was a Bulgarian-French theorist who contributed to a range of academic disciplines, including literary theory, anthropology, history and philosophy. Todorov is best-known in media studies for his theory of narrative.

Tzvetan Todorov was a structural theorist, whose work on narratives in culture has been used in the fields of literary, film and media theory. He described narratives as having a chronological quality outside of plot; a process shared in common.

1. A state of **equilibrium** is present at the start of a narrative. This can be considered a stable starting point for the rest of the narrative to flow from. At times, the equilibrium can only be discerned from the disruption to it.
2. Some kind of **disruption** occurs to the equilibrium. This is the jolt that drives the narrative, which gives us a story and sense of movement.
3. A **recognition** of disruption occurs next (sometimes this is almost simultaneous with the disruption itself). Someone realises that something has gone awry or discovers a need. This then sets the scene for the next stage.
4. The **attempt to repair** in a narrative can be extensive. It may be broken down into a series of narrative segments. This stage will persist until the final one is reached.
5. A new **equilibrium** is reached at the end of a narrative. This is not a simple reinstatement of the original equilibrium – even a cyclical narrative will be typically a metaphorical journey for those featured within it. Lessons will have been learned, and losses and gains incurred.

Apply it

Apply Todorov's narrative theory to a double-page feature from a celebrity or 'true life' magazine and an interview with a prominent person in any lifestyle, sports or entertainment magazine.

How easy was the theory to apply? Were there any texts that didn't seem to fit comfortably with the five stages and, if so, were elements of it still useful – or would you choose different enabling ideas to support what you wanted to say about the narrative organisation?

■ Barthes' narrative codes

We have already encountered Roland Barthes in the earlier discussion of semiotics. Barthes is also renowned for his work on narrative, and particularly his organisation of aspects of narrative into five different **narrative codes**. Barthes described these codes as functioning like a 'braid'. No single code is prioritised in the functioning of a narrative – they all take on their own comparative significance and then recede at different points in the text. These codes and their key features are outlined below. Further details are given for some in Chapter 2.

- **Hermeneutic code** (HER) – these are sometimes known as enigma codes. They are used to describe any element of a narrative to which the audience requires answers. The function of the hermeneutic code is connected with

CHAPTER 1 READING PRINT MEDIA

narrative chronology, since it functions in print media to keep the audience interested until the end of an article, to make them look closer, or to encourage them to buy the next issue.

- **Proairetic code** (ACT) – these are sometimes called action codes. They describe small, quickly resolved units of action that drive the narrative forwards and maintain the interest of the audience. Any proairetic code suggests that another will follow. Proairetic codes are also connected with chronology since they are often about cause and effect. All 'plots' are composed of numerous units of completed actions.
- **Semantic code** (SEM) – Barthes uses this term to define anything that is strongly connoted by a particular element of a text; meanings that go beyond the denotations that are present in any text.
- **Symbolic code** (SYM) – these are also present in text outside of structure. Symbolic codes tend to be the deeper meanings we can draw from a narrative, sometimes as a result of repetition of particular semantic codes, or contrasting ideas in a text.
- **Cultural/referential code** (REF) – these relate to our shared understanding of how the world works and the established understanding of its properties. These could be behaviours or events that have psychological realism, historical reference points, literary works or even medical or legal knowledge. Cultural codes can be a reference to almost anything in the body of human knowledge we can see being applied in the construction of a text. Genres can also be considered cultural codes.

Equilibrium
↓
Disruption
↓
Recognition
↓
Attempt to repair
↓
New equilibrium

△ Summary of Todorov's theorem

EXAMPLE: Film posters – *Polite Society* (2023)

Barthes' theory works well for film posters, for example one produced for the British martial arts film *Polite Society* (2023). The only code you will use less when analysing print media is proairetic, or action codes, which are more commonly seen when there is a clear **chronology** or sequencing to a narrative.

- Hermeneutic code (HER) – How have the protagonists been injured? Who or what are they fighting and what for? Who does the accusatory finger point to?
- Semantic code (SEM) – The posture of the women and their non-verbal codes strongly suggest they are determined and ready to fight.
- Symbolic code (SYM) – The lexical coding of 'Big trouble, little sister.' Draws on our understanding of sibling tensions and relationships as well as suggesting something paradoxical or surprising about the character.
- Cultural/referential code (REF) – Martial arts non-verbal and postural codes blended with South Asian cultural codes in dress.

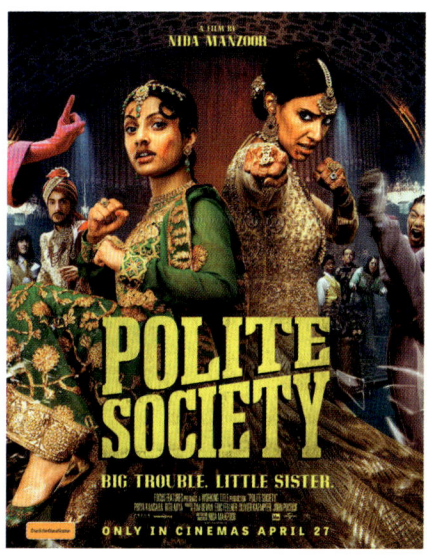

△ One of the film posters for the British martial arts film *Polite Society*

Apply it

Choose two posters for small British films currently on general release. How does each make use of hermeneutic and proairetic codes to engage the audience's interest?

Choose a more complex text, such as a magazine feature. Can you find any examples of the semantic, symbolic or cultural codes being used? Be aware that you won't necessarily find all in a single text.

1.3 Narrative organisation in print media texts

Key terms

chronology	this is the time order of narrative events	
	The narrative chronology is disturbed to show that the product could have helped the bride avert disaster in the final shot.	
cultural/referential code	one of Barthes' five narrative codes; the frame of reference that is human knowledge	
	The shadow shape of the wolf uses northern European fairytales as a cultural/referential code to signify danger to the children from their online activities.	
hermeneutic code	one of Barthes' five narrative codes; enigmas or puzzles in a narrative	
	Hermeneutic codes are established by the use of the slogan as well as the image which sets up the problem to be solved by the product.	
narrative codes	a collective term for Barthes' breakdown of the features of storytelling involved in the construction of narrative	
	Barthes' narrative codes help us to see the complexity of the ways in which this single-page advert communicates.	
proairetic code	one of Barthes' five narrative codes; units of resolved action through cause and effect	
	The first paragraph constructs a sequence of narrative chronology through proairetic codes describing the events leading up to the search.	
semantic code	one of Barthes' five narrative codes; connotations in a narrative	
	Semantic codes are used such as the close positioning of images of the two protagonists to suggest a relationship between them.	
symbolic code	one of Barthes' five narrative codes; deeper meanings and binary oppositions	
	Symbolic codes in the lexical coding of the magazine article reference the tension between the couple's troubled homelife and their public displays of unity.	

Quick questions

1. Which of the narrative codes is most often associated with narrative cause and effect?
2. Give three examples of cultural or referential codes.
3. Which stage comes after the equilibrium in Todorov's theory?

1.4 Genre and print media texts

Genres and their meanings are constructed through media language. The development of genres can be seen in the media language used, for example typical dress codes for characters or narratives.

■ Genre development

Print media products and genres have experienced technological changes in keeping with every other aspect of production and consumption.

One effect of market competition and globalisation has been to make content more homogenous and so to reduce variety. Simultaneously, the comparative cheapness of production technologies allows more access to digital production and distribution.

Print media is the only mass media form that has experienced a permanent and irreversibly negative impact on its sales because of the technological revolution. Despite dire predictions of its imminent demise in the early 2000s, print media still persists.

Some newspapers still retain a financially viable level of circulation despite losses to digital news sources – and magazines still offer the pleasure of having something tangible for your money. Genre texts in print – particularly magazines – offer something that is not yet being absolutely replaced by digital.

EXAMPLE: Genre development – a brief history of the film magazine

Film magazines have a long history in the UK. The first recorded example was only 16 pages long. Published in 1911, *The Pictures* proved very quickly that there was an appetite among fans of cinema – which was still very new at the time – for written material about their favourite movie stars and films.

These magazines really were the first celebrity magazines, often filled with gossip, Hollywood fashion and forthcoming releases. The industry was quick to capitalise on this for promotional purposes, and so a long-standing co-promotional relationship was born.

One of the most famous historical titles was *Picturegoer*, which was published first monthly and then weekly from 1921 for almost 40 years.

Although film magazines were initially popular with both men and women, television impacted their sales, as film entertainment lost its place at the heart of women's lives in particular.

In the intervening years, a number of magazines, such as *Film Review* for mainstream audiences and *Sight and Sound* for people with a specialist interest in film, continued to survive, with a number of titles appearing and disappearing as the market adjusted to who their target audience now were.

The brand leaders today, *Empire* and *Total Film*, launched in 1989 and 1997 respectively with very much a male target audience in mind. Both maintain good circulation figures despite online competition for film news, with glossy exclusives on upcoming releases of mainly blockbuster films, big director and star interviews, and privileged access to sets.

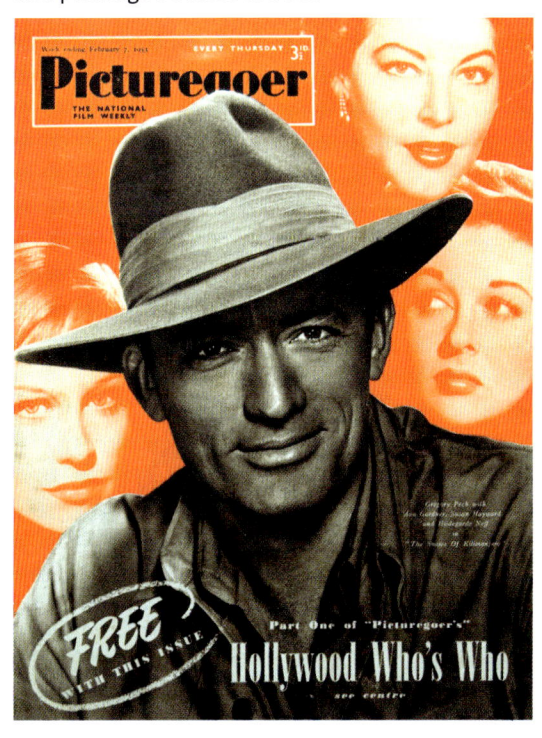

△ A 1953 issue of *Picturegoer* magazine

Exploring codes and conventions in print media texts

Print media genres are relatively straightforward to study. Magazines are often categorised by audiences and media producers alike according to their content – there are sport magazines, gaming magazines, lifestyle and so on, and some have clear sub-genres. Unlike audio-visual or digital media, these

Apply it

Choose a genre of product advertising and collect at least five examples from it. Identify any relevant sub-genres, common codes, and conventions and techniques used. How do you feel the audience might respond to these, and do they meet their expectations and need to familiarise with the product or brand?

🔗 Some of the theoretical approaches to genre are explored in more detail in section 2.4: Genre and audio-visual/audio media texts.

sub-genres have fewer members since the magazine business produces fewer individual titles than other media forms. When studying a print media genre, it is quite possible to collect all the examples on the market in the UK at any one time for analysis – something that would be almost impossible to do with digital or audio-visual media. They can also be grouped by target age range of audience or sometimes by gender of the majority of readership. Print advertising is often studied generically by looking at similarities between adverts for similar products – car advertising, for example, might be considered a genre, with family or luxury car advertising a sub-genre.

One interesting aspect of genre study is that print media genres do not exist in a vacuum – they will also borrow from other genres and be related to them. This is particularly the case with print media products that are advertising another media form, or functioning as a sub-promoter of that form, as do TV-themed magazines and film magazines.

Genres can be thought about in different ways – their usefulness to industry, audience and cultural commentators as well as students of the media mean the term can encompass different ideas about how we relate to media products.

Stretch and challenge

Much genre theory has evolved from film study and has been appropriated by media studies students for its interest and relevance in looking at a whole range of texts. One of these theories was proposed by Dudley Andrew in his book *Concepts in Film Theory* (1984). These definitions of how we understand the term 'genre', and the different ways in which the term is meaningful to both print media industries and audiences, are summed up here:

Genre as:

- **structure** – typical articles, content, technical codes and representations
- **blueprint** – useful to industry; the observation of previous successes and cultural trends
- **label** – the way in which audience and industry connect and understand print media titles
- **contract** – audiences exchange money for a media text in most cases; if they don't get what they expect, they won't repeat the purchase.

△ The front covers of these magazines arouse expectations about the contents

Use Dudley Andrew's ideas to discuss the ways in which these front covers use genre as a cultural code which is useful to both audience and industry.

CHAPTER 1 READING PRINT MEDIA

EXAMPLE: True crime magazines

Crime magazines are a niche genre of the form. It is difficult to define the readership, but the majority obviously has an interest in crime, the police and investigation procedures. This is not so strange when you consider how popular a genre television crime drama series are in that media form. There may be some overlap between viewers of the television genre, true crime podcasts and readers of this magazine genre.

There are five main titles on the market in the UK – *True Crime*, *Real Crime*, *True Detective*, *Master Detective* and *Murder Most Foul*. From looking at the series of images, we can see that each individual title shares some features with others. Historical crime cases from around the world form most of the coverline content. All the editions feature a crime focus, which in four of the five cases is positioned on the left-hand side around the sweet spot. Other secondary images are used in conjunction with coverlines to emphasise the human nature of the subject matter and to hook the readership in. The lexical coding uses frightening words with strongly negative connotations – *monster, lethal, hell, slaughter, rape, slayer*. These emphasise that the magazine covers the extremes of human experience of crime in a sensationalised way.

Most of the magazines use similar **iconography**, which refers to the visual style or repeated motifs in the design of media products. For example, black and white images indicating the starkness of the subject matter and the historical nature of some of the crimes. Fonts that look typewritten and 'torn' edges to graphical features are also common. Red and black, which can have a connotation of danger, and yellow – which combined with these can seem to be a sickly or disturbing colour – are present in the palette. The background selected in each case is dark and cold, blue or black. The cluttered look of the house style is not dissimilar to many women's weekly titles that feature a mixture of true stories, puzzles, some celebrity news and lifestyle elements, or even soap weeklies. This suggests an audience age range of predominantly middle-aged and older women in lower socio-economic categories.

Intertextuality and print media

> **TIP** ✓
> You will need to be able to recognise examples of intertextuality in media products throughout the course, to recognise their significance, and to think about how these are used to create meaning.

Intertextuality as a term first began to appear in writing about the mass media from the late 1960s onwards. It is often used in conjunction with **postmodern theory**. It is a difficult term to define with precision, partly because the nature of what it describes is often quite intangible. An intertextual product is one media text that is making a reference to another consciously and deliberately, to create a new meaning. This retains some of the reference text but imbues it with new qualities and meanings specific to the new text. Since all texts are part of a continuous cycle of the production of meaning, and continued cultural re-referencing, some critics suggest that the term is redundant in today's media climate.

🔗 For more on postmodern theory see section 4.3: Structuralism and post-structuralism.

Quick questions

1 Give examples of three genres of magazine.
2 How do we apply genre labels to print adverts?
3 Which significant change in media forms has most contributed to the decline in consumption of print media?

Apply it

Collect a range of examples from another magazine genre, such as sport and fitness or hobbies and crafts. Write a 500-word case study exploring the genre conventions and similarities as in the example above.

Key terms

iconography repetition of certain visual images or symbols, usually associated in media with particular genres
The scene borrows iconography from expressionist cinema.

intertextuality the process by which one media text consciously references another text or genre, therefore deriving further layers of meaning for a reader who has experienced both texts
The red cape worn by the influencer in the article intertextually references Superman.

postmodern theory a school of thinking that questions the idea of 'reality' as anything other than a collection of constructs apparent in any culture – the mass media is seen as playing an important role since it helps shape and reflect our understanding of our culture. The movement resists solid definitions and answers in many disciplines within the arts, humanities and even sciences
Postmodern theory can be used to explore our attitudes to celebrity culture.

1.4 Genre and print media texts

In print media, we sometimes see some very concrete examples of intertextuality. A magazine cover or advertisement might reference another famous media image, such as a propaganda poster. A feature interview with a celebrity might use a dress code associated with a film genre to depict them in a particular way. Although a lot of intertextuality can be seen in iconography, it can also be present in lexical coding, with conscious and deliberate referencing of any popular catchphrase from a sitcom or game show. Advertising slogans, long-gone television drama series and historical newspaper headlines continue to imbue the new text with an element of the original meaning, although this will often be conducted in a playful or ironic way.

EXAMPLE: *Wired* magazine and intertextuality

View the *Wired* magazine front cover from April 2016 (https://tinyurl.com/3nau8kru) which promotes its feature on China and technology and its interview with Chinese technology entrepreneur Lei Jun. What design similarities can you see between the cover and the Maoist propaganda poster below?

→ Exam-style questions

1. Analyse one of your close study print media products using Barthes' ideas about denotation, connotation, signification and myth.

2. Explain the relationship between the meanings signified by the types of sign used in one of your close study print media products and dominant ideology.

3. Explore the contribution made by the technical codes of print media to one of your close study print products.

4. Explore the contribution of narrative to the structuring of meaning in one of your print media products.

5. Explain the way in which genre codes are used to raise expectations about a print media product you have studied for your course.

→ Summary

- Semiotics, which is the study of signs, is an essential way of understanding how media products communicate with their audiences.
- Signs consist of a signifier plus the signified, which are regarded as being indivisible.
- Signs can be categorised into symbolic or arbitrary signs, iconic signs and indexical signs, which all function in slightly different ways.
- Roland Barthes added his ideas about different orders of signification that increase in complexity – the first order being denotative, the second connotative, and the potential third order operating on the level of ideology and myth.
- All main forms of media, including advertisements and magazines, have their own combinations of technical codes that allow them to be easily recognised by the audience. Each form may also have its own form-specific terminology.
- Narratives are present to some extent in all media texts, even those with the simplest form such as a single-page advertisement.
- Todorov's theory of narrative suggests that many narratives may be broken down into stages that describe the movement between two equilibriums. This is useful for newspaper stories and magazine features, but less so for print advertising.
- Barthes' five narrative codes work together to produce a holistic view of how narratives operate.
- Print media genres are often simple to demarcate, consistent in their conventions and very centred on content or product.
- Intertextuality is widely used in print media texts, and this is particularly evident in borrowed iconography.

Chapter 2: Reading audio-visual media

Enabling ideas

The following enabling ideas from the specification are introduced in this chapter:

3.4.1.1 Semiotics:
- paradigm
- syntagm.

3.4.1.2 Narratology:
- narration
- diegesis
- quest narrative
- 'character types'
- causality
- plot
- masterplot.

3.4.1.3 Genre theory as summarised by Neale:
- 'genre as cultural category'
- conventions and rules
- sub-genre
- hybridity
- genres of order and integration.

→ What you will learn in this chapter

Chapter 2: Reading audio-visual media covers:
- how audio-visual media language can communicate in different ways and be used to influence meaning
- the contribution of narrative to our reading of audio-visual media texts
- how genre theory can inform our understanding of audio-visual texts.

> Revisit the main theories and terminology associated with semiotics and the study of narrative in Chapter 1: Reading print media.
>
> For more on computer games see Chapter 3.

2.1 Technical codes and features used in moving image texts

TIP ✓

In Chapter 1: Reading print media, we explored the main theories and terminology associated with a structuralist approach to reading signs. It would be a good idea to revisit this section before undertaking any analysis of moving image texts.

Key terms

mise-en-scène term in audio-visual analysis that refers to individual codes and signs that contribute to meaning
The dress code makes a significant contribution to the mise-en-scène.

para-proxemics the perceived 'distance' between the audience and a character on screen that contributes to their meaning to the viewer
In terms of para-proxemics we feel closer to this character because of the use of a close-up shot.

proxemics the study of the comparative relationships of characters in a scene dependent on their position
Their close proxemics signify familiarity.

In the previous chapter, we considered some of the separate terminology associated with the three main print media forms. In this chapter, we will be looking at technical codes in a slightly different way to help us understand the codes common to all the audio-visual forms you study, which are: music video, television and audio-visual advertising. Computer games and apps are also audio-visual in their nature, and some of what you learn in this chapter is also relevant to their study.

■ Mise-en-scène

Mise-en-scène is the term used to refer to the placement of everything within a frame. It is one of the most significant decisions taken by directors and production designers of almost any moving image product. These elements are:

- setting/location, both interior and exterior
- dress code
- props
- lighting and colour
- non-verbal communication such as facial expressions and gestural codes
- **proxemics** and **para-proxemics**: the distance ('proximity') between people on screen and what that tells the viewer about their relationships, and the perceived distance between the audience and people on screen.

> **TIP** ✓
> One of the easiest ways to begin to analyse mise-en-scène is to take screenshots from a text to study, as picking out the elements of mise-en-scène while a moving-image text is playing takes a lot of practice.

> **Key terms**
>
> **gestural codes** the way in which we read expression through movement
> *His gestural codes are expansive, signifying confidence.*
>
> **lighting temperature** the feel lent to a scene according to how it is lit – warm or cool, for example
> *The cooler lighting temperatures in this scene emphasise the distance between the characters.*

Well-developed mise-en-scène analysis rarely focuses on all the signs within a single frame – it is used alongside the discussion of other technical codes, and selected significant elements are picked out for discussion across a whole sequence. Mise-en-scène analysis can also be useful in genre identification and contributes strongly to our understanding of the iconography of a genre, conventional symbols or images associated with it.

Mise-en-scène is controlled by framing. The positioning of props and people within the frame is just as important in visual media as it is in the photographic images used in print media texts. The same codes used in photographic images take on significance – dress codes, colour codes, décor, location and non-verbal codes. Non-verbal **gestural codes** and gait also become more significant when a person can be seen moving. Proxemics and para-proxemics are still significant, sometimes with more complex hierarchies as movement is introduced. Lighting is also significant and can be used to create a range of moods and effects through contrasts in **lighting temperature** between scenes, along with the control of highlight and shadow, and apparent time of day.

EXAMPLE: The mise-en-scène of the 'Kenzo: World' perfume advert (2016)

The 'Kenzo: World' perfume advert follows the recent trend of commissioning well-known directors (in this case, Spike Jonze) to produce extended and highly cinematic adverts featuring established celebrities. This often means a sumptuous and grand-scale mise-en-scène. Spike Jonze is known for making a range of high-profile films from the unusual romantic sci-fi drama *Her* (2013) to children's favourite *Where the Wild Things Are* (2009).

△ Spike Jonze, director of the 'Kenzo: World' perfume advert

The narrative features a young woman who escapes from a dull formal event in a large hotel or conference venue, only to playfully unleash herself on the corridors. She dances a riot around the venue to a specially commissioned and unconventional track before finally leaping through a huge model eye positioned outside. The main contributor to meaning within the mise-en-scène is the unusual use of non-verbal communication and gestural codes.

2.1 Technical codes and features used in moving image texts

Iconography of perfume advertising: This is apparent in the advert's focus on a glamorously dressed and physically attractive female celebrity. In this case, this is Margaret Qualley, an American television actor and formally trained ballet dancer. Throughout the advertisement, she dominates the frame, reiterating her status as the star.

Dress code: Qualley's hair is neatly arranged in an updo to suit the unnamed formal occasion she is attending at the start of the advertisement. Her make-up is low key but immaculate. She wears a long, formal ball gown, also matched to the occasion, which becomes more revealing throughout the sequence. The gown is deep green, a colour relating to superstition. It's also a strong signifier of nature in this context; Qualley fights back against convention in the text and her own 'nature' is unleashed.

Non-verbal communication: Qualley's performance style as an actor and dancer is highly energetic. At the beginning she is polite, sober in manner and subdued. The others around her appear to be absorbed by the formal event, which Qualley's character clearly does not feel any enthusiasm for; this is evident from her facial expression, which connotes disengagement. Once free to dance the corridors, stairs and stage of the venue her face contorts, puppet-like, into a series of outrageous expressions. Throughout, the character repeatedly directly addresses the audience by looking straight into the lens, reducing the distance between the audience and text, and making us feel complicit in her playful adventure around the venue. Energetic sequences in which elements of gestural codes are borrowed from action films – kickboxing and a range of dance styles and puppet-like movements – are used to transport her from one part to another. These gestural codes combine elements of the masculine and feminine. They culminate in her final graceful leap and landing to where she rises and beats her chest.

Location, décor, props: The location uses a vast and luxurious (connoted by the plentiful floristry and chandeliers) but bland hotel or conference centre. A significant prop used in the advert is the mirror, which has a long tradition of being used symbolically for reflection on the self and identity. The rose-covered wall-hanging against which she performs lends a stuffy, stale and claustrophobic backdrop. The pink flowers on the table at the start, and in the display stands inside and outside the venue, seem to symbolise a stifling femininity. Other aspects of the décor include a quietly feminine palette of peach, pink, pale gold and beige tones, against which Qualley's performance can really stand out. The other notable props are a bust of Winston Churchill, which is licked – symbolising a lack of deference to authority – and the eye that she leaps though at the end. This is open to interpretation, possibly symbolising all eyes being on her, expecting her to act her part. The generally muted lighting is broken using strobe as she attacks the man engaged in a serious mobile phone conversation.

> **Apply it**
> Select a range of frames from a television genre you enjoy by viewing them on a computer and pausing to take screenshots. Annotate the shots with the elements of mise-en-scène. You can combine the technical terminology relating to the codes above that you learned in Chapter 1: Reading print media regarding semiotic analysis.

2.2 Applying semiotics to audio-visual media

When working with audio-visual media analysis, you can continue to use semiotic analysis. At this point, it is a good idea to extend your use of semiotic terms to include two new terms: **paradigm** and **syntagm**.

- A **paradigm**, in semiotic terms, means a set of related signifiers and signifieds available to someone seeking to communicate meaning. It refers to a range of similar choices, from which the producer will choose the most appropriate one that best conveys the message. For example, a set designer for a home in a television drama can choose décor and props that make it feel comfortable and affluent, or sparse and dirty, which would signify completely different meanings for the scene.
- **Syntagms** are chains of meaning, that is the order in which signs occur and the way we make sense of them. The 'grammar' or codes of audio-visual texts and the order in which they are edited are a great example of syntagms, as they occur sequentially in time and follow certain conventions, such as an establishing shot being followed by a long shot of a character, followed by a close-up of their face or medium shot of their body in action.

> **Key terms**
>
> **paradigm** the choices of related signifiers and signifieds available in producing meaning
> *The jacket is selected from the paradigm of alternative dress codes.*
>
> **syntagm** 'chains' of meaning constructed by the grouping and association of signifiers and signifieds
> *The sequence of codes at the end, including the appearance of the slogan and pack shot, creates a conventional syntagm which encourages action from the audience.*

CHAPTER 2 READING AUDIO-VISUAL MEDIA

Camerawork

Shot types

Shot types are one of the most important codes in audio-visual texts. The basic shot types of **close-up** (CU), **medium shot** (MS) and **long shot** (LS) can all be modified to describe incremental changes in shot using terms such as extreme (for example, extreme close-up) and medium (for example, medium close-up).

Other shot types are named more for their function. A **two-shot** is the common term for a shot that has two people in it; an **establishing shot** is used to establish a change of scene. A **point-of-view shot** (POV) makes us feel as though we are seeing events unfold through someone else's eyes, and an **over-the-shoulder shot** gives us a sense of participation in a conversation. Other shot names – such as a **cutaway shot**, **reaction shot** or nodding shot only make sense in the context of other shots, so really form part of the codes relating to editing.

Some shots are named after specialist lenses that may be required to shoot them effectively – a **wide-angle shot** allows the audience to see more of an expanse of an exterior or interior location in one shot, with a **fish-eye shot** giving a distorted perspective that introduces even more extreme wide angles and can feel very claustrophobic.

> **Quick questions**
> 1. What aspects of a person's appearance in a scene would you analyse for non-verbal codes?
> 2. Explain the difference between proxemics and para-proxemics.
> 3. Give an example of paradigms in mise-en-scène that could be used to subtly alter meaning.

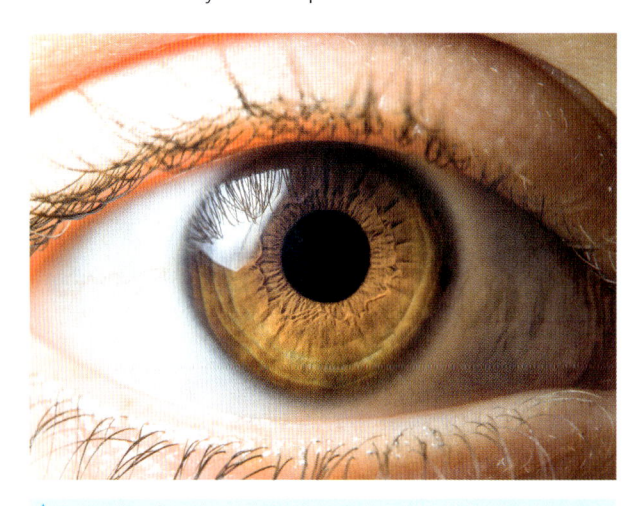

△ Extreme close-up

△ Medium shot

Key terms

close-up	often just face and shoulders
	A close-up effectively constructs him as a sympathetic character.
cutaway shot	footage that shows another subject before returning to the original
	The use of a cutaway functions as product demonstration.
establishing shot	often exterior locations, but can be interiors – used to set a scene
	The establishing shot shows a huge, barren fen.
fish-eye shot	a shot, usually using a specific lens for the purpose, which brings in a range of angles of view
	The fish-eye shot distorts the view and distances us from the events.

2.2 Applying semiotics to audio-visual media

long shot	full body at any distance
	Introducing the character in long shot makes him harder for us to relate to.
medium shot	mid-body shot
	The group are filmed in medium shot, allowing us to see them in the context of the classroom.
over-the-shoulder shot	a shot in which the back of someone's head and shoulder is partially in view – often used to shoot dialogue – and makes the audience feel they are sharing in the exchange
	The over-the-shoulder-shot feels intimate, as though we are part of the moment.
point-of-view shot	shot that allows us to share someone's perspective
	The use of point-of-view shot allows us to share her perspective more profoundly.
reaction shot	demonstrates a response to an event or person
	The use of multiple reaction shots signifies shame among the group.
two-shot	two people in the same shot, often implying a relationship between them
	The friends are shown in two-shot.
wide-angle shot	a shot, usually using a specific lens for the purpose, which shows a wide field of view
	The wide-angle shot allows us to see all of the hall in the frame.

△ **Fish-eye shot**

△ **Long-shot**

Camera angles

Just as important as the type of shot used is the angle of the camera. A camera placed roughly at eye level with its subject creates a sense of equality with it on the part of the audience. A **high angle** can easily make its subject appear inferior, and a **low angle** elevate it. A **canted angle** ('Dutch' angle) can feel edgy and disorientating in some texts, but in music videos these are very common. A **worm's-eye shot** is sometimes a point-of-view shot, either pointing directly upwards as though on the ground, or an extreme low angle that makes its subject loom. A **bird's-eye shot** offers the reverse perspective.

As with shot types, some camera angles are named after the techniques used to capture them – an **aerial shot** is used to show vast areas of a location, and usually requires air transport to shoot. Aerial shots span the categories of both shot type and movement. **Crane shots** also do this – a crane is used to provide some exceptionally fluid and unusual movements, often following action from perspectives that would be impossible from the ground. **Jib shots**, where the camera is positioned on a metal arm and operated remotely, are often used in studio shoots, such as those you might see in a studio-based television show.

Hand-held shot is a generic term for any use of camera operated by hand rather than situated on a mechanical steadying device such as a tripod or **dolly**. These are highly practical in documentary or news filming situations, where advance planning is not always possible, and spontaneity and portability are of the essence. This shot type can sometimes be re-appropriated in fictional media texts, where the effect is to create a feeling of instability in the subject matter or a documentary style that implies verisimilitude.

Specific movements

Other terms are used to describe very specific movements. A **tracking shot**, also called a **following shot**, is used to follow a moving subject by travelling alongside it. It can be filmed either by a vehicle with an on-board mount, or by a long track set up parallel with the line of movement, which then has a dolly move along it. A short tracking shot (often also slower) is called a **crab**. A **following pan** can also follow an object, but in this case the camera stays in one position and moves on its axis to follow the subject of the shot. Used at speed, this becomes a **whip pan**, denoting fast-paced action. A **surveying pan** can follow the same movement but is more languorous and has no foreground subject. When a pan occurs on the *y*-axis it is referred to as a tilt and is often divided into **tilt up** or **tilt down**, since it is unusual to see both movements in one take without an edit.

Although not strictly shot types, focus techniques and lens movements are often considered alongside these as they form part of the same paradigm. **Zooms**, both in and out, are strictly lens movements in which the subject is brought closer or made more distant. Zooms can be fast or slow, and the effect of speed on interpretation can be significant. Faster speeds are associated with action, and slower speeds with manipulating para-proxemics and sometimes contributing to the emotional response the audience experiences to a subject on screen. **Selective focus** is used to bring attention to a particular part of the frame to show its importance. A focus pull may be used to change this, and form a kind of in-shot edit, where the audience's attention is drawn first to one thing then another by changing the focus. Using this technique, a subject in the foreground may be defocused in preference to the background. The effect of this is usually quite contemplative, although very fast focus pulls can also be seen deployed in action sequences and point-of-view shots.

Music videos are interesting examples to use when beginning to study camerawork. They often use very dynamic shot ranges because of their innately bold visual style and feature a range of shots that can be explored out of the sequence.

Key terms

aerial shot from in the air, often shot from an aircraft
The use of an aerial shot gives a sense of magnificence to the landscape.

bird's-eye shot extreme high angle or directly from the sky downwards
The choice of a bird's eye shot is effective because …

canted angle sometimes known as a 'Dutch' angle – a shot that leans over to the side
The angle is canted and feels disorientating.

crane shot any footage taken using a crane – highly mobile and versatile in terms of movement
This crane shot allows us a privileged view over the action.

dolly a fixing for a camera that allows it to be moved smoothly over a set floor or on a track
The use of a dolly shot creates a smooth, hypermobile effect.

hand-held shot footage taken using a camera held and operated by a person
The hand-held shot feels unstable to us.

high angle a shot positioned slightly higher than the subject, which diminishes it
The high angle shot makes the child seem vulnerable.

jib shot any footage taken using a camera, remotely controlled, on a metal arm
The film uses a jib shot, which suspends our view close to the flowing river.

low angle a shot positioned slightly lower than the subject, which elevates it
We understand him to be the dominant figure in the room because of the use of a low-angle shot.

worm's-eye shot extreme low angle or directly from the ground upwards
The worm's eye shot allows us to absorb the sight of the small bomber plane coming into view.

2.2 Applying semiotics to audio-visual media

△ Working with the camera on a dolly

Key terms

crab	a short tracking shot
	The camera crabs to one side, revealing...
following pan	movement where the camera remains in one position but is turned on its axis to follow an action
	A following pan is used to draw our eye to where the ball lands.
selective focus	use of the lens where a particular section of the frame is in focus
	The use of selective focus draws attention to the snail on the leaf.
surveying pan	slow pan on the camera's axis, often to establish either exterior or interior environment
	A surveying pan conveys effectively the size of the quarry.
tilt down	movement where the camera is angled down on its axis
	The rapid tilt down makes the audience experience vertigo.
tilt up	movement where the camera is raised up on its axis
	The tilt up makes the building feel grand in scale.
tracking shot/following shot	follows action by travelling alongside or behind it
	The tracking shot keeps pace with the car.
whip pan	rapid following pan, widely used in action sequences
	The use of whip pan lends energy and frenetic pace to the scene.
zoom	movement of the camera lens to bring a subject closer or to distance it
	The slow zoom in intensifies the predicament the man is in.

EXAMPLE: Music video for *Angels*, Chance the Rapper featuring Saba (2015)

Music videos are interesting examples to use when beginning to study camerawork. They often use very dynamic shot ranges because of their innately bold visual style and feature a range of shots that can be explored out of the sequence. You can watch the video for *Angels* here: www.youtube.com/watch?v=eedeXTWZUn8

- **Tracking shot** – used in the opening to bring us on the boy's journey and allow us to sense his place in the city.
- **Establishing shot of the city** – shot as aerial footage, which feels like a POV perspective of Chance flying over the city.
- **Extreme low angles** – give an impression of the size and scale of the city, contrasting with the sky through which Chance flies.
- **On-board vehicle shots** – used on the top of the train, showing Chance's performance and lending a highly mobile and journey-like feel to the narrative.
- **Close-up of shoes** – signifying the introduction of dance moves to the sequence.
- **Tracking shots in the train** – both back and forth allow for focus on different characters and their performances.
- **Hand-held camera work on train** – reflects the movement of the vehicle.
- **Camera work** – reflects two spheres of action, the train/below and the train/above.
- **Numerous two-shots** – used on the street to film two performers dancing.
- **Crane shots, dolly shots and hand-held work including low-angle shots** – these elevate the importance of the performers and are all used in the dance sequence.
- **Bird's-eye shot at the end on the boy** – as though the 'angel' is looking down on him.
- **Video ends with a tilt up** – as the song finishes with the boy who drew us into the narrative at the start, we share his perspective on the city.

Apply it

Choose a music video from any genre you enjoy. Watch the video several times, pausing where you need to make notes. List some of the camera shots used, describing the effect of each.

Use your notes to write a 500-word, paragraphed analysis of how camera work contributes to the construction of meaning in the video.

Quick questions

1. What is the purpose of a focus pull?
2. What is the difference between a high-angle shot and a bird's-eye shot?
3. What is the most common usage of a surveying pan?

CHAPTER 2 READING AUDIO-VISUAL MEDIA

Editing

Many techniques are used in editing, and it is only possible to cover here a few that are seen most frequently. Most of the texts you study will use **continuity editing** style, the predominant type of editing in mainstream media. Continuity editing constructs time and space in straightforward ways that make sense to the audience because we have been reading its codes since childhood. It can involve selecting from a paradigm of similar shots taken on location and ordering these into a syntagm, a chain of meaning that helps to construct a narrative, build representations and many other functions. Most of the time it provides a seamless experience of viewing that does not draw attention to the **apparatus** – the physical nature of its construction.

The other common editing style you will see used is **montage editing**, which has many uses from film trailers to music videos. In montage editing we see a number of shots, which we understand are not occurring consecutively in the chronology played in close sequence. This creates a strong impression of a character's journey or an event, or can be used to create atmosphere. It is generally used quite sparingly.

Space is constructed according to technical laws and norms such as the **180-degree rule**, where the camera must not 'cross the line' in a cut from a film sequence to preserve the illusion of a particular perspective on a scene. If the perspective needs to switch to another side of the room, a connecting shot with a movement, such as a dolly or jib shot, will usually be included, or the narrative will cutaway to another scene before returning to a new camera position.

△ The 180-degree rule

Similarly, to preserve visual logic, we have the **30-degree rule**, which states that the camera must move more than 30 degrees when showing a new shot of the same subject. Failure to do so results in a **jump cut**, which is disorientating for the audience – and looks like a mistake. At times, this can be deployed for effect (usually with several jump cuts being edited together).

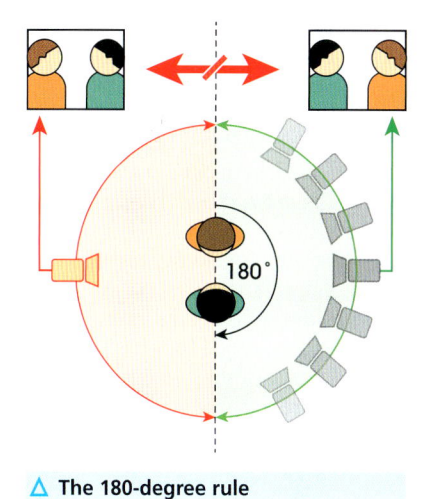

> **TIP** ✓
> Although it is important to understand how editing constructs space, you will rarely need to comment on this in an analysis. Understanding it will make you more aware of editing and more likely to spot other, more relevant techniques.

Key terms

apparatus term used for the equipment and methods used in media production
The apparatus of production is seen, which is unusual.

continuity editing dominant mode of editing that does not draw attention to itself, allowing the audience to focus on the subject matter
The sequence begins by disrupting standard continuity editing …

jump cut where the camera moves less than 30 degrees, creating an ugly and dissonant effect – sometimes used deliberately, but is not part of continuity editing style
The use of jump cuts feels jarring and causes anxiety in the audience.

montage editing an editing style where the audience is given a snapshot of different clips
The trailer uses conventional montage editing.

30-degree rule one of the rules that constructs space in visual language – the camera must move more than 30 degrees in order to avoid an ugly cut
The sequence breaks the 30-degree rule.

180-degree rule one of the rules that constructs space in visual language – the camera must stay one side of an imaginary line when filming a scene, unless a cutaway or visible movement leads the audience to another perspective
The rupture of the 180-degree rule has an unnerving effect.

2.2 Applying semiotics to audio-visual media

Key terms

accelerated motion the speeding up of footage during editing
This scene uses accelerated motion for comic effect.

compression of screen time the way in which media texts, through editing, reduce the real time in which events would unfold
Screen time is compressed considerably by the montage sequence.

decelerated motion the slowing down of footage during editing
The use of decelerated motion combined with a close-up shot makes the product seem more desirable.

multi-take non-continuity technique, where a dramatic event may be filmed from several angles and the moment duplicated for effect
The smashing of the cup is filmed as a multi-take to make the moment have more impact.

parallel development the apparently simultaneous presentation of another narrative strand in a text, which is actually achieved by alternating between the two spheres of action
The action cuts between the two scenes as the tension builds using parallel development.

screen time the amount of real time a character is present on screen for, e.g. two minutes
Screen time is manipulated to make the dive scene feel as though it's happening in real time compared with the moments leading up to it.

split screen simultaneous depiction of two events on screen by physical splitting of the frame
Split screen is used to show that the two people use the same product in different ways.

The way in which we experience the passage of time is also controlled by editing. The depiction of 'real' time is **compressed** – in fictional narratives, this is carefully controlled to manipulate our experience of the narrative. More **screen time** is given to certain characters at particular points, and events that unfold over a number of days – or would if they were real, in the case of fictional narratives – are compressed into an hour or 30 minutes. **Parallel development** may be used, where we understand that two events are supposed to be happening simultaneously, even though the edit requires that we cut between the two events alternately. The only real alternative to this is the use of **split screen**, which is acceptable for more experimental TV dramas but would appear odd in a soap opera.

Some other techniques that involve using editing to play with our perception of time include the **multi-take**, where the effect of an action is shown by repeating it several times, sometimes shot from different angles or distances. **Decelerated motion** (slowing down of the sequence) is frequently used to contribute to the emotional power of a sequence and is a convention so familiar we barely notice it. **Accelerated motion** (speeding up the sequence) adds to the audience's perception of speed, but usually must be deployed with a much lighter touch, since, unlike decelerated motion, it jars when used deliberately, and is only suited to deliberate use in a small handful of contexts, such as for comic effect.

Transitions are used to get from one shot or scene to another. The overwhelming majority of transitions you will see in audio-visual texts are straight cuts. Other common techniques are **fade in**, **fade out** and **fade-through-black**. These are subtle and slower-paced transitions. Also in this category is the **cross-dissolve**, where one image is slowly superseded by another, creating a whimsical effect.

Relationships can be created by editing. The juxtaposition of a high-angle with a low-angle shot can easily imply a relative power positioning between two characters. An **eye-line match** is created when we see someone looking, then see what they are looking at. **Matched cut** is another term used for pairs of shots that make sense together. Over-the-shoulder shots are used to film conversations, and reaction shots commonly allow the viewer to see the impact of almost anything else that has happened in the previous shot.

Key terms

cross-dissolve the gradual fading of one shot into another
The cross-dissolve connotes tenderness.

eye-line match usually means the pairing of a shot of a person with the object of their attention in the next frame
The eye-line match signifies equality between the two characters.

fade-in/fade-out the gradual dissolution of a shot
The fade-in follows the titles.

fade-through-black technique that allows the audience a moment to reflect, by placing a short breathing space over black between scenes
The transition between the scenes is slowed using a fade-through-black.

matched cut pairs of shots that have a logical connection
The door opens in one scene and cuts abruptly to the closure of the pool door in the next, using a matched cut.

transition the way in which movement from shot to shot is managed in editing, most often a straight cut
Shot transitions are unusual because they use many dissolves, meaning one image is superimposed over the previous.

CHAPTER 2 READING AUDIO-VISUAL MEDIA

Titling can be used in all kinds of versatile ways. Cutaway shots are used in factual media, sometimes to contribute additional meaning or add weight to a person's dialogue, at other times for illustrative purposes. **Cutting rhythm** and **cutting rate** are used to refer to the way in which footage is cut to create a particular pace. You should also remember that sound is also a significant part of the editing process. This is discussed further in the next section but is also relevant to audio-visual texts. Other post-production techniques include special effects, graphical elements and subtle post-production practices such as **colourisation**.

△ Over-the-shoulder shot

> ### Quick questions
> 1. What type of cut will you see the most as a transition in editing?
> 2. Give the common name for the technique of decelerated motion.
> 3. What is parallel development in editing terms?

EXAMPLE: Editing in the Bisto advertisement (2021)

You can view the Bisto advert on YouTube here: www.youtube.com/watch?v=TcOlDduqJ_I. The advertisement uses repeated shot types to construct a narrative about the role of an everyday food in the bond between two childhood friends. They are repeatedly shown in two-shot at different ages, as a montage that compresses their journey into adulthood by showing similar shots as the children grow up and are replaced by older actors, then eventually their own children.

It is a subtle example of editing that is very simple but cycles through the selection of similar shot types at a steady, rhythmic cutting rate matched to the beat of the soundtrack song, with only low-level, indistinct dialogue forming soundscape. Cutaway shots of childhood chatter give way to the formation of adult social relationships and activities, with repetition of the close-up shot of gravy being poured over the food to connect the audience consistently with the product. As a family orientated grocery product that has been in existence for decades, the editing style supports well the theme of longevity in friendships.

The end of the advertisement is very conventional, with a pack shot of the product in selective focus accompanied by a female voice uttering the simple slogan ('Ahhh ... Bisto.') and the logo superimposed over the final shot to reinforce brand identity.

> ### Apply it
> Choose an audio-visual advertisement from a well-known brand to study. Note down the key editing techniques you observe that are used at different points in the advert. Consider whether editing is used to represent the product in a particular way.
>
> Write your findings as a short case study, around 150 words.

■ Sound

Sound makes a huge contribution to audio-visual texts but is sometimes neglected by students during analysis in favour of the seemingly more dominant visual codes. **Aural codes** can contribute a great deal to our reading of a text if we listen carefully. The **sound mix** is an important part of post-production and can be considered alongside editing.

> ### Key terms
> **aural code** term used to describe all the techniques relating to sound
> *The sequence uses aural codes to signify danger.*
>
> **colourisation** the way in which the saturation or other elements of how we perceive colour may be altered post-production, either to harmonise footage from different shoots or locations, or to achieve a particular aesthetic
> *The colourisation is desaturated slightly.*
>
> **cutting rate** the way in which pace is controlled in editing – many shots of short duration lend a fast cutting rate; longer duration results in a slower rate
> *The fast cutting rate emphasises the frenetic action.*
>
> **cutting rhythm** the length of shots, particularly when edited to a soundtrack or score, when these appear to have rhythmic qualities
> *The cutting rhythm matches the track.*
>
> **sound mix** the combination of sound into a soundtrack, and the differing emphasis placed on certain sounds for effect
> *The sound mix prioritises the noise of the machinery.*
>
> **titling** the use of lexical coding over black or over image – has become very common in digital media texts
> *The titling uses discreet typographical codes.*

2.2 Applying semiotics to audio-visual media

Key terms

atmosphere/soundscape background sound, especially in fiction media texts, which is constructed to contribute to verisimilitude
The soundscape evoked is gentle and relaxing.

contrapuntal sound sound that does not seem to match the action, often deliberately used to unnerve the audience or even create a blackly comic effect
The contrapuntal sound of the child laughing creates an eerie effect.

diegesis the world of the media text, the story world, especially in fiction-based media
The score contributes to our sense of immersion in the diegesis.

diegetic sound refers to sound supposedly generated within the diegesis
The diegetic sound of the car engine.

extra-diegetic narration voice-over provided by an unseen person from outside the diegesis
The extra-diegetic narration distances us from the events.

intra-diegetic narration voice-over provided by a person or character from within the diegesis
As an intra-diegetic narrator, we trust her account of events when in fact she is unreliable.

non-diegetic narration voice-over created by an unseen person from outside the diegesis
The non-diegetic voice holds warmth and sounds affectionate towards the characters.

The term **diegetic sound**, meaning from the **diegesis** (the 'story-world', the construct) is often used to label the apparent source of sound and to understand how we should read it. A common mistake made by new media studies students is to assume that any sound which is added post-production rather than recorded on a location is non-diegetic. In fact, regardless of how it was technically integrated into the soundtrack, any sound that supposedly originates in an audio-visual text is diegetic. Parallel sound is a term used to describe sound that fulfils our expectations. Sometimes, sound that doesn't match the scene can be deployed – this is known as **contrapuntal sound** and has a disconcerting or even sinister effect.

> **TIP** ✓
> An easy way to remember what is and is not diegetic sound with texts is if the participants or characters in a recording can hear the sound, it would be classed as diegetic.

Very few sounds are commonly categorised as **non-diegetic**. The most significant of these are voice-overs, which can be provided by an **extra-diegetic narrator** (who is unseen) or an **intra-diegetic narrator**, who also appears in the text's diegesis. This second kind of narrator can bring an additional layer of uncertainty into a fictional text, as we might question the reliability of their interpretation of events. A score is also considered non-diegetic, although music can also appear diegetically, heard by characters and part of the scene.

Background sound, known also as **atmosphere** or **soundscape**, can be very interesting to analyse, as we rarely notice it, but it often makes a very significant contribution to our level of immersion in a text. At the other end of the scale, we can sometimes detect the use of selective sound, when one sound is deliberately amplified in the mix to draw attention to it.

Apply it

1. Choose a film trailer in a popular genre. Watch it first with sound, then without. Identify several sounds you hear used. Try to find examples of as many of the techniques mentioned on this page as you can.
2. Group your examples of sounds heard under diegetic and non-diegetic column headings. Are there any other ways in which you can group certain sounds? Try to decode the qualities of the sound.
    a. What can you decode from the soundscapes used in the trailer?
    b. What qualities are there in the range of vocal performances in dialogue?
    c. Which sounds are prominent in the sound mix?
    d. Does the trailer make use of a score? If so, what does the music contribute to meaning?
    e. Does the trailer use a voice-over?

Quick questions

1. Explain the difference between diegetic and non-diegetic sound.
2. What is contrapuntal sound?
3. Why do producers sometimes use selective sound?

CHAPTER 2 READING AUDIO-VISUAL MEDIA

2.3 Narrative organisation in audio-visual and audio texts

■ Approaches to reading narratives in audio-visual media texts

Most approaches to reading narratives distinguish between 'story' and 'plot'. Story refers to the overall narrative. Plot is the order in which information is presented organisationally in the text. In discussing plot, you may need to use the terms **analepsis** and **prolepsis**, meaning flashback and flashforward, referring to disturbances in the chronology of events.

When talking about the shape of a narrative, you should always consider what kind of ending and format it has. Is it an enclosed narrative, where all the loose ends are tied up? This kind of narrative often is said to have narrative closure, or narrative resolution. You might also consider whether a narrative is serial or self-contained. Remember that narrative study should be applied to both fiction and fact-based media.

Hook is another term widely used in **narratology** to describe any technique used to gain the interest of the audience. **Cultural tropes** are simple, over-used devices that, when connected with **universal themes**, help us constantly to re-evaluate our affiliation with a culture as well as what it means to be human.

Another consideration is the style of narration. Narration styles are sometimes described as either **restricted** or **omniscient**. Restricted narration means that some information is withheld from the audience to preserve suspense or enhance cognitive enjoyment in some way. With omniscient narration (the narrator is all-seeing), the audience occupy a privileged position where they can gain perspective on all the relevant events, although characters will not.

Narrative perspective is also important – the idea that we share a character's particular view of events as they unfold or sympathise with a particular group of characters. This is also connected with the idea of narration – the perspectives we gain on events through the way the story is told.

When reading complex fictional narratives, you need to have the terminology to talk about several things that may be going on at once. One of these is the **narrative arc**, which can be used to describe an individual character's journey through the narrative. You can use the term **narrative strands** to discuss separate contributory elements to the overall narrative. Another important idea when reading fictional narratives in audio-visual texts is the diegesis. The easiest way to imagine the diegesis, or story world, is as a bubble that contains the world of the text. We enter that bubble through the **suspension of disbelief**.

> ### Stretch and challenge
> Now that you have gained a familiarity with audio-visual codes, choose three scenes from one of your longer-form audio-visual Close Study Products.
>
> 1. For each scene, take six screen shots and analyse, in detail, for mise-en-scène.
> 2. Make detailed notes on the uses of three shot types and three edits or editing techniques you feel contribute most to meaning in each scene.
> 3. Make detailed notes on all uses of audio in each scene.
> 4. Use your notes to produce either an illustrated essay titled 'A deep dive into the role of media language in the production of meaning in [insert name of product].' or a presentation which includes clips from the scenes.

Key terms

analepsis	commonly known as a flashback
	The use of analepsis here is poignant because...
cultural tropes	plot elements, themes or figures of speech that are used repeatedly in literature or popular culture
	The image of a woman meditating is used as a cultural trope signifying a focus on wellbeing.

hook	any technique used to draw the audience into a narrative
	The pre-title sequence uses a hook to ensure continued viewing.
narrative arc	the journey of an individual character
	This contributes to the character's narrative arc by...
narrative strands	different 'storylines' or sub-plots that usually contribute something to the main narrative subject
	The episode has several narrative strands.
narratology	the structuralist study of narrative
	Narratology can be used to explore how the text sequences ideas for the audience in order to engage them.
omniscient narration	style of narration where the audience is privy to most contextual narrative information even where this is withheld from characters in the diegesis
	The use of omniscient narration effectively juxtaposes the action of the two scenes.
prolepsis	commonly known as a flashforward
	The use of prolepsis at the start establishes the genre as science fiction.
restricted narration	style of narration where information is withheld from the audience
	The use of restricted narration is conventional in the crime drama.
suspension of disbelief	allowing oneself to be immersed in a fictional world
	The sequence rapidly encourages suspension of disbelief through immersive effects.
universal themes	themes to which many people across cultures can relate
	The film review emphasises the universal theme of coming-of-age and it is this which makes it a truly internationalised product.

■ Applying narrative theories to audio-visual texts' sphere of action

> **For an overview of each of these theories and their origins see section 1.3: Narrative organisation in print media texts.**

Todorov's theory of narrative can be a useful tool for exploring longer narratives in either audio-visual or audio texts. Modern media texts are complex, and it can be difficult to apply the theory in its simplest form to complex narratives that may contain many sub-plots. This does not mean the theory is redundant – just that it can be applied in different ways to fragments of narrative and sub-plots that could be mapped across a longer text such as one of the high-engagement, high-budget television series that tend to be binge-watched on streaming services.

When approaching a text like this, you might even find that virtually all stages can be applied to an individual episode of a television series, to its respective sub-plots, or even to the overall narrative formed by all the episodes together. This is one of the most interesting ways of using theory, to see how it can be used to discover coherent units of narrative that build together like blocks to create a whole.

EXAMPLE: Todorov's theory of narrative applied to the first episode of *Stranger Things* (Netflix, 2016)

△ *Stranger Things* (Netflix, 2016)

Stranger Things is a Netflix Originals series that was broadcast in 2016. The science-fiction/horror series follows a mother's efforts to get back her missing son. This example clearly shows how Todorov's theory of narrative can be applied to a complex text, even though it is a serialised narrative.

EPISODE 1: Main narrative, 'The Missing Boy'

- **Equilibrium:** Four boys, firm friends, are playing Dungeons and Dragons in the basement of one of their family homes on a school night.
- **Disruption to equilibrium:** On his way home, one of the boys – Will – is accosted by an unseen creature, chased to his home and vanishes.
- **Recognition of disruption:** Will's mother realises he isn't at home the following morning; his friends miss him at school.
- **Attempt to repair:** Will's mother visits local law enforcement and a search party is called. The boys decide to form their own search without the knowledge of their parents, who have forbidden it.
- **New equilibrium:** It could be said that there is no true equilibrium to a first part of a serial narrative, as it relies on a continued state of disequilibrium to retain audience engagement until the next episode. Even so, often a situation will be left that has some kind of balance. Although the search party find Will's bike in the woods and fear the worst, Will's mother is convinced her son is still alive when she receives a strange telephone call in which she believes she hears his voice – and vows not to give up on him.
- Elements of further disequilibrium are suggested by clips from Episode 2, which hook the viewer in.

EPISODE 1: Secondary narrative/sub-plot, 'Eleven'

- **Equilibrium:** A girl appears in the woods near a secretive research facility, with a shaven head, an '11' tattoo on her forearm and wearing a nightgown.
- **Disruption to equilibrium:** Eleven, who seems almost non-verbal, is caught stealing fast food at a remote restaurant by its kindly owner, Benny.
- **Recognition of disruption:** Benny senses the girl is in trouble and is distressed but cannot get any information from her.
- **Attempt to repair:** Benny tries to help; he calls social services to collect her.
- **Disruption to equilibrium:** Fake social services workers arrive to collect Eleven, and shoot Benny dead.
- **Attempt to repair:** Realising she is in grave danger, Eleven defends herself using supernatural powers, and escapes.
- **New equilibrium:** Eleven is found by Will's friends, who decide to hide her in the basement, dovetailing the sub-plot with the main narrative arc and substituting the missing friend with a new, very intriguing one.

Apply it

Choose a serial television drama series you know well. Either re-watch the first episode or find a detailed episode synopsis online to help you.

Sketch out a map of the episode, showing a timeline of key events in the plot, and adding in any sub-plots. Try mapping the stages of Todorov's theory against these key plot events.

2.3 Narrative organisation in audio-visual and audio texts

Roland Barthes' five codes in narrative (see pages 16–17) are useful in decoding audio-visual texts, and you should remember that it is not necessary to identify every example of each type of code. You may also find that it isn't always possible to list all the ones you can identify, so focus on accuracy and care in identifying fewer examples and explaining fully how they contribute to the meaning of the text for the audience. The only two codes that refer to the chronology of the text are the hermeneutic (HER) and proairetic (ACT). You will often find it easiest to think of semantic codes (SEM) as the connotations of individual technical codes you are already used to identifying.

Symbolic codes (SYM) are often best expressed in terms of binary oppositions. Cultural/referential codes (REF) are very broad, and you will usually be able to find specific examples that relate to our cultural knowledge and practices without too much difficulty.

EXAMPLE: *Man on the Moon* (John Lewis Christmas advertisement, 2015)

The narrative of the two-minute advertisement features a young girl with a telescope who believes she can see a man on the moon, and wishes to contact him. As the advert progresses, we see her thinking through the problem and attempting to send messages to him in different ways, unsuccessfully. By the end, we see the girl send him a gift from under her Christmas tree using helium balloons. The man in the moon receives his gift, a telescope, and is able to see the girl waving back at him.

All of the five codes have been applied, although if you watch the advertisement for yourself, you will see more.

- **Hermeneutic codes (HER):** Close to the beginning of the advertisement, we ask ourselves, will the girl ever be able to communicate with the man in the moon?
- **Proairetic codes (ACT):** The girl adjusts her telescope and sees the man on the moon. The girl climbs a ladder to hold her letter up but isn't close enough. She shoots an arrow with the letter on it towards the moon, but it misfires. The letter is thrown from her window as a paper-plane but falls to the ground.
- **Semantic codes (SEM):** The man on the moon is shown from a high angle in long-shot, connoting isolation. His gaze is repeatedly shown as fixed on Earth, connoting his desire for contact. His facial expression connotes sadness in a close-up and an extreme close-up. The girl writes a letter, connoting that she wants to communicate with the man. The extreme close-up of the tear in the eye of the old man and the smile in the eye of the girl connote gratitude and a human connection/relationship.
- **Symbolic codes (SYM):** The Christmas spirit is contrasted with loneliness and isolation, the importance of cross-generational ties is emphasised through depiction of the relationship between someone at the start of their life and someone who is close to the end.
- **Cultural/referential codes (REF):** The children's story of the man in the moon, Christmas as a time for the ritual of gift giving, selflessness and charity.

■ Character types and causality

Character types can have an important role in narratives. These should be studied alongside representations to understand how certain types can have function in a narrative. Their roles can help to advance the story or promote **causality**. Causality can almost be thought of as the way in which the story runs itself, the way in which the events, usually driven by the desires and motivations of characters and the events that impact on them, drive the logic of the narrative forwards. **Archetypes** are shared across cultures and in human stories all around the world. They are basic, rather simple character types who appear over and

---

Apply it

Using YouTube, find examples of previous or subsequent years' John Lewis Christmas advertisements. Try to apply Barthes' five narrative codes to two of these. Are all the codes relevant? Some texts do not offer you an example of all.

Quick questions

1. Name the abbreviations used when describing Barthes' five narrative codes.
2. Describe two different ways Todorov's model could be applied to a television series.
3. Explain the difference between omniscient and restricted narration styles.

Key terms

causality the way in which the events, usually driven by the desires and motivations of characters and the events that impact on them, drive the logic of a narrative forwards
The behaviour of the model referred to in the magazine article constructs narrative causality as an explanation for her declining health.

archetypes basic, rather simple character types who appear over and over in narratives
The protagonist's rival is a 'black knight' archetype, whose strength is considerable but whose morals are questionable.

CHAPTER 2 READING AUDIO-VISUAL MEDIA

over in narratives. Heroes are archetypes, but so are jesters and sages. Note that most significant characters based on archetypes are male in classical stories and much of the canon of Western literature, and that this bias can still be seen in many media products – although their roles may of course be taken on by a person of either gender in contemporary texts. Tropes, on the other hand, are quite often gender-specific. Where they have a male and a female equivalent, there may be distinctions in how the trope is expressed depending on gender. Archetypes often give a recognisable but simple grounding for a character, but tropes can be more developed.

Tropes can be thought of as taking an archetype and placing it in a relevant contemporary context specific to the culture that produces the media text. Although many have their origins in archetypes, they are more modern – a single archetype, for example, might spawn more than one trope.

Three archetypes in traditional tales include the sage, the magician and the fool.

Another term you may come across when thinking about characters is stock characters. Many people use the term stock character and trope interchangeably, but, again, crucially their function is driven by narrative and their existence perpetuated by repetition in popular cultural products. Their purpose is to entertain us by providing a familiar framework of actions, behaviours and attitudes. A stock character is not intended to be sophisticated, and they do not need to be new or refreshing. Stock characters are interesting because their presence can tell us about the symbolic function they have in our culture – the manic pixie dream girl, for example, is defined by her spontaneity and impulsiveness, and at first glance may seem to be a more progressive female representation. However, narratively she often enables the hero to find his true self – while she may appear to be a free spirit, she is still a form of princess, subservient to the hero's greater need.

△ Three archetypes in traditional tales include the sage, the magician and the fool

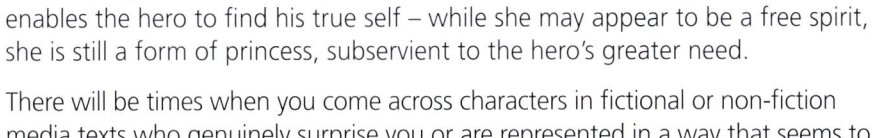

There will be times when you come across characters in fictional or non-fiction media texts who genuinely surprise you or are represented in a way that seems to run counter to dominant representations of similar people. They may form part of a concerted effort to contribute to the process of signification in a deliberate way, changing our minds and opinions about a group of people or an issue, and affecting the course of the narrative in surprising or unconventional ways.

EXAMPLE: *Jerk*, an alternative representation of disability

In BBC Three's hit black comedy *Jerk*, stand-up comedian Tim Renkow, who has cerebal palsy, plays a countertype to the more common tropes used of people with disabilities. These frequently represent them as saintly, objects of pity, victims of violence or heroic in overcoming day-to-day obstacles (see Chapter 5: Media representations for more on this topic). Instead, he plays a distinctive character who isn't particularly 'nice'. The series has been applauded for countering common stereotypes.

2.3 Narrative organisation in audio-visual and audio texts

> **Apply it**
>
> 1 Choose a fictional TV series or a reality TV show you know well. American television series with ensemble casts work particularly well for this activity, but any programme with a good range of characters or participants is suitable. List the main characters in the show – you can use a site such as IMDb initially. Can you identify any stock characters or archetypes without researching them?
> 2 Look online to find a source of stock characters, archetypes and cultural tropes. A particularly good site is http://tvtropes.org.
> Prepare a cast list for your show that gives a short description of the character and the trope they fulfil.

It is also worth thinking about what is meant by the terms plot and narrative. Although the term narrative is commonly used to describe any aspect of the story, the easy way to remember narrative is that it is the way in which a story is told. Think of the word narration – it tells you something about the style and perspective of the story and many other nuances. Plot is a term more commonly used in industry writing practice, but also has a function and meaning for audiences – it is the 'events' of the story in chronological order that constitute the 'backbone' of the story. The plot is what someone usually tells you if you ask them what a television programme or film is about.

■ Masterplots

A **masterplot** refers to an overarching narrative that is meaningful to a particular culture. It may be comprised of particular character types, plot events or conflicts that are explored over and over again. Many of these plots have universality to them – you can recognise elements of them in many popular texts. So established are masterplots that many writers have published checklists to use as a source. These tend to be rather more detailed and prescriptive than the backbone function most masterplots have on the organisation of narratives that are influenced by them.

The **quest narrative**, for example, is summarised as follows in Ronald Tobias's (2012) book on masterplots:

- Something must happen which triggers the hero's journey/quest.
- The journey should involve travel and movement.
- The protagonist should have a companion.
- They should discover something about themselves and mature as the journey goes on.
- The plot should end up geographically back close to home.
- The hero should realise that what they learned is not necessarily what they thought they were setting out to learn.
- The hero should mature and grow.
- The hero should pronounce his/her insight into their growth.

EXAMPLE: *American Gods* (Amazon Prime, 2017) and the influence of the quest narrative

The quest narrative elements of the plot can clearly be seen in this narrative of a young man whose life is thrown into disarray by tragedy but regains meaning through his journey.

- Shadow, an ex-convict, is released from prison, only to find his wife, Laura, has died. He is devastated to learn that she has also betrayed him with his friend.
- Unable to stay in their former home, he takes up the offer of work as a bodyguard from the enigmatic character Mr Wednesday.

> **Key terms**
>
> **masterplot** an overarching group of bare narrative elements that are meaningful to a particular culture
> *'Revenge narratives can be considered to be masterplots, since they have universal qualities to them which are understood globally.'*
>
> **quest narrative** an established narrative convention which comprises journey and maturation of a main character or characters
> *'The storyline of the episode establishes a classic quest narrative.'*

△ Shadow and Mr Wednesday undertake their quest in *American Gods*

- Mr Wednesday is on a journey to meet various people across America to recruit them for a cause – Shadow joins him.
- Wednesday can qualify as a companion, since, although he is a powerful agent in the narrative, the narrative perspective focuses on Shadow as protagonist.
- As he journeys, Shadow discovers strengths he was not aware he possessed, including forgiveness as he meets his wife Laura once more, now a zombie.
- He discovers knowledge about his environment that casts aside his perceptions of reality rather than himself – the people Wednesday takes him to meet are all rather unusual. Shadow begins to realise his travelling companion and his old acquaintances have supernatural powers. He loses his naivety about his relationship with Laura.
- Far from the journey being a distraction from Laura's death, Shadow discovers it is an unveiling of the supernatural dimension; the old gods brought to America by its immigrants are still surviving in some surprising places.
- Shadow admits his belief in the old gods and in Wednesday, who is revealed as the god Odin. He has a new purpose and an important role in Odin's battle against the new gods of Media and Technology, although we are not yet sure why he is so significant.

Apply it

1. Some other familiar masterplots in Western culture include revenge, transformation and forbidden love. Source a fiction media text as an example that makes at least partial use of one of these.
2. Journalists as well as fictional writers are aware of the existence of masterplots and the audience's receptiveness to them as cultural tropes. Find evidence of them in any fact-based texts, such as interviews with celebrities.

Quick questions

1. Briefly describe the key qualities of masterplots.
2. Explain the difference between tropes and archetypes.
3. Explain what is meant by causality in a narrative.

2.4 Genre and audio-visual and audio media

Genre development

Genre study becomes more complex when exploring audio-visual texts. In Chapter 1: Reading print media, we explored Dudley Andrew's idea that the term genre can have different nuances depending on the context in which it is used. In this section, we will be adding to your understanding of genre approaches to studying texts and equipping you with some new terms to use in writing about genre from enabling theorist **Stephen Neale**, as well as considering some of the problems with approaching study of a text through its genre.

KEY THINKER

Stephen Neale (1950–) is a British professor of philiosophy and linguistics. He has written numerous books about film and genre, and is widely reputed as an expert in the field.

Apply it

Choose an example of a television genre you are studying for your Close Study Products to research. Write a 500-word case study in which you trace its origins, identify its codes and conventions (and how these have changed over the years) and the influences on its development, and cite some key examples.

EXAMPLE: Situation comedy through time

The situation comedy (sitcom) is an enduring genre spanning both audio-visual and audio media forms. It is a series of episodes where each has an enclosed narrative, making it distinct from the comedy drama and sketch show. It usually features a group of main characters who are thrown together in some way. Families and workplaces are very common settings, and there needs to be a sense that the characters cannot avoid each other to bring out the best comedic situations.

A traditional sitcom should have humour and entertainment as its primary purpose. There are occasional serial elements to the narrative, but it usually resets at the beginning of each episode, with no reference being made to previous events. US sitcoms tend to run for long series, so are more likely to have serial elements and gradual changes to narrative or situation over time. The narrative shape sometimes varies across cultures, too – for example, in UK sitcoms we frequently see a character who is down on their luck gain an opportunity to escape their circumstances but ultimately be unsuccessful. US sitcoms vary this formula much more. Usually, stereotypes are heavily used to increase comic effect. Sitcoms are usually quite cheap to produce (with the exception of some of the star-studded casts, who have commanded some of the highest salaries paid in US television), and locations are limited with much filming taking place on a regular set.

△ The popular UK sitcom *Steptoe and Son*

Sitcoms were popular programming on the radio before becoming a mainstream part of television schedules. Some of the early popular radio sitcoms in the UK, such as *Hancock's Half Hour* (1954–61) later transferred to television. *Steptoe and Son* was made concurrently for both television and radio in the 1960s and 1970s, proving popular with listeners and viewers.

In recent years, the sitcom has seen many changes, such as the reduction of the laughter track, and increased hybridisation with the comedy-drama and even the spoof documentary. However, although audience tastes may be hungry for new incarnations of the genre, traditional sitcoms continue to be made.

△ The cast of *Ghosts* (2019). The British sitcom has shown that there is still an appetite in the UK for quirky situation comedies that satirise aspects of British social class and cultural identity. A US version of the programme has also been made

Neale argued that genre and its relationship with audience, industry and product could be described as **cultural categories**. Genres are widely understood by producers and audiences, and the category consists of dynamic aspects texts share. As such it can be understood as having a semiotic function in signifying meaning to the audience. It also allows them to use widely culturally agreed rules and norms to shape their viewing practices, but in addition has an economic role in informing production and commissioning practices in the industry according to audience tastes reflected by the market. Neale's work was conducted initially in the field of film theory but has relevance for media studies students because genres in other media forms behave in very similar ways.

Neale views genre as a process, rather than a collection of static groups that consistently draw on an identical **repertoire of elements**. These are conventions or rules that genres tend to follow which help arouse audience expectations of the product. Audio-visual genres evolve over time, meaning sometimes it is difficult to pinpoint exactly where a genre begins, disappears or evolves into a genre so different it is no longer considered part of the same genre category. Genres do evolve continually as new texts are added to the body of similar texts, which Neale calls the **corpus**. This may involve **hybridisation** between genres or the formulation of related **sub-genres**, such as action sci-fi or romantic comedy.

Genres are subject to change because of tensions of all kinds that push and pull texts. There is a dynamic relationship between audience, industry and text, which is constantly being renegotiated. The main tensions are between **repetition and sameness** versus **variation and change**. This means that genre text producers walk a fine line between repeating successful formulas with only minor variations – which may eventually bore the audience – and varying it sufficiently to still allow familiarity but also make the audience feel the product they are consuming is fresh.

Neale believes that genre labels are familiar to the audience and are important to them. They carry a **narrative image** that is communicated and perpetuated by word of mouth (other audience members) and marketing materials. This is closely connected with their **expectations and hypotheses** based on their previous experience of the genre. Audiences find the action of prediction based on generic

Key terms

corpus group of texts identified as belonging to the same genre
The film contributes to the corpus of coming-of-age stories.

cultural categories a way of understanding genre labels as products of both industry and audience
Genre identification helps us to navigate cultural categories in our media experience.

hybridisation the mixing of one genre with another
Both products show signs of hybridisation with other genres.

repertoire of elements identifiable aspects of texts belonging to the corpus in genre theory
The audience will recognise the locations because of their familiarity with the repertoire of elements.

repetition and sameness the tendency of genre texts to repeat aspects of successful formulas – always in tension with variation and change
Genres retain familiarity due to use of repetition and sameness.

sub-genres The formulation of a new sub-group within a genre which shares some of the qualities of the parent group but also has defining qualities of its own.
Within the magazine, action sci-film is marketed as a sub-genre appealing to a predominantly male audience.

variation and change the tendency of genre texts to reformulate with new qualities to prevent audiences from becoming tired of a formula
Genres are subject to variation and change, preventing staleness.

2.4 Genre and audio-visual and audio media

Key terms

cultural regime of verisimilitude our connecting of a genre text with our wider cultural knowledge
The representation of the court case requires us to draw on our knowledge of the cultural regime of verisimilitude.

expectations and hypotheses requirements to be fulfilled, and narrative and other predictions made by an audience based on their prior experience of a genre
The audience anticipates events in terms of expectations and hypotheses.

generic regime of verisimilitude the norms and laws of a genre; what is probable or likely in a genre text
The flamboyant setting is in keeping with the generic regime of verisimilitude.

narrative image the expectations of a genre text based on its label, often passed by word of mouth
The narrative image signified by the trailer strongly suggests the crime drama genre.

suspend disbelief the spectator must fully 'buy into' the film or TV narrative, characters, etc.
The viewer must suspend disbelief if they are to enjoy watching Lord of the Rings *films.*

expectations a crucial pleasure of some genre texts and are easily disappointed if these are not fulfilled, which can be a disaster for media producers.

In order to immerse themselves fully in a fictional diegesis, the spectator must **suspend disbelief** (i.e. 'buy into' the film or TV narrative, characters, etc.). In fictional media texts it is vital that we care about the characters and allow ourselves to share their world for the time allotted to the narrative to play out, whether that is a 45-minute radio play or a 26-episode television serial. We have all experienced an occasion when this has failed to happen, and distraction and disinterest wrest us from the narrative. At this point, when consuming a television text or radio narrative, we tend to switch off, transfer our attention to something else or switch to another channel.

The suspension of disbelief is associated with the two regimes of verisimilitude. The **generic regime of verisimilitude** refers to what is probable or likely in a genre text; the ways in which texts match up to both our experience of other texts and of the real world. We are happy for events to take place in a science-fiction television series using technologies that don't exist, because this is part of the norms and laws of the genre. The **cultural regime of verisimilitude** is connected with the spectator's experience of the 'real' world and can be subtle in its influence. Texts that are set in a real historical time or offer a fictionalised interpretation of real events may suffer credibility issues if the fictionalisation departs significantly from the known facts. This operates similarly to Roland Barthes' cultural code, which we encountered in Chapter 1: Reading print media.

Example

Outlander **(Amazon Prime, 2014) as an example of generic hybridity**

The television series *Outlander*, which began in 2014, defies generic categorisation, but simultaneously draws on conventions, themes, modes and tropes from a range of cultural categories. Listings across the internet attach a whole host of generic and sub-genre categories to the programme. These include science fiction, time-travel, adventure, drama, historical drama, fantasy, war and romance. This resistance to categorisation, while simultaneously showing the audience's desire to categorise, makes it an interesting example of the fluid nature of contemporary genre and the playfulness with which it may be exploited by its producers.

△ Action from Series 3 of *Outlander*

Quick questions

1. Why is it important that viewers can 'suspend disbelief' when consuming audio-visual products?
2. What is meant by the 'narrative image' communicated by genre labels?
3. What are two of the key qualities, usually stated as oppositions, that drive genre development and change over time?

■ Genre and technological change

Genre conventions change over time in response to two main factors: technological change and social and cultural factors. The form these factors take in affecting genre transmission vary across media forms.

The development of video-on-demand and increasing international reach of some audio-visual content providers through subscription packages, cable and satellite services has meant a big increase in the reach of certain television genres as part of the impact of globalisation on the mass media. New genres can spread from culture to culture more rapidly than at any other time in the history of the mass media.

Theorist Thomas Schatz (1981) proposed that there are only really two types of genre – **genres of order** and **genres of integration**. This is an idea that foregrounds the social and cultural uses of genre and attempts to address some of their ideological dimensions. The first is considered to be a 'male' mode of genre, where order is threatened and a power struggle must take place. Genres of integration are thought of as more 'female' and offer more exploration and resolution of emotional conflicts. Although his work relates to Hollywood film genres, it's a useful idea to bear in mind if you're thinking about the **ideological reading** of the nature of genres as a site for conflict and resolution.

Some genres certainly endure across media, with their popularity standing the test of time – although their conventions may change to reflect social and cultural attitudes and values.

△ Action films are a classic example of a genre of integration

Apply it

Choose a television genre that has been around for a long time. Research the genre and create a seven-slide presentation covering the inception of the genre including early examples, its conventions, key changes in the genre, its present-day examples and what you believe the future holds for it.

One final word about genre – some texts do genuinely resist generic classification. Others subvert the conventions of genres for their own ends or parody them in a way that could be considered as postmodern.

If genre conventions are not immediately obvious to you when studying a text, you might want to consider what the reasons are for this. Is it simply that genre is not as important an aspect of studying the text as other elements of media language? Neale himself cautioned against the idea of mechanistically using conventions as a checklist – in reality, many genre texts are quite subtle and make interesting use of their conventions beyond merely signifying categorisation.

🔗 **For more on postmodern approaches to genres see section 4.4: Postmodernism.**

Key terms

genres of order and integration systems of genre categorisation that foreground the social and cultural uses of genre and classes them as essentially 'male' or 'female'
Soap operas are primarily genres of integration.

ideological reading a conclusion that aims to expose how power relationships between social groups operate and manifest themselves in cultural production
An ideological reading of the homepage would take into account the lack of ethnic diversity.

2.4 Genre and audio-visual and audio media

Codes and conventions in audio-visual genre texts

Initially we tend to think of fiction texts when approaching the study of the media genres, probably because so much genre criticism has grown out of film theory. Fact-based media texts have just as many interesting genres, and their features can be identified as clusters of codes and conventions just as with any other text. When undertaking study of a genre in an audio-visual text, one of the first things you are likely to do is to research and/or try to define for yourself what the codes and conventions are based on your experience of a group of texts from the corpus.

This kind of approach produces a 'checklist' of generic codes and conventions that is a useful starting point. In keeping with the arguments you have already encountered, you should be aware that this method is only the beginning for generic discussion, albeit a useful one. It is worth including in your 'checklist' other factors such as audiences you associate with the products, and some of the economic factors affecting their production and scheduling. This will allow you to begin to access some of the other arguments about the genre you are studying that might be relevant in helping you to connect with the theoretical framework.

EXAMPLE: Adverts for male grooming products

Audio-visual adverts for male grooming products often make use of conventions that might include:

- use of **celebrity endorsement** by role models such as sportspeople
- use of actors who denote traditional masculinity in their physique
- masculine colour codes such as greys and blues, or technologically driven colours such as greens or orange
- high-key lighting to make the product seem appealing
- pack shots and slogans at the end
- a male voice-over
- foregrounding of technological qualities of products, together with close-ups of the working product which may use special effects or graphics
- use of a motivational soundtrack
- representation of any women in the narrative in heteronormative way as prizes or goals
- normalisation of interest in personal appearance as an acceptable part of 'new' masculinity.

This Gillette advert from 2022 features footballer and anti-racism campaigner Raheem Sterling in an advert that features most of the conventions listed above:

www.youtu.be/Q0YfJU4HB7M?list=TLGGXugfa5-GlBgxNjAzMjAyMw

Quick questions

1. Explain two other factors you should consider when studying genre, other than identifying codes and conventions.
2. What do we mean when we say genre is a 'cultural category'?
3. Explain the difference between genres of order and genres of integration.

Intertextuality in audio-visual media products

Intertextuality, which we encountered in Chapter 1: Reading print media, applied to print media products, is also found regularly in other media forms. This is often apparent in music videos, advertisements and television fiction. Learning to recognise subtle references to other media products will enrich your reading of the product, enhance the nuanced ways in which you can write about the production of meaning, and also develop your understanding of postmodernism.

Key term

celebrity endorsement the process by which a celebrity is paid to become the face of a brand. This might include appearing in advertisements, using the brand in high-profile places, being a spokesperson for the brand
In the campaign, the trainers are endorsed by a number of prominent sportspeople.

For more on postmodern approaches to reading media texts, see Chapter 4: Media language.

Example

Intertextuality and *The Simpsons*

The long-running US animated sitcom series *The Simpsons* is popular all over the world. It is also very well known for its conscious and deliberate referencing of a whole range of texts ranging from pop culture, political and social to the literary canon. Intertextuality in *The Simpsons* resides in many parts of the text – it can shape an overall narrative structure, be found in lines of dialogue, be evident in the construction of mise-en-scène, or dictate the reaction of a character to a situation. Sometimes it is subtle, at other times blatant.

Here are a few examples:

- 'Them, Robot': The narrative of this episode (and its title) makes conscious and deliberate reference to the 2004 film *I, Robot*. Mr Burns replaces the workers of his nuclear plant with more efficient robots that must abide by the three laws of robotics.
- 'The Tell-Tale Head': The title is a reference to Gothic American writer Edgar Allen Poe's story *The Telltale Heart*. Widely read in the USA, Poe's stories and poems feature regularly in *The Simpsons*. Lisa creates a diorama of a scene from the story in another episode, and in a Halloween episode a whole segment is devoted to the reading of the poem *The Raven*.

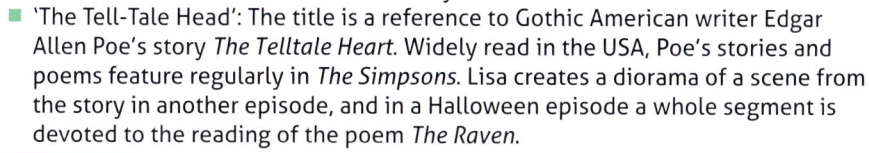

Intertextuality is so rich in audio-visual texts that it has almost become a redundant concept, since so many mass media forms constantly make references to others. This does not mean you should ignore it – sometimes it is used to greater effect than others.

Apply it

Choose an episode of *The Simpsons* to watch, looking for examples of intertextuality. Compile your answers as a class to see the breadth of intertextual sources used.

→ Exam-style questions

1. How useful are theories of narrative when analysing media products? Analyse one of your audio-visual media Close Study Products using two approaches of your choice.
2. Explain the relationship between audience, industry and the genre of one of your set products using the ideas of Stephen Neale.
3. Explore the contribution made by the editing and camerawork to one of your audio-visual Close Study Products.
4. Explore the contribution of mise-en-scène to the semiotic production of meaning in one of your audio-visual media Close Study Products.
5. Explain the way in which genre conventions help form cultural categories using examples from your audio-visual Close Study Products.

2.4 Genre and audio-visual and audio media

→ Summary

- The principles of semiotic analysis, explained at greater length in section 1.1, are readily applied to audio-visual and audio texts.
- The technical codes of audio-visual texts are combined in different ways in different audio-visual forms, but all these use the same codes.
- Mise-en-scène is used in both fact-based and fiction media to carefully construct meaning using dress codes, framing, props, décor, lighting, locations and non-verbal codes.
- Camera work is used to create relationships between subject matter and form in a text and the audience. Many aspects have to be carefully considered – shot type, camera angle, camera movement and lens used.
- Editing is fundamental to the audience's understanding of time and space in audio-visual texts. The two dominant modes are continuity editing and montage editing.
- Sound is often neglected in favour of the visual aspects of the text and its contribution should never be ignored in analysis.
- Audio-visual and audio narratives are time based, so narrative theories are used in a way that considers this.
- The theorists Todorov and Barthes are useful in decoding the narratives in audio-visual texts, and in this chapter you looked for the first time at some examples of how these theories might be applied to various popular texts.
- Stephen Neale is an important theorist in genre, and from his work terms and associated ideas have been gained that allow discussion of the relationship between audience, industry and text in a precise way.
- Intertextuality is rife in audio-visual texts, but analysis must still recognise the contribution made by it to meaning – the examples that seem most conscious or deliberate can still form an interesting part of a discussion.

Chapter 3: Reading digital media

What you will learn in this chapter

Chapter 3: Reading digital media covers:

- how to extend your knowledge and understanding of reading print and audio-visual media texts to digital media such as websites, social media and computer games
- the codes and conventions of some of the diverse world of digital media forms and products
- how to understand the unconventional ways in which narratives can operate in digital media texts
- how to approach the study of digital media genres.

3.1 Technical codes and features used in online texts

In Chapters 1 and 2, we looked at some of the ways in which we can access the meanings of print and audio-visual media texts. When approaching digital media text, you will be drawing on many of the same skills and much of the same terminology. Many digital media products, for example, draw on a combination of print media codes (for example, mise-en-scène) with audio-visual content and increased interactivity. Many of the significant differences lie in the way the user can also be a contributor to such media. In addition, digital media products demonstrate the user's ability to construct the text, within certain parameters, to suit their own aims and preferences.

> **TIP** ✓
> It's essential that you revisit Chapter 1: Reading print media and Chapter 2: Reading audio-visual media and consider what from those chapters can be applied to digital media.

Developments in website technology, codes and conventions

Websites deploy many of the features to attract attention that are used in newspapers, magazines and print advertisements. The majority offer the audience a familiar combination of a **banner**, usually positioned at the top, navigation features and clickable links (supplying interactivity). These are sometimes also placed as a **skyscraper**. On conventional sites, this is often on the left, but on blogs the convention is for a skyscraper of archived posts, adverts and links to be on the right. Single skyscraper adverts are also common. They use a combination of lexical codes, photographs, graphical images and large typography to sub-section content and draw the reader's

Enabling ideas

For this chapter, we will be considering how the enabling ideas we encountered in Chapters 1 and 2 can be applied to the study of digital media texts.

We will also be considering how developments in technologies affect media language in digital media products.

The following enabling ideas from the specification are introduced in this chapter:

3.4.1.1 Semiotics:

- sign
- signifier
- signified
- dominant signifier
- icon
- code
- symbol
- anchorage
- ideology
- paradigm
- syntagm.

Barthes' ideas and theories on semiotics:

- signification
- denotation
- connotation
- myth.

Key terms

architecture the structure and navigation of a website
The website's architecture is complex, meaning the audience needs to spend some time exploring its content.

banner commonly used term for any block of information at the top of a website; can also refer to the site's 'masthead', its identity
The banner signifies boldness through use of strong typographic codes.

dynamic content content that is regularly updated
The use of dynamic content makes the homepage appealing to repeat visitors.

hero image use of a large, dominating image that fills the majority of the viewable homepage before scrolling occurs
The hero image connotes authenticity through use of a natural landscape as background for the product.

hyperlinks links within a web page to other parts of the site or external content
Hyperlinks take the reader if desired to connected news stories on similar issues.

hypertextuality web 'intertextuality' – the linking from site to site of other content
Fan sites are rich in hypertextuality.

plugins additional features such as social media buttons or embedded players, for example for YouTube, that encourage sharing and connectivity
The website's use of plugins makes it a good example of a technologically converged product.

---

eye. The **hero image** has also become a feature of many contemporary websites, positioned centrally, sometimes filling the whole screen as a single image, video or rotating gallery. A slideshow such as this may also have clickable content and is a common design feature that allows the site's designers to order its most topical content in an attractive and appealing way. Similarly, many web designers now use cards to display dynamic content and encourage clicks, which have an image and a **slug** that creates enigmas that invite the audience to read further and draw them into other pages within the site.

Logos, house style (see Chapter 1: Reading print media) and branding are all as important to website design as they are to magazines, advertising campaigns or newspapers.

Web-page design has developed enormously since its early days, the main developments being faster communication technology speeds, the addition of more and more video content and images, and less reliance on text. They are also frequently much more digitally converged, with **plugins** linking to other content such as YouTube channels, podcasts and social media accounts. Some sites, however, still have longform articles designed to be immersive reads, emulating magazines which, in many cases, they have come to replace.

Embedded content, that is content which has been added from another site such as video, is common in blogs and other sites. Most feature numerous links, giving rise to a concept related to intertextuality known as **hypertextuality**, where the site's producers are able to physically link not only to other content within the site but also to external content. Banner adverts and pop-up ads are also a common part of the web-user's experience – often these are external adverts, and can be analysed as texts in their own right using standard print and audio-visual methodologies.

The way in which a website is designed and structured is sometimes referred to as its **architecture**. Other menus and **hyperlinks** are always provided as the online equivalent of a contents page. Most professionally produced websites try to avoid incorporating too much scrolling, so limit the content of the first page. This makes the rest of the site's content easily navigable from prominently placed and well-organised menus. Website design varies enormously, depending on the function of the site, its content and the design aims, but you tend to see the same basic elements present: interactivity, **dynamic content** (content that changes regularly), navigability and copy. Plugins, such as social media buttons, are also used, which increase web flow and ease of content sharing.

Key terms

skyscraper object positioned to run up the side of a website – sometimes a narrow advertisement
The skyscraper signifies the connection between real and hyperreal by promoting a festival featuring the act.

slug a line in larger print introducing a feature that acts as a hook
The slug draws in the reader by using a quote from the celebrity.

EXAMPLE: *The Art of Manliness* website

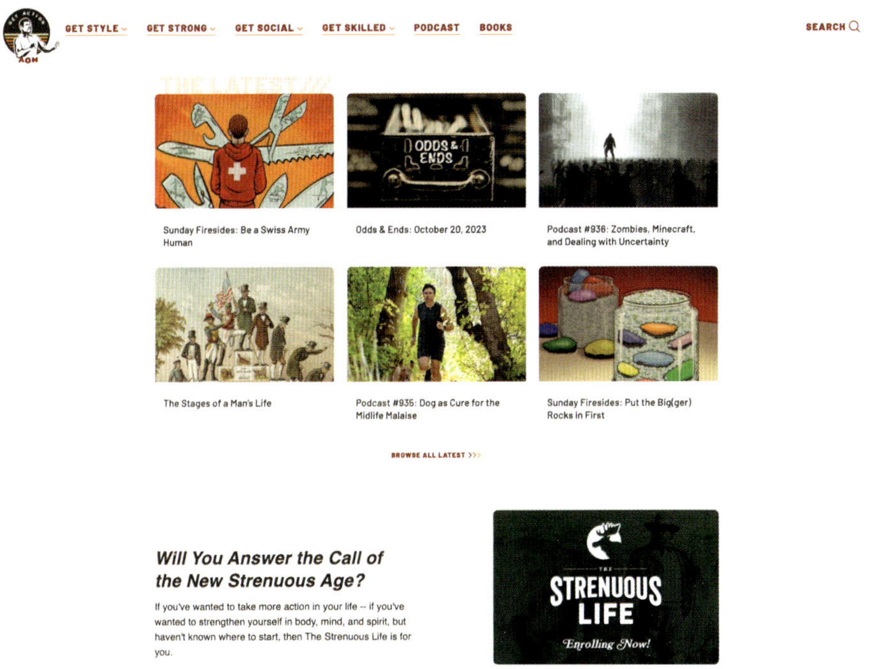

The Art of Manliness is a lifestyle website which uses conventional **card-based design** that readily adapts to different devices. The branding of the website, visible in the top left corner, features a wood-cut style image of a moustachioed man, bare-chested and fists raised, with the lexical coding 'get action'. This connotes traditional masculinity, presented in black and white with the simple addition of the warm neutral colour codes that harmonise the look of the site. Combined with other aspects of media language, these make traditional masculine qualities and interests feel relevant to modern men in an age where their interests may tend to shift towards technology. This nod to the past is reinforced throughout the featured articles using vintage-feel graphics and photography, consciously referencing an era where gender politics were less nuanced than today.

The content categories of style, get social, get strong and get skilled all encode masculinity as being about strength and capability but also appearance and self-representation. The site's podcast and e-books, formats that are likely to appeal more to men in their late twenties upwards, are promoted in the skyscraper to the right.

> **Key term**
>
> **card-based design** trend in web design that prioritises visual rectangular clickable links – 'cards' that often have a picture and captioning
> *The use of card-based design promotes a fashionable and vibrant visual aesthetic.*

Apply it

1. Choose a lifestyle website. Take screenshots of the full scroll on the homepage. Annotate them to show which features of analysis can be used from print media, and which aspects clearly follow the design conventions of a website. You should also pay attention to hyperlinks, elements of the site that move, such as galleries and slideshows, social media buttons and feeds, and other opportunities for the user to interact with the text.
2. In addition, choose a short piece of video from the site. Analyse the contribution it makes to the audience's experience of the text.

3.1 Technical codes and features used in online texts

51

Quick questions

1. Why would it be useful for a magazine publisher to retain a print edition as well as an online version?
2. What is the purpose of a 'hero image' on a website?
3. Explain what is meant by 'hypertextuality' as used on many websites.

Apply it

Create a mind map showing as many uses of the presence of digital video online as you can.

Key terms

post-broadcast era term sometimes used to define the shift away from scheduled media consumption
Audiences are freer to select content and time of viewing in the post-broadcast era.

viral the electronic passing of images, information, etc. between users. Before digital and social media, the term was used to describe the spreading of information by word of mouth

citizen journalism the passing of footage or photographs taken by witnesses as events to either mainstream or alternative news distributors
Citizen journalism can foreground the stories of minority groups in the news agenda.

Apply it

Use the four numbered points above combined with screenshots to create a five- to seven-slide presentation of an online video of your choice.

Present it to the rest of the group, including a screening of your video at the beginning.

■ Online magazines

Online magazines are an interesting example of how new technologies have developed traditional media. These may exist alone or form part of a bi-media publishing strategy. This means that the print edition continues to be published, but the online content is also widely and, in some cases, exclusively read. In this case, you are likely to see strong continuity not only of subject matter but also branding between the two.

EXAMPLE: *Dazed* online magazine and its print edition

Dazed magazine successfully retains a coffee table-style bi-monthly print format magazine that features art, fashion and culture alongside a web edition that explores trends and soft celebrity news and reviews. The clean look of the website (https://www.dazeddigital.com) with simple black and white colour codes and use of white space, replicates the strong visual/copy divide of the heavily art-influenced aesthetic of the print edition. The simple branding of the website, signified only by the lexical and typographic coding, is understated but very recognisable to its audience.

■ Video content on the web

The length of internet video content is often very short. Initially, this was due to connection speeds and bandwidth limitations, but it also quickly became clear that abbreviated forms of audio-visual text were highly suited to the internet environment. Short videos are now an established part of our internet experience, whether we are consciously seeking them out through a dedicated video-sharing platform such as YouTube, we are using social media or visiting a news site. Video is such a popular and powerful feature of the new media age that web video has become a defining feature of an increasingly **post-broadcast era**. Video has become an important way of enriching any other digital presence.

The ability of audio-visual codes to deliver high-impact content in a short space of time makes it very suited to web-browsing habits. The impact of the **viral** video (simply meaning one that has been shared and viewed many times) on popular culture is a dramatic one. When you are analysing any kind of video content online, you should start by asking the following questions:

1. What are the **stylistic conventions** of this kind of video? This could be location, mode of address, camerawork, mise-en-scène editing.
2. What is the **purpose** of the video? Does it belong to an identifiable genre? If so, what are its conventions?
3. What kind of **duration** is typical for online video content, and how would you describe the content's **narrative progression**?
4. Where is the content typically **posted** initially, and does it **move** from platform to platform?

Online video

Online video content is a mixture of professional and amateur texts, ranging from user-generated prank or cat videos on a range of platforms to highly polished promotional content. Short video can even be used in war zones or protests as **citizen journalism**, countering authorised versions of events or documenting abuses of human rights. The rise of TikTok as a platform has led to an explosion in short-form video, which transmits readily across all social media platforms, leading YouTube, Facebook and Instagram to respond with their own short video categories.

CHAPTER 3 READING DIGITAL MEDIA

Video logs, often referred to as vlogs, are aimed at a youth audience and are one of the most popular genres on YouTube. Similar to podcasts, users can subscribe to vlogs in various ways to ensure they are notified of the latest instalment from a favourite vlogger. Vlogs feature personalities, often with big followings. Like blogs, which reach a much older target audience, their content can be about almost anything. Popular genres include game walkthroughs and release reviews, beauty, and lifestyle – where the personality of the vlogger and their opinions are usually of great significance. Some topics are less pop-culturally focused, such as popular science vlogs, where scientific principles are often tested out in entertaining ways. One of the key presentational devices in vlogs is that they are dominated by the personality of the presenter – it is the combination of the presenter and their take on their subject matter that earns them subscribers. The presenters also frequently host from a familiar environment, often their home studio, which again builds rapport and familiarity and replicates real-world personal relationships where a person might visit a friend they know well in their domestic space.

EXAMPLE: Olajide Olatunji aka KSI, YouTube personality

Olatunji, known to many of the millions of followers of his two channels as JJ or KSI, is a British rapper, boxer and vlogger who started his career making FIFA game videos but soon branched out into other lifestyle and technology content. Like many YouTubers, he uses his brand to promote other income streams, such as his 'Prime' soft drinks and his music career (as rapper KSI).

On his personal channel, the mise-en-scène of recent videos at the time of writing feature him in the same room for each, wearing the same headphones in the same medium shot. The home setting and informal distance of the para-proxemics contribute to the conversational feel of the videos. Props in the background include the range of drinks he markets with previous YouTube rival Logan Paul, trophies from his boxing career and a large plant, often used to signify trustworthiness and calm. The décor is modern and the lighting low in the background, foregrounding the personality. Olatunji himself appears relaxed in his seat, headphones connoting his role as content producer, and he wears clothes conforming to a bright, fashionable, casual dress code, which appeals to his primary audience of teens and young men.

Stretch and challenge

Choose three vloggers who, through their content, address different target audiences. For example, teenage gamers, 30-something mums and young people interested in travel.

Through the use of screenshots and close analysis, prepare a presentation comparing the media language techniques used by them to construct varying modes of address.

3.1 Technical codes and features used in online texts

Apply it

Choose an example of a vlogger you either regularly follow or one who your research shows has many subscribers. Watch two or three of their vlogs. Note the use of mise-en-scène, the editing style and the mode of address they use to communicate with their audience.

Write a 300-word case study, including three screenshots, which focuses on the use of audio-visual information combined with subject matter that makes the vlog appealing to its target audience.

Explainer videos

Another online video style with multiple variations in sub-genre and style is 'explainer' videos. These are short videos that can be distributed on any media platform. They can incorporate animation, photographs, graphics and video edited in montage, usually to a single music track. The 'explaining' is done using titles (**captioning**).

Sometimes, explainer videos may feature a person simply demonstrating a technique or tip, such as make-up or hair styles, or cooking hacks. Such videos often get heavily promoted on social media, where they appear to offer an entertaining solution to a common problem or promise some kind of short-cut tip that will drive more traffic to the user's main content.

> **Key term**
>
> **captioning** the adding of subtitles to a video, sometimes used as another term for titling
> *The video is captioned, making it readily shareable on social media.*

🔗 For more about soft news see Chapter 5: Media representations.

Apply it

Choose an example of an amateur-produced and a professionally produced explainer video. For each, analyse how the lexical coding and soundtrack interplay with other technical codes to produce meaning.

In another variant of the explainer, a person will speak simply and directly to camera as they would when vlogging. These simple videos are popular with brands wanting to employ sales techniques that make people feel they have a 'face' – the representative could be a brand ambassador, for example.

Quick questions

1. Why is short-form video so popular online? Give two reasons.
2. What is the defining quality of all 'explainer' videos?
3. Describe a common feature of the mise-en-scène technique in vlogs.

Apply it

Choose three genres of website, such as fan wiki, celebrity news and film review. Explore some examples online. List five conventions (methods/styles) of each.

3.2 Narrative organisation in digital media texts

Some digital media narratives function in a way that is quite different from traditional media. This is due to the interactive nature of many digital narratives. While a viral or user-generated video can be analysed similarly to any other short audio-visual text, some digital narratives are more challenging to decode when applying traditional theories.

French philosopher Roland Barthes, whose ideas about myth and the five narrative codes we encountered on pages 16–17, also raised another issue about the ownership of meaning in media texts in his famous 1967 essay 'The Death of the Author'. Barthes suggested that the Western habit of taking meaning as set by the author over the reader's experience of the text in interpreting it was losing its relevance in contemporary culture.

This signified a move away from the earlier structuralist theories of narrative, which tended to see the meaning as being inherent in the text. It began to move us towards an era of participatory and gaming culture where narratives can be used in all kinds of non-linear and non-traditional ways.

This might include the reappropriation of game footage in *Machinima*, for example, where new narratives are created from recorded and re-edited game footage. This is an interesting approach to apply to digital media texts, which are often highly intertextual and derivative. Narratives that exist in many digital forms may be fragmentary, have many contributors and be open-ended, with many opportunities for variation in between.

Conventional narrative theories can be applied in a modified way to digital media texts, but you might find yourself doing this in a much more fragmented way. Before considering how narratives work, it is worth revisiting the sections on Barthes and Todorov in Chapters 1 and 2.

> **For further discussion of participatory culture see section 6.7: 'End of audience' theory.**

> **For further discussion of fan responses to digital media products, see section 6.6: Fandom and the media.**

EXAMPLE: Exploring narrative in the *On Our Radar* alternative news website

On Our Radar is an alternative news agency which aims to empower citizen journalists as the owners of their stories and help people from marginalised communities' voices to be heard.

On the 'Manifesto' page of the website, a narrative is built in the following way, which can be interpreted using Todorov's ideas about narrative structure:

- **Equilibrium:** Western media reports on marginalised communities using privileged, often white middle-class journalists who visit for a short period of time then leave, gaining only a partial picture of the events, people and places they report on.
- **Disruption:** a loss of trust in Western media can be seen across the world, both in Western countries and in the communities reported on.
- **Recognition:** that change is needed and there should be a move towards a new style of journalism that promotes real lived experience over the views of outsiders.
- **Attempt to repair:** *On Our Radar* is formed with the aim of empowering people from these communities to become powerful owners of their own stories using digital platforms.
- **New equilibrium:** Journalists now use their storytelling expertise to engage with local communities and to support them to tell their own stories in their own words in both traditional and non-traditional ways and using new technologies.

3.2 Narrative organisation in digital media texts

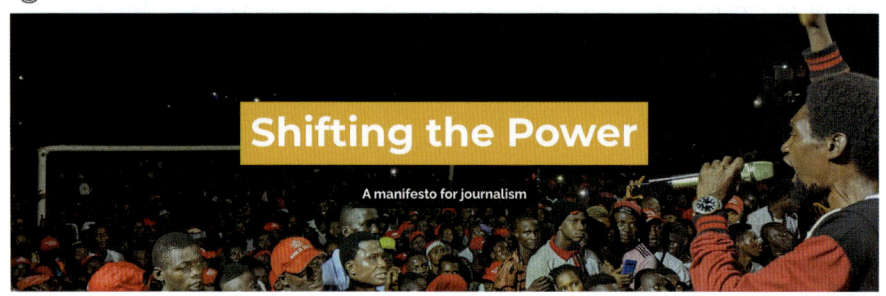

Media language, narrative and genre in social and participatory media

Social and **participatory media** involves the use of platforms that allow users to make themselves heard. These are based on the idea of **virtual communities**, and operate through profiles, a digital projection of a person's individual identity in that community. There are image-sharing sites, video-sharing sites, social networking sites, micro-blogging sites, communication-based apps, discussion and news aggregation sites, idea cataloguing sites, fan wikis and so on. They are a medium that is generated by the masses and consumed by the masses. Highly accessible and often free at the point of consumption since they rely on advertising as a funding model, they differ significantly from traditional media in their ease of access, self-regulation and immediacy. To some extent they are less permanent than traditional media, subject to trends in use among their majority youth audience.

> **Key terms**
>
> **participatory media** digital media that the audience interacts with, helps construct and distribute
> *Online videos encourage responses and interaction from the audience, which can be seen as a form of participatory media.*
>
> **virtual communities** groups of people who come together in cyberspace through a shared interest without geographical barriers
> *Fans of the show have formed a virtual community.*

For further discussion of the differences in consumption between consumer and participatory culture, see section 6.2: The impact of new technologies on patterns of media consumption.

Apply it
1. Find examples of sites that you think fit into the types of participatory media given above. Do some of them have more than one function? Where do they overlap?
2. Create a mind map, either in a group or individually, which lists as many functions as you can identify.
3. Write a sentence for each example, describing what you feel the main purpose of each site is.

Most social media platforms are used for similar reasons, even though the focus of membership might vary. Their users have generally come together to share content, either found elsewhere on the site or that they have created, to discuss things with other people and to network with like-minded individuals. All these things can be true of social features of websites such as message boards and forums. Most digital culture experts now believe that any content-sharing platforms can be regarded as 'social' media.

Social media usage can be a platform for communicating a person's identity and gives individuals a sense of a presence in the online world, of belonging to a community and a culture outside the daily grind of the real world. In this community, they may have a reputation that exists, at least in the first instance, exclusively online.

A significant aspect of social media in terms of media language is the way in which it creates narratives around personalities and brands and uses media language to construct an often strongly visual representation of its subject matter. Social media has been criticised for promoting unrealistic standards around physical appearance for both men and women. Perhaps this is because, in a world where the public images of celebrities are highly mediated in the mainstream media, followers who are used to accepting the use of special effects and the manipulation of images for years by the industry have different expectations of social media accounts. They may believe these to be more 'authentic' when they are often heavily curated and just as likely to feature images that have had modifications made to them.

Narratives in social and participatory media may be much more fluid and less well defined, often reacting to external events. It may be harder to identify the narrative in a social media account, for example, than in a 7-minute vlog entry where a new product is tested or an experience articulated.

EXAMPLE: Social media personality accounts – actor Michelle Yeoh

Many celebrities have heavily curated accounts, either run by themselves, their PR agents, or a combination of the two. These promote their celebrity persona and a glamourous way of life. Actor Michelle Yeoh's account is filled primarily with content of interest to her fans about her work – magazine articles, upcoming appearances in film and television, and appearances at awards ceremonies. It also promotes a range of social causes, such as charities, and features some candid home images that balance the more glamorous content and emphasise her 'ordinariness', which is highly appealing to fans.

In one image posted on 18 October 2022, Yeoh appears plainly dressed, bespectacled and with hair drawn up to front a campaign to fund COVID-19 vaccines for developing countries. Her dress code and serious non-verbal codes, coupled with the direct mode of address to camera, all reinforce the captioned piece to camera about vaccine poverty.

Another image from 12 January 2023 represents her glamorously dressed in designer gown and jewellery sporting a Golden Globe award for a film appearance, connoting her success as an actress.

In a further post, we see her in her living room after setting up a Christmas tree, a candid 'at home shot' where she appears relaxed and dressed in casual clothing. These kinds of 'diary shots' around festivities give followers a sense of identification with the celebrity.

You can also find an image that depicts her as *Time Magazine's* 'Icon of the Year' in synergy with the magazine.

All of the posts across Yeoh's grid cumulatively construct an age-positive narrative of an 'outsider' who has gained an extraordinary level of stardom, an actor belonging to a minority ethnic group who has achieved critical and commercial success and stardom, and has overcome typecasting in an industry that is predominantly white.

Apply it
Choose a social media account from a well-known person. Select four contrasting posts. How has media language been used to construct representation of their persona and lifestyle?

Genre and social media

Personal social media accounts of personalities often have similar conventions in their content which are like the accounts of private individuals. It is this familiarity with conventions that makes many followers feel such a level of familiarity with celebrities. Common conventions of these accounts, duplicated by many users, might include:

- pictures selected for their attractiveness in which they are the focus
- images that show them having fun
- social images that connect them with others to demonstrate their social capital
- domestic images, such as with family or pets
- travel, food, event and other general lifestyle images
- showing of new purchases (or sponsored content), promoting a consumerist ideology
- sharing of content that positions them in the context of the wider world as politically aware, environmentally responsible, compassionate, etc.

These conventions show both repetition and sameness and illustrate genre as a cultural category. There are numerous sub-genres of accounts for both prominent personalities and their followers, who often use them as inspiration for their own content. Sports personalities, for example, mainly post content of interest to people who follow the sport and their achievements, focusing less on their home and personal lives.

EXAMPLE: Sub-genre of social media personality account – Alexey Molchanov, sports personality

Like many good sport brands, the account belonging to Alexey Molchanov, a record-breaking sportsperson who is a household name within his niche sport of freediving and owns a high-end equipment line, targets both elite sportspeople and those who look up to them as role models.

Typically his account shows action-based images of him freediving, often in long or medium shot. These posts showcase his abilities as a sportsperson, allow his followers to benefit from tips and discussion of technique, and cater to followers interested in the niche aesthetic of underwater photography. Throughout his account, he frequently showcases his own brand's products. In the case of professional freedivers, showing or using equipment from sponsors is a common convention of their social media posts, as are shots of them competing in major competitions and of diving recreationally in the best locations worldwide. In this way, the audience has their expectations fulfilled by following the account.

Quick questions

1. Name three common generic conventions (methods/styles) of celebrity social media accounts.
2. Give an example of a 'virtual community' and explain why its existence depends on new media forms.

🔗 **Self-regulation of websites and social media is discussed further in Chapter 6: Media audiences.**

3.3 Computer games

The manner in which computer games are experienced is significantly more immersive than other mass media forms and requires many modifications of the traditional ways in which media texts are read to make sense of the space they have opened in popular culture. The best introduction into the study of computer games as media texts is to look at methods in which the technical codes of media language you have already encountered in reading other texts may be adapted to allow you to begin to explore the nature of these rich, diverse and interesting media forms.

An effective method of studying a computer game is to use one of the many examples of gameplay footage available on YouTube. Alternatively, you could play segments of the game yourself. Pause regularly to take notes on what you experience in terms of mise-en-scène, graphical information, framing and perspective, sound, narrative and so on. This should in turn lead to consideration of representations. Signification in computer games is layered, as suggested by Barthes' model. It is dependent on the interests of the player and their enthusiasm in engaging with the world created for the game. Its social and cultural contexts play a very important role in this process.

Mise-en-scène analysis has to be amended for computer game analysis, because very often the framing is being done by the player themselves in an environment. Props, location design, character design (including dress code) and non-verbal communication are all still relevant. Artificial environments can be procedurally generated in computer games – others are quite rigid and vary little as game progression occurs, with the key differences revolving around engagement with other characters and selected views of the environment.

Graphical information plays an important role, and in many games appears permanently on screen to give the player information and statistics about their progress, score and environment. Also highly significant in considering the mise-en-scène of computer games is the notion of 'simulation' – the blending of the real and virtual in visual style. Games that are based on augmented reality take this to a new and more literal level.

EXAMPLE: Mise-en-scène in Grand Theft Auto *V* (2013)

The environment of *Grand Theft Auto V* is huge, encompassing spatially connected desert, urban and mountainous environments. The style is hyperreal – there are very detailed dress codes and numerous small details in the environment, offering one of the key pleasures of the game. The appearance of the environment depends on how the player interacts with it – crashing into a lamppost will damage it – as well as whether the action is taking place during the day or at night, with sophisticated light quality generating realism. Weather is also simulated, adding to the sense of immersion.

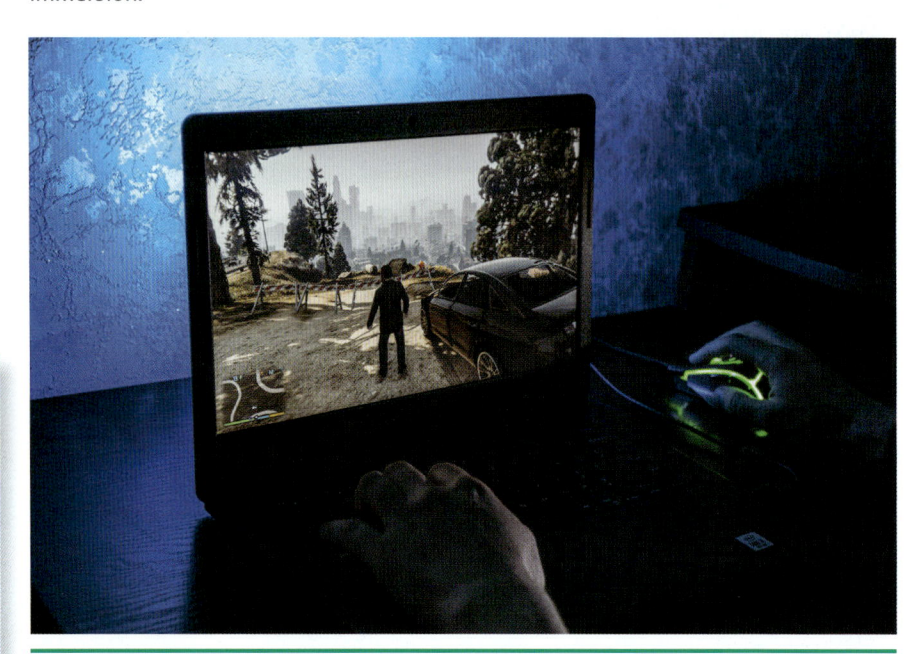

Apply it

Choose a computer game, either by watching gameplay footage on YouTube or playing your own game, and take some screenshots. Consider how mise-en-scène analysis can be applied in a conventional way to understand how it contributes to the gamer's experience of the game.

'Camerawork' and 'editing' are interesting aspects of computer games. In the absence of continuity editing (although some cut scenes observe its laws) the player essentially constructs the proxemics, para-proxemics and framing/view. 'Editing' takes place through a combination of player selection from a paradigm and responses in the game's programming to player interaction. Other optional views available for the player to choose from, such as maps, are a significant part of the gamer's rich visual world. First-person shooters almost always have weaponry in view, and the character in such games might only be seen at the start.

Since the gameplayer controls their own movement through the environment, we must consider the limited usefulness of applying the terminology of traditional camera shots to computer games. Graphic interfaces take on a much higher significance in many computer games; often the gamer is the character, so everything they see is a point-of-view shot.

Sound in a computer-generated environment may encompass effects, ambient music and character voice depending on the scenario. Aural codes are vital in gaming since they often provide essential feedback on gameplay, as well as having the usual functions of creating atmosphere and verisimilitude through soundscape. Some soundscapes in games differ from conventional media texts in that they are often more experimental and may seem to blur the boundary between extra-diegetic and diegetic. Ambient sound in an alien landscape may combine soundscape with score in interesting and evocative ways that contribute enormously to the gamer's experience of the game.

> **EXAMPLE: Game score – *Gravity Ghost* (released 2015 as a digital download)**
>
> US-based game score composer Ben Prunty, who has gained recognition for his work on indie games *Gravity Ghost* and *FTL: Faster Than Light*, sells his music for digital download on his website. You can preview the named atmospheric tracks generated for different points in the game at https://benprunty.bandcamp.com/album/gravity-ghost-soundtrack.

Apply it

1. Find a game score online to listen to, preferably one you don't usually play.
2. Research what you can about the game's genre, gameplay and narrative.
3. Listen to the score without visuals. Can you describe any of the techniques being used to evoke a particular atmosphere? Does the score signify genre? Are any sound effects integrated into the score? Since game scores are usually electronic, are there any acoustic sounds mixed into the track?

Narratives in computer games

Gameplay produces a different kind of experience compared with traditional media texts. Most of us recognise that computer games are more cognitively immersive than most mass media, but they are also very 'kinetically' immersive because of their sensory properties.

Another key difference is the experience of many computer games through a first-person narrative. This is especially relevant in role-playing games (RPGs), where the experience of creating an alternate 'self' can be especially powerful and personal. It may even be an expression of some or many aspects of a person's identity which only find a release in that environment. Even when the game allows control of an environment that features a third-person narrative, the audio-visual aspects of the interface often make the player feel as though they 'know' them. They feel a sense of ownership of the character(s) not usually experienced by mainstream viewers of other media forms.

The narrative of many computer games lies not so much in the sequential order or route through play, although for many games it is possible to identify a structure through the game's architecture. Some games also use **backstories** conveyed through **cut scenes**: non-interactive sequences of action that often provide contextual information about the next section of gameplay. Backstories (or 'lore') may often be the subject of YouTube videos and fan wikis, where it is clear that narrative immersion is a key pleasure, driving players to stay with a game. Cut scenes can be more easily analysed using traditional narrative theories, although the actual cut scenes experienced by the player may be dependent on the route through gameplay. Because of the limited capability of the game experience to generate complex characters, narratives often depend heavily on the predictably in behaviour of character archetypes. These in turn signify a broader cultural understanding and consensus in reading the text to engage fully with the narratives presented.

Some elements of traditional narrative theory have retained a certain level of usefulness when beginning to explore games. Todorov's theory, for example, could be applied to a game that has a strong 'plot' that drives the gameplay and a defined resolution or outcome. Lévi-Strauss' theory is non-linear, and works well when analysing any computer game narrative (see Chapter 4: Media language). Of Barthes' five codes, proairetic codes (ACT) are obviously of most significance, but symbolic (SYM), semantic (SEM) and even cultural/referential codes (REF) can also be applied.

> **Key terms**
>
> **backstories/lore** (in computer games) contextual narrative information, often fed in through cut scenes and used by fans to embellish the narrative and increase immersion through fan behaviours
> *The backstory may be analysed structurally through conventional theoretical approaches.*
>
> **cut scenes** non-interactive animated sections of games that contexualise an element of play
> *The game uses cut scenes to generate new hermeneutic codes that engage the player.*

3.3 Computer games

> **Key term**
>
> **ergodic narrative** a digital narrative that has different outcomes according to the interaction between the 'user' of the text and the 'rules' of the game
> *The narrative is ergodic, with many different potential endings to the game.*

EXAMPLE: Narrative in *Hollow Knight* (2017)

Like many computer games, the narrative in *Hollow Knight* is reliant on a combination of the backstory, lore developed from this in the gameplaying community and the possible **ergodic** routes through the game which the player participates in constructing. The backstory provides a stable narrative for exploration of the world and is revealed through use of cut-scene conversations with characters encountered by the knight. It also provides rich material for the development of 'lore' associated with the game, strengthening the player's online relationship with the game in a participatory way.

Key points about the story:

- The player controls a newcomer to the kingdom, known as the Knight.
- It is set in the Hallownest, an insectoid world which has been overrun by an infection that attacks free will, giving its victims extra strength but removing their goodness and free will.
- The infection began with a malign force called the Radiance, who appeared in dreams.
- The Pale King created the Hollow Knight as a vessel made from a power called Void, which has no will of its own, to trap the Radiance.
- The Infection was once partially contained by the Pale King in a temple which is sealed by three boss figures, the 'Dreamers', but still managed to escape.
- The Knight must confront the source of the infection and fight the warrior Hornet, defeat the Dreamers and battle the Hollow Knight.

In different game outcomes, the Knight can defeat the Hollow Knight and take over to successfully contain the Radiance in the Temple, defeat the Hollow Knight with help from Hornet or defeat the Radiance in the Dream, another realm. Throughout the game, there are numerous side-quests and sub-narratives, such as defeating some previously faced enemies in the Colosseum of Fools and the 'shade', a dark version of the Knight created by the death of the player in previous game attempts.

Hollow Knight can be defined as a quest narrative. The Knight, who may or may not be an escaped vessel from the Abyss, must work to defeat the source of the infection. Along the way, the hero is tested numerous times.

Todorov's theory can be applied readily to this game, despite its non-linear qualities. Using this model demonstrates a common feature of computer game narratives – that the backstory tends to introduce the player to an equilibrium, along with disruption and recognition. The majority of gameplay forms an attempt to repair, with the final act and outcome varying according to different routes to successful completion of the game – or its abrupt termination.

- **Stable situation:** Hallownest is a successful, thriving kingdom.
- **Disruption:** the Radiance sends the infection in dreams.
- **Recognition:** the Pale King realises and seals the Radiance in the Temple, but is only partially successful.
- **Attempt to repair:** the entire gameplay is filled with numerous setbacks and additional conflicts.
- **New equilibrium:** is one of the three endings to the game.

Barthes' theory is useful for decoding gameplay and looking at the aesthetic of the game.

- **Hermeneutic code (HER):** encounters with characters in the game in the form of cut scenes. For example, why is the Grubfather crying? Who imprisoned the grubs and why? What will happen when the grubs are returned by the player to him?
- **Proairetic codes (ACT):** cut scenes, codes actioned by the player to control the gameplay such as battles, acquisition and use of soul or spells.
- **Semantic codes (SEM):** the use of sound and graphics in the battle to connote effectiveness of gameplay.
- **Symbolic codes (SYM):** tensions between the Knight and his environment.
- **Cultural/referential codes (REF):** orchestral score, hand-painted backgrounds and hand-drawn animation – Japanese-influenced aesthetic.

It's worth mentioning that the entire game can be played and progressed without engaging with the main narrative, although no narrative closure would be available.

Apply it

Use conventional narrative theories to analyse games in order to answer the following questions:

1 Find a synopsis of a computer game plot from a source such as a games wiki. Print it out. Highlight the synopsis and annotate it to see whether and where Todorov's five stages of narrative can be applied.
2 Research one of the top ten current best-selling games in the UK. Choose one, then read reviews and a synopsis of it. Which binary oppositions can you identify in it?
3 Choose one game which has a setting that relates to the 'real' world, such as a combat-based game or a sim game. View a couple of game walkthroughs and cut scenes. Can you observe any use of hermeneutic codes (HER) in the cut scene? Which proairetic (ACT), symbolic (SYM) and cultural codes (REF) are used?

Digital media texts populate a space created by technologies that are constantly on the move. Because of this, new genres are often emerging and old ones disappearing. You can apply the genre theories you encountered in sections 1.4 and 2.4 in just the same way to explore digital media genres. At the beginning of this chapter, we explored the typical features of some websites and other digital media forms, such as social networks and content-sharing sites. Using this information, you should be able to work out the conventions of most websites and other digital texts with relative ease.

■ Genre and computer games

There are some broad genre labels used in computer games, which can be understood even by people with a limited knowledge of the medium. Some game genre labels also evoke genres in other media in describing a setting, such as science fiction, war or sport. These have only a limited usefulness, since innovation in genre constantly leads to genre mixing and very little generic stability. View the table on the next page for some typical examples of computer game genres.

3.3 Computer games

Apply it

1. Look at Table 3.1. Find three examples for each of the categories. What do they have in common?
2. Can you think of three further examples that are generic hybrids of these categories? What does this suggest to you about genre labels and mode of play?

▽ Table 3.1 Computer game genres

Category	Description
Combat	Games where beating opposing forces is the primary goal.
Sport, fitness and dance	Games that require very active physical participation.
Role-playing	Games where the player has a strong role in creating the appearance and persona of the character they play.
Simulation-based	These games focus on the simulation of an environment or situation. May also be a mode of play within other games.
Strategy	Games that need a combination of cognitive skills and knowledge of the game's challenges.
Platform/environment/metroidvania	Games that often cluster around levels and are driven by certain repeated skills and how to overcome new challenges, which are offered progressively.
Puzzles	Games that require problem-solving to complete.
Racing	Games where speed and competition are the primary pleasures.

EXAMPLE: Metroidvanias – genres as cultural categories

Stephen Neale described genres as 'cultural categories', meaning they are not fixed but open to movement between labels, shifts in popularity, dynamics such as audience and industry tastes, and increasingly the role of audiences in defining, popularising and curating genre categories through online activity. A cultural category can be thought of as being affected by shifts in power structures within the industry as well as changing audience tastes. This all fits with Neale's ideas about the tensions between repetition and variation, sameness and difference, a state of flux in popular cultural products that subtly changes the ways in which we experience genre products and recognise them.

Metroidvania games are an intriguing example of some of the ways in which genre categorisation may function slightly differently within computer games, including the way in which genre labels may evolve or be coined by audiences themselves in a participatory way. This is perhaps more likely to happen in this medium, where audiences may be more heavily invested in discussion of games online. The name comes from two words put together to create a new meaning – *Metroid* and *Castlevania*. These are two games dating from the late 1980s. Therefore, although the term may be more recent, the lineage of the genre can be traced much further back.

The genre itself demonstrates hybridity, as it is a combination of both action and adventure. Beyond that, the conventions of the genre's best-known games do vary but would be expected to display some of the following features:

- side-scrolling/platform-based game mechanics
- 2D graphics
- map-centred exploration that means the game is non-linear
- acquisition of tools and abilities that help advance gameplay
- the defeat of enemies
- exploration of interconnected parts of a world, discovery of secret areas
- cohesive worlds that may have much 'lore' and discussion attached to them beyond the playing of the game
- a distinctive aesthetic that is one of the pleasures of the game, for example in the design of the environment.

However, not all Metroidvania games share these features. Some have 3D environments, while others have additional elements of gameplay, and although many draw on fantasy conventions as well as action and adventure, this is not the case for all. This illustrates the dynamic and fluid dimensions of genre.

△ *Ori and the Blind Forest* (Moon Studios, 2015) is a typical Metroidvania game and fulfils all of the conventions listed above

Game genres are sometimes clustered around what are known as the 'pillars' of game design, and the modes of play with which the players engage. Players and designers alike understand the broad language of design pillars and play modes, and definitions of what these are vary from source to source. Pillars include world design, game mechanics and game writing. Other generic labelling language used by players might refer more closely to the modes of play – the actions that preoccupy the gameplayer in using it.

EXAMPLE: Genre and play modes in *No Man's Sky* (2016)

No Man's Sky was a much-anticipated indie game released in 2016. Players were excited by the alleged complexity of the world design it's a science-fiction exploration game in which players explore and conquer different worlds in a procedurally generated 'universe' and its highly appealing aesthetic.

The four modes of gameplay in *No Man's Sky* are combat, exploration, trading and survival. Players can specialise in any of these four areas to progress through the game or focus on different skills at different points in their gameplay.

3.4 Intertextuality in digital media texts and computer games

Intertextuality in digital texts is so widely used that many cultural commentators have coined a different term – hypertextuality – to describe the endless interlinking practices of digital media forms. However, you will still be able to identify instances of intertextuality in a more conventional sense – the conscious re-referencing of existing texts in other media forms or other digital forms. Many memes are examples of intertextuality, where the original meaning of an image is reappropriated time and time again until it is almost entirely self-referential. Computer games offer rich opportunities to see connections and influences across popular culture more generally, and within digital and gaming culture.

Quick questions

1 Explain the function of backstories in computer games.
2 What role might be played by a cut scene in the overall narrative of a game?
3 What similarities and differences are there between computer game genres and those in other media forms? Write three sentences to explain some of these.
4 Explain what is meant by an 'ergodic' narrative.

EXAMPLE: Intertextuality in *Life is Strange* (2015)

Life is Strange is an episodic third-person adventure game/sim, which is strongly focused on characterisation and narrative arc. Its protagonist, Maxine Caulfield, is named after Holden Caulfield, the protagonist in the classic American novel *The Catcher in the Rye* (1951), which covers the themes of teenage angst and alienation. Therefore, this signifies to the audience that the game has an the off-beat, youthful appeal.

Forerunners to *Life is Strange* can be seen in other media. A key part of its gameplay is the pop-cultural interpretation of 'the butterfly effect', which has provided inspiration for many television serials and films featuring time-travel, alternative universes and the notion that small events can change entire histories.

Other essential aspects of the gameplay include Maxine's special skill – that she can rewind time – and the high-school setting. These are both explored in the Japanese anime, *The Girl Who Leapt Through Time* (dir. Mamoru Hosoda, Japan, 2006), which in turn was based on a serialised narrative that appeared in a teen-oriented Japanese magazine in 1965. A live-action version of the film was also made in Japan in 1983.

Apply it

Find three examples of games that make conscious and deliberate references to a textual world outside the game.

Where is the intertextuality located in the game? Is it in the narrative and themes, the iconography or the characterisation?

Create an infographic to map your findings, using screenshots and other visual reminders of intertextual links.

△ **Visitors playing *Life is Strange* at a games fair in Cologne, 2017**

→ Exam-style questions

1. What are the similarities and differences in applying narrative theories to digital media products compared with the traditional media products you encountered in Chapters 1 and 2? Choose one theory of narrative and apply it to one of your Close Study Products (CSPs).

2. Explore the unique features of the ways in which media language has been used in an online publication compared with its print media predecessor or edition.

3. Explore the role of the game-player in controlling the elements of mise-en-scène in one of your computer game products.

4. Explore the creation of meanings using semiotics in an online product you have studied.

5. Explore the positioning of one of your computer-game CSPs within genre as a 'cultural category' and consider how audiences respond to genre labels in marketing.

→ Summary

- Many digital products, including video content and websites, can be analysed using strategies you are already familiar with from your study of print and audio-visual media. Much of our work on the process of signification, narrative theory and approaches to genre can be adapted to help you understand digital media texts.

- Digital texts have their own codes and conventions, and it is important to understand these. You also need to recognise the unique way in which digital media are designed to promote their nature as interactive media, consumed in new ways.

- Social and participatory media are a crucial part of the way in which you encounter much digital media content.

- Some traditional media forms have made the transition to a digital existence: serialised audio-visual narratives previously encountered only on television now appear as made-for-web series; short documentaries and self-contained international news stories fly around social media sites; and web-only comics continue to develop huge followings.

- Computer games are experienced by the audience in a different way from other media, and some conventional techniques of media analysis have limited usefulness to assess them.

- New types of narrative are emerging in digital culture, which may require us to modify our use of narrative theories. This is particularly true of social and participatory media, where narratives may be highly fragmented.

- Genre study offers different challenges when studying digital media texts due to their evolving and participatory nature. However, genre analysis of digital media forms, such as websites, videos, for example on YouTube, and computer games, is possible.

Chapter 4: Media language

Enabling ideas

In this chapter, we will pause to consider what we have learned so far about media language in its various forms, using some further examples of the theoretical framework in action and providing additional opportunities for you to try out what you have learned. We will also be looking a little more closely at the issue of genre and technological change.

New to this chapter is the structuralist theorist Claude Lévi-Strauss, and the following concepts associated with his work:

3.4.1.4 Structuralism

- binary oppositions
- mytheme
- cultural codes
- ideological reading
- deconstruction.

Moving on from structuralism, we will further your study of postmodernism, which we learned about in the earlier chapters, through the idea of intertextuality. You will learn more about these postmodern characteristics of media products:

3.4.1.5 Postmodernism

- pastiche
- bricolage
- implosion.

You will also be introduced to a major postmodern theorist, Jean Baudrillard, who contributed the following ideas to the field of postmodern studies:

- simulacra
- simulation
- hyperreality.

→ What you will learn in this chapter

Chapter 4: Media language covers:

- examples of how to develop and apply your understanding of media language, including narrative and genre
- how media language constructs and incorporates values and ideologies
- structuralism and post-structuralism
- postmodernism and media language.

4.1 What we have learned so far about media language

In Chapters 1–3, you explored the key methods and theories used to explore media texts. This helped you to understand how they communicate with their audience, and that there are many different approaches we can use to understand the significance of media texts in contemporary culture. You learned the terminology that describes the technical codes associated with decoding audio-visual, print and digital media texts, and the contribution made by semiotic theory to this process. You applied some important theories associated with studying narrative and genre to the texts you studied. This section provides a reminder of your learning so far and some examples of that learning in action, as well as some activities which get you to apply your knowledge to ensure you have really mastered it.

You should be able to use some of the principles and terminology of semiotic analysis with confidence and be aware of the contributions made by key thinkers to the field, including understanding the process of signification (Saussure and Barthes), categories of sign (Peirce) and denotation/connotation/myth (Barthes). All these theories have enabled you to deconstruct media products, to access their meanings through methods such as semiotic analysis. In turn, this allows you to make judgements about the meanings of the text in relation to society, its tensions and hierarchies.

By now, you will be confident in your ability to decode a range of print media texts, such as magazine covers and features, and advertisements, with confidence and using appropriate terminology. You will also be happy decoding a range of audio-visual and audio texts, including television, advertisements and trailers, radio, podcasts, and contextual material embedded in digital media forms, such as web video content.

EXAMPLE: Analysis of technical codes in the trailer for *A Series of Unfortunate Events* (Netflix, 2017)

In the case of technical codes, you may have a specific focus you are looking at – or you may be looking for what is interesting about the technical codes you see and using the codes themselves to find a focus for something to say about the text. In this situation, you don't need to comment on everything – this example shows how picking out just five points per type of technical code gives you plenty of evidence you can use to support a solid response to this kind of analysis.

In this example, let's imagine that the focus in the form of a question is:

Explore how technical codes construct meaning in the marketing materials for one of your television programme Close Study Products.

Camerawork

- An extreme close-up of the Count's eye through the peephole signifies suspicion, along with the anti-social tendencies of the character and his lack of suitability as a guardian.
- The whip pan that follows the bird from the beautiful neighbourhood to the gloom of the house signifies the rapid change in their circumstances and loss of the children's freedom.
- The frequent framing of the children in two-shot (plus Sunny held in Violet's arms) reinforces the strength of their bond.

Mise-en-scène

- The ashen desaturated tones of the interiors in Count's house signify that their situation will not improve if they remain there.
- The Count sits in long shot at a huge table, with a plate of food before him, on a throne-like chair. In terms of proxemics, the children are right at the opposite end of the frame, and their non-verbal communication is hunched and intimidated; nothing is placed before the children.
- The light source in every frame shot in the Count's house is externally sourced, connoting that there is no hope for the family if they remain inside – but that escape could offer them a chance.

Editing

- The montage of bleak situations the children find themselves in at the Count's home is shown in rapid succession – cleaning the filthy bathroom, preparing food in a cluttered kitchen, sitting on a single bed in a leaky attic, all emphasising their bleak prospects.
- The mise-en-scène of the exterior neighbourhood is colourised in the editing post-production to highlight the soft tones of pastel pink cherry blossom, green turf and blue sky, which are swiftly juxtaposed with the filthy and grey interior of the house.
- The abrupt change of soundtrack from jazzy upbeat lyrical song to the sound jerks of the score signify again the abruptness of the children's change in situation.

Apply it

Choose a current TV show that has an interesting or extended title sequence. Practise using the terminology of sound, camerawork, editing, mise-en-scène and other relevant technical codes to identify key meanings in the text.

Audio codes

- The selective use of certain diegetic sounds (see Chapter 2, page 34) above the score contributes significantly to meaning because they are used so sparingly – for example, the ominous tone of the doorbell.
- The quality of the Count's vocal performance signifies dislike of the children from the moment of his greeting, as he sneers the word 'children'.
- The full orchestral score borrows from the intensity and scale of a cinematic production, signifying the dramatic nature of the disaster that befalls the children.
- Lemony Snicket's reverent vocal performance and the verbal codes he uses in voice-over quickly signify that the tale is to be filled with misfortune.

Although the range of forms in which they appear makes the decoding of various digital media forms quite challenging, you should by now be feeling more confident about how to use technical codes and adapt them to the form you are exploring. Websites, games, apps and social media, including emerging and experimental texts, should all form part of your exploration and growing familiarity with the ways in which texts work, even when these are not as common or confined to a specific use in digital media production.

In studying narratives in media texts, you should be able to apply relevant terminology commonly used in discussion of narrative organisation. More of this will be introduced in this chapter to help deepen your understanding of ways in which you can write about narratives.

By now, you will be able to discuss how narratives are organised in texts and how audiences make sense of narratives, using appropriate terminology and the specific theories of Todorov movements between two equilibriums (Todorov), five codes (Barthes) and masterplots.

Apply it

Choose a cut scene from a computer game and decode it using any relevant technical codes and the language of semiotics. You may need to draw not only on terms specific to the study of digital media codes, but also those from print and audio-visual media, depending on the content and stylistic presentation. Identify key meanings in the text.

EXAMPLE: Narrative analysis of the Green & Black's Velvet Edition television advertisement (2017)

Even a 30-second television advert can be very fruitful for testing your understanding of the narrative theories you have learned so far on the course. This Green & Black's chocolate advert features a girl in a red velvet cloak on a bicycle, who is pursued by wolves. The end of the advert reveals a twist – they are playing hide and seek, and now it's the wolves' turn to hide. The slogan is, 'Not everything is as dark as it seems'. Watch the advert here: www.youtube.com/watch?v=VV06pVdviRU

Let's apply Todorov's and Barthes' theories to this advert.

▽ 1 Todorov's five stages of narrative

Equilibrium	The girl is on her bike taking a break from a journey (enjoying a bite of chocolate).
Disruption	She hears a twig snap.
Recognition	She realises someone is watching and possibly following her.
Attempt to repair	She cycles away at speed. She leaves the road for the cover of the trees, then hides behind a rock.
New equilibrium	Found by the wolves, she despatches them to take their turn to hide and takes her time to enjoy the chocolate.

This text is very short, but nonetheless, Todorov's model still works to describe the advancement of the action through a series of stages.

▽ 2 Roland Barthes' five codes

Hermeneutic code (HER)	What has Red Riding Hood heard? Will the wolves find and catch her? What will she do when she is cornered?
Proairetic code (ACT)	Units of action can be defined, such as Red Riding Hood hears the noise, and pedals away as fast as she can. She drops the bike at speed and runs through the wood to hide. She meets the gaze of the wolves, and then begins to count. The wolves turn and run.
Semantic code (SEM)	Red Riding Hood's fast breathing is heard as a selective sound, signifying that she is exerting herself and possibly in fear.

4.1 What we have learned so far about media language

> **Apply it**
>
> Choose a 30-second advertisement for a confectionary product, food or drink and use it to practise applying all the theories you have learned so far on the course. Critique the theories as you use them. Do they all work equally well?

Symbolic code (SYM)	The redness of Red Riding Hood's cloak, against the natural background of the woodland, signifies that she is in danger.
Cultural/referential code (REF)	The advert relies on our understanding of the traditional European tale of Little Red Riding Hood.

The theory works well and is in fact underexplored here – given its length, this is a rich text for Barthes' codes.

In terms of genre studies, your confidence should be increasing in your ability to identify codes and conventions for yourself of any genre and be aware of the limitations of any genre analysis that relies purely on convention identification.

By now, you will be able to use the terminology of genre analysis (Neale) and understand some of the different ways in which genre can be understood as a concept by both audience and industry.

EXAMPLE: Genre analysis of the trailer for *The Keepers* (Netflix, 2017)

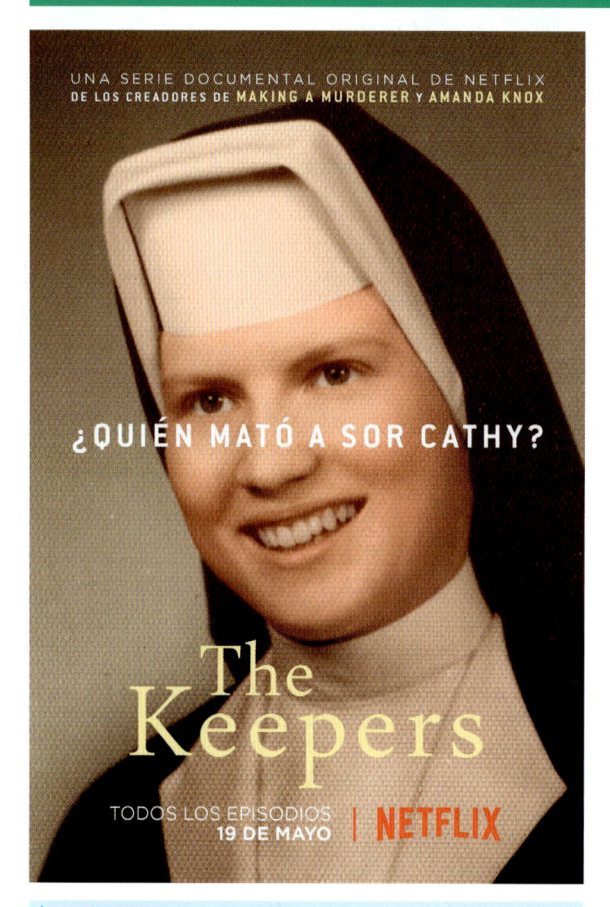

△ A Spanish poster for *The Keepers*

Documentaries focusing on the investigation of criminal 'cold cases' or suspected miscarriages of justice are currently a popular genre, spanning both audio and audio-visual production. Netflix's *Making a Murderer* performed extremely well in the video-on-demand (VOD) market in 2016, perhaps forming a blueprint for further additions to the corpus. *Serial* topped podcast charts. In the UK, Radio 5 Live broadcast their own investigative crime series, *Beyond Reasonable Doubt*.

The Keepers is a Netflix Originals web-television documentary series. The documentary focuses on the murder of a nun decades ago in a small American town.

Conventions common to many texts in the corpus of investigative crime-based documentary include:

Linear narrative chronology based on the investigation of a crime and/or its prosecution	There is the suggestion that *The Keepers* may vary this convention, and that the focus will not be on the death of Sister Cathy, but its alleged cover-up.
A possible miscarriage of justice or unsolved case at its heart	It is implied that her killer has not been found, fitting with the audience's generic regime of verisimilitude, i.e. their expectations of what is probable or likely in the genre. This forms a structure that audiences can relate to and expect contractually from the genre.
New insights or fresh evidence, witnesses or documents associated with the case	Many documents are seen – photographs from the time period, newspaper headlines viewed on microfiche, a medical report – and form part of the iconography of the genre. One subject in particular makes a statement claiming their father confessed to burying the body. These all contribute to the manipulation of the audience's expectations and hypotheses.
Passionate commitment to the case and determination to 'find the culprit'	On the case is a team of amateur investigators who knew Sister Cathy or were taught by her – seems to be a variation of the single investigator model.
Engagement with mainstream ideologies about crime and punishment, although not necessarily about law enforcement and the justice system	Engages with our sense of fair play: Sister Cathy is represented as the embodiment of kindness and Christian values. She is young and innocent. The Roman Catholic Church, on the other hand, is represented as the villain of the piece. This might run counter to conservative Catholics' values but resonate with the wider community's experience of news stories and sex abuse scandals involving the Roman Catholic Church, fitting with our cultural regime of verisimilitude.
Documentaries of this kind have a ritual and ideological function	Reminds us that, even when justice has not been served, a wrong may yet be made right.

> **Apply it**
>
> Choose a trailer for a film or television release. Explain what you think the conventions are both of a trailer for that type of product and the signifiers of the genre itself. Explore whether your example conforms to these, making sure you integrate some of the key terms used to present discussions about genre.

Repertoire of elements common in documentary trailers:

Soundtrack	Dramatic score punctuates the montage, emphasising proairetic codes encoded in the inter-titles and pausing dramatically for witnesses to utter key phrases.
Use of titling	Helps to cultivate a narrative image for the series; examples include 'a story buried for 50 years' and 'abuse, murder, conspiracy'.
Soundbites from participants	Positive representation of the team is generated by their collaborative efforts to pursue the case.
Locations	Locations around Baltimore, mainly exteriors, are used as iconic signs of place.
Archive footage	A separate investigation relating to the murder is presented.
Hand-held camerawork	This is used to bring a sense of spontaneity and also immediacy to events.
Re-enactments	A priest viewed from the back in close-up, suggesting he is up to no good; two nuns walking together lend atmosphere; however, it is unclear how much of a role re-enactments will play in the actual documentary.
Voice-over/narration	Narration is created using soundbites from participants, and meanings anchored by footage of locations, reconstruction and so on.
Montage editing	Technique is used in a conventional way in this trailer.

> **Apply it**
>
> Early on in the course you practised applying some of the terms used in semiotic analysis. Combine these with your understanding of genre codes to work out the contribution made by print media codes to our recognition of print media genres:
>
> - a newspaper front page
> - a magazine front cover
> - a print advertisement.

4.1 What we have learned so far about media language

Revisiting genre and technological change

One of Neale's most influential ideas about genres is that they are not stable – they fluctuate over time because they are always responding to a crucial tension between sameness and repetition, variation and change.

These tensions give rise to hybrids and sub-genres. Hybridisation (see Chapter 2) is becoming increasingly common in television. The huge investment by production companies in well-funded, long-lasting drama series means even more potential for experimentation and stretching of what one might expect from genres. Sub-genres, where a group of conventions identify a sub-group within an overall generic category, can sometimes develop to an extent that they can outgrow the genre that spawned them. They then become well-defined categories in their own right: hybrids. This is what we mean by genres as cultural categories – we love to categorise things, and new genre labels are as likely to spring up from audience participation and response to media texts online as they are in media marketing or critical circles.

△ See the example box on hybridity in *Outlander* on page 44

Genre conventions change over time in response to two main factors. These can be separated into two broad influences: technological change and social and cultural factors, although this is a slightly artificial division. In this section, you will be breaking these down a little further and exploring them in more detail.

One of the factors that impacts on genre is technological change. Factors affecting genre transmission vary across media forms.

The way in which video-on-demand (VOD) services categorise and label genres is not necessarily how audiences would use genre labels.

The development of VOD and increasing international reach of big audio-visual content providers through subscription packages, cable and satellite services has meant a large increase in the reach of certain television genres as part of the impact of globalisation on the mass media. New genres can spread from culture to culture more rapidly than at any other time in the history of the mass media (see Example box on page 72).

Like television, radio has gained more of an international audience with the advent of the internet. However, podcasting has ushered in entirely new

CHAPTER 4 MEDIA LANGUAGE

genres specific to the form. The technology of podcasting distribution and the distinct way in which podcasts tend to be listened to when compared with radio has also allowed for transmission of genres that have traditionally worked well on television but less so on radio.

Most newspapers have made the leap from print to digital platforms, but at the same time new news-based sites have emerged. An almost entirely new genre is the satirical news website, which provides a constant, almost real-time social commentary on world and domestic affairs. News websites such as *HuffPost*, which exist only online and are designed to be experienced through other social media feeds as much as through the main site, have also become commonplace.

Magazine genres have remained fairly stable, since their digital versions are consumed in similar ways and they use similar subscription models to print editions. However, comics – in decline over the years in print form – have become a popular genre online. Fan comics have emerged, as have other genres.

The emergence of genres in digital media

Digital video, especially in short forms embedded into social media sites and on YouTube, demonstrates an almost constant emergence of new genres. Prior to the digital age, the only short forms in existence tended to be animations, children's programming and short film. In the digital age, short video forms are everywhere. Because digital video is so quickly distributed and because of the huge global reach of social media networks, new genres can be spawned over a matter of days rather than the years or even decades it could have taken in the past, for example, for a film or television genre to evolve.

Computer-game genres also move incredibly fast, and gaming is one of the forms where genre is closely integrated with the technological experience of the game. In some cases, the development of new gaming technologies, such as virtual reality (VR) headsets, may simply change the way in which a genre is experienced – other changes, such as augmented reality (AR), may spark new genres for which there are no real antecedents.

△ The emergence of new gaming technologies brings new genres to audiences as well as developing familiar ones

Blogs and websites also have their own genres. An influencer, for example, may also make lifestyle content specific to their interests on YouTube and be followed on Instagram, with each manifestation of their digital persona appearing in different platforms.

■ Genre and social and cultural change

Most genre theorists believe that there is a connection between the popularity of genres in specific time periods and the social and cultural contexts that produce them. Although they may disagree about the way in which genres grow and change, you need to remember that genres are always a product of the relationship between audience, industry and text. This relationship is a dynamic one – social and cultural conditions can almost be seen as a force that gently exerts influence over this relationship.

The appearance of some genres and the decrease in popularity of others cannot always be explained in a straightforward way, and when studying texts in relation to others you should think carefully about what social and cultural influences could account for their increased presence or absence.

4.1 What we have learned so far about media language

EXAMPLE: The soap opera and reality TV

A great example of how rapidly one genre might take over another can be seen in the movement of television audiences, traditionally female, of soap operas towards reality TV. The two genres may initially appear to be unrelated, but they share a number of pleasures in common, which might account for the relatively easy poaching of audiences from one genre to the other, despite one being a fictional text and the other non-fiction – audiences for the soap opera have been in decline for a long time, possibly due to younger audiences in particular preferring the reality genre.

Soap operas rely on loyal audiences, and this may, in fact, be their greatest weakness when faced by competition from reality TV. Let's look at how the two genres measure up to one another.

Soap opera	Reality TV
• High investment in regular viewing – loyal audiences have time to get to know characters and families, and become familiar with their quirks and histories; compulsive, with viewers afraid of missing out. • Single platform, with some dedicated soap magazines for fans who watch most; appeals to mainstreamers. • Older audience. • Long history born out of early advertising in the US; began in the UK on radio in 1950, with *The Archers*. • Different tones to different soaps, but some are notorious for treating controversial subject matter in a responsible way. • Offers uses and gratifications of social relationships and personal identity. • Single genre with stable boundaries and with repetition and sameness. Few sub-genres (e.g. medical soaps) due to high investment in set and salaried cast. New examples of the genre rarely appear – sustained drops in viewers can be catastrophic.	• Binge viewing – shorter seasons which have a narrative resolution. • Synergy with tabloids, celebrity magazines and gossip websites, aspirational lifestyles which may have cultural resonance and appeal to aspirers. • Youth audience. • Genre exploded in around 2000 and was quickly considered to be 'low-brow' TV. • Producers unafraid to push boundaries of taste and decency and to court controversy. • Uses and gratifications of social relationships and personal identity. • Huge array of genres and opportunity for variation and change – easily exploited by producers and low investment costs. Failures can easily be cancelled.

Apply it

Choose a television genre that is very well established, such as the crime drama. Research the genre and create a presentation of at least seven slides covering the inception of the genre including early examples, its conventions, key changes in the genre and present-day examples.

One final word about genre – some texts do genuinely resist generic classification. Others subvert the conventions of genres for their own ends or parody them in a way that could be considered as postmodern.

Be careful not to apply genre labels just for the sake of doing so, and if the genre conventions are not immediately obvious to you when studying a text, you might want to consider what the reasons are for this – or is it simply that genre is not as important an aspect of studying the text as other elements of media language? Neale himself cautioned against the idea of mechanistically using conventions as a checklist – in reality, many genre texts are quite subtle and make interesting use of their conventions beyond merely signifying categorisation.

Quick questions

1. Why do television programmes often hybridise over time?
2. Give one reason why computer game genres evolve differently from other media products.
3. Which two wider contexts do you think are most significant when considering the evolution of genres, and why?

4.2 How media language constructs and incorporates values and ideologies through ideological reading

All media texts contain ideologies, messages about society and culture. Learning about politics and the mass media helps you to be able to identify and decode messages. Many media texts contain a political bias, meaning they promote either a left- or right-wing political stance. Many also engage with a single political agenda or issue (such as gender equality, racial equality or climate change). Political bias is most evident in the **news agendas** of national newspapers, but fictional media texts can also engage with political ideas and can be a powerful tool for promoting political thought and engagement.

EXAMPLE: Political bias in newspaper supplements, current affairs and lifestyle magazines

Lifestyle sections or supplements of major newspapers may publish interviews of politicians from the party whose stance the newspaper supports – but also, surprisingly, politicians from opposition parties who may be represented as more 'moderate', or having something that potentially appeals to floating voters who read that paper but may not have a strong political affiliation to it.

> **Key terms**
>
> **ideological reading** a conclusion that aims to expose how power relationships between social groups operate and manifest themselves in cultural production
> *An ideological reading would reveal a patriarchal bias in the repeated selection of male authority figures.*
>
> **news agenda** the priority given to particular news items by a news organisation
> *The issue has featured prominently on news agendas.*

△ Labour leader Sir Keir Starmer on the cover of the *Sunday Times Magazine*

Magazines focused on current affairs sometimes feature coverage of politicians, but often focus on the 'person' and tend to represent them in such a way that, although their status in society is linked clearly to a specific political party, the reader's assumed interest is neutral rather than politically engaged. This is important so as not to alienate a section of the readership.

Distinct from a newspaper's readership, a lifestyle magazine's audience might be expected to constitute a cross-section of political viewpoints. This can also serve the interests of the politician – the magazine can act as a platform to bring their ideas to a new audience in a way that tends to represent them in a positive light.

Most political standpoints on key issues can be seen as a series of oppositions and are therefore associated with Claude Lévi-Strauss's ideas about structuralism and the **ideological reading** of products (see section 4.3, page 79). After all, in the UK we even refer to the largest political party in parliament not in government as 'the opposition'.

As a general overview, in the UK, Conservative, right-wing politics can be summed up as 'conserving' traditional values/promoting traditional morals. Labour, left-wing politics are more people-centred and supportive of the rights of workers/minority groups. More centrist politicians, such as some Liberal Democrats, tend to adopt a middle way though these, selecting from them on an 'issue-led' basis. In reality though, there are many overlaps in the day-to-day politics and policies of government and opposition at any one time.

Be aware that some of these ideologies have contradictions within them – for example, right-wing ideologies might seem to be anti-class mobility, but in fact it is important that Conservative voters (many of whom are working class) feel that class mobility, for example through small business ownership or entrepreneurship, is available to them.

You can find out more about the political spectrum here:
www.unifrog.org/know-how/understanding-the-political-spectrum

---

The ways in which media language can be used to advance a political perspective include:

- images selected to portray an issue or a person in a positive or negative light
- lexical or verbal coding taken out of context, content juxtaposed in a particular way or heavily edited
- agendas in coverage of issues – selection, focusing and combination
- emotive content used to sway the audience's feelings
- soundtracks used to underscore particular moments in fictional texts.

This list is not exhaustive and you should always be on the lookout for the nuances in media language used whenever you have identified the presence of a particular political ideology. The examples given are hypothetical, but you will easily be able to find real ones of your own by using these as a starting point.

4.3 Structuralism and post-structuralism

■ Saussure and Barthes

Saussure's semiology (see Chapter 1: Reading print media) is an example of early structuralism. Barthes is usually considered a post-structuralist, and his ideas about denotation, connotation, myth and the signification process have already been embedded into your understanding of how to read the media.

Barthes' study of the codes of narrative and work on narratology have also been a significant part of your studies so far. Structuralists attempt to find

---

Quick questions

1. Why are neo-Marxist theories critical of mainstream media products? Explain in one sentence.
2. Explain what we mean by a 'liberal pluralist approach' to reading ideologies and the media.
3. Why is the study of dominant ideology often critical of media industries? Give one reason.

meanings in human cultural production and interaction by analysing the frameworks that support them. They believed there was an intermediary point between 'reality' and abstract concepts of it, and this was what they sought to understand – the process that connects the two. This could be understood as the **deconstruction** of the text – using the tools of structural analysis to find its meaning.

Saussure was one of the founders of structuralism, and semiotic theory in its earliest forms is a structuralist theory. Later developments in structuralism, which took some of the original ideas but also rejected others, became known as post-structuralist approaches. Barthes is the best-known post-structuralist thinker on this course. You will notice that Barthes progressed, for example, the idea of the signifier and signified, and the way they combine to form a sign, into the idea that there were orders of signification – a first, a second and a third – that related to ideology and myth. You can think of post-structuralism as being both an evolution of structuralism but also a rejection of some of its aspects, which may be considered in later thinking as either underdeveloped or too rigid.

> **Key term**
>
> **deconstruction** accessing the meanings of a media product about society using the tools of structuralist analysis
> *Deconstruction of the advert reveals a society fascinated by celebrity culture.*

■ Lévi-Strauss

One of the much-valued ideas in **Claude Levi-Strauss**'s work was **binary oppositions**. These could be, at their most basic, light versus darkness, good versus evil, or death versus life. According to Lévi-Strauss, we all understand the world in terms of opposites. He theorised that this way of viewing the world was common to people across all cultures, and that the stories we tell in all societies are heavily driven by opposite qualities and characters of all kinds. As someone who studied the similarities between myths (in the fantastical story sense of the word) across cultures, he found that many of them had very similar qualities and, particularly, presentations of recurrent conflicts. Let's take, for example, the Green & Black's chocolate advert we examined on page 71 as an example of narrative analysis. Here we see the usefulness of structuralist theory in decoding narrative:

> **KEY THINKER**
>
> **Claude Lévi-Strauss** (1908–2009) is renowned as a structural anthropologist. Lévi-Strauss was heavily influenced by Saussure. He is considered a key figure in modern anthropology, mainly because of his belief that the 'savage' and 'civilised' minds were no different and both held the same essential humanity.
>
> Strauss's work in this field was considered revolutionary for its time and had strong implications for anyone studying culture, including how narratives function in media texts.

Example

Binary oppositions in the Green & Black's advert

Rest versus motion	The advert offers us the contrasts between the symbolic action of the chase, and the more languorous moments when the chocolate is being consumed.
Traditional tale versus modern interpretation	The wolves are bad in the original tale, but the bicycle already signifies to us that we might expect an updating in some way. The advert uses the traditional tale as a reference point, then subverts our expectations, suggesting that our preconceptions of a dark chocolate as 'bitter' may in fact be unfounded.
Red Riding Hood versus the wolves	This opposition is used to signify danger and threat, drawing readily on our understanding of the wolf signifying danger in this story and many other European folk tales. The threat is then resolved in an unexpected way – this is pleasurable for the audience.

The theory works well and is an interesting one to use, since Lévi-Strauss's original work explored traditional tales and myths in different cultures. There are potentially more oppositions to be found, or the ones selected could be redefined or restructured in different ways.

Binary oppositions are especially useful as an approach to reading narratives when examining those print media texts that may not be sufficiently long or complex enough to apply Todorov's or Barthes' theories. Binary oppositions can be usefully applied to whole genres as well as to the individual text, making them a very interesting way of approaching meanings of whole clusters of signs.

It is the tension between oppositions – or the imbalance caused by the presence of one thing and the absence of a countering opposition – that drives all our stories, with the pairings acting like counterweights, pushing and pulling the narrative ebb and flow. These tensions are more important than the chronology of a narrative – the order in which things happen.

Binary oppositions can be used to explore themes and expose dominant ideologies in a text. It is a highly adaptable theory to use with any moving image text.

> ### EXAMPLE: Music video for *Letter to the Free,* Common featuring Bilal (2016)

You can watch the video for *Letter to the Free* here: www.youtube.com/watch?v=KO7tVuPHOxA

This music video shows the complexities of applying binary oppositions to formulate an ideological reading of a text. It was produced as the soundtrack to the 2016 documentary *13th* – the documentary explores the mass incarceration of black Americans and its connections to the abolition of the Atlantic slave trade, and is heavily politicised.

Binary oppositions in the video can be found both by watching the video and by decoding the lexical codes of the lyrics.

Liberty versus incarceration: the cotton fields shown at the end of the video remind us that enslaved people were forced to work in cotton fields, even as they tasted 'freedom', and provide a stark contrast with the previous mise-en-scène.

Justice versus injustice: the supposed end of the Atlantic slave trade versus its perpetuation in the modern prison system and the over-representation of black Americans in the prison system is explored lyrically and seen as a continuation of white institutional exploitation of black people.

Power versus vulnerability: the lyrics and claustrophobic camerawork all contrast the power held by the white-dominated justice system with the claustrophobia of the black experience of incarceration and the historical weight of the Atlantic slave trade.

Key term

interpellation the normalisation in media texts of certain ways of thinking, attitudes and values, so powerfully that they become part of a person's identity
Consumers are interpellated by these kinds of advertisements into a belief in the role of make-up and beauty regimes in perceived attractiveness.

In the process of using Lévi-Strauss's approach, an ideological reading could be obtained from a text – a conclusion that aims to expose how power relationships between social groups operate and manifest themselves in cultural production, and therefore normalise certain ways of thinking, attitudes and values so powerfully that they become part of a person's identity. Lévi-Strauss considered binary oppositions to be the foundation of this ideological reading – that we constantly seek to understand the world around us and the narratives we encounter about it through our media consumption. This process was described by French philosopher Louis Althusser as **interpellation** – the creation of a subject of ideology.

△ **The Force Manchester** interpolates the viewer as a subject of an ideology which favours law enforcement and naturalises the police force as an ideological state apparatus

Mytheme

Another important aspect of Lévi-Strauss's work involves the analysis of **mythemes**. Mythemes are small units of myths that he identified in the traditional stories of the tribal groups he studied. Another term he gave to them was gross constituent units. In this way, a narrative could be understood as being comprised of units of relationships between characters, actions they undertake and the themes that result. Lévi-Strauss was interested in the relationships between these units. Each element of a narrative does not, therefore, have its own fixed meaning but operates within a framework of ideas and cultural meanings. It is in relation to other elements of the story that a mytheme takes on its role in the production of meaning – mythemes are part of the functioning of binary oppositions. They cannot be read in isolation but have a meaning when the whole overview of the narrative is considered.

Lévi-Strauss called mythemes 'bundles of meanings', clearly showing the interconnectedness of the individual units in creating meaning. Oppositions are played out in myths because they help to resolve contradictions that a culture may experience in day-to-day living. They are therefore meaningful to the context of the cultural codes that produce them, and although myths may be similar across cultures, the way in which mythemes are organised varies according to the function of the myth in that culture.

The relevance of this work to studying narratives in contemporary media is still considerable, since media texts arguably have the same role in contemporary culture – they render the world comprehensible to us.

> **Key term**
>
> **mytheme** small unit of myths that Lévi-Strauss identified in the traditional stories of the tribal groups he studied
> *The advert uses a recurring mytheme of transformation to signify the effectiveness of the product and its effect on those around the protagonist as part of its narrative construction.*

> **Quick questions**
>
> 1. Name two other theorists aside from Lévi-Strauss that you have studied on the course whose ideas are relevant in structuralist thinking.
> 2. Explain in your own words why binary oppositions are a useful tool.
> 3. Why are mythemes crucial to a contextual reading of a media product?

4.3 Structuralism and post-structuralism

4.4 Postmodernism

■ Postmodernism and media language

Postmodernism is an approach to reading media texts that is useful to consider in relation to media language. It is often through aspects of media language that you can most clearly identify the postmodern characteristics of a text and use these to consider different possible meanings or ways of understanding it. It explores a media-saturated world and concludes it to be a fragmented world of signs that have little meaning and are ephemeral. Postmodernism isn't confined to media language as an area of the theoretical framework, since it considers the nature of how you read representations and the role of the audience in making meaning as crucial factors. There is some overlap between theorists who are regarded as postmodernist and and those regarded as post-structuralist.

Postmodernism is a famously ambiguous critical area, with poorly defined boundaries and a resistance by some of its main theorists to being categorised as postmodern at all. It is a critical approach that has been applied to almost every aspect of intellectual pursuit, art and culture, but in this section you will be trying to apply its overall precepts to a media-specific context.

In his introduction to his anthology *From Modernism to Postmodernism* (2003), Lawrence Cahoone draws out some of the ideas in postmodernism as 'themes', which is a good way into understanding it. He presents these as oppositions, showing us some of the interesting overlap sometimes seen between postmodernism and post-structuralism. These form part of the way in which postmodernism critiques aspects of culture and society.

Presentation versus representation and construction

Postmodernists generally agree that in a sense there is no originally 'present' idea or image. Everything is represented, mediated and interpreted in various cultural, social and historical ways that may be interpreted differently from person to person. This doesn't mean that postmodernists don't believe that the real world exists, but that everything encountered is subject to the various ways it has been mediated and represented to us in our experiences.

Origin versus phenomena

Postmodernism denies the validity of any approach that tries to identify a definite, original, contextual meaning to a media text. In rejecting the idea of an original meaning that holds some kind of 'truth', postmodernism deals instead with the idea of phenomena that do not have any kind of permanent relationship to a deeper 'reality'.

Unity versus plurality

Postmodernists propose that there is no single unified definition or meaning of any text that is understood by everyone in an identical way. Postmodernism, like post-structuralism, focuses on the plurality of meanings offered by media texts, where everything is related to everything else. It does, however, push this idea to its very limits. This includes our understanding of the self, and it has interesting implications for the study of identity. Theories of identity that view identity as fragmented are influenced by postmodernism.

'Truths' that we hold to be universal, such as goodness, justice and courage, are all seen as serving other social or intellectual agendas rather than having inherent qualities which mean the same thing at different points in history.

Postmodern analysis means resisting all the hierarchical organisational structures by which we usually recognise cultural products, seeing some as innately 'better' than others, and instead seeing them as subjects of systems that attempt to define one thing by privileging it over another. Postmodernism makes no distinction between popular culture and high culture because it makes no value judgements about texts. Because of this, postmodern theorists try to look beyond the commonly studied aspects of texts, to what is marginalised or absent, rather than obvious.

Some of these ideas may be difficult to grasp, but that is the nature of postmodernism – it is a completely different way of reading media language from the structuralist theories you encountered earlier on the course. However, there are some aspects of texts that are most easily recognisable as postmodern. It is more likely you will need on the course to be able to recognise texts that have postmodern features than to critically apply a complex postmodern approach to a text. We will now look at some key terms and their associated ideas, which are useful when identifying techniques used in a postmodern text.

■ Intertextuality

In the preceding chapters you spent some time looking at examples of intertextuality. It is the easiest aspect of postmodernism to identify in a text and refers to the process where a media producer consciously or even subconsciously references another text. This may be a conscious attempt to repurpose the connotations of that sign in a new order of signification, or a subtler interaction of signs from the referenced text and the newly created one. You not only need to be able to recognise where intertextuality is present in media texts, but also to understand *why* it has been used, the meanings it borrows and how audiences might respond to its uses.

Pastiche

Pastiche involves the making of a new media text from components of another. In the case of pastiche, this is done in a positive and respectful way to bring new meanings, rather than in the case of parody, where the original text is mocked and derided.

> **Key term**
>
> **pastiche** the making of a new media text from components of another
> *The series title sequence makes such strong use of intertextual references and genre codes it may be considered a pastiche.*

△ Although they border on parody because they are humorous, there are numerous visual recreations of the famous cover for The Beatles' 1969 album, *Abbey Road*, that are in fact examples of pastiche, since they are reverential

Bricolage

Bricolage describes a product made from other media texts, or that borrows signs from them. The term comes from the French for do-it-yourself, or DIY, meaning that the product made has been assembled with what was at hand to create something new. Many fan products, however, use bricolage in a productive way within their own semiotic productivity, re-appropriating signs to give them meanings that are not oppositional but alternative. Bricolage is therefore an interesting element of some practices in fan culture and highly participatory. Internet memes often also use bricolage. Advertisers frequently appropriate existing artworks or cultural references in a bricolage style. In this Lufthansa advert, da Vinci's *Mona Lisa* is given the Moulin Rouge treatment (https://tinyurl.com/48s499da). The effect is irreverent, as is often the case with bricolage – remember that postmodernism does not recognise hierarchies of high or mass culture.

Implosion

Implosion may be seen as part of bricolage – it is the media's constant recycling of itself and its signs because it has no new material to feed it. Meaning 'implodes' – we have information circulating through communication, but this is more of a process for recycling rather than the creation of new meanings. Cultural forms and structures emerge, flourish briefly, then collapse in on themselves.

Although the French sociologist and philosopher Jean Baudrillard (see below) saw implosion as something that affects wider social structures worldwide – business, politics, even law – he saw the media as playing a role in implosion and a place where it can be seen to manifest. For example, TV news, crime dramas and television series all reassure us that the real violent world out there is at a distance or confined to a fictional realm. Presented alongside these genres and content are light entertainment, a bombardment of advertising, and product consumption that make us feel secure and removed from the threats of the world.

> **Key terms**
>
> **bricolage** a product that is made from other media texts, or borrows signs from them
> *The fan videos produced on the channel are a form of bricolage.*
>
> **implosion** the media's constant recycling of itself and its signs
> *The phenomenon of the reality contest show can be seen as an example of implosion.*

> **Apply it**
>
> It can be hard to distinguish between different forms of postmodern media-making techniques and styles. Many of these techniques can also be referred to as intertextual as well as being more specific about the way in which this intertextuality manifests itself at a textual level.
>
> Research an example of pastiche and bricolage. Source images and write a short case study of each text and the text it refers to in order to help you see the mode or style of connection between them and the differences between those connections.

■ Jean Baudrillard: *Simulacra and Simulation*

In *Simulacra and Simulation* (1981), **Jean Baudrillard** explored philosophical ideas about the relationship between human understanding of existence and the role of culture and the media in constructing those ideas. There are three key terms you will need to be familiar with to apply Baudrillard's ideas: simulacrum, simulation and hyperreality. Baudrillard believed that each of these aspects of the modern world and human condition are related to our increased urbanisation and culture of consumption. These established the pre-conditions of the simulacra because they distance us from the reality of the production of goods, made thousands of miles away, and the experience of the natural world – which we may just now perceive as another part of the

simulacrum. His ideas have even more implications for the evolution of gaming technologies and ways of navigating our environment, such as augmented reality apps, which literally overlay the landscape of our existence with the signs of consumption.

Simulacrum

The simulacrum is a state of semiotics where a sign no longer refers to any original meaning but to other signs, like a hall of mirrors. It no longer represents a thing itself but means nothing more. Baudrillard saw this process as happening in stages, like a game of broken telephone, where the original message becomes something else entirely.

This is known as the **precession of the simulacra**:

- First, a basic copy is made of something that exists in the real world, in which we have trust because we can see a resemblance to the original.
- Second, a corrupted second is made that obscures the 'truth' of the first copy – which we no longer trust.
- Third, the sign presents to us as representing something that did not exist to begin with.
- Finally, we arrive at the signs and symbolisation processes of contemporary culture and late capitalism; we accept signs as part of the simulacra, where there is no longer any reference to reality.

△ A hall of mirrors – the idea of multiple reflections and distortions - is commonly used when trying to understand the relationship between objective reality and the simulacrum

EXAMPLE: The precession of the simulacra and scripted reality television

Baudrillard's ideas can be applied in all sorts of interesting ways to contemporary culture. We could see the development of scripted reality television shows as an analogy for the precession of the simulacrum.

1. First, we have the origin of the genre in **fly-on-the-wall documentaries** with an observational mode, which could be seen as the basic copy. They seem to bear some resemblance to reality – we trust the copy and believe it stands in for something that has actually occurred in the real world.
2. Over time, programme-makers offer us **mock documentaries** – the parody that obscures the truth of the first because it is 'malevolent', in that a mock documentary is often satirical and therefore perverts the meanings and the 'truth' apparently offered by the earlier predecessors it parodies.
3. Perhaps emboldened by the acceptance of the mock documentary and its deliberate posing as reality, despite being a falsehood, programme-makers offer us a third stage – **'reality' television**, the very name of the emergent genre making a claim about the relationship between the show and reality. Scandals initially appear about the relationship between the shows' content and 'reality', but these quickly die down as audiences lose to some extent the expectation that there is a straightforward relationship between representation and reality in the text and come to a new contractual understanding of the genre. Distinct from its documentary predecessors, there is often a competitive aspect to reality TV shows, which is purely driven by the product, is highly constructed and does not refer to anything outside itself as imitator spawns imitator. This takes us back to the idea of the hall of mirrors, where we no longer perceive a true original but simply accept distortion itself. The contestants become short-lived D-list celebrities, perhaps with their own associated product lines and feeding other media products for subject matter. Reality television purports to offer us a version of reality, but this is a pretence the audience quickly comes to accept.

KEY THINKER

Jean Baudrillard (1929–2007) was a French philosopher who contributed the key ideas of simulacra, simulation and hyperreality often debated in relation to postmodern thinking. Baudrillard is sometimes also regarded as a post-structuralist thinker because of his interest in semiotics and new ways of understanding how signs are interrelated in a complex web of meanings.

Key terms

simulacrum state of semiotics where a sign no longer refers to any original meaning, but to other signs, like a hall of mirrors
The narrative of the video has lost its original reference points and is understood by the audience as part of the simulacrum where original meanings have been diluted and disappeared.

precession of the simulacra the series of stages between simulacrum and simulation
Development of the genre may be seen as an example of the precession of the simulacra.

4.4 Postmodernism

4   The fourth stage is the endless making of **scripted reality shows**, where the participants are part actor, part participant, and the whole genre has become improbably self-referential. The audience accepts and no longer cares how much of the show's content is scripted, because the scripted reality is a sign that does not refer to anything else, and the D-list celebrities it makes of its contestants or participants are empty signifiers in a hyperreal world – another simulacra within a web of simulation. Viewers may accept the hyperreal representation of the participant characters and their narratives as 'real' even though they bear little resemblance to reality.

Apply it

Source examples of the genres and sub-genres mentioned in the example. To what extent do you think they fit the idea of the precession of the simulacra? Use them in the following discussion:

1   Can you see any problems in using this genre as an example? Is it too simplistic?
2   Does the precession of the simulacra, for example, need to happen in a specific order, since media genres don't always behave in this way?
3   Since postmodern approaches are fragmentary, how might you be able to relate this to the existing genre theory we covered earlier in the chapter?
4   Could the ideas in simulacra and simulation be used to understand other media genres?

Simulation

This is the end product of the precession of the simulacrum. In the **simulation** we no longer perceive any difference between representation and reality. Consumers of cultural products inhabit this world without the need to refer to reality, because all of us are so far removed from its original reference points.

Baudrillard uses a fable to explain simulation of an empire that created a map to be laid over the physical space it occupied. When the empire crumbled, all that was left was the map. Baudrillard suggests that the hyperreal world, the simulation that is the end point of the precession of the simulacrum, is like living on that map despite the land having crumbled away beneath it. It is this world that he suggests we all inhabit. We continue to overlay our culture on the map, but there is no longer anything beneath it to which it refers.

> **Key term**
>
> **simulation** end product of the precession of the simulacra. In the simulation we no longer perceive any difference between representation and reality
> *The audience find themselves in a simulation, inhabiting a digital world encoded with the signs of social media content and gameplay that come dominate their social interactions in the real world.*

EXAMPLE: Augmented reality and simulation

Consider the way in which augmented reality apps and digital navigation/mapping systems, full of signs relating to consumption, literally overlay the ground beneath our feet, the homes we live in and the cities or spaces we walk around with cultural signs, in a composite that combines the real and the virtual. Even the term 'augmented reality' is fascinating – it suggests that the world we overlay with its cultural signs is somehow 'better' than the world without it, and that we are dependent on the apps to navigate this world.

The augmented reality game *SpecTrek* lets players 'capture ghosts' as they walk around their environment, 'try-on' apps allow people to try out new tattoos or hairstyles without the bill (or the regret!), and the iPhone app *Yelp Monocle* allows users to overlay real maps to see reviews of goods and services. *Quiver* enables children to see their colouring pages in 3D; *iArtView* makes it possible for artists to see how their work would look in real spaces, and *Star Chart* allows stargazers to see mapped constellations overlaid on the night sky.

CHAPTER 4 MEDIA LANGUAGE

Hyperreality

The term **hyperreality** relates to a state of living in Western culture populated by simulacra, meaning we inhabit a simulation where we no longer have any connection to a 'real' world but live instead through a commodified world that never existed to begin with. This merging of the real and media is constructed from a merging of consumerist signs and meaningless cultural practices that we feel are 'real', but that do not connect with reality or have true meaning – they are a 'simulation' of human experience.

EXAMPLE: Disneyland and Disneyfication v *Black Mirror*

The gap between the aspirational images projected to us in the simulacrum and the real world of austerity today, defined by globalisation, war and terror, it's no wonder we are comfortable in hyperreality and the diversions it offers us. Think about the way in which Disney culture is such a huge part of childhood, especially for many young girls. They know the films and songs by heart, they wear the costumes and they sport the brands on their personal effects. Baudrillard uses the example of Disneyland to show how the supposed boundary between representation and reality is voided in hyperreality. For many families, the ultimate dream is to visit Disneyland itself, arguably one of the biggest symbols the world has of the commodification of childhood, in order to immerse themselves fully in the experience.

An interesting feature of hyperreality is its ability to offer us critiques of itself as part of its network, embodying the often-problematic issues we come across when trying to apply postmodern interpretations. *Black Mirror*, a television series of one-off stories the first of which was released in 2011, is a fascinating representation of our relationship with technology, media images and materialism, and its impact on our culture. Incredibly pessimistic and dark in tone, it savagely critiques our increasing social and cultural dependence on media technologies.

△ In 'Nosedive', an episode of the TV series *Black Mirror*, a person's advantages in life and work are all impacted by their social media rating

> **Key term**
>
> **hyperreality** merging of the real and media worlds to the point where it is difficult to distinguish between them
> *The actor's social media posts contribute to the hyperreal presence of the star in the digital landscape.*

> **Apply it**
>
> Search for an augmented reality app that is free to download on your smartphone. Try it out. In what ways does it 'augment' an experience? How much use does it make of the 'real'?

> **Apply it**
>
> Can you think of any other examples of the ways in which hyperreality can be seen manifesting in individual cultural signs?
>
> Create an A3 collage or moodboard of a young person's media consumption, showing visually the numerous ways in which their reality could be viewed as the cultural simulacra they encounter and interact with every day.

4.4 Postmodernism

Quick questions

1 What do we mean by intertextuality in media products?
2 What does Baudrillard see as the connection between hyperreality and capitalism?
3 Why do digital media forms provide particularly productive examples when studying Baudrillard's ideas? Give one example and one reason.

→ Exam-style questions

1 To what extent do media products demonstrate changes in the way genre is expressed due to developments in technology? You should respond to the question using two of your Close Study Products.

2 How does narrative contribute to the construction of a version of reality? Explore this idea using detailed reference to two of your Close Study Products.

3 'Media products construct ideological meanings in favour of the status quo.' Do you agree? To what extent? Respond using evidence from two of your Close Study Products.

4 How does structuralism allow us to deconstruct the ideological meanings of texts and understand the relationship of the audience to them? Refer to two Close Study Products in your answer.

5 How can postmodern ideas contribute to our reading of digital media products? Explore with reference to two relevant Close Study Products.

→ Summary

- An understanding of types of sign and the signification process as described both by Saussure and Barthes is central to the way in which we decode texts, and should be considered as a contributory factor in the creation of meaning, no matter which further methodologies and critical frameworks one then goes on to apply.

- Understanding narrative perspective and how this impacts on the audience is an integral part of narrative studies.

- Genres evolve to keep up with social and cultural change, although many have continued to endure. Genres of order and genres of integration are also central to our understanding of how genres evolve.

- There is a distinction between structuralist and post-structuralist approaches to media texts, as defined by key thinkers Roland Barthes and Ferdinand de Saussure, and the ideas of Claude Lévi-Strauss.

- Postmodern thinking contributes to the ways in which we might read some contemporary media texts and the way audiences make sense of them. Postmodernism is characterised by a resistance to fixed and finite readings, without inherent truths and only shallow meanings and fragmentary forms, often borrowing consciously or unconsciously from other sign systems.

- Bricolage, pastiche and implosion are three important ways by which we might recognise postmodern features in a media text – although, there may be crossover in these techniques.

- Key thinker Jean Baudrillard put forward the idea of the precession of the simulacrum, by which the process of representation becomes such that there is no longer any real-world reference point for media representations and everything becomes simulation. As such, modern living can be seen as its own hyperreal experience.

4.4 Postmodernism

Chapter 5: Media representations

What you will learn in this chapter

Chapter 5: Media representations covers:

- how to approach the study of representations
- the way events, issues, individuals, groups, places, events and abstract concepts are represented through processes of selection and combination
- the way the media through representation construct versions of reality, including claims about realism
- how and why stereotypes can be used positively and negatively, and why countertypes exist
- how media representations convey values, attitudes and beliefs about the world and can inform our sense of our own identity
- how media representations can invoke discourses around gender and ethnicity.

Enabling ideas

The study of representation builds on the foundations of what you have learned already about how media language is used to construct meanings across a range of media forms and product types. The ideas you learn will be interconnected, so this chapter categorises these broadly into sections.

The specification states that you will need to understand the following, more general theories of representation:

- constructed reality and the positioning of audiences in relation to representation
- issues relating to misrepresentation and the selective nature of media representation
- dominant ideology and hegemony
- positive and negative stereotypes and countertypes
- Stuart Hall's theory of encoding and decoding
- the ideas of David Gauntlett. Specifically, these are:
  - fluidity of identity
  - constructed identity
  - negotiated identity
  - collective identity
- theories and ideas from the critical field of gender studies, including some of the best-known debates in feminist theory as follows:
  - the male and female gaze
  - patriarchy
  - sexualisation and raunch culture
  - postfeminism
- specific theorists from this field include feminist theorists Liesbet van Zoonen and bell hooks about:
  - gender as power
  - gender as discourse
  - intersectionality

- the more recent field of critical thinking around gender, including:
    - the role of sex and gender
    - queer readings of media products
    - Judith Butler as the key theorist
    - gender as performativity
    - gender as historical situation rather than natural fact
    - subversion
- theoretical approaches to ethnicity and postcolonialism, including how power structures in society are present in ideologies about race and ethnicity which may either be reinforced or challenged by the mass media. General theories include ideas around:
    - cultural imperialism
    - multiculturalism
    - imagined communities
    - marginalisation
    - Orientalism
    - otherness/alterity
- a specific theorist in the field of ethnicity is Paul Gilroy, whose ideas about black identity have been hugely influential in recent years. You will need to understand the following concepts associated with Gilroy's work:
    - diaspora
    - double consciousness.

5.1 General theories of representation

The process of representation is the essence of media studies. Meanings in these texts are not fixed in a particular way, and do not necessarily have one single interpretation in our culture. They are constructed through what we call **signifying practices**, which include the study of semiotics (interpretation of signs and symbols). Other signifying practices include genres and narratives, and their connections with cultural myths and ideologies. Study of the values of the sector of the industry that produces and distributes the text also contributes to meaning. Producers will guide the audience towards the preferred reading of a particular text – the one intended by them and accepted by the majority.

■ Constructed reality and the positioning of audiences in relation to representations

Media texts are **polysemic signs** (they have potentially more than one meaning depending on who interprets them). Elements of the sign and the signification process will show variations in interpretation between consumers. Not everyone will accept the preferred reading, or even read a sign in the same manner. The social and cultural factors that come into play when reading a media text are important for us in understanding the broader significance of the media texts we consume.

We often think of the mass media as relying heavily on **stereotypes** in creating representations, but it is important to remember that stereotypes are not necessarily negative. In his 2013 book *Representation: Cultural Representations and Signifying Practices*, **Stuart Hall** refers to stereotyping as a form of **cultural shorthand**. It allows the audience to quickly assimilate ideas. However, it is not the only factor in how an audience reads a media text. If stereotypes of a social group are used in a persistently negative way, this could of course be harmful. Media producers can play in a sophisticated way with our understanding of stereotypes, or even consciously challenge them.

Key terms

cultural shorthand a way of understanding how stereotypes communicate ideas quickly to the audience
It's thought that this use of cultural shorthand communicates meaning faster and more effectively.

polysemic signs possible multiple meanings of a sign
The figure of the woman is polysemic.

signifying practices techniques used to construct representations
Television producers may use a range of signifying practices to construct meaning.

stereotypes reduction of a social group to a limited set of characteristics
The artist himself conforms strongly to stereotypes in his dress code.

KEY THINKER

Stuart Hall (1932–2014) was a prominent cultural theorist. Born in Jamaica, Hall spent most of his life in the UK, and became a highly influential thinker respected for his writing about cultural practices in many disciplines, including sociology and media studies.

Apply it

Think of the difference between a tabloid newspaper's coverage of 'migrants' compared with a documentary telling the story of a 'refugee' family from Syria such as *Exodus* (see page 109, later in this chapter). Both texts nominally represent the same social group in completely different ways.

Choose a social group or issue, and source two texts that represent them/it in contrasting ways. Write a 1000-word case study exploring the reasons for the contrasting representations. Make sure you use your knowledge of the relevant technical codes and analysis techniques for your medium as evidence, as encountered in the first three chapters of the book.

Key terms

counter-representation/ countertyped a representation that offers an alternative to stereotypes
The protagonist is countertyped when contrasted with more common stereotypes of teen girls.

representation the way in which people, places, abstract concepts and events are mediated in a particular way in media texts
Representations are significant because they communicate ideas about our culture and society.

In his book *The Matter of Images* (2002), Richard Dyer explores some different ways of understanding what we mean by the term **representation**. If we think of it in terms of representation, reality is mediated to the audience in various ways, and is constructed using media language. The world both within and beyond the audience's experience is represented to them, often in ways that seem familiar or match their existing ideologies.

Dyer also considers the process as a presentation of what is 'typical' of a given people, place, time, etc. This can be understood in terms of stereotypes and is perhaps most obvious when the complexity of representations is secondary to narrative or generic factors.

Sometimes, a great deal of care is taken over the process of representation as a way of speaking for or on behalf of a group of people or person. Deliberately signifying certain values often creates what is termed a **counter-representation**. This idea is explored in more detail later in this chapter. We can also recognise audience reactions to different representations and consider them in terms of these and how they might vary from person to person.

It's essential that you are familiar with the technical codes of the media form you are trying to analyse. You will also need to be able to use semiotic analysis and genre and narrative theory to evidence your ideas.

The relationship we perceive between representations and reality will always be a complex one. Producers of media texts

△ We are normally drawn to people first when looking at a media text

CHAPTER 5 MEDIA REPRESENTATIONS

make deliberate choices about how they reconstruct the world in limited time and space in print, in audio or on screen. These choices are encoded to guide the reader to the preferred reading. Assumptions are made about how the audience will read a text all the time, and producers rely on us having attitudes and values that they can either reinforce or counter, depending on the intended meaning.

Almost all study of representation has to begin with some simple exploratory questions. The following sections will look at each of these questions in detail to understand why they are so significant.

■ Who is being represented?

People are the main focus of the majority of media texts. This is why who appears in the text and how they are portrayed is so significant. First, we can consider how many representatives of a social group or treatments of a theme we see. Many research studies have used this idea as a tool to explore visibility, meaning the profile given to these groups and the frequency with which they appear, or measuring as a sub-category the prominence their appearance has. Are they on the front cover? How long are they on screen for? Quantitative representational analysis does not usually explore in detail the nature of the representation. Results of quantitative studies are sometimes impressive, but they are still open to a range of interpretations and reasons for them.

EXAMPLE: Researching crime, ethnicity and television news representations

In 2010, a study was conducted into the reporting of ethnicity and crime in the USA, which is very typical of a quantitative study. *Race and Ethnic Representations of Lawbreakers and Victims in Crime News: A National Study of Television Coverage* conducted a review of findings already given by other researchers, and then used quantitative methods to check its findings. The study concluded that black people were over-reported in television news stories as being the perpetrators of crimes.

The study draws its conclusions from a random sampling of television news stories, both local and national, from all over the USA and shows clearly the usefulness of quantitative methods.

Qualitative representational analysis is the set of tools, including semiotic theory and related ideas, that we use to understand the quality – the nature – of the representation. This kind of analysis is often more useful, since it allows careful evaluation of the possible messages encoded within a particular representation.

Key terms

qualitative representation using techniques such as semiotic analysis to draw conclusions about the nature of media representations
Qualitatively the representations in the series are complex.

quantitative representation using techniques such as content analysis to draw conclusions about representations in media texts
The advert has limited diversity and features only one person from a minority group.

visibility how high profile a particular issue, group or event is in media analysis
People with disabilities have limited visibility in the media.

5.1 General theories of representation

The significance of different technical codes of media language vary depending on the media form. For example, radio representations are constructed primarily through vocal performance, soundscape and audio cues. Computer graphics in a game almost always have a hyperreal feeling to them, and colour codes are deployed in evocative ways that are far richer than we would see in other media forms. However, when you are exploring representations of a person or people, try to consider the following questions:

- What gender are they?
- How old are they?
- What is their ethnicity?
- What does their dress code, including their hair, accessories or make-up, suggest about them?
- Is there anything distinctive about the way in which they speak or the language they use?
- What do elements of their non-verbal communication, such as facial expression, posture or gait, communicate?
- What sense do we make of the behaviours and actions?
- How are technical codes such as framing contributing to the production of meaning?

Apply it

Find a selection of vox pops (see Example box) on a television programme from a current schedule. Vox pops are sometimes used in light investigative documentaries (e.g. food programming) and local news broadcasts. Consider the mix of people used by their age, gender, ethnicity, etc. Summarise briefly the range of views they express. What kind of representation of the subject of questioning is created by their responses?

EXAMPLE: Vox populi

Vox populi (known as vox pops) are used to give viewers of news, documentary or magazine programmes on television a sense of other people's opinions. They involve the cutting together of a broad sample of people's responses, usually to the same question or approach by an interviewer. The interviewer may or may not be present in the final edit. Excerpts are then edited together to suggest a range of opinions and, where possible, a social mix. Vox pops are not as equitable as you might think – quite often they are edited to a particular bias required to match the preferred reading.

■ What else is being represented?

It is not just people who are represented in media texts. Almost every aspect of our lives and the world around us has to go through similar processes of mediation.

Think about how the places you see are represented. The settings chosen for any one media text are highly significant. They might be historical, present day or futuristic. They might be small or large. They might be interiors or exteriors. If you're listening to a radio show recorded in a studio, even that studio is signified through the reactions of the audience (if there is one) or the relationships between presenters. There may be excerpts recorded elsewhere, and the way in which that sound has been mixed further contributes to our impression of the place.

It is also really important to consider the way abstract concepts are represented. Marriage or romantic love might be represented quite differently in a crime drama featuring a storyline about domestic violence, a situation comedy featuring a married couple, a banking advertisement or a trailer for a romantic comedy. You should be able to identify relatively quickly what the dominant themes and ideas are in factual media texts. In the case of fiction texts, these sometimes take longer to emerge. We can sometimes think of abstract concepts in terms of themes, and there are close connections between themes and narratives.

Key terms

mediation the process by which the mass media represents aspect of reality
Stereotypes are often heavily mediated versions of real-world representatives of social groups.
vox populi soundbites and/or visual clips of different respondents discussing a topic or answering a question intended to reflect a range of opinions
The use of vox populi suggests this attitude is widely shared.

Events are also represented in particular ways, for example:

- A sporting event, where the winning team is heralded as heroes in their own region, the losers being either denigrated or represented in a melancholy or contrite way.
- Historical events are interpreted and reinterpreted: the same stories are retold in different time periods in different ways.
- News providers constantly have to consider how they are presenting events to their audience. What one news source chooses to highlight may differ from that of another depending on their angle.

> **Apply it**
>
> Look at the list of forms in Table 5.1 and choose five to work with. Find a textual example for each and evaluate the nature of the representations it contains. Create a grid modelled on the table. Sum up the nature of the representation and explore ONE important representation in each text using some of the techniques used to create it.

Issues relating to misrepresentation and the selective nature of media representations

Selection, focusing and combining play a vital role in constructing a representation. Numerous techniques are used to influence how we read a text. Selection of material is essential to the process of representation. Without selection and focusing, texts would be difficult to make sense of. In audio-visual media, camerawork and sound as well as editing combine to create meanings. Non-verbal communication in actor or participant performance can be essential in encoding meaning. In factual media, such as news and documentary, shot selection is vital.

The following list suggests some of the ways in which the main media forms you study on the course control the selection and focusing aspects of representations, mainly through technical, narrative and genre codes but also institutional factors. The list is not intended to be exhaustive but serves to highlight some of the most important processes.

> **Key terms**
>
> **combining** using elements of more than one aspect of media language and form to achieve a desired representation
> *The muted décor of the room combines with the sombre dress code to signify mourning.*
>
> **focusing** building of a representation through techniques such as repetition or elimination of comparisons
> *The advert uses focusing on female uses of technology as a strategy, as no men appear.*
>
> **selection** choosing to represent one thing over another
> *The rural lifestyle is represented only through idyllic landscape shots and large houses.*

▽ Table 5.1 Forms and techniques used in differing media types

Form	Techniques
Television	• Editing – screen time can be manipulated and relationships implied through editing. • Shot types and angles – close-ups make us more likely to empathise with someone; high angles can make someone look either inferior or vulnerable. • Mise-en-scène and para-proxemics – the context in which people appear or events take place, and relative positioning within a frame or perceived distance from the audience (proxemics); how people and places are lit. • Inclusion – who appears and the social group they represent; shot selection • Sound – who speaks the most; selection of score; social class or region conveyed through accent; voice-over
Film marketing: trailers/ web/print	• Narrative image and compression of screen time • Genre conventions embody the focusing process; selection of numerous elements from a particular paradigm because of audience expectations and hypothesis • Voice-over and titling; lexical codes • Typography • Use of composite images to establish key character hierarchies and relationships as well as locations • Menus that select material such as press reviews and awards for positive content and elevate the profile of particular characters or personalities

5.1 General theories of representation

Form	Techniques
Music video	• Mise-en-scène and dress code • Lyrical content • Camera angles; screen time; editing; repetition of visual motifs • Locations • Signification of artiste or band • Form – the majority of music videos fit into the style of performance-driven or concept-driven
Radio	• Vocal performance • Music • Atmosphere/soundscape; signposting • Lexical coding – audiences are far more attuned to language use and its nuances in radio than any other medium • Scheduling and running order
Online and participatory media	• Profiles and shared content • Marketing algorithms and tracking; moderated content; censorship via filtering • Selection based on personal engagement and preferences; most-read – 'echo chamber' effect • Alternative voices can be heard; new communities emerge with their own powers of selection
Computer games	• Embedded behaviours in characters • The player/character/agency and power • Binary categorisation, e.g. of genders, can lead to simplified representations • Hyper-masculinity • Which characters have a voice • Self-representation in role playing games
Newspapers	• News values • Headlines • Selection of images and captioning (anchorage) • Choice of quotations • Experts • Bias
Magazines	• Coverlines • Features and column space • Inclusion – who or what appears in the magazine • Lexical codes in slugs, captions and pull quotes • Illustrative photography and artwork accompanying an article • Non-verbal codes
Advertising and marketing	All of the above may be used depending on the form in which the promotions appear.

EXAMPLE: Evaluating the nature of representations

Cancer Research UK advert, Channel 4, September 2016	Advert features a middle-aged woman talking about her hopes and dreams	Advert represents an organisation making a difference to cancer sufferers, but still needing support	• Personal mode of address; positive non-verbal communication – smiling • Selection of 'ordinary' person • No mention of cancer itself, which can have negative and frightening connotations as a disease • Head shot, one continuous edit – like being in conversation. High level of focus on subject matter

One-page article about media personality and model Katie Price, *Heat* magazine, 2016	Article describes Katie Price's alleged behaviour in response to marital breakdowns	Represents Katie Price as being taken over by her 'party girl persona', 'Jordan'	• Two close-up paparazzi shots taken in club locations 17 years apart, in which Price appears to be inebriated • Copy uses quotes from a 'friend' close to Price and the subject herself in a previous article to create a present-moment narrative of self-destruction • Archive photographs of Price partying after each marriage has broken down support the representation of her as her alter-ego, 'Jordan'

Important questions to ask yourself when considering the nature of a representation:

- Is the representation positive?
- Is it negative?
- Is the representation neutral?
- Is it simple or complex?
- Does it fit with mainstream ideologies about the social group, individual or subject matter?
- How open is the representation to alternative readings?
- Does the text conform to established stereotypes, or offer any counter-representation(s)?

■ Why are these representations the way they are?

Once you have done the work of identifying what the representations are and how they are being constructed using media language, the next stage is perhaps the most important.

You need to explore what the maker of the media text is trying to convey about their subject matter – what is the preferred reading? You don't have to agree with the preferred reading, but you need to be able to identify it.

What factors might have influenced their decision to represent their subject matter in a particular way? Do these relate to the institutional values of the media organisation that produced the text? Are they trying to promote something? Is there an informative aspect to the text, or does it exist purely for entertainment value?

Apply it

Choose a reality TV show episode. Draw up a single-page profile for each participant. Include a screenshot of each of them. Explore the representation of each participant using both the individual episode and any wider knowledge you may have of the show. Bullet point five clear examples of how media language is used to construct the representation.

EXAMPLE: Reality TV's image problems

As a genre, reality TV is one of the most criticised for its selective use of editing and construction of particular narratives, often from many hours' worth of footage. The problem is a perceptual one, in that the genre has its origins in the documentary format, which audiences expect to be offered as a factual perspective. It is easy for media audiences to forget that media products, whether factual or fictional, can only ever offer us a 'version' of reality. This idea is explored in much more depth in section 5.2: Constructing 'reality' through representation – Stuart Hall's encoding and decoding.

All documentary makers must create narratives and decide which stories they want to tell from the footage they have, whether their purpose is primarily to inform or to entertain.

5.1 General theories of representation

△ The Kardashian–Jenner family starred in the reality TV show *Keeping Up with the Kardashians*, which ran for 20 series between 2007 and 2021.

5.2 Constructing 'reality' through representation – Stuart Hall's encoding and decoding

Apply it

Discuss what features you would associate with any collection of mythical beings – ogres, giants, mermaids, angels and so on. Consider where you might have gained these ideas from. Most of our knowledge of mythical beings comes from ancient narratives retold in different ways within cultures. Identify a cluster of signs you would associate with each being. Search the internet and collect three visual representations of the beings. Do their features correlate with your conceptual map? Do they contribute to it? Annotate the images with your reactions to them.

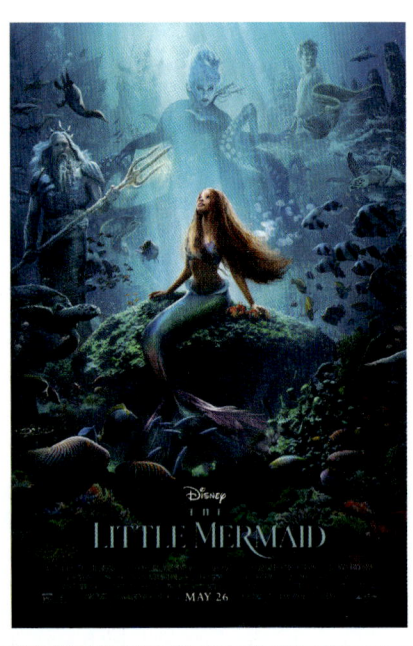

△ These images both use representations of a mythical creature but in different ways. Try to reflect this in the examples you choose of your own.

CHAPTER 5 MEDIA REPRESENTATIONS

Stuart Hall outlined two **systems of representation**. The first correlates with our **conceptual map** – the way in which we group representations in our minds, using features such as similarities or differences. This can be applied not only to social groups within our direct experience, but also to ideas outside of it. In his book *Representation: Cultural Representation and Signifying Practices* (2013), Hall uses the example of angels or mermaids, which we all have a clear representation of in our minds even though we could never have seen either of these mythical beings.

The second system of representation is the language we use – the signs that stand for the concepts. This process was covered more fully in Chapter 1: Reading print media, where we looked in detail at the process of the production of meaning through semiotics.

Hall outlines three approaches (referenced below) that explain the relationship between reality and representations. These approaches take differing stances on the way in which we understand how the process of representation works.

Reflective approach	This approach to representation suggests that meaning is inherent in the aspects of the real world that are being represented. Media language therefore simply 'mirrors' the real world as we experience it.
	This approach has limitations, because it doesn't account for a whole range, from slight to significant, of variations in readings of a text. It ignores the fundamental process of mediation.
Intentional approach	This approach has the producer of the text constructing the world as they see it, and the audience accepting those values encoded in the text at face value. Since signs are polysemic, any sign system is open to variations in interpretation. There would be no room here for a negotiated or oppositional reading.
Constructionist approach	The constructionist – or sometimes 'constructivist' – approach is the one most useful to us, and the process Hall believed best described the relationship between representation and reality.
	Concepts and signs do have some shared meanings, but they are not all inherent, and the audience for a text play a large role in their active interpretation and use of conceptual interpretation of signifying systems.
	Hall says, 'We must not confuse the material world, 'reality', where people and things exist, and the symbolic processes and practices through which representation, meaning and language operate' (*Representation: Cultural Representations and Signifying Practices*, page 25).

Apply it

Choose a Close Study Product from any of the forms you are studying on the course. Try writing a paragraph that uses the reflective approach to discuss representations. Then do the same with the intentional approach and, finally, the constructionist approach. How does each change the significance of the encoding process? Discuss your findings with the rest of the group.

What is very clear from Hall's work is that sign systems can never reliably depict 'reality'. All sign systems are open to differing interpretations across and within different cultural groups. All signs in the media are representations – a version of reality that subtly steers audiences towards a particular reading, but can never guarantee that they will respond quite as intended.

Key terms

conceptual map the reference point for people in interpreting media texts according to their individual world view
Younger women may read the advert differently from the older generations because of differences in their conceptual maps.

constructionist approach approach that suggests readers of a text or its producers can wholly fix meaning
By adopting a constructionist approach, we can see that meanings are made as a result of both the intentions of the producer and the audiences. Their interpretations may differ.

intentional approach approach that suggests meaning is imposed by the producer of the text
This would suggest an intentionalist, fixed meaning to representations but does not allow for differences in audience interpretation.

reflective approach approach that suggests meaning is inherent in what is being represented
We would not consider a reflective approach to be valid since it suggests that meanings cannot be subject to change by the process of representation or the medium it appears in.

systems of representation identified by Hall – our conceptual map, and the language we use to navigate it
Hall's systems of representation describe both the way we make sense of communications and the signs we use to construct them.

Quick questions

1. Explain in your own words what Hall meant by two 'systems' of representation.
2. Which of Hall's three approaches is the most useful to media studies students and can be taken when interpreting representations?
3. Why do we say media products can only offer a 'version of reality'? Write a couple of sentences exploring this idea.

5.2 Constructing 'reality' through representation – Stuart Hall's encoding and decoding

■ Encoding and decoding

Hall developed his model of **encoding and decoding** to help interpret media representations as he found previous, more linear models of communication to be outmoded. Previous communication models tended to focus on the idea of a sender or source originating a message, which is distributed by a channel and received by someone (the audience). Although a broadly correct description of the process of someone (the producer) creating a media product and getting it out to audiences, this does not sufficiently account for the polysemic nature of signs and the different ways in which audiences could be steered towards a particular reading – but ultimately might differ in their responses to it. For this reason, these earlier models are sometimes called **transmission models**.

> **Key terms**
>
> **encoding and decoding** the process whereby a producer of a text generates a meaning and the audience interprets it
> *The sign of the wolf encoded in the opening titles may be decoded by the audience as signifying threat.*
>
> **SMCR/transmission model of communication** simplistic early approach to communication study
> *The SMCR model is considered linear because the message travels very simply and in one direction from sender to receiver.*
>
> **transactional model of communication** used to describe models of communication such as Hall's which build more subtlety and feedback into the stages in a communication chain
> *Hall's circuit of culture is a transactional model of communication.*

△ Berlo's model of communication, a 'linear' model of communication

Criticisms that could be made of the **SMCR model** (Source/Message/Channel/Receiver), such as Berlo's model in the illustration above, begin with its assumption of a fixed meaning. If media products were all encoded simply with a message which was understood in the same passive way by everyone who viewed it, there would be no space to argue that people interpret products in different ways.

Hall's model allows for a more subtle and dynamic understanding of the processing of the message and the relationship between those who produce and consume it. It has been widely adopted by cultural theorists because of its robustness and flexibility in acknowledging the role of the audience in making meanings (interpreting what is placed in front of them). The process is not as 'one-way' as earlier models suggested. Because of its flexibility, it is often referred to as a **transactional model of communication**, suggesting more give and take in the relationships and that the production of meaning may be happening at different points in the model.

Hall's model is that of a '**circuit of communication**', where individual moments in the process of communication can feed back into each other, each time subtly affecting the meanings being made and the feedback received by the producers, which may also affect future production. Hall saw each stage in the communication model as being a transaction, with information potentially flowing in many directions. These moments could be understood as follows:

1. Production could include research into the audience and cultural trends undertaken by commissioning producers as well as pure production methods.
2. The circulation of media products is the broader term for the ways in which audiences may encounter products and differing conditions of reception as well as technologies.
3. Distribution becomes much more about the different ways audiences make sense of the product itself – importantly, this is not seen by Hall as a given, but as something that is unpredictable and can't be guaranteed to remain intact as the producers may have intended.
4. Perhaps less familiar – 'reproduction'. Hall viewed this as the outcome in the circuit of culture and it is closely linked to other ideas we are already familiar with about the dissemination of ideologies via media productions and their relationship with dominant ideologies. The reproduction stage is where we see what sense audiences make of products in relation to the world around them, and to what extent the media products they consume actively shape their own communication of ideas or their rejection of them.

> **Key term**
>
> **circuit of communication** Hall's model of communication, which identifies experience of a textual product as a series of 'moments' in the communication process
> *The circuit of culture is a more flexible way of interpreting how meaning is produced, as well as the relationship between producers and audiences.*

5.3 The relationship between representations and reality

■ Why does it matter how individual people are represented?

Media studies assumes as a starting point that representations in the mass media are important. Some of the discussions you will be having will consider the relative importance of these. No two media theorists agree completely on the extent to which media representations are thought to affect the treatment of social groups in the real world, since this is impossible to measure.

Some texts seek to actively shape or change public perceptions of an individual public figure through the way in which they are represented. In the case of prominent public figures, journalists and documentarians, who seek to portray the individual in any way that challenges their mainstream media portrayal, typically encounter obstacles. These might range from legal challenges to difficulty in gaining access to subjects.

■ Gender and sexuality

The field of gender studies and the mass media is hugely significant because it has such wide-ranging implications for all of us. We often find that stereotypes associated with gender and sexuality are remarkably slow to make progress in keeping with societal attitudes.

△ On the television show *Dragons' Den*, the representation of Deborah Meaden may be considered to conform to the stereotype of the 'ruthless businesswoman'

For more about cultivation theory see section 6.4: Cultivation theory.

Key terms

emasculate to remove masculinity
The antagonist is represented as being angered and emasculated by his female boss.

patriarchy a system where men predominate in power structures
The magazine represents a challenge to patriarchy by focusing on powerful women and avoiding sexualisation.

Traditionally, women in the media have been the focus of a great deal of representational study. This is because of the unique position they occupy in our society. Women constitute 50 per cent of the population, yet are still treated very differently from men in the mass media. Most of the feminist explanations for this relate to **patriarchy** as a social system. Traditional femininity is based on the role of women as child-bearers and at the heart of domestic activity. On the other hand, women are often sexualised, portrayed simply as 'beings' to be looked at and appreciated by men and valued according to their perceived attractiveness. These examples demonstrate to us just how contradictory stereotypes can be – that they can simultaneously embody many different qualities. This is related to the concept of myth, since several myths can co-exist about a social group, and are perpetuated by repeated exposure.

Representations of women in more powerful roles in the contemporary media frequently depict women as having to make sacrifices for their role. They can degenerate into unflattering stereotypes. An example of this might be the 'ruthless businesswoman', who is cold and unfeeling, inflicting misery on her employees.

Much of the focus in gender studies over the last few decades has been on women because they have gone some way to challenging some of the pervasive historical stereotyping of women that is a product of patriarchy. Increasingly, more critical studies have been undertaken in the field of masculine representation.

Traditional masculinity perceives men as breadwinners, and authoritarian and paternalistic figures in the family. Outside the family they are macho heroes who are independent, capable and fearless. Showing emotion is generally frowned upon.

Although newer stereotypes relating to masculinities are emerging, the media struggles to keep up with the changes men have experienced in real life in their roles. Many newer modes of masculinity are still often depicted as though they are **emasculating**. Reading masculinities in media texts is therefore complex. Plural masculinities that are a blend of old and new are

CHAPTER 5 MEDIA REPRESENTATIONS

apparent in some contemporary media texts, and those that draw exclusively on traditional masculinity are becoming fewer. Nonetheless, as with female representation, it seems that it is simply easier to represent both men and women in a binary way as having very different, often stereotypical attributes and behaviours.

Apply it

Collect a range of images from across the media that signify more traditional modes of femininity and masculinity. Create a collage as a class, using large sheets of paper taped together to display your findings. Discuss what you notice.

EXAMPLE: The marketing for *Jason Bourne* (2016)

The online trailer for the action/spy film *Jason Bourne* (2016) uses codes associated with traditional masculinity to signify the action genre. The film hit the headlines when it was released, partly because the lead actor, Matt Damon, only says a total of 288 words in the film.

Despite the appearance of a seemingly powerful female ally in the trailer, traditional masculinity is very much in evidence. Bourne continues to signify the macho hero, able to cope with anything while showing no emotion and with immense physical strength combined with combative skill. He represents the qualities theorists studying masculinity in the Hollywood hero have identified over and over again: coolness, toughness, hardness – and silence.

Another important area of gender representation of often marginalised people is the LGBTQ+ community. Just as it is sometimes difficult to find progressive representations of new masculinities and femininities in the media, so it is equally difficult to find examples of LGBTQ+ people being represented in a positive and rounded way. Common historical representations in the media have tended to portray people in this social category as deviant, dangerous, victims or a source of comic relief. Sadly, many of these stereotypes persist, despite some changes in social attitudes.

■ Race, ethnicity and religious representations

Race representation in the media and their relationships to real groups in society continues to be a source of productive discussion. The race and ethnicity representations that predominate in a culture tend to vary according to the make-up of that culture and its histories.

In the USA, representation of African-Americans is considered a contentious area. This is partly because African-Americans represent a significant proportion of the population, but also due to social issues relating to power and poverty. This includes the disproportionately high level of incarceration of young black men, and ongoing social problems such as police shootings of black people. Historical sensitivities still exist in both white and black communities around the legacy of the Atlantic slave trade.

In the context of the current climate of global terrorism and conflict in the Middle East, negative representations of Muslims as a people and Islam as a religion have become more prominent. Where negative stereotypes are

5.3 The relationship between representations and reality

repeatedly reinforced by media outlets and alternative representations are not sufficiently visible or absent, it can contribute to Islamophobia. Concerns have also arisen over the representation of eastern European migrants and workers in the UK, with some blaming negative tabloid representations of this group for inciting persecution.

▲ A Black Lives Matter protest in New York City, 2014

Age

Stereotypes relating to age tend to affect mainly those at the higher or lower end of the spectrum – older people and teenagers.

Teenagers are often particularly negatively portrayed, using stereotypes relating to youth crime. History shows us that youth, as a time of exploration of new-found independence and risk-taking, has always been viewed with suspicion by older generations. Over-representation of youth crime and other negative factors associated with youth are often at the root of moral panic, in which news media give over a greater proportion of reporting time to stories that have currency, such as abuse of legal highs and gaming addiction.

Older people also suffer from entrenched stereotypes – that they are bored, lonely, senile or physically infirm.

Social class

As a society, the UK is hugely class conscious, and many areas of media representation, from comedy to news, still reflect this. We are especially sensitive to signifiers of social status and class, such as outward displays of wealth, cultural practices, dress code, education and profession, manner of speech and regional background. Even as a developed country, the UK still has wide variations in standards of living, from the uber-wealthy to families living below the poverty line, even if some of the signifiers of these situations do not match traditional structures and delineations of social class.

Apply it

Using age, race, ethnicity or social class as the basis for choosing, select a text from the range of forms you are studying on the course. Write a 500-word case study exploring how the text uses either stereotypes or countertypes associated with that social group.

CHAPTER 5 MEDIA REPRESENTATIONS

■ Disability

For a long time, people with disabilities have been categorised as an out-group (see page 106), despite the fact that the majority of people with disabilities live fully integrated with the rest of society. And like other marginalised groups, people with disabilities tend to suffer from recurrent reductive stereotypes in the mainstream media.

> **EXAMPLE:** *Meet the Superhumans* (Channel 4, 2012) and *The Undateables* (Channel 4, 2016)

Trailers advertising the Paralympics are always interesting in their representations of people with disabilities.

In the award-winning trailer for Channel 4's coverage of the games, athletes are seen in footage that shows them at the top of their game, as well as flashbacks showing disability resulting from injury, or being present from birth.

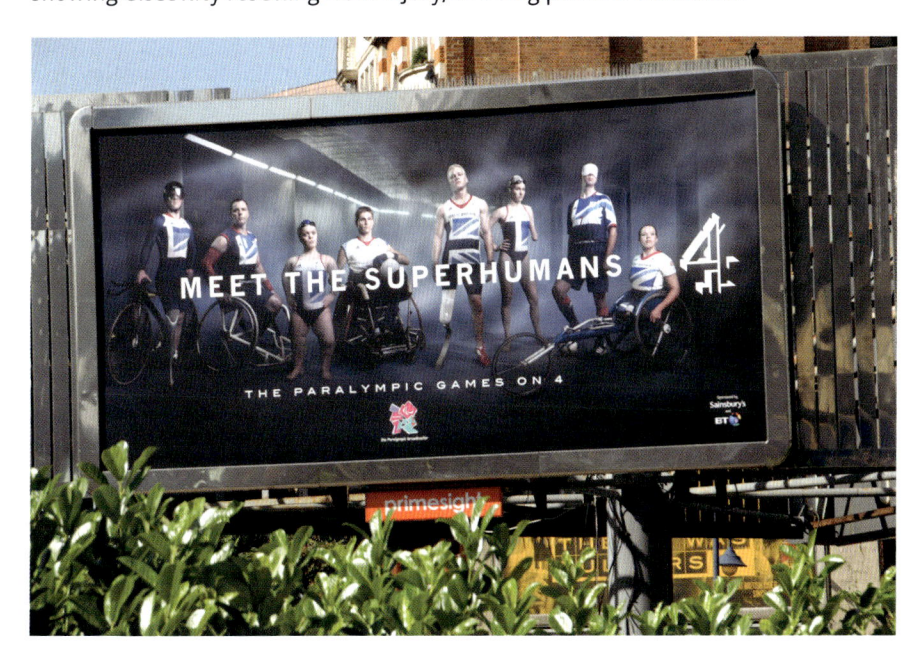

There is a danger that this advert could be considered to be lacking in complexity and perpetuating a 'triumph over tragedy' stereotype, limiting the representation. Of course, athletes without a disability have also been marketed in similar ways in mainstream media. Nonetheless, the writer of this article in *Prospect* magazine points out not all people with disabilities are 'exceptional' performers, and broader representation is needed: www.prospectmagazine.co.uk/culture/45860/stop-using-the-paralympics-as-inspiration-porntheyre-elite-sports-stars

The Undateables (2012–17), also broadcast on Channel 4, is a reality dating show that follows people with physical disabilities and/or learning difficulties. The show initially met with controversy for its suggestion that people who belong to these groups are unwanted or cannot participate in day-to-day life: a claim that was denied by the show's producers, who intended the title to reflect mainstream attitudes rather than reality. However, critics praised the show's warmth and positivity in the portrayal of its subjects.

> **Apply it**
> Source and view other trailers for the Paralympics and an episode of *The Undateables*. Do they conform to the media or the social model? Do they reinforce certain stereotypes or attempt to counter them?

5.3 The relationship between representations and reality

Apply it

Choose an audio-visual media text that represents a particular historical time period or place. Think about how it represents that place or period through mise-en-scène.

Quick questions

1 Give an example of a social group that may be subject to stereotypes in the media, together with a short explanation of why.
2 What do we mean by 'marginalisation' in mass media terms?
3 What do we mean by a 'pariah group' in society, and why could stereotyping be particularly damaging to people in these groups?

Apply it

Using an example of a moving image, and an audio, web and print advertisement, identify four stereotypes that are common in the popular media. The stereotypes should not be limited to gender or age – try to cover as much ground as you can across the texts. Considering working or familial roles is a good way to ensure variety.

Key terms

in-groups members of a dominant culture
Men are often seen as an in-group despite making up approximately half of the population.

out-groups minorities living within a dominant culture
Ethnically Chinese-British people are represented in the article as an out-group.

Place

In our culture, place is often defined in a structuralist way using binary oppositions (see Chapter 4: Media language). For example, the countryside is quiet and dull while the city is loud and vibrant; or the countryside is a place of beauty and connections with nature while the city is an ugly sprawl and an unnatural environment. We often read representations of place as points of contrast with our own experience, a representation of certain events or values, or as a projection of our desires and imagination.

EXAMPLE: *Poldark* and Cornwall

Cornwall is frequently represented in both fiction and documentary in a highly romanticised way. As a popular UK holiday destination, the county enjoys a largely positive reputation of clean beaches, great surf, pretty harbours and rugged landscapes. In reality, many Cornish people struggle to make ends meet and economic poverty is rife. This side of Cornwall is rarely shown as it fails to match the entertainment values of the programmes using it as a location.

Poldark is a historical 'period' drama based on the novels of the same name by Winston Graham. The original series was broadcast on the BBC in 1977–79, and the remake in 2015–19. Part of the reason for the show's success is its use of location filming and the depiction of a wild and romantic setting (Cornwall) as the backdrop to an intense family saga. Although avidly watched by many Cornish people, the series as a whole is intended to appeal to a cross-section of the BBC's audience.

5.4 Stereotyping and counter-representations

Stereotyping refers to the practice of reducing a group or an individual to a limited set of preconceived ideas that already circulate about this group within society. Stereotypes are a means of quickly constructing representations in an accessible way for the audience. They are constructed in many of the ways discussed above, and may have more significance in some genres than others.

Most theorists agree that stereotypes are based on a limited set of ideas and assumptions that stand in for a whole, rich and varied representation.

In-groups and out-groups

When looking at social groups, an important concept is **in-groups** (the dominant culture) and **out-groups** (usually the minority). It is not always about numbers of people in a society, but about who holds the power. For example, women have historically been considered an out-group within patriarchal systems of representation. In-groups often hold stereotypes about the out-groups as a way of understanding their presence in the context of their own group; stereotypes are often based on difference – a set of binary, contrasting qualities that the in-group may use to compare the group characteristics with their own. Sometimes this process consciously defines the out-group as inferior. There is then a danger that this treatment in the mass media either reflects or reinforces real treatment of members of that out-group in society. Out-groups can be instrumental in the formulation of alternative representations and countertypes. These alternative representations can begin to make their presence felt in mainstream media; more often they are confined to alternative media.

EXAMPLE: Two advertisements from *Attitude* magazine

In September 2016, the two advertisements below appeared in *Attitude* magazine, an established lifestyle, fashion and culture magazine targeted at gay men. In the magazine, a range of advertisements appear targeting this audience. Some are for mainstream companies who seek the custom of a gay audience; others are for companies that exclusively cater to the gay audience's needs. This demonstrates how an out-group in British culture can redefine itself outside of the imposition of stereotypes held by the in-group, in this case heterosexuals. This is also known as counter-representation.

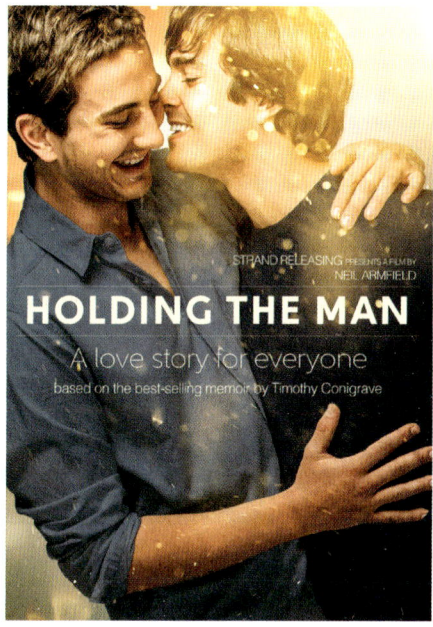

- *Emerald Life Insurance advert (left):* reinforces the idea of the committed, loving, long-term gay relationship, countering the out-group's belief that gay relationships are transient.
- *Holding the Man film release advert (right):* promotes the release of a romantic drama that centres on two gay characters and their *desire* to be together. It counters the idea that romantic love is entirely the province of the heterosexual norm.

Another important idea is the notion of **otherness**, or **alterity**. This is a well-established concept in postcolonial theory, which explores representations of different ethnicities in Western culture (see section 5.9: Ethnicity and postcolonial theory). In the case of **the other**, people belonging to the out-group are defined exclusively by their differences from the dominant culture. This can be used in political justification for repression of groups or limitations of their rights within a host culture. It is also used in other demeaning ways, such as sexualising black women by portraying them as 'exotic'.

■ Problems of misrepresentation in a global culture

In Chapter 7, we will be discussing more about the global nature of media industries and how this affects media consumption. It is certainly true that today's media audiences are exposed to more varied representations of people from other cultures. Although the Westernised values embedded in these representations predominate, you will be considering media that is produced by other cultures, and also media that is produced by out-groups. These alternatives often challenge the dominant representations encountered in other texts.

Apply it

As a class, source a copy of *Attitude* magazine or another magazine that caters for an out-group. Choose three advertisements in the magazine and explore how these may challenge stereotypes held about that group by the in-group.

Key terms

alterity in a media studies context, the state of being 'other' in representations from dominant representations of in-groups
The alterity of the women is signified by their dress code.

otherness the state of being defined as 'different' – views of an out-group held by an in-group
The earthquake victims in the report are defined by their otherness, signified for example by multi-generational accommodation and the destruction of the food market.

the other the state of being defined as 'different' due to cultural differences
The women in the camp are defined as 'other', potentially narrowing the range of possible readings of their situation.

5.4 Stereotyping and counter-representations

A number of the issues presented by the global nature of some representations are outlined below:

- A reduction in diversity of representations occurs due to their repetition in dominant media forms, for example English language content, particularly from the US.
- There is transmission of negative stereotypes from one culture to another – bad news travels faster than good.
- Media censorship – the state censoring of some content may lead to skewed representations that are difficult to make sense of.
- Reduction in perceived value of indigenously produced media content – the indigenous groups struggle to find a platform for self-representation in a competitive media industry.
- Value judgements – alternative representations and modes of self-representation are perceived as less important than the dominant representations we are exposed to on a regular basis.

■ Are stereotypes fixed?

Some stereotypes are certainly more persistent than others in both society and media histories. Since society and culture are constantly changing, the mass media is also in a state of perpetual flux. New stereotypes and sub-categories emerge all the time while others remain surprisingly constant.

> **EXAMPLE: 'Geek or Chic? Emerging Stereotypes of Online Gamers' (2012)**
>
> In their article 'Geek or Chic? Emerging Stereotypes of Online Gamers', Rachel Kowert and Julian Oldmeadow explore a new stereotype relating to digital media – that of the online gamer. In the article, the authors argue that the social stereotype of 'isolated and lonely couch potatoes' is less interesting than what it can tell us about what they term the 'cognitive stereotype' – society's attitudes towards gaming as an activity. In the study, they propose that online gamers are:
>
> *stereotypically unpopular, unattractive, idle, and socially incompetent, a characterisation that seems to match common stereotypical portrayals in the media, television and internet fora.*
>
> The study, which tested a range of supposed traits associated with gamers among both gamers and non-gamers, found a marked distinction between gamers, who tended to refute the stereotype, and non-gamers, who appeared to have internalised it.
>
> Today, how popular game vloggers are with their youth audience has gone some way towards challenging this stereotype, although in traditional media things may be slower to change.

Tessa Perkins, a sociologist and lecturer in communication theory, wrote an important article called 'Rethinking Stereotypes' in 1979, which explains the significance of stereotypes in the media. It still represents some of the most powerful and focused consideration of the nature of stereotypes and the problems with them that can be found anywhere. Perkins makes these points:

- Stereotypes do not come from nowhere.
- Stereotypes can be both true and false at the same time.
- Some stereotypes are simple, others are more complex and attached to complex social meanings, for those who both replicate and decode them.
- Stereotypes are always held by a particular social group about another social group.

Apply it

Explore a stereotype relating to new digital media: examples could be the mum blogger, beauty blogger, stereotypes relating to teenagers and social media use, the comic and fan-fic 'nerd'. Try to collect at least two textual sources that help you to assess the nature of the stereotype.

Set up three photographs: one, a portrait of someone who represents the stereotype, and two others showing behaviours you might associate with them. Present them as a 'wanted' poster. Discuss with your classmates how they all look displayed together.

CHAPTER 5 MEDIA REPRESENTATIONS

Another well-known aspect of Perkins' work was her identification of some of the problems with the way in which stereotypes are understood. She questions whether stereotypes are always **pejorative** (negative) – many are, but not all. Positive or **laudatory stereotypes** can also play an instrumental role in elevating the visibility of an oppressed group, as well as validating a group that is already powerful or respected in society.

Stereotypes are often used in the media because they support another aspect of the product's form. Stereotypes recur commonly in genre-based narratives. Industry values can also be highly significant in dictating the observance of stereotypes. These are central to the success of the tabloid press in the UK. Often accused of vilifying social groups and individuals, some mainstream media texts nonetheless persist in using stereotypes because the formula works.

■ Counter-representations

Counter-representations are sometimes present in mainstream media texts. They can work to increase suspense, promote awareness of an issue or simply to serve a niche audience. Counter-representations are often far more consciously constructed than stereotypes, and structurally reinforce a stereotype by opposing it. Counter-representations are therefore interesting to study alongside a structuralist theory of narrative, such as that proposed by Claude Lévi-Strauss.

The term countertypes is used to mean much the same as counter-representations, except it is applied more commonly to an individual.

Countertypes may have an educational role in the media, challenging prejudices and increasing awareness of issues relating to stereotypes. Like stereotypes, they may also appear more commonly in some genre texts than others. Countertypes are particularly likely to emerge in social media, shared as viral messages that provide an alternative to dominant representations. These may attempt to raise awareness or galvanise social change. Although better than no representation at all, it should be remembered that often this kind of video does not reach the people (people who subscribe to stereotypes) it is intended to, and tends to be more readily shared among those who are already receptive to alternate viewpoints. Documentary is another common genre in which to find the countertype, as documentaries usually aim to inform people about certain topics. They sometimes also aim to expose something, or leave the audience thinking about a subject from a new perspective or re-evaluating attitudes.

EXAMPLE: *Exodus: Our Journey to Europe* (2016)

Exodus: Our Journey to Europe is a three-part documentary that was shot by refugees on their own smartphones as they made the treacherous escape from Syria and broadcast on BBC One in 2016. The documentary challenged many people's views of 'migrants' by showing the desperate reasons they are fleeing war zones, allowing audiences to connect with the stories of individuals. This allowed for self-representation for a group who, because of its obvious lack of power and status in society, does not usually have a voice. It is also a powerful reminder of the potential that digital media and mobile devices have for helping people to tell stories that otherwise might not be heard.

It would be too easy to dismiss stereotyping as a cultural signification practice, which is mostly harmless. Sometimes, perhaps it is. Given we know that the relationship between stereotypes and the real-world attitudes and values of media consumers informed by them is a complex one, media

Key terms

laudatory stereotypes stereotypes that contribute positively to views of social groups
The refugees are represented in a laudatory way, focusing on their bravery and humanity.

pejorative stereotypes stereotypes that demean their subject
Pejorative stereotypes of young South Asian men are sometimes used in the tabloid press.

Apply it

Think of three different laudatory stereotypes we hold about people in society. For each type, identify an example of this being reinforced in a mainstream media text. A good place to start is with Perkins' 'salient groups', since there is often a pre-existing neutrality about these compared with, for example, pariah or opponent groups, which tend to bear more ideologically significant aspects to their associated stereotypes.

△ Syrian refugees arriving in Greece from Turkey, 2015

> **Apply it**
>
> Storyboard a 60-second video that constructs a deliberate countertype of teenagers. The video should be suitable for distribution on social media.

producers have an ethical responsibility to try to represent people in a fair way. Derogatory stereotypes can inform attitudes and have been used to form negative propaganda campaigns throughout the relatively short history of the mass media.

> **Quick questions**
> 1. What is the difference between a laudatory and pejorative stereotype?
> 2. Why are counter-representations necessary? Give three reasons.
> 3. Write definitions of the terms 'in-group' and 'out-group' from memory. Then check your answers against the Key terms box on page 106.

5.5 The ideological nature of common media representations and how we respond to them

■ Ideologies and hegemony – what they are and why they matter

The study of **ideology** is a complex field. For the purpose of A-level media studies, we will use the term ideology to mean the shared value and belief systems of a culture. Mainstream media texts tend to support the dominant ideology in a culture. They have a role in both maintaining the status quo and reflecting the values held by a large part of a population. The resulting problem is that not everyone within a particular culture shares the same values and ideologies. Popular ideologies often lean conservative and pro the role of the individual and traditional family structures in society. They tend to be predominantly **heteronormative**, pro-work, and supportive of the government and democracy. These kinds of values pervade our media texts.

Some political theories of the mass media go even further. Marxist theorists suggest that the mass media is a tool of the state, serving the wealthy and powerful, and protecting the interests of the ruling class as a **passive ideological state apparatus (ISA)** by naturalising values that preserve their power (an idea first proposed by French philosopher Louis Althusser). Marxist theorist Antonio Gramsci referred to the process of coercing the population into conforming with mainstream ideologies as **cultural hegemony**. Texts that have a hegemonic function may simply convey mainstream ideologies in a simplistic way, or they might test out alternatives and then resolve them in favour of the ruling elite.

Mass media products are important to everyone and affect our lives in ways we may not have previously considered because they can contribute to hegemony in many different, subtle ways. Through repetition, they constantly reinforce values that are relevant in a society using the other signification practices and processes you have already learnt about.

> **Key terms**
>
> **cultural hegemony** the process of indoctrination through cultural products of the dominant ideologies in a society
> *The magazine reinforces cultural hegemony through the mode of address used in the headline of the article.*
>
> **heteronormative** using the perspective of heterosexuals (and therefore omitting alternative perspectives)
> *Marriage is represented in a heteronormative way as being between men and women.*
>
> **ideology** in the context of A-level study, dominant ways of thinking in a society shared by many people within it
> *The text communicates through shared ideologies about childhood.*
>
> **passive ideological state apparatus (ISA)** according to Althusser, the function of the mass media in maintaining the status quo
> *In this sense, the media can be seen as a passive ISA that reinforces the positive handling of the crisis by the government.*

> **Apply it**
> 1. Identify some popular ideologies around the following in society: work ethic, the family, the monarchy, body image, consumer culture, and celebrity.
> 2. Now find evidence for each of these in a range of print media products. Include magazines, newspapers and print adverts.
> 3. Collate your findings as a slide presentation to share with your group.

> **EXAMPLE: The portrayal of positive role models in *Hello!* magazine**
>
> This publication is well known for its positive portrayal of society's role models, such as celebrities and particularly the British monarchy. It publishes exclusive interviews and photoshoots with the wealthy, which are positive in tone and uncontroversial. Because of this, *Hello!* is often the only invited media presence at celebrity weddings and therefore it has a higher-than-normal level of access to the younger generation of the monarchy. *Hello!* could be considered to play a role in upholding the status of the wealthy and powerful in society, reinforcing their significance in the lives of ordinary readers, promoting values such as patriotism and validating distinctions in social class.

This idea was also explored by the American professor Noam Chomsky when he wrote in 1988 that the mass media helps to **manufacture consent** in a society by playing out and resolving in favour of the ruling class any contentious issues. Chomsky believes that a galvanising force is necessary as a background to his **propaganda model of communication**, which unites the majority of a population in the face of a threat that is real and can be maintained over a long period of time.

Not all political theorists share this left-wing perspective. The dominant mode of considering the relationship between audiences and the media they consume in most Western capitalist countries is liberal pluralism. Liberal pluralists do not think that the media controls people's beliefs about society, more that they offer choices and can even reflect diverse identities and ideologies. This approach suggests that media consumers, when faced with a multitude of ideologies, select those that match their own and reject others that don't. Consumers tend to ignore texts that challenge their way of thinking, seeking out instead those that reinforce their view of the world. This appears to support the idea of preferred readings – a consumer who encounters a text that disturbs their view of the world may simply disengage from it.

△ Fans of *Star Wars* attending a *Star Wars* convention are expressing an aspect of their identity

This is most important when considering the relationship between how we respond to dominant ideologies in the mass media and how they might contribute to our sense of our own identity.

5.6 Theories of identity and the role of the mass media

There has been a great deal of critical thinking in recent years, particularly considering developments in participatory and digital media, about the role of the mass media in shaping and reflecting multiple identities in society.

Identity is often separated into **cultural identity** and **personal identity**. Aspects of cultural identity are common across large groups of people – personal identity is much more individual. The way in which these combine uniquely in every person is one of the reasons media texts are so open to

Key terms

manufacture consent the process, as identified by Noam Chomsky, that media institutions use to persuade audiences of the validity of national policies
Chomsky would argue that the newspaper helps to manufacture consent on the issue of funding the NHS.

propaganda model of communication the sustaining in media profile of a genuinely threatening event for political purposes
News coverage of the war on terror following 9/11 fulfils Chomsky's definition of the propaganda model of communication.

Key terms

cultural identity aspects of our identity that are derived from cultural influences such as region, religion or family
Aspects of the main character's cultural identity are used to define them in the opening sequence.

personal identity identity made up of individual preferences and views
Young women may engage with the broadcast to differing extents according to their personal identity.

> **Key terms**
>
> **collective identity** aspects of our identity we share with others
> *The advertisement reinforces our sense of collective identity.*
>
> **individuality paradox** a known philosophical quandary in studying identity, that most people wish to simultaneously be seen as an individual while experiencing commonality and social belonging.

> For more on identities see section 6.1 How the media industry targets audiences.

> **KEY THINKER**
>
> **David Gauntlett** (1971–) formulated ten influential criticisms of media effects theory.

△ David Gauntlett (1971–)

different readings of the same content by various people, especially when the text seems to force a conflict between the two. It is certainly true that conforming with mainstream identities creates feelings of acceptance by society and is very reassuring for significant numbers of people.

Most research into identity over the past few decades makes the assumption that identity is a fluid concept. Some believe identity is fractured or fragmented. Many individuals do have a complex identity, made up of several components. If we accept that the mass media offers us role models and ways of being that we can select from if we choose, then this renegotiation process has a far wider frame of reference at this point in history than ever before.

Some people may choose not to conform with mainstream identities and reframe their own identity in alternative ways. The internet offers numerous spaces where people can build and share alternate ways of being or select from more eclectic media influences. People can also take pleasure from having a **collective identity** – feeling that they are sharing values or even just acts of consumption with others. This can be seen in the case of fan sites and forums.

A more pessimistic view of identity formation would suggest that this happens only infrequently, and that the majority of people frame their understanding of their own identity from a narrow range of media representations and societal roles.

■ David Gauntlett – enabling ideas

In the second edition of his book *Media, Gender and Identity* (2008), the British sociologist **David Gauntlett** considers the relationship between representations in the mass media and how people construct their own identities. Although his main interest is gender, much of what he says about gender is more widely applicable. Gauntlett's book makes interesting reading, partly because he evaluates the thinking of other key thinkers as he works through ideas relating to media representations and our sense of identity.

In his book, Gauntlett considers why media influences are important in thinking through how representations affect people's sense of self and relationships with others in society. Gauntlett does not suggest that we can prove media influence on identity; more that we should be aware of the power and prevalence of representations in the media that are frequently repeated.

Towards the end of the book Gauntlett tries to make sense of some of his exploration both through his own experimentation and the ideas of other prominent theorists. These are some of his conclusions:

- People tend to view their identities as a single thing rather than perceiving them as fragmented. They may see what some theorists term fragmented or multiple identities as co-existing within a whole.
- Most people actively dislike the idea that they are the same as everyone else, and try to differentiate themselves from the masses in some way while at the same time wanting to feel a part of society. This is known as the **individuality paradox**.
- The media does not exist in a vacuum – it is a part of most people's everyday social reality and not a separate field that they enter and then leave. In order to study the media's contribution to our sense of identity through representations, we need to understand how it fits into people's worlds.
- Media studies tends to treat audiences as a faceless mass – and even though it is often acknowledged that audiences are made up of individuals with their own tastes and ideas, this only touches the surface. The real issues of complexity of the individual and how that affects the ways they make sense of their media consumption are almost infinite.

- Most people don't actually rate influence from the media all that highly when questioned about influences on their identity, unless the media is specifically mentioned.
- Despite all these issues, the media does influence how we feel about our identities, because it offers us frames of reference and ways of understanding how people fit into society – the stories we tell about ourselves use some of the points of narrative and symbolic reference we gain from the media, even if we find that a hard thing to acknowledge.

The issue of media and identity forms an overlap between two of the areas of the theoretical framework: audiences and representations. People do not encounter difficulties in building an outwards representation of their identity, suggesting that the concept of identity is readily understood by anyone.

There are several key terms in identity theory you need to be confident in using when discussing issues relating to representation and identity:

- **Fluidity of identity**: this idea, currently a key component of critical thinking about identity, suggests that people do not have a fixed identity that is wholly and permanently a part of them, with only superficial changes being constructed by that individual. Where this seems to be the case, this is perhaps because people have willingly chosen a part, for example, of their cultural identity and subsumed it as a dominant feature of their personal identity. There is a strong groundswell of critical thinking from a range of disciplines that suggests there is a big influence from society as a whole that affects how aspects of our identity are expressed according to mainstream norms and values. The idea that identity is fluid informs a lot of contemporary critical thinking about gender.
- **Constructed identity**: the mass media constructs identities in the representations it offers us – many theorists believe that we then assimilate various aspects of these in building our own identities, which we may then display in various ways, for example, through online group memberships or mainstream social media.
- **Negotiated identity**: this refers to the ways in which we negotiate the various influences on our composite identities and relate to others in relationships – how we perceive ourselves in relation to others. The idea of identity negotiation is active in the fields of Sociology and Psychology, but has currency also in media studies. You can use it to try and understand how we relate not only to real, present 'others' in society but also the constructions of other identities seen in the media, whether fiction or fact based.
- **Collective identity**: media representations and fandoms, or the sense of belonging to a sector of a media audience, form just one factor in the construction of individual identity. In general, in media theory the phenomenon of collective identity is widely accepted as the sense of belonging to an audience for a media product, drawing on ideas often repeated in active theories of audience or the social relationships aspect of uses and gratifications. Gauntlett believes that people easily navigate the identities available for them to choose from in the media – assuming some and rejecting others – but that the media is only one influence of many on their lives.

> **Key terms**
>
> **collective identity** sense of ownership of media representations and fandoms, or the sense of belonging to a sector of a media audience
>
> **constructed identity** the view that the mass media constructs identities in the representations it offers us
>
> **fluidity of identity** the concept that people do not have a fixed identity that is wholly and permanently a part of them
>
> **negotiated identity** ways in which we negotiate the various influences on our composite identities – how we perceive ourselves in relation to others

Quick questions

1. What is the difference between cultural and personal identity?
2. What do we mean by the individuality paradox?
3. How has the development of the internet helped to facilitate collective identity in media audiences?

5.6 Theories of identity and the role of the mass media

> See Chapter 7: Media industries to help you link ideas about how industry contexts affect representations.

Key terms

cultural imperialism the domination of mostly English-language, well-funded products of the global media market
Popular genres can play a role in cultural imperialism by saturating indigenous markets.

cultural relativism judging of other cultures against white European values
Failure to represent both sides of this news story is an example of cultural relativism.

△ RuPaul is a good example of a popular television personality outside the heterosexual 'norm' whose audience extends beyond the drag and LGBTQ+ communities

5.7 How industry contexts impact on representations

Who produces a media text and why it is produced can have a significant effect on the representations it contains. The commercial drive to make a profit, coupled with political pressures, doubtless has a significant impact on the nature of the representations produced by newspapers in the UK. Public service broadcasters such as the BBC are more likely to represent minorities or offer a wider spectrum of more complex representations of diverse groups than a commercial broadcaster such as ITV or Channel 5.

Globalisation and **cultural imperialism** can result in cultural content globally becoming very similar despite being produced in different parts of the world that could be expected to have their own distinct cultural identities, usually apparent in their domestic media. Connected to this is **cultural relativism** – the idea that mainstream media products may reflect in their creation the tendency to judge other cultures based on the values and ideologies of white Europeans. Reframing other cultures in this way is potentially very damaging to them.

A number of other significant aspects of industry practice have an effect on representations. In studying representations, we should be careful that the methodologies we use do not overemphasise the content of those representations identified through semiotic analysis (see Chapter 1: Reading print media). They must also take into account broader contexts of study, considering issues relating to audience reception and industrial production, and how these shape the way representations manifest.

5.8 Discourses around representation and ideology: gender studies and the mass media

A **discourse** in academic terms means a discussion in academic thinking, often taken in different directions and explored from different angles by different theorists. Some of these theorists may disagree, others develop and reinforce each other's ideas.

The fields of queer theory and studies in masculinity are relatively small when compared with feminist theory. The reasons for this are complex. Feminist thinkers were the first to question how patriarchy shaped our values as a society, and how media texts might contribute to the maintenance of this hegemony. Queer theory also developed as a critical field, as the visibility of lesbian, gay bisexual and transgender (LGBTQ+) people grew. Awareness of the qualitative nature of this group's representations has since increased in our society.

Following behind both feminist and queer theory are studies in masculinity, which evaluate the role of men in this changing society, as their superior status under traditional patriarchy and older modes of representation of traditional masculinity fade. There have been many interesting individual writings about masculinity in cinema, and David Gauntlett undertook some very interesting work in researching contemporary images of masculinity in *Media, Gender and Identity* (2008). However, there is not yet an equivalent body of rich discourse on masculinities, as is the case with feminism.

■ **Feminist approaches to media representations of women**

Feminism is a huge field of study in critical thinking. Its relevance to media studies is significant, as it allows us to consider the nature of female representations,

CHAPTER 5 MEDIA REPRESENTATIONS

and also to question who makes and owns the media we consume and how this might affect the text being produced at a representational level. One way of understanding the progress of feminist thinking over the past few decades is to understand it in terms of waves – patterns of thinking and analysis that have distinctive characteristics which change noticeably over time. (see Table 5.2)

All feminists are united in their ideological opposition to patriarchy, a system where men exert control at every level within the power structures in society. Under patriarchy, men are over-represented in almost every sphere where power is wielded – politics, business, etc. Feminists argue that power structures in society need to be more inclusive of women and, until women are equally represented in every sphere, they will continue to be oppressed by the system.

Some critics have even identified what is known as the post-feminist era. However, the summaries offered here are necessarily broad and quite generalised so as to offer a way of contextualising the movement.

▽ Table 5.2 Historic waves of feminism and what they have involved

First wave 1800s–early 1900s	• Concerned about political equality • Socio-political issues surrounding women's rights
Second wave Post-Second World War–early 1990s	• Disruption to women's lives and roles during and after the Second World War • Dissatisfaction with domestic life and roles • Freeing-up of leisure time for women due to advances in technology, such as household appliances (1950s) • Reproductive rights (1960s)
Third wave 1990s–present	• Feminism as a unified movement begins to fragment • Begins to focus on more marginalised groups of women as opposed to privileged white, straight women • Women as owners of their own sexuality not vessels of male desire
Fourth wave 2000s–present	• Digital activism • Continued strong focus on gender inequality, the calling out of stereotypes and abuses of power by men over women

EXAMPLE: Political suffragette poster, UK, 1913

The 1913 Prisoners (Temporary Discharge for Ill-Health) Act, commonly known as the 'Cat and Mouse Act', was a move by the government of the time to defeat hunger-striking suffragettes in prisons and prevent them from dying while incarcerated and becoming martyrs. The Act worked by releasing them when they became too ill through refusal to eat, then sending them back to prison when they were considered to have recovered sufficiently.

Apply it

Collect six examples of pro-suffrage for women posters, UK or US, using an online image search.

- What is the issue or focus of each poster?
- What is the mode of address in terms of both images and any lexical coding?
- What messages do they send about the problems facing women in society at the time?
- If men or children are represented in any of the posters you chose, how are they represented?
- How does the poster draw on aspects of real women's lives to persuade the audience of the political message?

5.8 Discourses around representation and ideology: gender studies and the mass media

A typical 1950s household product advertisement targeting women

■ The male gaze

In 1975, feminist Laura Mulvey, who was heavily influenced by psychoanalytical film theory, wrote a hugely influential essay called 'Visual Pleasure in Narrative Cinema'. In this essay, Mulvey argues that women are present to be looked at by men, therefore women who view films are forced to see themselves in the same way.

Mulvey coined the term the **male gaze** to describe the way the audience is positioned to look at women in film. She also noted that powerful female characters, perceived as potentially threatening by the male audience, must undergo punishment.

△ This iconic shot of Gloria Grahame in *The Big Heat* demonstrates a classic cinematic example of the male gaze as defined by Mulvey

Today, there is still an argument for the existence of a **female gaze**. It is certainly true that men may now be filmed in a similar way.

> **Key terms**
>
> **female gaze** the subversion of the male gaze in which men become the subject to be looked at by women
> *The band are photographed in such a way as to appeal to the female gaze.*
>
> **male gaze** describes the way we all are conventionally positioned to look at women in film in an inferior, and often sexualised way
> *The young women are all represented submissively to appeal to the male gaze.*

EXAMPLE: Media coverage of the Harvey Weinstein scandal and #MeToo

Following a spate of accusations of sexual misconduct against Hollywood producer Harvey Weinstein in Autumn 2017, #MeToo began trending on social media, as more women shared their stories of sexual assault and male intimidation. The consequences of the Weinstein scandal and its coverage were huge, with ramifications not just for the film and media industries, but in UK politics and business. For a time, accusations were made almost daily against high-profile men. It was widely reported that both ordinary and well-known women felt empowered

CHAPTER 5 MEDIA REPRESENTATIONS

by the groundswell of unity surrounding the campaign. The rise of #MeToo also resulted in negative reactions from some sections of the internet community and contributed to visible hate speech towards women online.

Apply it

Create an A3-size digital collage of news headlines, images and extracts from social media and the internet about the #MeToo campaign.

- What impression do you get from this of the scale and reach of the reportage and sharing?
- What are the messages conveyed by seeing all these extracts together in terms of third or fourth wave feminism and its relationship with the mainstream?
- Which groups or perspectives are neglected? Is it a local, national or global issue? Does it only affect women?

Raunch culture and post-feminism

Raunch culture is the sexualised performance of women in the media that can play into male stereotypes of women as highly sexually available; whereas its performers believe they are powerful owners of their own sexuality.

In her book *Female Chauvinist Pigs* (2006), writer Ariel Levy proposes that the sexual objectification of women in images, once confined to the private male sphere in areas such as erotic art, has become a dominant representation of women across the mass media. She described this phenomenon as raunch culture, which plays into the same dated objectification of women under patriarchy, while positioning it critically as female empowerment. Levy suggested that raunch culture positioned women in the following ways in society:

- Representations of women in an overtly sexualised way, more usually associated with the sex industry, become more mainstream and culturally acceptable.
- Women become complicit in these representations, misconstruing them as empowering and contributing to their subjugation to patriarchy.
- It began to emerge in the 1990s and was possibly a backlash to the perception that earlier feminists were dismissive of female sexuality and saw sexual agency as being the province of men and part of the exploitative nature of patriarchy.

Closely linked to the idea of raunch culture is **lipstick feminism**, which is also seen as a brand of third wave feminism that allows women to portray themselves as equal to men in terms of their sexuality by expressing it in any way they choose. This is viewed as a counter-ideology, in that it challenges notions of decency and purity demanded of most women and policed by other women in a patriarchal society. It also takes ownership linguistically of chauvinistic terms for women, which can be seen in political protests, asserting the right of women to look or behave how they wish without fear of male reprisal or abuse. The validity of third wave feminism's ownership of sexuality through control of their image as sexualised is one that still divides feminists and is an ongoing debate surrounding raunch culture.

Key terms

lipstick feminism a brand of third wave feminism that allows women to portray themselves as equal to men in terms of their sexuality by expressing it in any way they choose
The celebrity's statement defending the photoshoot could be interpreted as an example of lipstick feminism.

raunch culture specifically associated with music videos, but with cultural resonance seen elsewhere – the overt sexualisation of female artists
The shots of the artist performing are highly sexualised and in keeping with raunch culture.

5.8 Discourses around representation and ideology: gender studies and the mass media

Critics of raunch culture suggest that it may position women as powerful owners of their own sexuality in posturing, but it does so in a way that validates chauvinistic attitudes to women and continues to commodify them. Its pervasiveness in the mass media can impact on male expectations of female sexual availability and it pits women against each other in a competition to be the most sexually appealing and, therefore, most powerful.

Post-feminism is a term used to define any critique of feminism at any point following a particular manifestation of feminist thinking. Therefore, it is a difficult concept to explain in a definitive way, since it is more a collection of critiques of feminism, which may be contradictory rather than a single ideological stance on gender equality. The term post-feminist is sometimes used to suggest that, because feminism has tended to form splits in debate and take on many fragmented new forms, it is in some way weakened, when in fact these new, more diverse feminisms could be taken as evidence that feminism is actually thriving.

EXAMPLE: Female music artists and raunch culture

Many critics of raunch culture believe that the only benefit to women of the proclaimed 'liberation' of overtly sexual musical performance and expression by these artists is the financial one to themselves. In reality, their message is far from empowering for women but simply a repackaging of the traditional commodification of women's bodies in the media and in society as a whole.

△ A waxwork model of Miley Cyrus on her wrecking ball – powerful owner of her own image or sexualised subject of patriarchy?

Quick questions
1 What is meant by 'raunch culture' and what is its connection with post-feminism?
2 Explain in a short paragraph the defining qualities of one of the waves of feminism.
3 What did Laura Mulvey mean by 'the male gaze' and how might this be apparent in any given media product?

An overview of some key aspects of the perspectives of the key thinkers named in your specification on the topic – van Zoonen, hooks and Butler – are offered here, but it is recommended you take your reading beyond this book to gain a more developed and contextualised understanding of what these theorists have to offer you in your study of gender representations.

Apply it
Analyse a video track by a female music artist mentioned in the Example box. Try applying both perspectives – one reading the video as an empowering example of lipstick feminism, the other viewing the performer as a subject of patriarchy. Can you use semiotic evidence to justify both perspectives from the audio-visual, generic and narrative codes, and what they signify?

Liesbet van Zoonen – gender, discourse and power in the mass media

Liesbet van Zoonen's book *Feminist Media Studies* (1994) is an influential collection of explorations into a range of issues connecting dominant modes in feminist thinking, specifically with issues of media representation. Van Zoonen takes a close look at the main issues affecting female representation in the media and assesses the usefulness of feminist approaches to the study of the mass media. She acknowledges the complexity of a 'feminist' approach to studying the media, arguing that there are many different ways we can approach it, all with their own strengths and weaknesses. Although mainly focusing on traditional media, van Zoonen's ideas are readily transferable to the study of contemporary media in the digital age. She feels that feminist **discourse** is still very much dominated by a symbolic conflict about definitions of femininity. She suggests that the mass media has a huge amount of power in constructing gender representations that are broadly stereotypical, but also that there has not been any close study of what women actually do with these messages when they receive them. At the end of Chapter 3 (page 42) in her book, she asks some important questions which can help to shape the reading of gender in media texts. Following this way of enquiring into gender representations will give you thoughtful and engaged interpretations of your close study texts:

- *How are discourses of gender encoded in texts?*
- *Which preferred and alternative meanings of gender are available in media texts, and from which discourses do they draw?*
- *How do audiences use and interpret gendered media texts?*
- *How can these processes be examined and analysed?*

Van Zoonen broadly agrees with Stuart Hall's ideas about the process of signification in media texts – the encoding and decoding model. In looking at his model, however, she argues that although media texts are polysemic, their means are not infinite. They are constrained by the producers of texts. She draws on and finds connections with the ideas of both bell hooks and Judith Butler, both of whom are referenced key thinkers within this book. Many of van Zoonen's ideas centre on issues of power and inequality in a media industry where much of the production process is controlled by men.

Some of the issues van Zoonen identifies as the way feminists have attempted to make sense of discourse surrounding meaning in the mass media are as follows:

- All feminist debate is in some way about gender and power. However, women are not a homogenous group. Feminists therefore struggle to agree on a definition of femininity. Approaches to understanding how women are represented need to take account of differences between women and their real-world experiences who belong to different social strata and ethnic backgrounds. Gender is not the defining quality alone for women; it intersects with race, sexuality and class.
- The practise of constructing gender identities is constantly being played out not only symbolically in media texts but also in everyday life. Gender is seen by van Zoonen as a vital aspect of culture at all levels, and one that is institutionalised by factors such as genre and the domination of the industry by rich, white men on the level of mass mediation. However, gender is also evident in all the ways in which we interact with others in our daily lives.

KEY THINKER

Liesbet van Zoonen (1959–) is a Dutch author of feminist media studies. She developed a wide-ranging theory of the importance of looking at all aspects of media production and content in exploring representations of women.

Key term

discourse an academic discussion or debate about a subject embodying a range of perspectives around a similar subject
Exploring feminist discourse around music videos is a productive form of analysis.

△ Liesbet van Zoonen

5.8 Discourses around representation and ideology: gender studies and the mass media

- Stereotypes and socialisation by the mass media (see page 153) have often been important components in understanding how the media represents gender. They were historically accepted as the norm, and it is only in more recent decades that people began to question how stereotypes about gender developed, were reinforced or how they continued to circulate. The mass media tends to reflect the real-world issues women face and, as a result, *'symbolically denigrate women, either by not showing them at all, or by showing them in stereotypical roles'* (van Zoonen, page 17). This, however, does not factor in how women make use of the media – their understanding of it, and other complex factors such as narrative and generic contexts.
- Feminism is a product of left-wing thinking because it offers a cultural critique. It asks us to question the signs we see all around us. Strongly socialist feminists use the ideas of Gramsci and Althusser (see page 110) to support their view that gender is an important construct in ideology, since the media is the primary source of cultural hegemony in our society which allocates a place to women economically and socially, and its messages strive to maintain that status quo.
- The concept of **distortion** is significant in understanding just how difficult it is for feminists to come to an agreement as to what needs to change in terms of female representation in the mass media. Most people would agree that the way in which the media usually represents women's lives does not reflect the reality of many real women. There are plenty of women living complex and interesting lives who do not encounter similar types of women on television. Stereotypes, however, do reflect the reality of some people's lives. For example, because many women really are housewives whose main roles are child-rearing and domestic duties, we can question whether this is problematic. There is no universal agreed replacement for these stereotypes, so constructing countertypes that satisfy everyone who wants to see more progressive representations of women is always going to problematic.
- Gender has always been dynamic, varied across cultures and full of contradictory meanings. In our own popular culture in recent years, there are plenty of examples of celebrities and and other high-profile figures who draw on more androgynous or ambiguous notions of gender identity. It seems, then, that the mass media can be open to the transgression of traditional notions of gender boundaries between male and female. If the mass media could begin to reflect this possibility and go beyond the socially constructed paradigm of how we see men's and women's roles in a binary way, distortion would no longer be an issue.

> **Key term**
>
> **distortion** the phenomenon by which the way the media usually represents women's lives does not reflect the reality of many real women
> *The all-female investigative team in the drama can be seen as an example of distortion.*

EXAMPLE: Verizon *Inspire Her Mind* digital video advertisement (2016) and John Lewis *She's Always a Woman* television advert (2010)

The Verizon *Inspire Her Mind* and John Lewis *She's Always A Woman* adverts use similar techniques, with each offering a montage of moments in a girl or woman's life, respectively, but with quite different perspectives – one challenging the way girls are often raised in Western culture, the other reinforcing dominant ideology.

The Verizon advert seems to reinforce van Zoonen's idea that the construction of gender identities does not just happen symbolically in media texts but is a key aspect of our cultural exchanges every day. This is contrasted here with an advert for John Lewis, which represents some of the defining romantic notions of womanhood, another area van Zoonen cites as being most frequently explored by feminist critics of the mass media.

> **Apply it**
>
> Find two contrasting examples of advertisements that feature women. How clearly do they seem to act as examples of such symbolic reflection of women's real lives? Use them to explore some of van Zoonen's ideas about a feminist approach to reading the roles of women in media texts.

The John Lewis advert was very popular with its female target audience, despite its restrictive portrayal of a woman's life as revolving solely around the (luxurious) domestic setting, marriage, pregnancy, child-rearing, the nurturing of family ties and grandchildren. This suggests that many women accept the preferred reading that women should be proud of their centrality to family life.

In contrast, the Verizon advert is a hard-hitting critique of the way in which girls are socialised by the world around them into disbelieving that they are scientifically and academically capable. It attempts to use the mass media to promote this message, counter to van Zoonen's observation that advertising is a prominent purveyor of stereotypes about women and their roles in society. It draws on the absence of portrayals of 'ordinary' women working in disciplines such as science without being turned into stereotypes of 'geeks'.

You can watch the John Lewis ad at **www.youtube.com/watch?v=jYOsWWKHZVw** and the Verizon ad at **www.youtube.com/watch?v=QZ6XQfthvGY**

KEY THINKER

bell hooks (1952–2021) was an important contemporary American feminist and social activist. She wrote extensively about issues relating not only to gender representation but also its connections with race and social class, so is considered an important thinker on intersectionality.

■ bell hooks – intersectionality

Gloria Jean Watkins was a prominent African-American feminist thinker. She wrote many books, all under the pen name **bell hooks**, which she chose not to capitalise in order to emphasise her ideas over her persona. Her ideas are not only central to many issues of gender representation, but can also be applied to issues of race representation and postcolonial thinking, and political theory relating to social class.

hooks was preoccupied throughout her career by the **intersectionality** of race, social class and gender issues. She believed that they work together in differing power structures to limit the opportunities available to black women. Her writing is important as a reaction to the predominantly white middle-class concerns that preoccupied early feminists, some of which seemed to have little relevance to the lives of black American women struggling with issues relating to other aspects of their oppression in American society. Many of her ideas translate equally well to the treatment of women from minority ethnic groups in predominantly white European culture, and as a feminist who disliked the separating out of different schools of feminist thought, her work is of interest when looking at any female representation.

hooks believed that equality of the sexes is not possible without the participation of men in feminist thinking. As a media studies student, you need to consider whether the imbalance of men to women in key roles of the media industry affects female representations. Also consider whether men within the media industry are thoughtful, and whether or not they are engaged with issues that affect women when they create representations (both on screen and within texts).

hooks' lecture on 'Cultural Criticism & Transformation' (1997), available online, is both an important insight into hooks' mode of critical thinking and a highly readable account of many aspects of popular culture.

Key term

intersectionality the acknowledgement that issues of power relating to gender, race and social class all intersect
The focus on black working-class women's lives acknowledges the issue of intersectionality.

△ bell hooks

5.8 Discourses around representation and ideology: gender studies and the mass media

Although hooks gave the lecture in 1997, many of the points she made are relevant in today's media climate and reflect her thinking about the role of the media in people's lives:

- Studying popular culture is hugely important as it is where the politics of difference manifest. Popular culture is a site of interplay between the various power relationships that exist in the real world.
- The individual, whatever their gender, class or race, is responsible for thinking critically about the world they live in and the media they consume.
- There may not be a direct causal link between portrayals of sexual violence in the media and real-world actions, but seeing these images can contribute to both men and women's perceptions of what is acceptable behaviour.
- The conscious construction of representations – media producers should be held to account by all of us for lazy stereotyping.
- Mass media representations in the late 1990s reflected a conscious backlash against feminism, and a deliberate attempt by a patriarchal business and power structures to put women back in their place.
- hooks' deliberate use of the term 'white supremacist capitalist patriarchy' reminds us of the links she sees between all these oppressive factors in society.
- The media industry is permeated at all levels by the prioritisation of the profit motive over fair representation of women or people from minority ethnic groups. hooks believed that the profit motive gets the better even of those who begin with good intentions.

EXAMPLE: Intersectionality – Michael Burnham in *Star Trek: Discovery* (Netflix, 2017)

Star Trek: Discovery is part of a series franchise that stretches back to the 1960s. *Star Trek: Discovery* shows clear progress in attitudes to women from minority ethnic groups. The main protagonist, Michael Burnham (played by Sonequa Martin-Green), is a powerful black female lead, on whom all the series narratives are centred. Writer and co-creator Bryan Fuller said he wanted to continue *Star Trek*'s legacy of looking through a 'gender- and colourblind' prism.

hooks' ideas seem to have come to fruition in Michael Burnham – a positive, complex black female character who resists many of the more habitual stereotypes. It is debatable whether this series or any of the others in the *Star Trek* franchise can be said to be truly 'gender- and colourblind', but the aspiration is present.

△ Michael Burnham, right, played by Sonequa Martin-Green

Judith Butler – gender performativity

Another well-known theorist is **Judith Butler**, primarily for her book *Gender Trouble: Feminism and the Subversion of Identity* (1999). In this book, she challenges the notion that gender is a biological fact that places masculinity and femininity in binary categories. The book became highly influential not only for the impact it had on feminism, but also its contribution to the field of **queer theory**. Her work is exciting because of the way in which it encourages discussion about the perception of masculinity and femininity in society and how they manifest in media representations.

△ Judith Butler

Butler suggests that sex may be biologically defined at birth but that gender is learned through society and, in fact, is a performance. She refers to gender as a 'stylised repetition of acts' that we perform every day, most of the time without being conscious of our actions. We refer to this theory as **gender performativity**. Butler also recognises that to bypass this hegemonic state is an act of subversion that is very difficult for individuals to undertake, since society constantly reinforces and socialises us in a heteronormative way – and this is reinforced by many media products.

Butler's original book is a highly complex read, but her overall challenge to traditional ways of thinking about gender politics is not too difficult to grasp. These are just some of the points you can gain from reading her work:

- Many traditional approaches to gender and the way we understand it in society are governed by the notion that 'heterosexuality' can only be defined in a binary way by the existence of an 'other', 'homosexual' state.
- Feminist strategies that identify men and patriarchal structures as oppressors mimic the divisions and creation of barriers in society they would like to see removed.
- 'Women' are a huge array of people. Traditional feminism focuses on unity and tries to suggest that the sharing of biological sex is a trans-cultural phenomenon dictated by reductive qualities such as sexuality and child-bearing, which excludes a whole range of other aspects that influence the formation of gender identity.

KEY THINKER

Judith Butler (1956–) is an American feminist and author of *Gender Trouble: Feminism and the Subversion of Identity* (1999). She is well known for her theory of gender and performativity.

Key terms

gender performativity the idea that men and women 'perform' gendered behaviours and roles due to acquired cultural expectations
The main characters all demonstrate to some extent gender performativity.

queer theory critical approach that explores LGBTQ+ perspectives on culture and the media
Queer theory is sometimes neglected in approaches to the study of gender and the media, but is a useful tool.

5.8 Discourses around representation and ideology: gender studies and the mass media

- Most previous work on identity politics requires a known, categorised identity to be fully formed in order to be included in debate.
- Exclusion and hierarchies are present in almost every debate about gender and identity.
- Transformative approaches to identity politics can only emerge if we resist categorisation and start debates about gender and politics,
- Society should move towards and accept less 'stable' manifestations of gender identity.

EXAMPLE: Transgender characters – Buck Vu in *The OA* (Netflix, 2016)

The OA is a science fiction series that was shown on Netflix in 2016. It is based on the premise of a young blind woman, Prairie, who reappears seven years after she went missing and has recovered her sight. The character of Buck and the actor who plays him, Ian Alexander, form an interesting case study because it shows just how far media producers can go to represent characters from minority groups in a positive and thoughtful way. The show's writer/producer team, Brit Marling and Zal Batmanglij, were determined that the character should be cast as written – a young, transgender character with mixed Asian heritage. Initial casting calls were unsuccessful, so the producers put out a call on social media. Ian Alexander recorded his audition tape on his smartphone in his bathroom. The 15-year-old actor was immediately cast in the role despite his lack of formal acting experience, and has since been critically lauded for his performance.

△ Ian Alexander as Buck Vu in *The OA* (Netflix, 2016)

Apply it

Choose a representation of a transgender person or character from anywhere in the media. Explore the qualitative nature of the representation in around 300 words.

- To what extent does the representation accept that gender is just a performance? How inclusive is the treatment of the person or character?
- If the text is fictional, is the transgender character played by a transgender person?
- Does the representation centre on their perceived 'difference' from social norms of gender, or does it have other more complex aspects to it?

Studying representations of masculinity in the mass media

Many social commentators and some academic theorists have suggested that changes in gender roles in the last decades have led to what is sometimes termed a 'crisis' in masculinity. Certainly, this has become a popular cultural trope, with angry emasculated men seeking revenge on women or society in general being a popular device in cinematic and crime narratives. Some theorists, however, suggest that in reality there is no crisis in masculinity, and that the majority of modern men are perfectly equipped to deal with the changes in their roles and those of the women around them.

While there are fewer that explore the nature of masculinity in media texts compared with those that look at the role of women, it is a very interesting line of enquiry. Masculinity used to be considered a single set of traditional representations, with qualities that varied in their proportions and the way they were expressed but very little in other ways. Any deviation from these models was represented as negative. Portrayals of male emotion have to be properly contextualised historically, such as limited expression of grief being appropriate if a comrade-in-arms has fallen.

One error often made by new media students is to not recognise the versatility of feminist theories in decoding representations of masculinity in media products. Rather than being an overt way of challenging patriarchy and drawing attention to its power structures, feminist theories can also accommodate and validate more progressive representations of masculinity and celebrate these where they are more complex for what they can contribute to the debate.

Today, masculinity is generally expressed in a plural way. Many media texts are more progressive and diverse in their exploration of masculinities, but others remain which draw on conventional archetypes. The following example explores two advertisements in this interesting range.

EXAMPLE: A television advert depicting masculinity – Hugo Boss eau de perfum advert featuring actor Chris Hemsworth

The 2020 advert for Boss by Hugo Boss (available to watch here: www.youtube.com/watch?v=sPi0UbYtv9Y) is a much more traditional portrayal of masculinity rooted in the 'English gentleman' stereotype, which has in turn much older roots in the archetype of the knight and the chivalric code in Western culture. The colour codes of the mise-en-scène are cool and masculine, and the significance of Chris Hemworth's strong physique and designer clothes signify the image of a businessman who has as his core values 'integrity' and good behaviour towards others.

5.9 Ethnicity and postcolonial theory

Postcolonialism as a field is closely allied with race representations and is useful when considering how power structures between groups are represented, as well as to evaluate the significance of who has created a representation of a particular group or individual. It describes a collection of ideas that come out of the legacy of colonialism. It also attempts to define attitudes and values that can often still persist, including an assumption of the superiority of Western values in relation to other cultures. This can lead to marginalisation of other cultures in being either absent from media representations at all, or worse, represented in a crudely stereotyped way.

Stretch and challenge

Choose five of your CSPs from different media forms. Using the feminist thinkers you have encountered on the course, consider how these would interpret representations of masculinity and individual men.

Quick questions

1. Explain what van Zoonen means by 'distortion' in female representation.
2. Which three categories in society does hooks' concept of intersectionality claim interact with each other in determining a woman's treatment in media representations, as well as informing attitudes prevalent in society as a whole?
3. What does Butler suggest is the main difference between gender and biological sex?

Apply it

Choose two television adverts for products aimed predominantly at men. Identify how the media language draws on codes relating to traditional and new masculinities. Which cultural myths are present about the role of men in our society?

Colonial attitudes remain influential in Western culture long after the withdrawal of most colonial occupations. They are a deeply ingrained part of the legacy of the historical Western economic, social and political exploitation of other cultures. Historically, there has been a tendency for Western cultures to ignore the complexity of other cultures when studying them, holding them up for scrutiny against Western values that label them as 'strange', 'primitive' or 'deviant'. This imposing of what we might think of as an external value system onto other cultures suggests that Western culture and societal values represent a kind of 'norm' from which other cultures deviate.

Another significant concept in postcolonial studies is **multiculturalism**. Multiculturalism is a political policy, adopted notably in the UK, that acknowledges the unique contributions made to British culture by people from minority ethnic groups.

■ Imagined communities

Related to the idea of multiculturalism and the understanding of national identities is the concept of **imagined communities**. The book of this name by political scientist Benedict Anderson was first published in 1983. It contributed a great deal to debates about ethnicity, patriotism and the role of nationhood, and works well in analysis of media products alongside the theories of identity discussed earlier in this chapter. Anderson explains in his introduction that there is no easy way to define what we mean by 'nation' or 'nationalism', yet the phenomenon exists in people's minds culturally. We can certainly see it in media products in terms of representations of national identity.

The 'community' has boundaries that are geographical and political and are an invention of sovereignty (the exercise of power or authority by a monarch or government). It is 'imagined', because individual members of the community can never all know one another, but in their minds the relationship with others within the nation is real.

In his writing, Anderson draws on the tradition of Marxist thinking but also critiques it, as he finds it problematic that Marxism cannot easily accommodate the phenomenon of nationhood – yet Communist leaders over the decades have frequently constructed ideas about nationhood to promote their ideologies in propagandist campaigns. This works since, despite inequalities and exploitation, members of the community still experience feelings of comradeship with others. This is particularly the case in times of conflict or hardship, when authorities may appeal to people's sense of nationhood and their role within the nation to encourage certain behaviours seen as being in the interests of the nation, such as during the Covid-19 lockdowns. But the use of imagined communities goes far beyond this every day in media products; it is used to sell us products and foster a sense of identity that serves dominant ideology and promotes hegemony.

> **Key terms**
>
> **imagined communities** the way in which a nation is imagined by the people who live within its national boundaries
> *The front page coverage of the Queen's funeral addresses an imagined community of pro-monarchy patriots.*
>
> **multiculturalism** a politically inclusive policy towards ethnically mixed nations/communities that welcomes diversity and respects cultural differences
> *The broadcast represents multicultural Britain by choosing vox populi from a range of people from various minority ethnic groups.*

> **Apply it**
>
> Research and collect examples of three advertisements that represent British identity – either print or audio-visual. Make notes on the ways in which representations in the products address the 'imagined community'. Who are they? Are they mainly of white people, or are they more diverse or inclusive? Using the examples you have collected, do they suggest that the imagined community is ethnically white and British or do they address a more modern, multicultural idea of the UK?

CHAPTER 5 MEDIA REPRESENTATIONS

Orientalism and otherness/alterity

Academic **Edward Said**'s 1978 book *Orientalism* describes how Western cultures have always sought to define countries in 'the East'. Said also looks outside 'Western' culture at ways that seem to justify Western values and attitudes to them, including political agendas and narratives of exploitation and colonialism, which could be justified if a culture was seen as sufficiently different and, by default, 'inferior' or 'strange'. This is apparent historically in high cultural artefacts such as art and literature, which depict these places and people in a subservient way and patronise their heritage. These ideas dominated the approaches of scholars in the 18th and 19th centuries and shaped the ways in which these cultures were studied, always from a point of difference and comparison with Western society. Said's work was a turning point in attitudes to the study of other cultures and their artefacts, and is a key text for anyone studying postcolonialism.

The idea of 'otherness' or alterity (constructing cultural identities by comparison with an 'other') is central to postcolonial studies. Attitudes to race in media consumers can be, in part, shaped by the consumer's experience of them being represented as 'alien' to white Westerners rather than being represented as having things in common with them. Difference can be emphasised in a voyeuristic way, or otherwise negatively define the culture being represented. 'Otherness' in media representations can result in the eroticisation of minority ethnic groups and other demeaning stereotypes or reductionist portrayals. It can also be used negatively in cases where ethnicity is made to seem more important than other dimensions of a character, public figure or criminal. It can romanticise aspects of a culture, highlighting a kind of purity of spirit and naivety – the 'noble savage' stereotype, which has a long legacy in the European imagination. However, 'otherness' can also spark interest in a positive way by engaging a majority-white audience with issues and insights relevant to other cultures, such as through emphasising commonalities between races and cultures, rather than differences.

Postcolonial studies have been a popular approach in literary theory and criticism, but many of the ideas can readily be applied to any cultural product. The approach allows you to ask fundamental questions about cultural identity and meanings in media texts, and the power relationships between who is doing the representing and who is being represented. It allows you to review narratives and power structures, particularly when considering historical and present-day racial stereotypes that persist in the mass media. Different Western countries may have distinctions in the ways in which they represent different cultures due to their own colonial histories and associations with them. It is a good idea when studying postcolonialism to think about how globalisation and cultural imperialism have forced some of these issues even higher up the social agenda. For example, if we are **transnational** media consumers, how does that impact on consumers in other countries, and the way they see themselves being represented in media texts?

Representing race in multicultural Britain today

Why does postcolonialism matter if it's connected with power structures that have long since been dissolved or centuries-old values? It matters because colonialism led to people of multiple ethnicities living in Britain today whose cultural heritage may be deeply intertwined with the colonial past. These people have every right to see fair representation of themselves in the media texts they consume, and better cultural understanding could be reached if media representations could be more carefully considered.

KEY THINKER

Edward Said (1935–2003) was a Palestinian-American postcolonial theorist whose ideas about how we perceive 'the Orient' in the West transformed cultural studies in the second part of the twentieth century.

Quick questions

1. What kinds of ideologies and narratives were constructed in colonial representations of indigenous people in historical media products? Give two examples.
2. Write a definition explaining in your own words the concept of an 'imagined community'.
3. What is meant by 'otherness' in the construction of media representations?

Key term

transnationality in the case of text, having a presence or value that crosses cultural and geographical divides
The series has transnationality in its appeal to audiences due to its use of widely recognisable genre codes.

5.9 Ethnicity and postcolonial theory

> **Apply it**
>
> Source a print copy or view the website for a niche publication other than *The Voice*.
>
> Analyse a single article from it, exploring the way its perspective differs from mainstream media, in a case study of around 300 words.

In particular, public service broadcasters have taken deliberate measures to improve the quality and diversity of their representations of people from minority ethnic groups in recent decades – progress has been made. There has been an increase in the presence in the mass media of people from minority ethnic groups and their casting/presence in more significant roles or high-status broadcasts signifies a quantitative improvement. More diversity in the niche media market shows recognition that mainstream media products may not always cater well for people from different cultural backgrounds or racial groups.

EXAMPLE: Niche media products aimed at minority ethnic groups in the UK

There has been an increase in media products that cater for the specialist interests of minority ethnic groups in the UK, such as the BBC's *Asian Network*, *Black Beauty and Hair* magazine, *Eastern Eye* and *The Voice* newspapers.

Today there is more awareness of the language used to discuss race across media forms to show more consideration for consumers from minority ethnic groups. More awareness of racial stereotypes and more caution in referencing or repeating these, coupled with a greater effort to portray people from minority ethnic groups in a positive light or in more significant roles, means that qualitative representation has improved.

CHAPTER 5 MEDIA REPRESENTATIONS

Racial representations have often historically viewed men, in particular, as threats to the dominant white culture, as criminally deviant and so on. This is still the case today and can be seen in the abrupt rise of Islamophobia in the UK in response to the global terrorism threat.

EXAMPLE: Situation comedy: *Citizen Khan* (BBC Two, 2012–present)

Citizen Khan is an interesting example of a text made for a public service broadcaster for a diverse audience, and it attempts to light-heartedly explore cultural tensions and build bridges between different elements of British culture. Written by and starring comedian and presenter Adil Ray, the sitcom features the larger-than-life character Mr Khan, who was first created as a comic entity outside of the series.

The series exaggerates to comic effect the lives of an ordinary Pakistani-Muslim family from Birmingham, making numerous cultural references to values, lifestyle and in-jokes relevant to that community.

> **Apply it**
> Watch an episode of *Citizen Khan* or a clip of a scene from it on YouTube. Compare it with a historical or more recent example of a all-white family sitcom, such as *2 Point 4 Children*, *My Family* or *Outnumbered*.
>
> Draw up a list of similarities and differences between the two episodes. What elements of cultural distinctiveness make *Citizen Khan* unique, and what does it borrow from more established examples?

> **Key term**
>
> **double consciousness** two aspects of black experience; living within a predominantly white culture and having an aspect of identity rooted somewhere else
>
> *The text could construct a sense of double consciousness given the reductive use of racial stereotypes.*

■ Paul Gilroy: Double consciousness

In sociologist **Paul Gilroy**'s book *The Black Atlantic: Modernity and Double Consciousness* (1993), Gilroy explores the idea of **double consciousness** first proposed by American academic and civil rights activist W.E.B Du Bois in 1903. Du Bois described a vision of black identity that has since been explored by numerous writers and critical thinkers 1903. Double consciousness describes two aspects of black experience. The first of these is the challenges black people face in reconciling living in a predominantly white culture and having an aspect of identity rooted somewhere else. Second, it can also refer to the experience of living in a white culture that consistently represents black people from a white, often racist perspective, and of being essentially forced to look at one's self through the eyes of a white, often racist society.

△ Paul Gilroy

> **KEY THINKER**
>
> **Paul Gilroy** (1956–) is a contemporary British cultural theorist who writes about race relations in the UK and US.

5.9 Ethnicity and postcolonial theory

Gilroy explores this idea further by arguing that black experience is transnational, a hybrid of multiple influences and cultural forms that come from the movement of black people around the 'Atlantic', which he uses as a term to encompass diverse experiences of black people in the USA, UK and Caribbean. He suggests that cultural production across networks is relevant to and contributes to the making of black experience that is international and does not fit with pre-defined notions of cultural or national boundaries to black experience. He also, importantly, sees cultural and artistic production by black artists and practitioners as politicisation – a way of resisting white Western capitalism. The legacy of the Atlantic slave trade is seen by Gilroy as highly significant in the double consciousness of black experience. The movement of people and the cultural mixing and influencing of people who were displaced without any deference to their roots or original cultural identity is seen as crucial to the notion that black identity is complex.

The term **diaspora** means a scattering or spread of people, and it is not exclusive to the history of black populations in the USA and UK. For example, the Jewish diaspora has been written about a great deal. Gilroy advanced the use of the term critically to describe the experience of black people in the UK in his influential book, *There Ain't No Black in the Union Jack* (2002). In Chapter 5 of the book, Gilroy makes the following points, which are useful to help a media studies student understand his concept of the diaspora:

- The terms race, ethnicity, nation and culture are not interchangeable. They all have very specific politicised meanings.
- The black British experience can be seen as diasporic – its culture is a blend of different experiences from different places and includes influences from black America. Black culture in the UK is in constant flux, being 'actively made and remade' (page 202).
- He rejects what he refers to as **cultural absolutism** (sometimes also called **racial essentialism**), which relies on linking a person's cultural and racial heritage to a place of national or ethnic origin.
- The culture of black Britain can be understood as a critique of capitalism – as you saw earlier with feminism, oppression of any social group can be linked to white patriarchal structures endemic in capitalist society.
- 'Contingent and partial belonging' and 'ambiguous assimilation' are both phrases Gilroy uses to describe the black experience in Britain.
- **Cultural syncretism** is the blending of different influences to form a new means of expression.
- Gilroy explores the idea of cultural exchange and commodification (the spread of new ideologies through the distribution of music, for example, worldwide, including back in the directions artists have their roots), new uses being made of these ideas, and their reappropriation and absorption into other geographical spaces.
- Gilroy's exploration of cultural products produced across the diaspora focuses mainly on black musical genres and artists and their relationships with a predominantly white industry.
- He also explores the political power and influence of black culture and music in responding to events worldwide, and the way in which these function within the diaspora as a call to action for people with diverse black heritage.

The diaspora refers to the geographical spread of people from Africa, both in terms of recent migration and historically, for example due to the trade in enslaved people. It's an important concept underpinning much of Gilroy's other work about black identity, and takes into account both historical and

> **Key terms**
>
> **cultural absolutism/racial essentialism** the linking of a person's cultural and racial heritage to a place of national or ethnic origin
> *The text avoids cultural absolutism by careful selection of a range of news about people from different communities and backgrounds.*
>
> **cultural syncretism** the blending of different influences to form a new means of expression
> *The influence of different musical styles in the video as well as dress codes signifies cultural syncretism.*
>
> **diaspora** a scattering or spread of people
> *The text is mindful to appeal to a broad section of communities descended from the African diaspora.*
>
> **postcolonialism** the study of the many ways in which the legacy of colonialism affects race representations
> *Postcolonialism is a vital tool in decoding representations of race and ethnicity.*

contemporary issues affecting the power structures that underlie race representation. Gilroy's ideas about double consciousness and the diaspora can be used in a number of ways when applying a **postcolonial** reading to a media text and in exploring race representations. They can also be used to look at ways in which different black identities merge in representations, to understand the polysemic way in which race representations may be read by different social groups, and to understand how power relationships in society manifest in media representations.

5.10 The social, historical and cultural dimensions of media representations

> **Quick questions**
> 1 What is the difference between cultural syncretism and cultural absolutism?
> 2 Why is the concept of the African or black diaspora important when studying black representation in media products?
> 3 In your own words, explain which two aspects of black identity are described by the term 'double consciousness'.

As you will have gathered from reading this chapter, media products don't exist in isolation. They are part of the fabric of our culture and society and of particular moments in history. If we apply Hall's constructionist approach, we can understand that they neither wholly reflect reality, nor do they 'create' it. All they can ever do is offer us a 'version of reality'. The process of representation is complex and dynamic, and subject to numerous influences. The specification requires you to be aware of the wider contexts of media studies – the situation of media products within the contemporary or historical media landscape. When writing about representations, you will be considering a range of contextual factors that may have influenced both who or what is being represented, and how, as well as the diverse ways in which they may be read by audiences.

Historical context is a significant factor, since reading a text that is produced in a different time period will require an understanding of any differences between dominant ideologies in that time period compared with today. Variation in hegemonic attitudes towards gender and ethnicity are some of the most obvious aspects you may notice. However, sometimes knowledge is required of other national or global issues affecting people at the time of production. War, disease, level of education among the population, the types of employment people had, domestic roles – any of these factors could impact on the ways in which representations meets their audience's needs. You can also consider within historical context the form of the product and how it was distributed or accessed by people at the time, for example the conditions of reception. A television programme broadcast in the UK in the 1980s would have only three other competitors among the majority of the audience, lending greater weight to the representations it constructs than would be the case in the post-broadcast era we see today.

Social contexts may include many issues and debates that are specific to the era in which a text is produced. Both fact-based media and fictional media tend to select representations and content that resonate with their current target audience. Media products can be seen as a barometer of social issues. For example, for many years soap operas would race to be the first to explore storylines relating to same-sex relationships, domestic abuse or other social issues which may have become more prominent on agendas due to factors such as changes in legislation or high-profile news events.

For example, the first lesbian kiss between women to be screened on British television, on the popular soap *Brookside* in 1994, became notorious and caused controversy at the time. A detailed article on the kiss can be found here: https://tinyurl.com/8yjrf4j2. Today's media audiences are more used to seeing representations of LGBTQ+ groups due to changes in social and cultural contexts.

Cultural contexts share considerable overlap with social contexts, in that they are often ephemeral and connected with the interests and pursuits of people in a specific time period. Other factors that affect the cultural reading of products include the rise and fall of popularity of certain genres and therefore the dominant ideologies and representations these may construct, and the cultural relevance of specific celebrities and high-profile figures. It can also reflect the values and beliefs of people in a time period hegemonically as well as connecting with the uses of technology and the ways in which algorithms, for example in digital media products, may promote certain representations and content over others.

When you write about representations, keep these contextual factors in mind, as they will help you to stand back and see the bigger picture. No representation can exist in a vacuum: each is constructed as a series of relationships between the real world and product, industry and audience.

→ Exam-style questions

1 How do two of your Close Study Products illustrate, through uses of encoding and decoding, the role of hegemony in creating representations?

2 Explore how power structures are mediated in two moving image products you have studied on the course by considering the representation of minority groups.

3 How important is gender representation when understanding the relationship between the mass media and dominant ideologies? Explain with reference to two of your Close Study Products.

4 How are media representations constructed and understood by audiences? Using the ideas of Stuart Hall, explore the way audiences read two of your Close Study Products.

5 Explore to what extent you believe postcolonial thinking has changed the way we read media products and influenced production processes. Use two of your Close Study Products that include representations of people from minority ethnic groups as examples.

→ Summary

- The study of representation means studying the process of mediation. Representations are constructed using other codes, particularly the technical codes of media language and generic and narrative codes, but the process of reading representations is particular to the individual.

- In reading any representation, we must ask ourselves who or what is being represented, how they are being represented, and why?

- Gender, sexuality, age, race, ethnicity, religion, disability and social class are all interesting areas to explore when considering representations of social groups, but abstract ideas, places and time periods can also be represented through media texts.

- Stereotypes and countertypes are an important aspect of how representations work and often either reinforce or challenge dominant ideologies. However, they are not simple and need to be examined carefully, as they relate to power structures in society.

- David Gauntlett explored at length how identities and gender could be linked with the mass media. He discovered that the role of the mass media in shaping how people explained their identities to others was smaller than might have been expected. We need to understand media consumption as an influence on other people's identities in light of the role the media plays in their lives.

- Feminist approaches to reading gender representations are extremely important. Feminism is not a single movement, but rather a collection of approaches with a long history.
- The study of masculinity in the field of gender representation is also important. You should be able to distinguish, for example, between traditional masculinities and more contemporary representations, as well as to be aware of the concept of plural masculinities.
- You should be able to analyse representations of people from LGBTQ+ groups in a thoughtful way and be aware of some of the political aspects to the representation of out-groups defined by more fluid gender identities.
- Postcolonialism is an important field when considering race representation and any depictions of other cultures, as it has brought about widespread changes in the way other cultures are studied by academics in Western societies.

Chapter 6: Media audiences

→ What you will learn in this chapter

Chapter 6: Media audiences covers:

- how audiences are grouped and categorised by media industries
- how new technologies have changed the ways in which audiences consume the media
- theories that help us to understand how audiences interpret the media, including why audiences may interpret the same media in different ways
- how audiences interact with the media and can be actively involved in media production
- understanding the relationship between media products and media audiences
- how the application of media effects debates, cultivation theory and reception theory to media products
- how audiences use media in different ways, reflecting aspects of demographics, identity and cultural capital
- fandoms and participatory culture and the role of specialised audiences, including niche and fan
- 'end of audience' theories.

Enabling ideas

Studying audiences means developing a rounded understanding of who consumes media products, what shapes their consumption behaviours and their relationship with the media. We will also be considering audiences from the perspective of the media industry – how they are targeted and what that means for audience choice. In addition, we will be considering how audiences make sense of meanings in the media and the role media plays in their lives.

In the specification, a range of enabling ideas are outlined for you to use to understand any media audience and debates associated with audience and that support your understanding of other areas of the theoretical framework.

Theories of media effects that you will study on the course include:

- uses and gratifications theory
- hypodermic needle model
- cumulation
- media literacy
- Albert Bandura's ideas about social learning and imitation
- John Fiske's bardic function.

In addition, we will be exploring George Gerbner's cultivation theory:

- socialisation
- standardisation
- enculturation

- cultivation differential
- mainstreaming
- resonance
- Mean World Index.

We will be considering the ways in which audiences receive media products, known collectively as theories of reception. These include:

- framing and agenda setting
- myth making
- considering the conditions of consumption
- Stuart Hall's hegemonic, negotiated and oppositional readings.

We will also learn how to understand the nuances of the ways in which media audiences have changed in the digital age. These include:

- ideas about the prosumer and interactivity, as well as 'end of audience' theories
- Henry Jenkins' ideas about participatory culture and textual poaching
- digital natives
- 'we the media'
- convergence
- Clay Shirky's theories of mass amateurisation.

6.1 How the media industry targets audiences

■ Constructing audiences

The media industry is sometimes said to 'construct' audiences. This is an interesting idea, since as audiences we tend to think of ourselves as having free choice over what we consume without really considering that we can only choose from content that is available to us. Often we are subtly steered towards particular content by a whole range of **profiling techniques**.

Genre is one of the most powerful tools available to media producers in 'constructing' an audience. This was originally discussed in the first three chapters from a media language perspective, but is integral to the dynamics in the relationship between audience, industry and text. Reality television and its sub-genres, for instance, constitute one of the most popular genres in television viewing today. Television producers have built on the successes of early examples and deliberately refined earlier formats to appeal to a whole range of audiences (see Example box on pp.85–86).

Audiences are not always predictable in their tastes, and ensuring a product is a hit can be challenging. Traditional marketing, such as billboards, print advertising, radio and TV spots, and trailers, is still important, as is word of mouth (including social media), as it increases the audience's sense of having a foreknowledge of the product. This enables the audience to feel as though they identify with the content. Crucially, audiences do not want to feel targeted. They want to feel as though someone is catering for their needs and desires, not selling them something. Manufacturing this illusion drives the entire marketing machine that shifts a media product from concept to product.

> **Key term**
>
> **profiling techniques** ways by which media producers discern their target audience
> *Profiling techniques are used to focus on a youth demographic.*

Apply it

Produce a report on all the different ways in which mass media products and services are marketed. Do this by considering each media form in turn: radio, television, websites, computer games, magazines and newspapers.

More detail about how media industries measure their audiences is available in section 6.2: The impact of new technologies on patterns of media consumption.

Market research techniques as well as mass media proliferation have both been revolutionised by the advent of digital media and **media convergence**. Information gathering has become increasingly sophisticated, meaning media producers have better access than ever before to complex data about who is consuming their products. Once a media producer knows who they think their audience is and what similar content they might be consuming, they have to consider carefully how the audience will engage with that product and market it accordingly.

The mass media industries are finding increasingly sophisticated ways to reach the right audience for a particular product. Often, there is a good financial incentive to do so where media industries are driven by a dependence on advertising revenue for their profit. Other subscription-based media products or public service producers, which are not answerable to advertisers, still need to ensure that their products get to the right audience sector in order for people to continue to subscribe, or to justify their reach to trustees or stakeholders.

■ How audiences are grouped

Publishers of print media in particular have often used **demographic** information about their audiences to increasingly target them more directly. Demographics means the simpler measures of characteristics of audience members such as where they live, their gender and their age. These are common factors used to identify and target audiences that help media producers and advertisers to reach the right people. Some categories initially seem too unwieldy and broad to be useful, but when combined with others they can segment the audience powerfully. Producers of mainstream media rather than niche products are most likely to use demographics, although they are important to both.

Key terms

demographics studying how populations may consume the media in different ways according to where they live
Audience data from marketing tools gives insight into demographics.

media convergence the coming together of many aspects of media businesses, including commercial, technological and cultural
Convergence culture has resulted in an increase in leisure time consuming a range of media.

Age and gender

Age is a significant factor in targeting audiences. A simple way into understanding age-centred targeting is to look at media products that target children. Some large media producers may produce products that cater for quite distinct banded age ranges.

Apply it

Write a 500-word report on the television shows you have found most memorable, from the early years of primary school to your first experiences of viewing your own choice of television shows. Which TV channels did you watch as a child, and what were your favourite programmes?

When did you stop watching dedicated children's programming, and what did you watch instead?

What do you think had the most influence on the TV channels you watched when you were a child?

EXAMPLE: How the BBC caters for its younger audience

△ The BBC targets different ages with its output. For example, *Bluey* (left), an animated series for younger audiences, is shown on CBeebies, while older children may enjoy watching family serial dramas such as *Doctor Who* (right)

The BBC has two channels that target three different age ranges – CBeebies, which is for three- to six-year-olds, and CBBC, which states its age range to be 7–12. A version of the video-on-demand (VOD) service iPlayer, containing only the content for these two channels, is available for children to use independently. The age of the child is added to a profile at set-up, and this is then used to offer age-appropriate content.

Somewhere around the time of transition to secondary school, tweens and then younger teenagers begin to join their parents in family viewing, and teens will also find their viewing habits diverge from their parents' – if they are viewing much television at all. Tea-time and early evening viewing on various channels now begins to dominate. This age group may enjoy family viewing of big reality contests such as *Strictly Come Dancing* and *Masterchef*, soaps and long-running serial dramas, such as *Eastenders* and *Casualty*, sport and pre-watershed drama series such as *Doctor Who*. **Scheduling** is therefore really important when targeting a family audience.

The **British Film Institute (BFI)** commissioned a survey to explore the effects of age and gender on television genre preferences, which appeared to show that men preferred sports, factual entertainment and culture programmes. Women were found to enjoy more reality television programmes, soaps and chat shows. In some areas, though, such as sitcoms, news and wildlife or nature programming, as well as music concerts, no significant gender gaps in viewing were found. For all of these genres, variations were significant in terms of age. This means that gender and genre may both be useful considerations to schedulers looking to cater for a wider range of audience members on their channels.

While of course not everyone fits into a binary, a clear gender divide can be seen in purchasing patterns in the magazine market and, in terms of primary readership, there is quite clear delineation between the male and female market. The exception to this is the sports rather than fitness sector, where some popular titles that sell worldwide aim to appeal to all genders.

Key terms

British Film Institute (BFI) organisation that promotes the work of British cinema and studies cinema as a pastime among British people
The film was part-funded by the BFI.
scheduling in traditional television viewing, choosing the optimal time of broadcast to reach the highest potential target audience
The viewing of scheduled television is in decline.

6.1 How the media industry targets audiences

Social class, income, location and political leanings

Social class is a complex area and, just as with age and gender, it is difficult to make broad generalisations. Clear delineations no longer exist in the way that they did a few decades ago. Increased access to education beyond 16 and higher education beyond that for working-class youth initially led to an expansion of the middle class, but more recently to an increase in educated adults doing jobs that no longer fit comfortably into old definitions of working-class or middle-class jobs, some of which are lower income, for example, call centre work and IT services.

Some sectors of the mass media face criticism for being focused on the interests of people living in the south-east of the UK, and ignoring the issues and interests of people living in other parts, where there may be subtle but important cultural differences. Income is also a factor in targeting audiences. The cover price of a magazine may be a significant factor in an audience's purchasing decisions. It does not necessarily follow that the more expensive a product or service is, the wealthier the uptake of the target audience who consume it. Some lower income families may choose to spend a significant proportion of their money on, for example, a comprehensive satellite subscription package, because it represents good value for money for something the whole family can enjoy.

One of the places in the media industry where the divide in social class is still quite apparent is in national newspaper readership. Newspapers are traditionally divided into tabloids and broadsheets Traditional tabloids such as the *Daily Mirror* and the *Sun*, as well as the 'quality' tabloids such as the *Daily Mail* and *Daily Express*, have a majority working-class and retired working-class readership. Content is matched accordingly with the perceived interests of the social class, with a heavier focus on entertainment, domestic and **soft news** stories. Traditional broadsheets such as the *Guardian*, *The Times* and the *Daily Telegraph* tend to be read by a more middle-class audience, who may have a stronger interest in current affairs, international news and the **hard news** stories. Soft news tends to be relegated to **supplements** and in most cases appears mainly in weekend editions, the weekend being a traditional time for leisure in the middle-class lifestyle.

Key terms

hard news news that focuses exclusively on serious issues relating to domestic or world events *Hard news is often seen as having less appeal to the target age range of the audience.*

soft news news that can be seen as focusing mainly on entertainment or celebrity-focused stories *Soft news stories are given prominence to increase entertainment value.*

supplements extra inserts to newspapers that tend to have a specific focus; issued particularly at weekends or on a certain day of the week. May be themed by finance, business, arts or other categories *The arts-based content of the supplements implies high cultural capital in the readership.*

EXAMPLE: Crossing class boundaries with *the i*

The introduction of *the i*, which is aimed at 'readers and lapsed readers' of all ages and commuters with limited time, marked an interesting development in the traditional notion of social class being signified and even in part constructed by newspaper owners. Defying the odds in a culture where all traditional newspapers are experiencing a decline in circulation of their print editions, *the i* has been very successful.

Originally produced by the politically middle-ground newspaper the *Independent* and now owned by Johnston Press, *the i* has appealed to both working-class and middle-class audiences, with its blend of contemporary layout, mixed selection of news, lack of strong political bias and moderately in-depth reporting. Crucially, it also has a cheap cover price.

CHAPTER 6 MEDIA AUDIENCES

Ethnicity

Ethnicity is a consideration for targeting audiences in the UK, with contemporary producers in some sectors becoming more aware of cultural distinctiveness and consumption preferences among sections of their audience. Some traditional research into ethnicity and the mass media is problematic, because it often comes from a white **ethnocentric** approach, which can draw conclusions that have more to do with preconceptions about a culture than the reality of the varied cultural diversity and readings within it.

Targeting a minority ethnic group does not necessarily mean providing those belonging to the minority ethnic group with access to imported satellite or cable shows from their own culture, or the publication of newspapers such as *Eastern Eye* and lifestyle magazines such as *Black Beauty and Hair*. It also involves considering which kinds of mainstream programming are appealing to different cultural groups as part of the wider audience, and increasing that share of the market by making subtle changes to content and representations to make them more socially inclusive and appealing to a broader audience.

■ The 'reader'

To help them to promote their publication to advertisers, most magazines include in their **press packs** information about their market share – its size, nature, interests of readers and so on. By regularly commissioning polls of their subscribers, the magazine industry is able to discern its readership, and draw logical conclusions about the content that will keep them buying, therefore continuing to generate advertising revenue.

△ British-Asian newspaper *Eastern Eye* is an example of a media product that specifically targets a sub-section of the UK population based on ethnicity

EXAMPLE: *GQ* magazine's press pack

GQ refers to itself as:

the only brand in Britain dedicated to bringing together the very best in men's fashion, style, investigative journalism, comment, lifestyle and entertainment. GQ is the go-to brand for discerning, affluent men, delivering award-winning content across multiple platforms: in print, digital, online and social.

Key terms

ethnocentrism seeing an issue from the perspective of a specific cultural heritage – usually refers to a white European perspective
In neglecting diversity, the producers leave themselves open to accusations of ethnocentrism.

press packs information released by a company to promote its work, often to prospective investors or advertisers
The magazine's press pack contains its mission statement and a clear definition of its target audience.

6.1 How the media industry targets audiences

High cultural capital

First quadrant	Second quadrant
Low economic capital but high cultural capital	High economic capital and high cultural capital

Third quadrant	Fourth quadrant
Low economic capital and low cultural capital	High economic capital but low cultural capital

Low cultural capital

(Low economic capital ← → High economic capital)

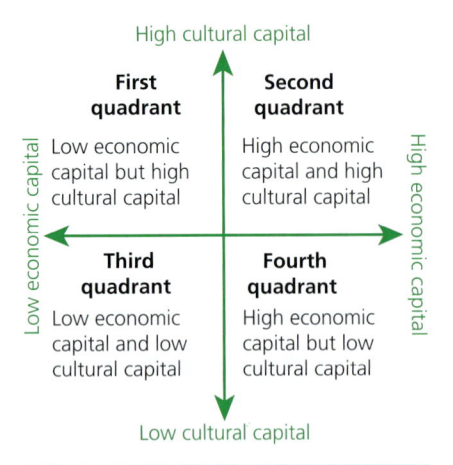

▲ Bourdieu's conceptualisation of social classes

Source: F.P.A. Demeterio III (2003) *The Grammar of Class Conflicts in Philippine Electoral Process and the Task of Filipino Philosophy*

Key terms

cultural capital the ability to mix in higher levels of society because education has given the individual qualifications, ownership of cultural products or access to works of culture
The broadcast assumes high levels of cultural capital on the part of its listeners.

embodied cultural capital the acquired knowledge of culture experienced and outwardly presented by a person
The article uses representations of embodied cultural capital as part of a narrative of success in theatre prior to film.

institutionalised cultural capital recognised qualifications that symbolise someone's worth in terms of cultural capital
The magazine is a niche product that appeals to those who have institutionalised cultural capital.

neo-Marxist critiques of culture and the media that have a left-wing bias
A neo-Marxist reading of the text would critique the representation of the working-class characters as petty criminals.

objectified cultural capital a cultural artefact that confers status on the person who owns it
The villain's art collection is a signifier of objectified cultural capital.

Pierre Bourdieu and cultural capital

Looking at categories of audiences raises some questions. How do audiences view their own participation in media consumption? How do they see the relationship between the media and their own lives? It is likely that demographics play a role in this – the perception, for example, that a media production is made for a particular gender may either actively discourage or encourage someone to feel it is addressing them. But what other factors might be at work?

Bourdieu's model works on two axes and is closely allied with the idea of social privilege attained through the capitalist class system. It is a **neo-Marxist** theory, as it critiques the way in which capitalist society allows the movement of some people up social rankings within the class system, while others are held back. Essentially, Bourdieu sees what he refers to as **cultural capital** as the ability to mix in higher levels of society because education has given that individual qualifications, ownership of cultural products or access to works of culture – a frame of reference that includes familiarity with and appreciation of aspects of high culture such as music, art and literature.

Bourdieu identified three types of cultural capital:

- **Embodied cultural capital**: the acquired knowledge of culture experienced and outwardly presented by a person, for example, knowledge of classic literature.
- **Objectified cultural capital**: can be classed as something like a work of art or some other cultural artefact, such as a valuable musical instrument, which confers status on the person who owns it, and can be transferred to someone else.
- **Institutionalised cultural capital**: recognised qualifications (either professional or academic) that symbolise someone's worth in terms of cultural capital, and can be used to gain higher employment status or accumulation of material wealth.

It can be argued today that Bourdieu's categories of art, music and literature can be expanded to include art house film and cultural practices such as fashion, elite brand awareness and choices of travel destination/types of holiday, food and so on. We could, in a sense, think of Bourdieu's cultural capital in modern terms as middle and upper-class 'tastes' and education.

The Great British Social Class Survey (2013)

In 2013, the BBC surveyed around 161,000 people and asked them about their cultural and leisure pursuits, income, occupation and other aspects of lifestyle to produce a complex picture of how social classes are comprised of trends in the differing types of capital suggested by Bourdieu. New class definitions and categories were drawn up as shown in Table 6.1:

■ Table 6.1 New class categories deriving from The Great British Social Class Survey (2013)

Category	Class definition
Traditional working class	Contains more older members than other classes but also scores low on all forms of the three capitals. They are not the poorest group.
Technical middle class	A less culturally engaged new class with high economic capital. Small in numbers, they have relatively few social contacts.
Established middle class	Not quite elite but members of this class have high levels of all three capitals. They are a gregarious and culturally engaged class.
Precariat	The poorest and most deprived class in Britain. With low levels of economic, cultural and social capital, everyday lives of members of this class are precarious.

CHAPTER 6 MEDIA AUDIENCES

Category	Class definition
Emergent service workers	Young and often found in urban areas, this new class has low economic capital but has high levels of 'emerging' cultural capital and high social capital.
New affluent workers	Generally young and active, members have medium levels of economic capital and higher levels of cultural and social capital.
Elite	This is the most privileged class in Britain, with high levels of all three capitals. Their high amount of economic capital sets them apart from everyone else.

Cultural capital is important because it allows people to move freely in the upper levels of society where those tastes are shared – where people have similar cultural capital. Economic capital, the accumulation of material wealth, is described as falling into different sectors. For example, someone can have high economic capital but low cultural capital – be a professional person but disinterested in the arts and high cultural products – and this person would be distinguished from someone who possesses both economic and cultural capital. It is possible to have low economic capital but still be higher in cultural capital.

EXAMPLE: BBC Four and cultural capital

The BBC promotes cultural capital through two niche services: BBC Radio 4 and BBC Four television, which is available on Freeview. Both these stations aim to cross Bourdieu's cultural axis by making higher cultural capital available for free at point of access to anyone. Since anyone can watch its scheduled content, it is accessed by people who fit into both the first and second quadrant in Bourdieu's model. Some drama series and comedy shows have higher entertainment value than the documentaries the channel is particularly renowned for, which might encourage viewing by those from the third and fourth quadrants. Historically, the BBC was associated with quality programming, and commercial television – represented by ITV – was seen as more entertainment-driven and therefore less focused on producing output of high cultural capital.

△ First World War poet Hedd Wyn, subject of a BBC Four documentary

Apply it

Can you think of any media products whose consumption is associated with people who have higher cultural capital? Create a case study of a media product or outlet that you believe appeals to consumers who have high cultural capital, regardless of whether they fit into the first or second quadrant. Consider too the interplay of social class and politics here – for example, the *Guardian* might be more likely to be read by people in the first quadrant, whereas the *Telegraph* might have a higher readership among the second quadrant.

Bourdieu's theory refers primarily to high culture, as mass or popular culture is not seen as part of cultural capital. Mass entertainment is produced for a mass audience, the majority of whom have a low to middle socio-economic status. However, there are numerous interesting ways in which we can see his ideas could be adapted to interpret modern audiences – and some theorists argue that models of popular cultural consumption actually replicate this model.

Objectified cultural capital could be seen as being present in ownership of technologies, particularly higher-status brands of electronic goods and services, which allows a differentiation in level of access to differing degrees of 'quality' in popular culture. It is apparent that there is a divide in ownership between the technological haves and have-nots in UK society, with economic

6.1 How the media industry targets audiences

> **Key term**
>
> **participatory gap** the effect of economic poverty, in particular, producing a divide in access to digital culture and the information age
> *Content produced by public services broadcasters can help close the participatory gap.*

poverty in particular producing a divide in access to digital culture and the information age. Henry Jenkins referred to this idea as the **participatory gap**.

> **Quick questions**
> 1 Why are the press packs used by magazines to sell their pages to advertisers useful for audience study?
> 2 What are some of the broader categories used to group a demographic?

6.2 The impact of new technologies on patterns of media consumption

Media audiences are changing. The way people use the media, the content of the media they are consuming, the access they have to the media and the devices they consume it through have all undergone rapid change due to the technological and digital revolution and convergence in media technologies, where the social and cultural uses of technologies, the businesses who run them, as well as the ways we access them, increasingly combine in new and interesting ways.

Previously elusive celebrity status is now within the reach of ordinary audience members. YouTube in particular acts as a showcase for talent or notoriety, which sometimes translates into a mainstream media career, albeit often short-lived. Celebrities are expected to engage with their audiences on social media.

It used to be commonplace for someone to watch a television programme and give it their full attention. Now, it is much more likely that they will dip in and out of the action, while connected to social media or even playing a computer game. Computer gaming technology is one of the fields that has really harnessed and integrated the social aspects of digital media, particularly in multi-player games but also online gaming communities.

> **Apply it**
>
> Produce a single-page infographic showing how technological advances have impacted on media consumption.
>
> What advantages and disadvantages do you believe changes in media consumption have brought about in society? Produce a bullet pointed pros and cons list. Make sure you consider both local and global audiences. To help you, consider these three questions – you could make notes in response to these and then find examples to support your points:
>
> - Do certain technologies disadvantage some and benefit others?
> - Do people within populations have different views on technology?
> - How many issues do technology and the mass media touch on that relate to other areas of people's lives?

> **Key terms**
>
> **globalisation** the increased interconnectivity of businesses and cultures worldwide
> *Globalisation has changed the face of the media landscape in the UK in recent decades.*
>
> **digital revolution** sweeping changes brought about by the internet and advances in digital technology
> *The digital revolution had a wide-ranging impact on television consumption.*

■ Globalisation

Globalisation began more than 100 years ago with the invention of the telegraph and improvements in the worldwide infrastructure of transportation. Today, the term usually refers to the increasing technological, economic and communications-based interconnectedness of the global community that has mainly resulted from the **digital revolution**. Another term widely used to refer to this is the **global village**, which was first coined by media and communication theorist Marshall McLuhan in the 1960s. Globalisation has had a clear effect on media consumers. Not only has technological connectivity given us more choice in how we spend our leisure time, but it has also provided us with rapid access to mass media production from other countries – most notably a sharp increase in the uptake of US-produced content.

■ Print media

The magazine sector has had to adjust to numerous changes. A standard publishing profile for a major magazine will now include digital editions, some of which are subscriber only, some of which are freely accessed through a website or app, and the production of videos, as well as a strong social media presence. This is in addition to the print edition. Newspapers have struggled to maintain income from their circulation, and some have moved to either online web subscriptions and paid apps, or open content that generates revenue from clicks on advertising.

> **EXAMPLE: How newspaper publishers are adapting to the digital climate – the *Daily Telegraph* and the *Guardian***
>
> The *Daily Telegraph* and the *Guardian* are traditional broadsheet newspapers that have responded quite differently to the challenges of freely available digital news.
>
> The *Daily Telegraph* was the first UK news provider to launch an online version in 1994. *My Telegraph* is a feature of the site, where users can sign up to have a blog hosted and connect with other readers. The online version requires a subscription to access all content. There are various packages available, but one that includes web access, e-reader and tablet access, rewards and giveaways plus the print edition currently costs around £470 annually.
>
> The *Guardian* makes all of its online content, including archived news stories, free and has a policy of equal and open access to its website. The *Guardian* has a strong culture of allowing moderated comments and discussion by audience on some of its content. A similar digital and print subscription to the package offered by the *Daily Telegraph* costs around £390 per year. A much cheaper app-only subscription can be purchased, which simply eliminates advertising.

■ Television

The ease with which video files can now be uploaded online has led to an explosion in piracy, which affects television producers as well as film copyright owners. The major change most consumers have experienced in recent years is a move away from traditional scheduled viewing, and increased use of **video-on-demand (VOD)**. The growth in the DVD box set and use of physical media to record in the home has slowed with the availability of **digital locker** systems and VOD services. Binge viewing has increased as an audience practice, leading producers to concentrate on high-budget and extremely immersive and lengthy series that are increasingly cinematic in style. Back catalogues of all kinds of classic programming are increasingly available to audiences thus broadening the popular cultural and generational experience of the mass media. Audience expectations of high-budget, computer-generated imaging (CGI) effects in television shows continue to grow. The vast range of competing VOD services gives audiences more choice and increased convenience.

△ Italian TV producer Walter Iuzzolino is responsible for selecting foreign-language content for the video-on-demand service Walter Presents, which is available on Channel 4's free digital streaming service. Specialising in foreign-language drama, Walter Presents typifies the output of a more globalised post-broadcast era

Key terms

digital locker system whereby a television show or film is purchased (sometimes as a physical copy) but also exists for that buyer to watch on other devices
Digital lockers have largely replaced DVD purchases of films.

global village term coined by Marshall McLuhan in the 1960s to describe the impact of media technologies on global culture
Instagram content related to the brand contributes to the global village effect on audiences, where national boundaries feel insignificant.

video-on-demand (VOD) any service where users can choose what they want to view and when
Many streaming services work on the principle of video-on-demand.

6.2 The impact of new technologies on patterns of media consumption

> **Apply it**
>
> Download and listen to three different podcasts. Try to choose a range of programmes, preferably including a converted conventional radio show, a professionally produced show that is for podcast distribution only, and a lower-budget but successful podcast perhaps originally produced by an amateur. How is it best listened to – at what time of day, or fitted around what other activities? How does listening to a podcast differ from listening to regular radio broadcasts? Make notes, and then compare your experiences with others in the class.

■ Radio

The main changes to radio are connected with digital broadcasting and the increase in both public service and commercial stations away from standard broadcasting. Audiences not only have more listening choice, but are in some cases also able to choose programmes to listen to again at their leisure. Podcasting is another significant growth area that continues to maintain a small but often devoted audience. This was caused in part by the development of MP3 players, meaning offline broadcasting was available for people to listen to anytime, anywhere. Streamed radio is also now much more common, and interactivity has become a key feature of modern radio, which has embraced the dynamics it offers.

■ Video on the web

Video upload sites are an entirely new feature of the digital age. They have allowed audiences to make and upload their own content and run their own channels. This has revolutionised not only the way in which younger media users spend their time, but also the relationship between the producers of media and their audiences. Many of the styles associated with short video production, borrowed from amateur producers of videos, continue to influence mainstream media organisations operating in digital spaces.

■ Gaming

Gaming is one of the areas that, because it is entirely driven by technological and communications advancements and has no legacy form, sees the most technological change. There is a high degree of crossover in effects technology development between the gaming industry and the film industry. One of the major developments in gaming has been the growth in communal gaming and the interconnectivity of players over broadband connections. Gaming has become much more of a social pastime, with gamers on major platforms using headsets to communicate with each other. The gaming industry is also at the forefront of virtual reality (VR) development. VR is revolutionising the gaming experience, and is likely to continue to be a huge growth sector in the near future. Another significant area is augmented reality games, which blend elements of the real world with graphical information that is artificially generated.

> **Apply it**
>
> If you were to interview a keen gamer, what would you ask them in order to find out more about their current gaming habits and how these have changed during the time they have been gaming?
>
> Use your questions to interview a gamer. Record the interview and write down key quotations that tell you about developments in gaming technology, the different pleasures of different games, and what matters to gamers when choosing a new game.
>
> Collate your quotes as a class. What common themes emerge? What do these tell us about the relationship between advances in gaming technologies and audience consumption?

> **EXAMPLE: The 2016 craze for *Pokémon Go***
>
> In July 2016, the augmented reality app *Pokémon Go* became the latest version of a game that has had various incarnations on different consoles since 1996. The game encouraged users to 'catch' Pokémon characters, which were positioned in various real-world locations using GPS. The app was available for free on both IOS and Android platforms, and was widely downloaded. There was also a temporary spike in negative media reportage of related issues, from muggings at 'Pokestops' to instances of careless driving by people using the app while in control of a vehicle.

CHAPTER 6 MEDIA AUDIENCES

The personalisation of news and other digital media content

News delivery is rapidly changing. News apps for smartphones and tablet allow people to effectively have more control over the news they consume. The set-up in news apps allows users to tailor the content they want to see, meaning they are now partially setting their own news agenda.

Many other websites, viewing services, producers using social media platforms to distribute content and so on also use information stored about their users to profile their use and offer similar content that might be of interest to the audience. Personalisation of content is therefore one of the most successful developments in connecting a wealth of content to the audience it appeals to the most. Clicking on suggested content refines this process and allows more precise targeting of the audience. Cookies and web tracking are used to follow audiences around the internet, with advertising spaces on subsequent sites filled personally with content from previously visited sites. This is one major way in which the digital media audience is constructed.

EXAMPLE: The *BBC News* app

The *BBC News* app for smartphones and tablets allows users to select from numerous categories, providing a great deal of opportunity for personalisation. Here are some recently listed examples:

TOP STORIES | MEDIA | EDUCATION AND FAMILY |

MENTAL HEALTH | MOST POPULAR | ENTERTAINMENT AND ARTS | SPORTS

Quick questions
1. What has been one of the main effects of globalisation on the media industry?
2. What do we mean by the personalisation of media content?

Apply it
Choose three digital services and/or websites that you visit or use regularly. Write 300 words on how their content is personalised for you as a consumer.

6.3 Theories of media effects

The ways in which we understand how media audiences make sense of the media products they consume have changed over time, and this is a widely discussed issue. The following section will give you an overview of thinking in this area of media studies, and allow you to explore each approach when applied to contemporary and historical media consumption. This will make it easy to select an appropriate theory to study the relationship between media audiences and their consumption.

Many effects theories assume a connection between media consumption and behaviour in the real world. Numerous examples exist of this assumption being made, and apparent links between violent acts in the real world and specific media texts thought to have been consumed by those who are responsible are a mainstay of tabloid news stories. Effects theory also often assumes that popular/mass culture is inferior to 'high' culture and art, and as such could have a pernicious effect on its individual consumers and society as a whole.

Key terms

effects theory the collective term for media theories that explore the correlation between media consumption and audience behaviours or interpretations of the real world
Effects theories suggest that media consumption can influence people in the real world.

hypodermic needle model simple effects model that assumes the audience to be passive recipients of media content
The hypodermic needle model is often seen as a very simple example of effects modelling.

moral panics term coined by Stanley Cohen to describe the press reaction to a negative event in the real world
The spate of recent dog attacks is presented as a moral panic over irresponsible dog ownership.

two-step flow communications-based model that highlights the significance of opinion leaders in the transmission of messages in the mass media
Influencers are a contemporary example of the two-step flow model in action.

The problem has always been that this is difficult to prove. It is very hard to separate the mass media from other influences. One of the other issues is that effects theory-based interpretations of social violence can contribute to **moral panics**. Some of the original research was politically conservative; researchers often already suspected the media to have a negative influence on society, and were looking for evidence that supported this assumption.

Despite some of the problems, it is rare to suggest that the mass media has no effect at all on people who consume it. Positive effects of the mass media are studied far less, yet they certainly exist. Think of the central BBC remit and its educational component. How could the media educate and inform if it had no effect on its audience? And what about other 'neutral' media effects, such as the transmission of cultural ideas such as fashions?

■ Hypodermic needle model

Approaches that explore the effect media have on audiences are known collectively as **effects theories**. In the early days of the mass media, much study of the supposed effects centred on anxieties regarding the changes in society and leisure time brought about by widespread access to media consumption. The earliest of these is the **hypodermic needle model**, which considered the relationship between audiences and media content to be a simple case of the direct inception of ideas from media texts into the ideologies of the audience. This approach views audiences almost like sponges, absorbing ideologies passively from the media they consume and engaging with them very little.

The **two-step flow** model of communication followed in the 1950s, which suggested that, rather than taking the mass media at face value, people have their interpretation of it formed by opinion leaders – those who reinterpret the mass media's messages who are trusted by the audience. Although treated with caution by subsequent theorists, the two-step flow of communication is quite useful in a limited way in explaining the campaigning by some celebrities or other prominent people in society about a certain political issue on social media.

EXAMPLE: Media influence and the Belstaff Millford coat

The Belstaff Millford coat worn by Benedict Cumberbatch in *Sherlock* (2010–17) sold out rapidly following the first broadcast of the series. *GQ magazine* ran a series of online articles about the sourcing of the mainly British clothing brands worn by the two actors in the show.

How do we explain the spike in sales of a coat worn by a particular actor in a drama series following its broadcast if the media had no effect at all on the audience?

Fiske's bardic function

John Fiske discusses a **bardic function** played by television in our culture. He argues that television simply fulfils an ancient role in society but in technological guise. He likens the role of television to that of a medieval bard, whose function was to tell stories in poetic form for their patrons, and to structure and organise ideas about what was relevant to people living in that time. Bards were influenced by all kinds of sources. They blended conflicting ideas and scraps of mythology, with nods to present fashions and trends. Through these texts, ideas which engrossed the audience could be produced and old content made to feel relevant. Crucially, the bard was not a representative of authority but a mediator, in the way we might view television today.

Fiske also used the term **clawback** to define the way in which television can give a sense of recognition of the self and cultural identity, and can function to make issues relevant once again to our own individual reality and experience of our culture. Texts that use clawback may take a character whose situation or aspects of identity might make them lack power in the real world and then represents them as significant in the text, therefore 'clawing back' their place in society.

△ Fiske found television to fulfil the equivalent modern role of the bard in the Middle Ages

Social learning theory, Albert Bandura

KEY THINKER

Albert Bandura (1935–2021) is a Canadian-American psychologist, and is credited with developing social learning theory.

Social learning theory was one of the earliest theories surrounding media consumption. It was derived in the early 1960s primarily from the experiments conducted by **Albert Bandura**. Through his famous Bobo doll experiment (where children in a controlled lab setting appeared to re-enact violent acts they had just seen on screen on an inflatable Bobo doll), Bandura concluded that children who viewed violent content on television or film might well go on to behave violently in the real world. This is called social learning, because it suggests that children 'learned' violent behaviour vicariously from the actions they saw on screen. The became a well-known study that appeared to validate the fears many social commentators already had about the effects of television. It still carries weight today, despite there being issues with the methodology.

Social learning theory is a little more complex than this element of the study might suggest. Bandura acknowledged that other processes also contribute to behaviours. In the real world, it is difficult to establish whether individuals with other social problems may seek out violent texts and have preference for them, rather than the viewing of violent texts causing a behaviour.

Social learning theory tends to be used by conservative commentators to justify criminal or deviant acts and blame the mass media as a main influence on such acts, but the positive effects of social learning theory as applied to the media are rarely heard about.

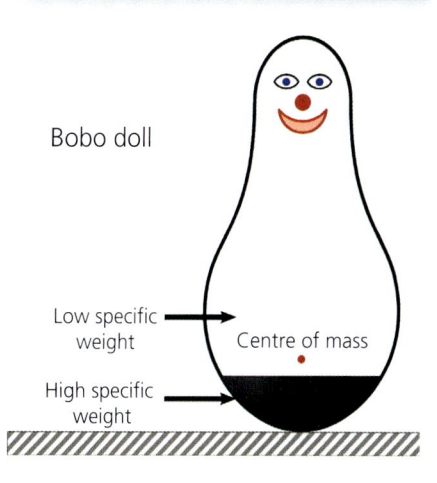

Key terms

bardic function the modern role of television in our lives as an aggregator of many different ideas and cultural influences
Crime dramas have a bardic function in our processing of moral issues facing society.

clawback the way in which television can give a sense of recognition of the self and cultural identity, our experience of our culture
For an LGBTQ+ audience, the programme has a clawback function in terms of constructing meaningful representations.

social learning theory branch of effects theory that considers vicarious learning to be a highly significant factor in how people respond to media content
Effects theories cover a range of approaches that seek to explore our relationship with the media.

Bobo doll

Low specific weight
Centre of mass
High specific weight

6.3 Theories of media effects

147

EXAMPLE: The positive side of social learning theory in action

In Afghanistan during 1994, the ruling party in control of the country, the Taliban, tried to ban a popular BBC World Service drama called *New Home, New Life*. The soap promoted women's rights, and also taught safe conduct around areas that were heavily land-mined. But banning the soap proved to be nearly impossible, since a number of Taliban senior figures were also said to be gripped by the popular series. Follow-up studies showed a decrease in the number of injuries and deaths caused by landmines in areas where people could access the broadcast.

Stretch and challenge

A mini-project exploring social learning theory

1. Research examples of contemporary outcries about media texts and their supposed influence on people or real-world events. Create a timeline of events, criminal acts or moral panics that have been linked causally to mass media consumption.
2. Research the Bobo doll experiment. What problems can you either identify yourself, or what criticisms can you find, of the conclusions gained from it?

Quick questions

1. What did John Fiske mean when he stated that television had a 'bardic function'?
2. Explain the difference between the hypodermic needle model and the two-step flow theories of audience.
3. What was the purpose of the Bobo doll in Bandura's famous experiment?

Key term

media literacy the level of awareness of the audience about factors affecting the production of meaning in media texts
Level of media literacy is a crucial factor when considering a historical media product's likely reception.

■ Media literacy

In the digital age, high levels of 'screen time' increasingly dominate our leisure time from an early age.

One of the issues surrounding some media effects theories is their presumption that audiences are not really aware of media effects but are passive subjects of them. It is therefore important that you begin to factor in the idea of **media literacy** when understanding how aware of media messages audiences really are, and that you consider how able audiences are to properly reflect on and understand content in context.

Media literacy can mean, in the most obvious sense, being taught to read and to critically evaluate the meanings of the media, as we do in our subject. Media literacy is vital because it enables people not to take mass media content at face value but to see it in a broader cultural context, and to understand media production as a business, often driven by a profit motive.

Apply it

In small groups, discuss the following contemporary issues, which all require some level of media literacy to understand. Reflect on your own media literacy and that of people you know. For each one, record two or three of the points that came up in your discussion to share in feedback to the class.

ISSUE 1
Does everyone understand that news agendas mean that some issues attract more coverage than others? Do they understand that the profit motive is driving what appears on the front page of their newspaper? Can they distinguish between real and fake news on social media?

ISSUE 2
Are both male and female consumers aware of the extent to which images of women's bodies are digitally manipulated to achieve an 'ideal' body shape and 'perfect' skin and hair? Are they aware that some models' body types are not only rare but can even be unhealthy?

ISSUE 3
Is everyone who plays computer games aware of issues relating to violent content, desensitisation and compassion fatigue? Are gamers really aware of the highly immersive or even 'addictive' properties of some gameplay modes?

> **ISSUE 4**
> Are we aware of the echo-chamber qualities of social media, in that we tend to connect with people with similar views to our own? Do we fully understand that complex algorithms are at work all the time to present us with a world view and products which align with what we already believe and are likely to like or buy, rather than giving us other perspectives or offering alternatives?

Many people argue that there is a more general 'literacy' relating to media consumption that can be linked with a broader level of general education, and skills in critical thinking. Do we really have a proper understanding of how the media is constructed and to what end? If we don't get our media literacy from education, where do we get it? How do most media consumers become media-literate? Is it through comparing some media sources with other, more 'legitimate' media? Or through an understanding of history, psychology or other academic subjects that foster critical thinking which can then be accessed in an abstract way? These are all important questions in thinking about whether audiences have the critical ability to understand the media-saturated world they inhabit.

If people have lower levels of media literacy, perhaps they are, in theory, more susceptible to media effects. Early sociological models, such as the simple hypodermic needle model and Albert Bandura's social learning theory, can be problematic to apply because of their apparent simplicity. Nonetheless, the media probably does have some effect on people in all kinds of subtle ways every day, for example attributing violent acts to media consumption is a popular social learning model for tabloids newspapers. The problem is that these effects can only really be reported as a possibility unless we find examples of large numbers of people who are willing to admit they have been affected by the media. Some effects are always going to be more readily admitted to than others.

For this reason, many theorists try to find a balance by proposing that short-term exposure to a particular type of media or a certain text is unlikely to cause an effect – but that with long-term exposure the likelihood of an effect occurring increases. This is known as **cumulation**. Looking at an overview of developments in effects theory is helpful for understanding how different trends have evolved over time, and that different elements of effects theory can co-exist.

Media studies students have historically drawn a distinction between 'passive' and more 'active' models of audience theory. In fact, all of them try to identify some kind of effect, even if the effect is that people 'use' the media to some end, such as integrating some of its messages into their own identity or using them in some way to benefit them socially or personally.

Key term

cumulation collective term for audience theories that consider longer-term exposure to media texts
Games consumption should also be considered in light of cumulation, with wide variation in hours of gameplay across the audience.

6.3 Theories of media effects

Stanley Cohen: *Folk Devils and Moral Panics*

Cohen's influential book *Folk Devils and Moral Panics* was first published in 1972. Since then, the preface has been updated a number of times by the author. In the 2002 edition, he cites a number of contemporary moral panics that were not around when he wrote the first edition of the book, but can be explored using his theory.

Cohen discusses an interesting dimension to the relationship between the mass media's coverage of an issue (this was at a time when the mass media had arguably an even greater influence than today) and perceptions of risk in society. This is relevant to our understanding of newspaper coverage, because it describes a negative dimension to the relationship between people's understanding of the nature of how newspapers represent reality.

He explores the ways in which the mass media can create 'folk devils' – people who act as a focus for people's fears in society. These folk devils in a contemporary sense can be located in a single personality – for example, Kim Jong-Un. The way in which they are represented often borders on the grotesque, and is overly exaggerated and simplified. Folk devils might also be more generalised – a section of society that is perceived as threatening to mainstream values or actual physical safety, such as terrorists.

Cohen also identifies what he termed a 'moral panic' that could be in part instigated or perpetuated by the tabloid press in particular. In the case of a moral panic, the population as a whole or in part may become hypersensitive to an issue. Its currency then leads to further reporting in the press, which appears to make the risk or threat posed by the original story greater in people's minds than the real-world risk posed by the source of it. The stages of a moral panic were identified by Cohen as follows:

1. Something or someone is defined as a threat to values or interests.
2. This threat is depicted in an easily recognisable form by the media.
3. There is a rapid build-up of public concern.
4. There is a response from authorities or opinion-makers.
5. The panic recedes or results in social changes.

Moral panics are also significant because they involve not only the media and public perceptions, but also the response of authorities to an issue. Aspects of a moral panic were defined by Erich Goode and Ben Nehuda in *Moral Panics: The Social Construction of Deviance* (1994) in the following way, and this update is acknowledged by Cohen in the preface to the 2002 edition of his original book:

- Concern – an issue is identified as a problem for society.
- Hostility – the issue is perceived as a threat to the fabric of society.
- Consensus – the story is presented in such a way that suggests everyone agrees the issue is a threat.
- Disproportionality – the facts relating to the issue may be distorted, misrepresented or fail to be properly contextualised.
- Volatility – the issue is seen as one that can flare up at short notice; the idea also that it can happen anywhere and affect anyone.

There is a sense, then, that moral panics are a very influential and important consideration when assessing the effects of the media on people's views of the society they live in. They may also have a powerful effect on institutions and governing/policy-making.

Apply it

Collect three examples of online news stories from tabloid papers about Kim Jong-Un. To what extent do they seem to construct him as a folk devil?

△ North Korean leader Kim Jong-Un is a contemporary example of a 'folk devil', with negative stories about him uniting the West hegemonically in supporting government foreign policy towards North Korea.

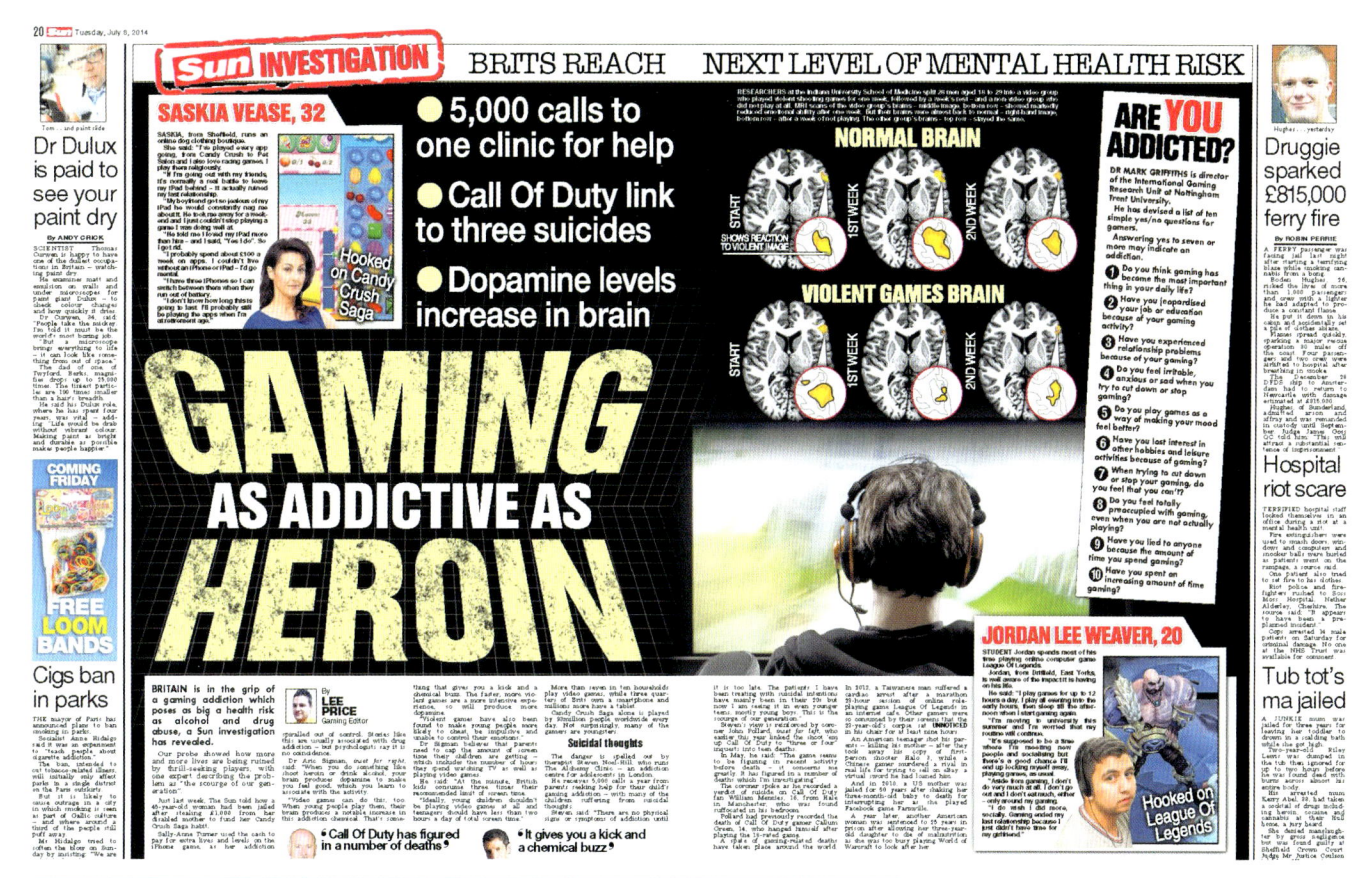

△ A double-page spread from the *Sun* newspaper shown in an online counter-article at *Den of Geek*. The article is attempting to spread moral panic around the subject of gaming addiction

The problem with both moral panics and folk devils is that they can potentially lead to vigilantism, since they grossly exaggerate the threats posed. They may come from highly conservative ideological standpoints and can often be considered to be moralising. They also frequently misrepresent the facts of a complex issue that deserves serious exploration by simplifying the aspects of it that best fit a narrow, sensationalist news agenda.

Quick questions

1. Why is media literacy increasingly important in the digital age?
2. What name did Cohen give to prominent figures in global or domestic culture who become a symbol of threat to a society?
3. Which word, beginning with the letter 'd', describes the exaggerated way in which moral panics are sometimes reported in news coverage?

■ Criticisms of media effects

Some of David Gauntlett's early work centred on critiquing social learning effects theories in particular, which he believed assume a simplistic cause and effect relationship between what the media audiences consume and behaviour in the real world.

Three of his criticisms of effects theory can be summarised as follows:

- Effects theories historically tended to focus on drama-based media texts when looking at violence in particular. It is assumed that fictional texts have a greater influence over audience behaviour than non-fiction forms of visual media such as the news or documentaries. This is clearly not the case – think, for example, of how television news coverage of social or political

Apply it

Identify three moral panics and/or folk devils you think are prevalent in contemporary culture. Find at least two front-page tabloid news articles or internet news stories from tabloid news sites that cover the issue.

1. How is it represented?
2. Can you think of any problems of representation in the way in which the issue is reported?
3. How does the mode of address and other aspects of semiotic analysis support a preferred reading that suggests consensus and signifies concern?
4. Which wider societal values seem to be connected with the issue?

Present your ideas in a grid format, using the questions above as headings.

6.3 Theories of media effects

151

issues or web-based content could potentially contribute to radicalising a young European-born with extremist ideologies.
- Effects theory has 'flawed methodologies' – Gauntlett suggests that many of the experiments related to effects theory, such as the Bobo doll experiment, simply do not scientifically prove the separation of the mass media from other influences and cannot measure this. Bandura himself was aware that subjects' learning from what they saw happening to the doll on screen was only one part of acquired behaviours, but perhaps he viewed it as more powerful.
- When questioned, many people hold a widespread belief that violence in media texts affects other people in a potentially dangerous way, but not themselves. This suggests that the vast majority of people can consume computer games or films with 18-rated content without exhibiting any subsequent signs of social deviance – so something else is clearly contributing when a person commits a violent act.

When you are studying the relationship between the mass media and its supposed effects on audiences, remember that you can only ever really identify an effect as a possibility. Make sure you learn the cases for and against the various approaches to studying media effects, and apply these to your own discussion.

By the 1970s, people in general were less suspicious of the potentially negative impact of an expanding mass media on society and this led to a change in the way in which the relationship between audiences and the media was understood. This made way for the development of more nuanced theories of audience.

Uses and gratifications theory – Jay G. Blumler and Elihu Katz

The early work on television viewing conducted by **Jay G. Blumler** and **Elihu Katz** led to a change in focus for media theorists via the development of uses and gratifications theory. This theory considers that audiences might not be passively consuming television, but instead are *using it* in some way – gaining social uses and psychological gratifications from it. The theory states that television in particular contributes in a positive way to people's personal and social lives. It famously divides these into four main groups:

- **Diversion** – this correlates with most people's understanding of the mass media as a form of escapism from the stresses and strains of daily life.
- **Personal identity** – the media is believed to supply people with role models, and ways of understanding their own place in society.
- **Social relationships** – many people seem to gain an element of sociability through the media. People discuss television shows with each other, giving the act of viewing a socially cohesive function. People often show an enthusiasm and liking for particular performers and presenters and enjoy the sense of familiarity they feel with them.
- **Surveillance** – the mass media contributes to people being informed about the world around them through the viewing of news and current affairs, and the consumption of documentary programmes, as well as allowing the audience to keep up to date with entertainment trends.

> **KEY THINKERS**
>
> **Jay G. Blumler** (1924–2021) and **Elihu Katz** (1926–2021) are credited as two of the key developers of uses and gratifications theory.

EXAMPLE: The application of uses and gratifications theory to four popular British TV shows first broadcast in 1979

Diversion – *The Paul Daniels Magic Show* saw magician Paul Daniels wow audiences with a glittering presentation of magic tricks, transporting them from the everyday grind. The magic, if not the ratings, was to last until 1994.

Personal identity – *Top of the Pops* (1964–2006) celebrated the UK's popular music scene. The show's viewing figures peaked in this year.

CHAPTER 6 MEDIA AUDIENCES

Social relationships – Generations and people of different backgrounds were brought together in their shared enjoyment of the second series of sitcom *Fawlty Towers* (see photo), whose mere 12 episodes were first broadcast in 1975. Numerous re-runs were shown, including in 1979.

Surveillance – *Brass Tacks*, a current affairs documentary series aired between 1977 and 1988, investigated issues close to the heart of the British public. This year saw the broadcast of one of its most famous and influential episodes, 'Are the Kids Alright?'

Apply it

Apply the four-part model to examples from current TV scheduling.

1 Does the model work when applied to other mass media forms? Try applying the uses and gratifications theory to popular magazines, computer games and video sharing sites, such as YouTube.
2 Think of examples for some of the more specific uses and gratifications suggested by Berger.

Uses and gratifications theory still has currency today, and is often used by media students to understand media content it was not specifically designed for, since the approach is transferable to other aspects of the mass media.

Many other researchers have gone on to identify the uses and gratifications for contemporary media device usage, such as mobile phones, social media sites and so on. This is a very interesting growth area for media students to explore.

Quick questions

1 Quickly jot down the four main uses and gratifications thought to be made available by media products.
2 In your own words, identify one possible problem with media effects theories.

6.4 Cultivation theory

Another exploration of media effects that seeks to interpret audience behaviours in the real world and their connections with the media is **cultivation theory**.

■ George Gerbner

The work of **George Gerbner** in the 1970s was interesting because it explored violence and crime on television for slightly different, more perceptual reasons. Gerbner's team of researchers considered television to be the foremost influence in modern American people's lives, ahead of religion and the state. Their research appeared to show that the more hours of television people watched, the greater their belief that the US was a violent and dangerous place. Television appeared to be literally 'cultivating' their ideologies and beliefs, acting as a form of socialisation and aligning them with the world they saw on television. This is known as **enculturation**. Gerbner

Key terms

cultivation theory branch of effects theory that looks at the effects of media saturation (particularly television) on the audience
Cultivation theory prioritises the time spent consuming a particular type of media.

enculturation the adjustment of people's values to mesh with the culture and society they inhabit
Enculturation is a form of socialisaton through the media.

6.4 Cultivation theory

153

KEY THINKER

George Gerbner (1919–2005) is credited with developing cultivation theory.

Key terms

cultivation differential the extent to which someone's world view and perception of their social reality is shaped by the volume of television they consume
Understanding the cultivation differential is vital when weighing up the likely size of a potential media effect.

mainstreaming in cultivation theory, the process of ideological alignment between media audiences and content
Mainstreaming may play in important role in the run-up to a general election.

mean world index in cultivation theory, a way of measuring the belief that the world is a more dangerous place than it actually is due to the viewing of violent acts on television
The programme could contribute to the mean world index through repetition of fictionalised acts of violence against women.

resonance in cultivation theory, the reinforcement of ideologies or experiences by mass media content

standardisation in cultivation theory, the proposal that norms and behaviours of people in the real world are modelled through repetition in televisual media
Standardisation of male and female roles in society is potentially influenced by traits of masculinity and femininity represented in television drama.

---

felt that television provided role models that **standardised** people into accepting certain norms, roles and behaviours through frequent repetition of representations in both faction and fact-based television.

The other finding of the study was that television appeared to be moulding people's understanding of issues and people around them, rather than real experience of life. This was termed by Gerbner as **mainstreaming** – a mainly political effect whereby people exposed to similar messages and viewpoints regularly on television find their own ideologies and those perpetuated in televisual texts beginning to synchronise, therefore affirming their views and shared symbolic language. Mainstreaming is also very useful to advertisers for economic reasons, since it means that brand and product awareness appear to take hold relatively easily in the minds of people who have frequent and lengthy exposure to television.

Another effect Gerbner identified was **resonance**. In the case of resonance, people find examples of aspects of their own lives that appear to correlate with what they see on television. This has an amplifying effect on perceptions of the world around them, where their own experiences, thoughts and feelings about society appear to be congruous (in agreement) with what they see on television. This could be seen in his research and tracking over a number of years of content in the **mean world index**, which demonstrated that people believe the world to be a more dangerous place than they actually experience in reality due to the sheer volume of violent moments experienced through television consumption. Also significant in Gerbner's work was the idea of a **cultivation differential**, which reflects the extent to which someone's world view and perception of their social reality is shaped by the volume of television they consume.

Gerbner's work has remained very influential. Although it was television that was the original subject of his research, his ideas have become extremely useful for studying digital media, which among younger members of society could be considered to have an even stronger influence than television. Social media and computer gaming are particularly interesting areas to explore using some of Gerbner's ideas.

EXAMPLE: Cultivation theory – *Bowling for Columbine* (2000)

Michael Moore's film documentary *Bowling for Columbine* (2000) is almost a visual essay exploring Gerbner's and Bandura's ideas. Moore is a left-wing documentarian, known for his outspoken critiques of US society and US government policy. In the documentary, Moore explores how moral panics, attitudes to race, perceptions of personal safety and gun violence can all be influenced by the mass media.

Moore claims that simple myths and a culture of fear and exclusion perpetuated in the mass media seem to have a real impact on the quality of people's lives, and that the absence of views other than the mainstream can be harmful to people who feel disenfranchised from society. At the same time, he refutes an absolute cause and effect link between media consumption and violent acts, arguing that other influences, such as US government policy and deeply held US cultural beliefs such as the right to bear arms, are neglected since the media is an easy target.

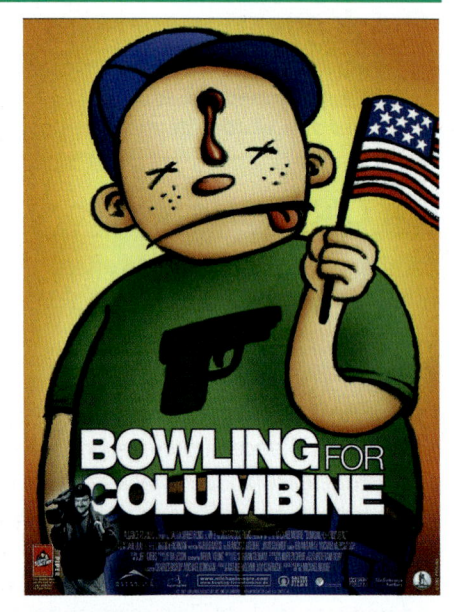

Desensitisation and compassion fatigue

Desensitisation occurs when a media audience is repeatedly exposed to shocking or violent content. **Compassion fatigue** is when a person who is repeatedly subjected to a situation or media content that would usually elicit an empathetic response ceases to be affected to the same degree. It can be caused by repeated exposure to either fiction or fact-based media. In a sense, compassion fatigue and other forms of desensitisation could be thought of as defence mechanisms. The human mind seeks to protect itself from things it finds disturbing or difficult to process in the face of continual exposure.

Both desensitisation and compassion fatigue are phenomena that appear to support cultivation theory, since they involve a lessening of the emotional or empathetic response to seeing traumatic events played out in mass media consumption. Whether either phenomenon would apply to real-world experience of these events is difficult to prove.

EXAMPLE: Desensitisation and compassion fatigue in routine television consumption

In the West, suicide bombings are considered to be shocking events. However, the increased frequency of their occurrence combined with greater exposure to the 24-hour news cycle could cause the audience to empathise less with the victims of such events and lead to the story dropping down news agendas.

Our fictional television consumption has also contributed towards our increasing desensitization to screen violence, with shows such as *The Walking Dead* and *American Horror Story* regularly borrowing from the body horror iconography of the horror film genre.

Associated with a cultivation approach are some other ideas that we can explore more here – the role of the media in socialisation and enculturation. Since most of us are exposed to the mass media from birth, it is assumed that it plays a contributory role in shaping our values and ideas about our culture alongside other influences such as family, education and peer groups. The media can provide role models for identity formation and circulate cultural myths in ways we are receptive to.

Quick questions

1. Why did Gerbner choose to focus on television when he was exploring cultivation theory in the 1970s?
2. Explain why desensitization is a cumulative media effect.
3. Briefly define 'enculturation'.

Apply it

Write a 500-word case study on an aspect of digital media of your choice. Apply and evaluate the range of media effects theories you have just read, and discuss how useful or influential they might be in informing public opinions about digital media.

Key terms

compassion fatigue the process by which the media audience loses empathy for victims of crime, disaster or war zones due to repeated exposure (especially to news)
Audiences exposed to a saturation of charity campaign advertising could develop compassion fatigue.

desensitisation the process by which media audiences can become used to seeing violent content and therefore are better able to tolerate it
There is concern that some computer games may desensitise players to real-world violence.

Apply it

Consider another issue where a cultivation effect of cumulative exposure might in theory affect perceptions or world view.

6.5 Reception theory

Theories of reception allow us to consider how the audience interprets products by considering the way in which audiences may respond differently depending on pre-existing aspects of their identity or mindset, the **conditions of consumption**. Some of these we have explored in considering lifestyle profiling and the role of identity in media consumption, which we looked at in Chapter 5: Media representations. Also connected with reception theory is the idea of cultural myth and the myth-making role of the media, which we explored in Chapter 1: Reading print media.

It matters whether the media is being used in a social way, or if it is consumed alone. When we consume media with others, we subconsciously modify our view of it when discussing it with them. This effect may also be seen on social media. We need to think about whether we are giving a media text our whole attention. For example, we might decide to sit down and 'devote' our evening to watching an episode of a favourite television programme – the reality for most of us, however, is that we might be engaging with or interrupted by social media while we do so. Consider the following issues:

- Does the divided attention we experience mean we miss the complexity of some media texts, or miss out on some layers of meaning?
- Is it different watching something on different devices? In the case of radio or podcasts, are listeners giving them their whole attention or dipping in and out of texts while doing other things, or listening when they can give their full attention?
- Does it matter what kind of device we view texts on? If 24-hour news is always on in the background on a screen in a workplace, are employees more susceptible to cultivation effects?
- Are people watching something because it is a scheduled broadcast, or have they sought the text out specifically to view at a time suited to them – and how many of the texts will they consume in one sitting?
- Do we watch something because it has been advertised to us, or because we know others are watching it? Think about how this affects the level of power media messages have to potentially influence us.

■ Agenda setting

Agenda setting is connected with the conditions of reception, since it attempts to steer the reader towards the hegemonic reading of the text. If expectations are established in the minds of the audience about what they expect to see, this makes the conditions of reception more fertile. The theory of agenda setting was first applied to the political uses of the mass media in covering election campaigns. This suggests that the media appeared to have an influence over people's perceptions of the campaign. Its theorists, Maxwell McCombs and Donald Shaw, compared news coverage of election campaigns with research into what people when interviewed perceived as the most important aspects of the campaign. They found a high degree of correlation between the two.

Since most people's only source of information about politics is the news media, it could be proposed that the media was literally setting the agenda of what was important. This theory therefore views the media as actively

> **Key terms**
>
> **agenda setting** theory relating mainly to news media that views the media as actively selecting certain issues and shaping public opinion of these by reporting on them more frequently
> *British newspapers play a role in agenda setting as the majority select similar news stories.*
>
> **conditions of consumption** a wide range of factors that can affect how a media text is interpreted by the audience, both in terms of ideological reception and physical consumption practices
> *Our viewpoint on the issue may differ from another's, resulting in different conditions of consumption.*

selecting certain issues and shaping public opinion of these by reporting on them more frequently. This aggregative effect happens because only a small proportion of people who encounter political stories pay much attention to them – the rest is picked up by the majority simply because it is something they have seen or heard frequently.

Audiences also tend to pick up more stories that affect them, and news producers tend to report on these because they encourage more sales or improve ratings if people feel that the issues being covered in the news – particularly political news reporting – are relevant to them.

Framing

The concept of **framing** is linked to agenda setting. However, framing concerns the content of a story – its bias and the way in which it is read by the audience according to their own interests and situation. Rather than the ease of accessibility that agenda setting focuses on, framing shifts this focus to how the individual can make sense of the issue or story – and how it is presented to them in a way that easily facilitates this. Framing means that we tend to interpret news stories according to factors that have already shaped our life experience. They determine how applicable it is to them rather than just how accessible the story is.

> **Key term**
>
> **framing** a news story's bias and the way in which it is read by the audience according to their own interests and situation
> *The audience tends to frame their understanding of the story in light of their political viewpoint.*

EXAMPLE: How much do the public trust their news sources?

In 2013, a poll was conducted for the BBC by Ipsos MORI. A thousand 'nationally representative' people were questioned about the BBC's trustworthiness as a news source compared with other sources.

The BBC scored significantly above any other news outlet available in the UK, with 58 per cent of the population trusting the news they saw reported on BBC programmes. However, rather than highlighting the BBC's comparative trustworthiness, these results actually show the wide consumption of BBC news by a range of individuals who also consume other media but would not necessarily take those other media, at face value.

Since 'one source' is stated alongside 'trustworthiness', this does not mean that people are not taking away messages from other news sources and absorbing other media organisations' agendas – it just means that when reliability is at hand, the BBC is the most popular choice. You also need to bear in mind that access to BBC content is free.

The BBC, then, clearly has a great deal of power to set political agendas, and this was seen during the 2017 election, when rows erupted repeatedly over the BBC's coverage being perceived to be biased in favour of the Conservative Party. If people are not conscious of agendas being set, then they are only able to take their news at face value – the effect of the presentation of a story may be cumulative, but if it comes from a trusted source, this may make the message that bit more powerful.

On the issue of bias and partiality, the BBC also scores the lowest for perceived bias, with tabloid newspapers and social networking at the other end of the scale. However, on a scale of 1–10 there is only around three points of difference between the highest and lowest scores, meaning that while people tended to rate the level of bias as less from television news outlets, there was not a huge gap in perceptions, and that there was an awareness of the issue of bias across the board. Again, if we are thinking about agenda setting, this matters very little. The news issues have to be selected first before people even get a chance to consciously consider how those stories are being presented to them – so, regardless of whether they 'believe' news stories or not, they have already had the content of their media consumption selected for them.

The BBC is the news source that the public say they trust the most. Of all the news sources, which one are you most likely to turn to for news you can trust?

6.5 Reception theory

Apply it

A good way of understanding both framing and agenda setting is to look at the front pages of a range of news sources on a single day. These might include: two or three newspapers; two different news broadcasts, for example on Sky News and Channel 4; and two news sites, such as the BBC and *HuffPost* (UK). Explore the way in which different news stories are sequenced in the agenda, positioned and framed. Consider what assumptions are being made about issues such as the audience's political views, their prior knowledge of the story, their understanding of international events and so on.

■ Stuart Hall

Stuart Hall extended his work on encoding and decoding to form a simple model that allows us to consider that different audiences do not necessarily respond to media texts in the same way. Hall suggested that this is partly due to each person having a different **conceptual map**, meaning that they bring their own understanding of the world. This then affects the conditions of consumption of any given media text. Hall also proposed that texts are polysemic, meaning that they can carry more than just the meaning encoded by the producer. Hall's ideas therefore challenge the thinking behind the hypodermic needle model, where the audience is passively 'injected' with the meanings of a particular text and decodes these meanings exactly as intended.

Reception theory suggests that when audience members consume a media text, they actively choose how they respond. Their own conceptual map, affected by variations in social class, gender, ethnicity, political leanings, life experience, education, cultural preferences and so on produces a decoding of the text, which correlates with this sum of experiences.

Three types of response are described:

- **Hegemonic reading** – the most common response to the text. It is the dominant meaning encoded – or 'preferred' – by the producer of the text.
- **Negotiated reading** – some of the audience may partially accept and partially reject the text. Negotiated readings can happen for all sorts of reasons, and can vary a great deal from person to person.
- **Oppositional reading** – some of the audience completely rejects the text. This might occur because of conflict with their values or ideologies, or may be as simple as a matter of personal taste.

Hall's theory reminds us that we should not make simplistic or reductive assumptions about audience members based on generalisations such as age or gender, as they can – and do – have complex and differing responses to texts. Some texts are more likely to provoke a strong reaction than others.

> See Chapter 5: Media representations for more on Stuart Hall's media theories.

Key terms

conceptual map our inner reference points dictated by the sum of our social and cultural experiences
We interpret the text in different ways according to our unique conceptual map.

reception theory considers that different audience members may interpret a single text in varying ways
Reception theory gives us differing possible audience responses to the product.

△ Stuart Hall

Apply it

Choose one print, two audio-visual and two digital media texts. Using reception theory, write a 600-word case study that explores the differing ways in which audiences might hypothetically receive the media texts you have chosen.

Quick questions

1. Discuss two conditions of consumption that could affect how a person responds to a media product.
2. How might we see agenda setting in action in a newspaper prior to a general election?
3. What is meant by a hegemonic reading of a text?

6.6 Fandom and the media

One of the most significant changes to occur with the impact of new technologies is the shift in audience expectations regarding their right to respond to and interact with media texts in such a way that their voices are heard.

Media consumers now experience the highest level of autonomy and control over their consumption than at any previous point in history. Web forums, fan sites and social media, which can be considered a channel for this feedback, are examined here in light of other forms they are connected with, rather than in their own right.

The makers of contemporary newspapers have found themselves needing to produce online editions in order to keep up with free news websites such as the BBC. Audiences increasingly share news stories that interest them on social media. Some news websites and apps allow comment facilities, with varying levels of moderation, allowing audience members to respond to news stories and lend their views, thus contributing to the entertainment value of the content. At their worst, such sites can be used for political ends in the same way that reviews on commercial sites can be hijacked for promotional purposes. Magazines have adopted social media as their primary participatory mode.

Elsewhere, television has clearly moved away from traditional scheduling as its only means of reading the audience, with viewers able to add favourite programmes to their profile. It is online where we have seen the biggest growth and changes in the ways in which audiences interact with the shows they love – review sites, fan sites and forums covering broad televisual entertainment or dedicated to particular shows and social media communities are readily accessible to anyone interested in finding out more about a show. There is evidence that producers sometimes even listen to these legions of fans.

Radio has always been to some degree an interactive medium, from listeners writing in to stations and taking part in phone-ins, to emails and text messages, which are read out on air. BBC Radio 1 is an excellent example of a station that has fully embraced interactivity, transforming both production values and the way in which it is consumed.

Computer games are clearly the most interactive of all media, since much of the progression and action in many games is directed by the players themselves. This is particularly true of 'sandbox' games, where the pleasure of the game is derived from the roaming, choosing of tasks and interaction with the gameplay world rather than a set progression. But all digital media forms have interactivity at their heart – it is this that distinguishes web destinations of every kind, from music and fan sites to user-generated video channels, from traditional media.

> **Apply it**
>
> Find three examples of different television shows that have been continued beyond their anticipated lifespan due to fan intervention. What techniques were used?

EXAMPLE: Fan power in the USA – *Chuck* (2007–12)

When rumours began circulating that US comedy-drama *Chuck*, which first aired in 2007, would be cancelled due to falling ratings, fans leapt into action. Beginning on social media and fan forums, such as ChuckTV.net, they launched the 'Save Chuck' campaign with the aim of persuading producers to keep the show on air.

Fans employed traditional tactics during the campaign, such as letter writing and petitions, but some of the tactics were more usual. The 'Have a Heart, Renew Chuck' campaign involved raising over $17,000 for the American Heart Association on behalf of NBC, which became newsworthy. Another tactic involved directly targeting one of the sponsors for the show, the global fast-food chain Subway. On the day the second-season finale aired, fans came out in force to purchase footlong subs from the chain and write positive comments about the show on store comment cards, causing a huge spike in sales and creating a stir in the news.

The show eventually reached a natural conclusion with the series finale airing in 2012.

Fan culture is one of the most interesting and dynamic aspects of studying popular culture, and one that is becoming increasingly important, especially since the visibility of fan culture has increased online. We will be exploring fan culture through the idea of two theorists: John Fiske and Henry Jenkins. Both have written about the relationship between fans and cultural products.

Central to contemporary thinking about fandom and participatory culture is the concept of the **prosumer**, the media audience member who also makes their own media. This development in society was being predicted as early as the 1970s by futurologist Alvin Toffler. Toffler perceived prosumption as a positive move in society, which he believed meant people would feel less alienated. This is interesting in the light of contemporary research into the effects of social media usage, where we are constantly connected with others but that connectivity – if not meaningful – can still give rise to a sense of alienation.

People who support prosumerism, seeing it as a positive contribution to human expression and industry, argue that it has given increased ideological and creative freedom and modes of expression to people who before may have lacked a voice. However, its critics argue that it merely supports the consumer economy, and that the freedoms it gives are actually illusory. They see prosumerism as a veiled part of the exchange mechanisms of capitalism that have made the most of sales of technological goods and the promotion of brands.

Key term

prosumer media producer who spans the categories of both audience and producer of media texts in variable proportions
The portability of the smartphone camera has greatly enabled prosumers to quickly produce content.

CHAPTER 6 MEDIA AUDIENCES

Somewhere between the two arguments there is a compromise. Perhaps there is a harmony overall between the sense of identity, self-esteem and connection with others gained from engaging with capitalist production in a way that benefits the consumer. Perhaps it reconciles their place as part of the commodification of internet users, and allows them to feel they are participating in a shared culture over which they feel ownership.

> The prosumer, although a concept first introduced a long time ago, is intimately connected with the development of Web 2.0, explored in more detail in Chapter 7: Media industries.

Example

Prosumers on YouTube – revenue over creativity?

Prolific YouTube genres, such as make-up tutorials and game vlogs, are good examples of products made by prosumers. The platform itself is a mass media institution, but content may be anywhere from amateur to professionally produced. On the level of the individual text producer, they may or may not have a formal relationship with business linking them to the products they test out, demonstrate or promote – but their activities can be seen as promotional whether or not a formal agreement, such as exchange of material goods for positive reviews, exists. They may also accumulate advertising revenue from clicks or views and external content appearing on individual posts. All these issues make the status of the prosumer and their positioning within the media industry difficult to place with precision. But the question is: do audiences really care about the distinction?

△ Make-up artist Jaclyn Hill demonstrates make-up techniques – and promotes beauty products – on her YouTube channel

Apply it

How much actual content is genuinely creative and detached from economic activity in the prosumer content you consume yourself? Choose an example, either of one of the genres above or another from YouTube, and explore the transparency and other dimensions of your chosen producer's relationship with both YouTube as a platform and business and the wider media industry.

The ways in which fandoms manifest have changed since the 1970s and 1980s, when fan culture began to really emerge as a form of self-expression among media audiences. The behaviours fans demonstrated then included wearing T-shirts with images of idols emblazoned on them, writing fan mail, attending events where their idol might be present, the creation of fanzines and membership of fan clubs – either official or unofficial. Collecting memorabilia and objects such as signed photographs was a true expression of fandom.

In the 1990s, the internet allowed fans to become more organised. Fan conventions, where fans can get together to celebrate their favourite films, TV shows or comics and meet their idols, have now become a mainstream cultural practice, with some, like Comic Con, attracting thousands of devoted visitors with a huge range of interests. Fandoms have almost always historically been associated with youth culture – and closely linked with the expression of identity.

John Fiske's essay 'The Cultural Economy of Fandom' (1992) describes fan culture as something that people who are otherwise marginalised by society can take part in, and they achieve status and a sense of belonging as a result. He discussed the ways in which fans can become producers and distributors of their own texts, which, although rooted in popular culture, stand largely outside its conventional forms. He describes the space in which fan culture exists as the **shadow cultural economy**.

Key term

shadow cultural economy the space in which fan culture exists
Fans are able to gain status within their community in the shadow cultural economy.

6.6 Fandom and the media

Key terms

enunciative productivity sharing the meanings and ways of talking about the text – 'fan-speak' – and wearing clothing or styling hair or make-up in a particular way
Integrating character sayings into everyday conversation can be seen as a form of enunciative productivity.

semiotic productivity the meanings made from the source texts by the fan
A fan's emotional affiliation for the celebrity could be seen as a form of semiotic productivity.

textual poaching the act of reappropriating a cultural product which may result in new meanings
The re-cutting of the series titles on YouTube may be seen as an act of textual poaching.

textual productivity fan-made texts as sense of ownership of the source text
The game has stimulated textual productivity in the form of fan art and even fan fiction based on its characters and narratives.

Fiske finds that fan culture exists alongside and in dialogue with mainstream cultural practices. He refers to the idea that fandoms produce a sense of self-esteem and social prestige. Interestingly, Fiske identifies those participating in fan culture as lacking in what he calls official cultural capital – that they are seeking a way of gaining it through alternative means. He also points out that many young people who participate in fandoms may not lack cultural capital, but use their affiliation with fandoms as a way of exploring their identity and setting themselves apart from parental influence or societal expectations of them. Importantly, Fiske sees the shadow cultural economy as rejecting the values of the official cultural economy. He points out that it exists purely to validate the interests of and receive feedback from peers within the fan community, and that this is its end gain.

Fiske characterises fandoms using three perspectives – discrimination and distinction, productivity and participation, and capital accumulation. These are summarised briefly below.

■ Discrimination and distinction

The tendency of fans to strongly define themselves as a group, and the tendency of others to also be able to identify that group, is a significant characteristic of fandoms. Fans also like to establish and debate the content of their fandoms in hierarchical ways – to create their own canons relating to aspects of the dominant, popular culture that is the subject of the fandom. These in a sense legitimise the fandom, and promote the aesthetic, in particular, of the cultural product. Fiske noted that white male fans were more likely to do this than other groups 'subordinated' by gender, race or class.

■ Productivity and participation

Fiske identified different forms of fan productivity, while acknowledging that there can be crossover between all three categories:

- **Semiotic productivity**: the meanings made from the source texts by the fan.
- **Enunciative productivity**: sharing these meanings and ways of talking about the text – 'fan-speak' and wearing clothing, or styling hair or make-up in a particular way.
- **Textual productivity**: fan-made texts and the sense of ownership of the source text. This can also be known as **textual poaching**.

■ Capital accumulation

Fiske points out that fan-based acquisition of cultural capital cannot be translated into economic capital, since the subject of fandom – popular culture – is excluded generally from mainstream education and the qualifications that can advance economic status as part of it. Fan knowledge does, however, still confer privilege, and sets the fan apart from wider consumers of popular culture, therefore still replicating a hierarchy.

Fiske uses the example of a Shakespeare play compared with the script for the *Rocky Horror Show* – a Shakespeare expert uses their knowledge to differentiate between performances of a text, whereas a fan uses their

△ Cosplay (dressing up as characters) at conventions is an example of enunciative productivity

CHAPTER 6 MEDIA AUDIENCES

knowledge of a script to 'participate' – to feel part of the performance and the fandom associated with it. Fan collecting behaviours are also addressed by Fiske – the memorabilia associated with popular culture are often cheap to collect and do not require a high amount of economic capital, compared with the collecting of works of art, so the emphasis is on volume of artefacts rather than their individual worth. Again, there are times when fan culture coincides with the traditional intersection of cultural and economic capital, such as in the status that might be gained by owning a rare comic – an objectified part of cultural capital.

△ Owning a rare comic is an example of objectified cultural capital, an intersection between the mainstream and shadow cultural economy

So far, you have considered fans to be a specialised sector of the audience. You have observed the ways in which, through Fiske's uses of Bourdieu's theory of cultural capital, fans can be distinguished from audiences and the ways in which fandoms can be seen to model some of the patterns of behaviour seen in the acquisition of conventional cultural capital within the shadow cultural economy.

■ Participatory culture

There are fundamental differences between participatory culture and **consumer culture**, a model of culture where the audience receives texts but does not 'interact' with them. The study of consumer culture does take into account the meanings of texts and the ways in which audiences relate to brand identities and particular media products, but it lacks visible evidence of action on these meanings.

In some ways, the digital age has relegated the status of purely consumer culture as the primary mode of consumption, but it's important to acknowledge that it does still persist. We can therefore think of consumer and participatory culture as co-existing. One is controlled by industry but subject to the dynamics of trends and consumer tastes, while in the other there are many more dimensions and complexities in the dynamic between producer and audience. Audience power in consumer culture is limited to economic expression – the decision to purchase or otherwise.

In their introduction to *The Participatory Cultures Handbook* (2012), Aaron Delwiche and Jennifer Jacobs Henderson identify four phases of participatory culture. They are summarised in Table 6.2.

> **Key term**
>
> **consumer culture** a model of culture where the audience receives texts but does not 'interact' with them
> *Magazines are a form of consumer culture.*

▽ Table 6.2 Four phases of participatory culture

Phase 1: *Emergence* (1985–1993)	• Personal computers begin to find their way into homes • ARPANET and other connected networks began to appear • Laser printers and DTP software • Nascent computer subculture and the hacker ethic • Academic research into *textual poaching* (Jenkins); increased interest in what fans do with products
Phase 2: *Waking up to the web* (1994–1998)	• Graphical browsers allow people to start making their own web pages and navigate the web more easily • Huge increase in speed of transformation in digital technologies • Increase in academic interest in human connectivity online, including studying gaming • Recognition that online cultural expression was important and worth studying
Phase 3: *Push-button publishing* (1999–2004)	• User-friendly web publishing services arrive, so participation reaches a much wider audience • Platforms appeared that were early social media, and the MP3 player revolutionised the portability of some media content • Both lead to the increased ability of audiences to publish, share and 'remix' • More studies began to focus on fandoms and the collective uses and sharing of information
Phase 4: *Ubiquitous connections* (2005–2011)	• Changes in broadband technology brought video-sharing platforms • Transmedia publishing • The increased take-up and rapid development of the smartphone • Academic recognition of some of the critiques of the networked era as well as Jenkins' *Convergence Culture* (2008), a hugely significant work

Quick questions

1 Give one reason the rise of the prosumer can be seen as a benefit to media audiences as a whole.
2 What is the difference between consumer culture and participatory culture?
3 What reason does Fiske give for young people engaging with fan behaviours?

■ Henry Jenkins: Participatory *Culture and Convergence*

KEY THINKER

Henry Jenkins (1958–) is a notable contemporary American academic theorist whose work has focused on fandoms and participatory culture, as well as the impact of digital connectivity on society and the cultural artefacts it produces.

The ideas of **Henry Jenkins** have been considered enormously important since people really began to study participatory culture. He has written extensively on convergence culture and participatory culture. It is highly recommended you take your reading of Jenkins beyond this book – his style is accessible, and his writing is full of interesting examples from popular media that help to embed his ideas.

'Textual poachers'

In his 1992 article, '*Textual Poachers: Television Fans and Participatory Culture*', Jenkins begins by exploring the popular stereotype of the *Star Trek* fan in other media, summarising the perception of them as desexualised social misfits who cultivate worthless knowledge, are unable to separate real life from a TV show and are emotionally immature.

△ The ability to share a pop cultural artefact, news story or meme at the touch of an icon defines the age of ubiquitous connections

CHAPTER 6 MEDIA AUDIENCES

This is the starting point for a number of points he makes about fans and fandoms:

- Fans are often stereotyped as mentally unbalanced in news media and in fiction as psychopathic. Fans are represented as an 'other' in popular media because their '*cultural preferences and interpretative practices … must be held at a distance so that fannish taste does not pollute sanctioned culture*'.
- Referring to Bourdieu, Jenkins points out that fan culture is seen as distasteful because it values pop cultural artefacts over more traditional signifiers of cultural capital.
- Much of the condescension surrounding fan culture is actually symptomatic of our anxiety around issues of the 'violation of dominant cultural hierarchies', which are transgressed by fans. Fans do not have the 'aesthetic distance' experienced by consumers with high cultural capital, and readily transgress and blur boundaries between fact and fiction.
- Fan culture challenges cultural hierarchies partly because they often seemingly possess cultural capital and come from middle-class, educated backgrounds. They are active producers of meaning who are able to manipulate the texts they encounter for new social bonds and transform the meanings of television shows into a rich and participatory culture.
- Fans are aware of their perilous position on the fringe of the original texts and the meanings encoded by their producers, and sometimes react with anger at narrative decisions taken by the programme-makers.

△ *Doctor Who* is an example of a television programme with a very active fan community going back many decades

Jenkins explores the meanings of the term textual poaching, originally suggested by Marcel de Certeau. If you were to apply Hall's model, then this would be the process by which fans encroach without authorisation on the hegemonic meaning encoded by the producers of a text. In this way, we can see the notion of a received meaning that is passively being accepted by the audience being challenged by fans. Jenkins suggests that textual poaching is an even more complex process than this. It resists the idea that there are identifiable meanings somehow already present in the text, and accepts that there are multiple positions in the meanings fans make which are not necessarily oppositional ones. Instead, they are alternatives to the dominant reading, ones that subsume the dominant reading and repurpose it to fit their own ideologies, since fans like a text in the first instance because it appeals to their way of interpreting the world. He suggests that because fans

6.6 Fandom and the media

cannot (in terms of television production – in the 1990s) own the means of production or direct it themselves, they are culturally marginalised. Jenkins believes that this creates a sense of dependence that is rejected by some, who then reappropriate cultural products and use them for their own, alternative purposes:

Fans possess not simply borrowed remnants snatched from mass culture, but their own culture built from the semiotic raw materials the media provides.

Apply it

Choose a television series or film franchise that inspire fandoms. What content can you find on fan sites that supports Jenkin's assertions about textual poachers? What examples can you find of fans 're-appropriating' meanings to match their world view, or where they feel marginalised by producer decisions?

Try:

www.fanpop.com

www.fanforum.com

https://archiveofourown.org/

Example

The enduring appeal of Sherlock Holmes

Jenkins refers to the example of Sherlock Holmes fans, who wrote to Sir Arthur Conan Doyle to beg him not to retire his character. It's an interesting coincidence that the modern television updating of Sherlock for the TV series of the same name has also inspired passionate fandoms, perhaps illustrating Jenkin's point that fans may also possess mainstream cultural capital, which they contribute to the shadow cultural economy.

△ Sherlock Holmes fans in London for a Guinness World Record attempt

In between these two texts, one published in 1993 and the other in 2016, Jenkins continued to explore participation through his book *Convergence Culture*. Written in 2008, this book looks at the ways in which traditional media has not been entirely replaced by new media but co-exists with it, and the myriad of interesting ways audiences can use new media to interact with old. It considers the old media's attempts to harness the power of new media for its own purposes, and the rise of huge media conglomerates that are multi-platform in their reach. Collective knowledge and play are considered as important aspects of the power that media consumers are able to express.

In *Participatory Culture in a Networked Era* (2016), Jenkins joins forces with two other key theorists in the field, Mimi Ito and Danah Boyd, to explore and debate some of the key ideas active in the field of participatory culture study today. It is a very readable book, with chapters that are themed in which each theorist presents their ideas in a conversational way, as suggested by the title. The most relevant chapter is the first, debating, for example, the differences between participation and interactivity. Jenkins identifies the key questions that the debate hinges on as follows:

- Can meaningful participation take place when the nature of contributions is controlled by big media and technology businesses?
- Is participation exploitation, where clicks generate not only access to content but also generate money for advertisers?

Jenkins makes clear that his first usage of the term in 1993 was about describing the dynamics between fan, producer and text, and their relationships with other fans. All three academics agree that what is meant by participatory culture has changed enormously and acknowledge that participatory culture may have started out as a study of fans, but that it now has academic usefulness in exploring networked connections way beyond these.

Jenkins says that he does not believe that technologies are participatory, but that cultures are. He believes that people are doing with social media and platforms such as YouTube what people have always sought to do – to connect social experience through their use. He feels that interactivity itself is not participatory – it is the use of interactive tools that makes them so. Participation means to take part, to share experiences and creative production. Technology therefore facilitates participation – it is not participation itself.

Jenkins does not believe that participatory culture necessarily stands in opposition to mainstream cultural values or that it resists them – but it does offer alternative sources of status and social belonging to people who may otherwise feel that they are low status in the world beyond their use of networks. Participatory culture exists alongside mainstream culture but does not necessarily challenge it.

> **Apply it**
>
> Choose a television series that has inspired fandoms. Search online for evidence of fan activities based on the show. What kinds of products can you find based on the 'semiotic raw materials' sourced by fans from the shows? Try to find three solid examples of contrasting fan-made artefacts. They might be costumes, videos, fan-fics, artwork, comics and so on. How do fans use the original material in their own ways? What do you think appeals about the show to fans, based on both the fan materials you found and the dominant messages contained in the original?

> **Quick questions**
> 1. What did Jenkins mean when he said fans were 'culturally marginalised'?
> 2. Write your own definition of the term 'textual poaching'.
> 3. What does Jenkins see as one of the benefits of participatory culture to those who most engage with it?

6.7 'End of audience' theory

The changes in the producer/audience relationship have been so extraordinary over the last couple of decades that it is not surprising the way in which we conceptualise audiences and understand how we should even define audience has come under scrutiny. A term for some of these collective ideas is **end of audience theory**. Most theorists do not literally propose that media audiences, in the sense we used to understand them, no longer exist. Instead, they suggest that we need to re-evaluate almost everything we assumed to be true about them because they no longer engage with the media on the same terms that we understood historically. A lot of thinking about the end of audience focuses on the **digital native**, the community of media users who have grown up with the internet, rather than **digital immigrants**, the older generation who have had to acquire the skills to participate in the digital world more consciously.

End of audience theory draws a line under older traditional practices of media industries and audiences and puts emphasis on the changes to these. Media production as an industry has historically been very hierarchical and difficult for 'outsiders' to gain entry to as production processes were very professionalised and ordinary people might be excluded by reasons of expense, technological skills or lack of access to distribution channels to gain the expertise necessary to compete.

> **Key terms**
>
> **digital immigrants** the older generation who have had to acquire the skills to participate in the digital world more consciously
> *Digital immigrants will feature less in the demographic of TikTok.*
>
> **digital native** community of media users who have grown up with the internet
> *Digital natives are more familiar with celebrity influencers.*
>
> **end of audience theory** changes in the way in which we conceptualise audiences and understand how we should even define audience
> *End of audience theory helps to account for changes in audience dynamics between producer and consumer.*

The media industry for much of its existence prior to the advent of digital technologies was heavily based on consumer culture, and the only audience feedback being received was that assessed by its own highly selective rating services or market research. Physical media that could be owned in some way was also a large part of the industrial process, and the costs of producing this made it prohibitive for any audience member wanting to challenge these companies with alternative content to do so.

Other issues that have become more complex today by comparison include regulation – with a media industry based on established sanctioned networks and higher proportion of content being domestically produced, regulation was simpler in the past than it is today.

By contrast, today's media world is riddled with complexity. Prosumers have access to both the technologies and distribution platforms at a very low cost to reach global audiences, leading to a huge increase in volume of media available for consumption and time spent consuming it by audiences. Physical ownership of media products has decreased, and digital convergence has changed the way we access previously discrete forms and content. Although regulation still exists, large volumes of the media we consume are self-regulated or communally moderated. All of these facets mean we need to radically re-assess what we thought we knew about the audience and its relationship with products.

A thorough introduction to this issue is 'The End of Audience?' (2009), an article by Sonia Livingstone and Ranjana Das. In their writing, the authors ask whether we can still define media audiences in the same way now, as the way in which they consume the media has changed so radically. The change from receiving mass communication to belonging to networks impacts enormously on *'the mediation of identity, sociality and power'* (page 1), yet some aspects remain a constant. Livingstone and Das caution us to reject the notion that the audience is 'dead', but point out that the conditions of consumption and the ways in which we interact with texts have changed the way we need to explore audiences, and perhaps the way we understand what audiences are doing with texts when they interact with them, form networked communities based on them or become prosumers.

Here are some concise points taken from the essay, although it's well worth reading yourself for its depth of exploration of the issue:

- In the age of digital media it's important we continue to recognise the *'mutuality of text and reader'* – in other words, texts are still open to different readings and what audiences do with those meanings can and does vary from person to person.
- We have reached a point in time where we are bombarded by media exposure, just as representational issues are higher on the political agenda than ever before, and we are a part of the constantly circulating messages in our culture.
- Because content is spread across media platforms, there is no neat boundary by which we can define a 'text'.
- Audiences are situated between text and context, with the technology that supports it and the text itself becoming increasingly indistinct from each other.
- Many theorists writing about the end of audience focus on the idea of a consumer becoming a citizen, and a lot of debate surrounds just how much power this new relationship with the media actually brings the consumer.

Livingstone and Das conclude that both social and semiotic approaches need to continue to work in tandem if we are to understand the complexity of the audience's new relationship with media. Audience theorists still face the same problems today that they did in previous generations – that we struggle to join up the meanings people make from what they see on screen with the context of the society that shapes those views. This continues to be a very difficult argument to grasp.

In addition to older models of reception, the digital age brings with it the audience as makers of not only meanings but also texts – that we should neither privilege the audience nor the text but try and acknowledge the duality of approach needed to really understand the relationship between the two.

■ Dan Gillmor: *We the Media*

Dan Gillmor's 2004 book *We the Media: Grassroots Journalism by the People, for the People* was an assertion of the changes that were happening in news media, where the impacts of a more participatory culture were just beginning to make themselves felt and shaping the future of news. In his book, he proposes that the de-professionalisation of the news industry and increased participation of the semi-professional or amateur 'grassroots' journalist is to be welcomed rather than perceived as a 'dumbing down' of journalism.

In his introduction, Gillmor talks about the changing roles of news providers; he views the evolution of journalism as the difference between moving from being in a lecture to being in a conversation. He puts the point quite strongly that news should not be a commodity solely owned by the most powerful media organisations. Gillmor discusses three groups of people who are changing in response to the rise of citizen journalism – journalists, newsmakers, and the former audience. Now that access to publishing technology has become democratised, there are implications for all. Journalism is no longer the hierarchical profession it once was, newsmakers have to be aware of the treatment of the subject matter they create by new, more grassroots news providers, who may not follow the old 'rules', and the audience are no longer the passive recipients of news but are in dialogue with it, or even reporting it and contributing to it themselves.

■ Clay Shirky: mass amateurisation and cognitive surplus

KEY THINKER

Clay Shirky (1964–) is an American writer, professor and influential contemporary thinker who specialises in the field of how digital media and communications may be shaping our society. He has written and lectured extensively about the new dynamic between media producers and audiences.

In his books – *Here Comes Everybody: The Power or Organising Without Organisations* (2008) and *Cognitive Surplus: How Technology Makes Consumers into Collaborators* (2010), **Clay Shirky** speaks in favour of collaborative crowdsourcing. Two of his key ideas applicable to your studies are outlined in the following section, but it is worth reading for yourself some of what he has to say about how we are learning to engage as audiences with a new, far more participatory media world.

△ Clay Shirky

> **Apply it**
>
> Watch one of the following Clay Shirky TED Talks online:
>
> - How social media can make history
> - Institutions vs. collaboration
> - How the internet will (one day) transform government
> - How cognitive surplus will change the world
>
> Make notes as you view your chosen talk. Look back over your notes, and do the following:
>
> 1 Write a summary of the talk in one sentence. What was its subject?
> 2 What were Shirky's main points?
> 3 Did you feel he was optimistic or pessimistic about social change brought about by media technologies?

Mass amateurisation

Shirky's work centres on the premise that the audience–industry hierarchical relationship of old, where professionally made media was consumed by audiences in a fairly simple model, no longer predominates. He sees this new world as not yet full-fledged, and loaded with issues as the crossover and blurring of lines between audiences and producers is not yet completely resolved.

An important aspect of Shirky's work centres on the idea of **mass amateurisation**. Shirky, in exploring this aspect of mass media change in relationship between audience and industry, treads similar ground to the ideas we have encountered already – the prosumer, citizen journalists, the fan producers of texts.

Shirky sees the shift in roles and the loss of distinction between producer and audience as one of the most significant changes in media consumption and production history. He defines this shift as being from 'Why publish this?' to 'Why not?' He points out that the selection of what can be published is no longer as highly structured and regulated as it was within the old media 'profession'. Amateurs simply don't need to follow any rules since there is no cost or low cost involved in distributing their content. He also explores the idea that, although the individual small producer of a blog or minor social media alternative news outlet may not individually be held in high esteem by the audience, there is an amplifying effect to their repetition in numerous places.

> **Key terms**
>
> **cognitive surplus** the way in which people globally now use their free time to develop collaborative online projects
> *The fan wiki has been developed using the cognitive surplus of fans.*
> **mass amateurisation** state of the media today, where professionally made media that was consumed by audiences in a fairly simple model no longer predominates
> *The tablet computer has become a facilitator of mass amateurisation.*

Shirky does not necessarily imbue the term 'amateur' with negative associations. At the end of his third chapter, 'Everyone is a Media Outlet', he points out that the profession of scribe was once hugely important in an age where the printing press, and therefore mass reproduction of texts, had not yet been invented and the majority of people were illiterate. The ability to read and write was imbued with huge significance and status. However, the advent of movable type and the increased literacy of the population meant reading and writing became commonplace tools that were available to all. Shirky sees this as a metaphor for the transformation of the relationship between people and the media.

Cognitive surplus

In his second book, Shirky uses the term **cognitive surplus** to describe the way in which people globally now use their free time to develop collaborative online projects that demonstrate diverse collective creativity. Two main perspectives seem to drive this use of time – the desire to be recognised and respected as a contributor to a project, and to join with a group who share interests and common goals.

The purposes of these groups might vary from pure entertainment to the formulation of groups who are serious about social activism of some kind. Fan wikis and online media archives are good examples of this in media terms, but Wikipedia and Kickstarter could also be seen as examples of how technology can be used to get momentum together by using the collective knowledge and intellect of a large number of contributors.

Apply it

Choose a website that demonstrates Shirky's notion of cognitive surplus being put to use. It could have as its focus environmental activism, or it could be a fan wiki or science project – there are all kinds of different texts and a huge range of subject matter.

Take screenshots of your site, and include them when preparing a five-slide presentation on how the collaborative nature of the site is apparent in its mode of address, its statement of intent (this often can be found in the 'About' section of the website) and user interactivity/ contribution mechanisms.

Quick questions

1. What analogy did Dan Gillmor use to explain the biggest change in journalistic style and practices in recent decades?
2. Why does Clay Shirky see mass amateurisation as a benefit to society?
3. Can you explain the difference between a digital immigrant and a digital native?

→ Exam-style questions

1. How do media producers ensure their product appeals to the audience they hope to attract? Explore this using your two television Close Study Products.
2. Why can we only ever identify a *potential* effect of media products? Using your knowledge of effects debates, explore the relationship between audiences and product using two of your Close Study Products.
3. Why do the conditions of reception of a media product matter? Discuss using two of your Close Study Products.
4. How and why have fans become an increasingly important sector of the audience to media producers? Explain the role of fandom in relation to two of your Close Study Products.
5. How has the way we understand the role of the media audiences in consumption changed in the digital age? Explore using one of your pairings of Close Study Products that includes a historical media product.

6.7 'End of audience' theory

→ Summary

- Audiences are constructed by media producers.

- Audience interactivity has changed some of the dynamics of the relationship between producer and consumer in recent decades, but fundamentally they are still reliant on the choices offered to them through media channels.

- The methods used to target the audience appropriately vary across media industries, and almost all industries now use digital technologies to their advantage in monitoring, in some way, who consumes their products.

- Effects theories are important concepts in audience studies – although each model has its own weaknesses, all of them can help us to access debates and discussions about the relationship between the audience and their consumption practices.

- Media audiences are becoming increasingly fragmented, and media producers are having to find more and more creative ways of reaching them in light of increasing specialisation of audiences whose experience of consumption reflects the fragmenting of popular culture.

- Cultivation and social learning theory were introduced as key ideas about potential links between the mass media and audience behaviours, attitudes and values.

- Agenda setting and framing are interpretative effects theories that seek to understand the extent to which news media influence people's perceptions of political and social agendas and issues.

- Hall's reception theory, and exploring reception in general, forms an important part of how you approach the relationship between the encoded message and the decoding process, as well as the idea of a hegemonic, negotiated or oppositional reading.

- Gillmor described the changes happening in the relationship between journalists, audiences and traditional news outlets.

- Shirky and Jenkins introduced us to the related ideas of mass amateurisation, integrating ideas about the prosumer with commentary on the changing relationship between audience and industries brought about by new technologies.

Chapter 7 Media industries

→ What you will learn in this chapter

Chapter 7: Media industries covers:

- an overview of significant changes in the media industry spanning a number of decades
- what is meant by processes of distribution and circulation in the mass media, and how these vary across industry sectors
- the importance of ownership and control
- the significance of economic factors, such as commercial and not-for-profit public funding, to media industries and their products
- how the media is regulated in the UK
- how digital technologies have changed the demands of media regulation, distribution and circulation, including the role of individual producers.

7.1 The ever-changing nature of the media

Just a couple of generations ago, the media landscape looked very different from the one we know today. Pre-television, most people's main sources of news were the radio and printed newspapers. Leisure time in terms of media consumption was dominated by the cinema. From the 1950s, audiences for television programming grew and, by the 1970s, UK television broadcasters were routinely broadcasting the majority of their schedules in colour.

In the 1980s, some homes had satellite television in addition to the four terrestrial channels and some newspapers included colour pictures for special editions. The magazine industry had continued to expand into health and lifestyle titles, while many traditional town cinemas were closing due to competition from out-of-town multiplexes, video recorders and video rental. Young people were spending more and more of their time in gaming arcades, which were largely superseded by games consoles in the home. Music was still being bought on vinyl, but there were plenty of fans of the cassette, which had introduced another real headache for the music industry – widespread music piracy. By the end of the 1980s, the younger generation and plenty of older cash-rich **early adopters** were buying their favourite albums on compact discs (CDs).

Moving on another 15 or so years, digital technologies had begun to impact on people's lives and consumption habits in ways they could only have dreamed of a couple of decades previously. Social media, cheap digital cameras, digital television, huge leaps in computer gaming technologies, the internet, streaming, Freeview and cable television, and devices such as smartphones and tablets changed the media landscape forever.

Key term

early adopters individuals who take advantage of technological developments before they become mainstream

Apply it

Write a 1,000-word article on the ways in which you experience the mass media compared with the media consumption practices of your parents and grandparents. Use a range of contrasting authoritative web-based sources, including at least one article or book found using Google Scholar. Gather interview material from a sample of subjects from different generations. Record the interviews using your smartphone, and be sure to supply a list of your internet-based sources at the end of the piece.

Key terms

circulation amount of copies of a print media publication sold (paid circulation) or distributed (free publications funded entirely by advertising)

content providers individuals, groups or organisation who create the content of media products; they may or may not be media producers

convergence the use of different technologies and/or platforms to produce and distribute media products

cultural industries the industries that are involved in the production, distribution and circulation of cultural artefacts, including media products

distribution methods used to make media products available to audiences

diversification media companies' move into the production of a range of different types of media product

free market trading based on unrestricted competition between private companies

monopoly when one corporation dominates the provision of a specific product or service so there is no choice for the consumer

neo-liberalism political values that prioritise individual freedom of choice and the power of the free market

production the manufacture of media products

shareholders groups or individuals who are part owners of a company, as they have invested money by buying shares

Traditionally, the **cultural industries** which produced the media products that audiences read, watched, played and listened to were large media corporations. This was because **production**, **distribution** and **circulation** were so expensive that only companies with access to money and resources were able to create media products that had any chance of finding a large audience. Traditional media industries still produce a lot of media content, but since the mid-2000s more and more media products have been produced and distributed by independent and amateur **content providers**. Traditional media institutions and industries are under enormous pressure, as they are increasingly competing for audiences and advertising revenue. In addition, technological developments have created new audience behaviours and expectations. Clay Shirky (see page 169) argues that the internet 'challenges existing institutions by eroding the institutional **monopoly**' (Hesmondhalgh, 2012). This puts pressure on the existing industries, who are finding it harder to find audiences and compete with a wide range of producers, all of which seek to attract audiences' attention.

The relationship between audiences and industries is primarily economic. As they exist within a capitalist framework, cultural industries seek to find a way to commodify their product or service and then attempt to attract an audience to buy or buy into whatever they are selling – even if this is advertising space. Most media industries exist to serve their **shareholders**. Companies such as Sky, BMG, Columbia Pictures, YouTube, Global Radio, Rockstar Games and so on all exist to create profit. In a **neo-liberal**, **free market** environment, all media industries are in direct competition with one another for our time, attention and money. This means that media industries must constantly try to innovate, **diversify** and engage in **convergence** practices to help them respond to changing audience demands so that they remain viable.

△ A billboard for *L.A. Noire* by Rockstar Games

Studying media industries means engaging with the structures and economics that support the production of media artefacts. Understanding the industrial context of the production of media products gives an insight into *why* media products are the way they are. At the heart of this is the culture of **commercialisation** (Hesmondhalgh, 2012), which leads to the **commodification** of both media products and audiences.

Put simply, media studies is the study of the relationship between audiences and industries. At the centre of this relationship are the media products themselves.

■ Technological changes across media forms

The history of the media is the history of technological change. From the invention of the printing press to today's virtual reality headsets, we can see that methods of production, distribution and circulation have developed with the technologies that are available.

Newspapers

The printing press made possible the mass reproduction, and consequently distribution, of the written word and images, and through them, the dissemination of information and ideas. Literacy was once limited to members of the powerful institutions of the time (the Church and the legal profession) and then to a wealthy, educated elite. The invention of the printing press, however, led to a rise in literacy, and, slowly, more and more ordinary people learned to read.

Printing and distributing written materials is, however, a costly endeavour:

- Writers and journalists offer a specialised skill that traditionally attracted a professional salary.
- Print media businesses needed to have access to specialised equipment to be able to produce the materials and distribute them.

This means the power to produce was traditionally in the hands of large companies or individuals with personal wealth, or those who could attract large amounts of investment. This paradigm of industrial production and ownership can still be seen in UK newspaper industries. Most national titles are

> **Key terms**
>
> **commercialisation** the practice of running an institution or creating media products specifically with an aim to generate financial gain
>
> **commodification** to turn something into a product that can be sold

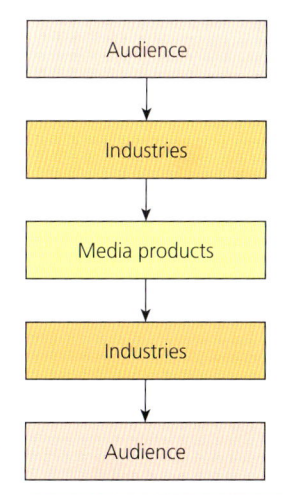

Audience
↓
Industries
↓
Media products
↓
Industries
↓
Audience

△ Media products are at the centre of the relationship between media audiences and industries

7.1 The ever-changing nature of the media

175

owned by members of the English aristocracy (Jonathan Harmsworth, the 4th Viscount Rothemere, is the chairman and majority shareholder of the Daily Mail Group), multinational media businesses (the *Sun* and *The Times* are owned by News UK, a subsidiary of News Corp, founded by billionaire Rupert Murdoch) or entrepreneurs (the Telegraph Media Group is currently owned by the Barclay brothers). The only national British newspaper that is not a for-profit business is the *Guardian*, which is run by the Scott Trust Limited. The Trust, which was created in 1936 to secure the financial and editorial independence of the *Guardian*, has no individual owner and does not pay dividends to shareholders.

As the newspaper industry developed, generic expectations began to be established. Local newspapers reported primarily on local news. Some of the newspapers founded in bigger cities began to focus on national affairs. Eventually, three main types of newspaper emerged with quite different **news values**: local papers with a regional focus that reported only on national events that concerned local people; broadsheets with a hard news agenda that debated politics and reported on global affairs; and tabloids, which became increasingly entertainment and soft-news oriented, tending to focus on domestic issues and headline-grabbers such as crime and the latest moral panic. In recent decades, this trend has been magnified.

The distribution of hard-copy newspapers requires a delivery network to ensure 'today's paper' arrives in newsagents and supermarkets early in the morning. All of this is labour intensive, costly and time-consuming, and means that daily newspapers need to recoup their substantial costs if they are to survive. There are two ways newspapers can make money:

- by selling advertising space
- by selling the newspaper itself to its audience.

In recent years both of these income sources have been hit. Newspapers have found that the competition provided by free online news sources has meant that fewer people are prepared to pay for their news and, as circulation has dropped, the amount a newspaper can charge advertisers has also steeply declined, reducing their income even further. All British print newspapers have an online edition and, in 2016, the *Independent* became the first newspaper to go 'internet only'. The *Independent* closed its print edition because the cost of production and distribution became unsustainable: its survival could only be ensured if costs were reduced by limiting the distribution of content to the website and social media only.

△ A newspaper printing press in action

Magazines

Modern lifestyle magazines developed from shopping catalogues and offered a range of content often targeting a female audience with domestic interests. The history of the popular magazine title offers a fascinating insight into the study of culture, leisure and other areas such as gender politics. It is also inextricably linked with the history of print advertising, since most magazines make their **commercial revenue** not just from their circulation but also primarily from the advertisers they can attract who have a message for that magazine's readership. The exception to this is comics, and some **niche publications** where publishers rely instead on high turnover and profit from a smaller number of units sold.

> **Key terms**
>
> **commercial revenue** profit generated by a media organisation
>
> **niche publications** print media publications serving a special interest or with a small circulation

CHAPTER 7 MEDIA INDUSTRIES

Magazine publishers, in common with newspapers, have struggled with the growth of the internet and the information age. With much of their editorial subject matter now available elsewhere for readers to access for free, it has been a challenge to maintain readership and continue to sell what many view as an outmoded concept for which they are reluctant to exchange money.

Some magazines have responded by moving part of their publishing to **digital subscription platforms** such as Zinio, where readers can access their archived back copies and re-read any issue when signed in. Forays into providing exclusive digital content for e-platform readership have had mixed results. This is partly because there is little understanding as yet of what consumers really want as additional benefits from a paid-for digital magazine subscription that they cannot already access readily elsewhere online.

Radio

Radio sets used to be the centre of the family home and, in many cases, were the sole provider of popular entertainment and news. The technology required to be able to access radio broadcasts was relatively cheap. The BBC was set up in 1922 to create radio programming to be broadcast to the UK public with a view to inform, educate and entertain, and, as the use of radio spread, it became the first electronic mass media form. It was an important technology that allowed audiences to hear the voices of their leaders, for instance, famously, Prime Minister Neville Chamberlain's declaration of Britain going to war with Germany in 1939. During this period radio could be seen as a unifying force, as it formed the first shared culture, with people accessing the same programming at the same time. This brought people together through their shared media experiences.

Radio, unsurprisingly, was hugely impacted by the arrival of television in people's homes. For years, ratings went into decline – yet public service broadcasting, community radio and commercial radio all persist today. Many popular genres we know on television have a predecessor on radio. Well-known examples we still watch today on television include the crime drama, situation comedy (sitcom), panel game show and soap opera.

Radio's popularity further reduced with the advent of television and then the internet, which offers audiences more varied ways to obtain information. But, nearly five million people listen to the Radio 1 *Breakfast Show* every week. Many TV programmes struggle to attract audiences of this size but such numbers are on a slow decline. Radio has always been a relatively mobile form of media but internet radio shows and podcasts mean that 'radio' programmes can be accessed via smartphones and tablets anywhere and at any time, and access is not limited to specific broadcast times, which has the potential to increase the circulation of radio programmes or podcasts. Podcasts also provide far more specialised content, leaving them even better able to compete with broadcast radio for listeners.

> **Key term**
>
> **digital subscription platform** content provided digitally for a monthly or annual payment

△ Radio was the primary form of in-house entertainment and news delivery before the invention of the television and, later, the internet

7.1 The ever-changing nature of the media

> **Key term**
>
> **viral** the organic sharing of information by word-of-mouth and sharing on social media

Serial Season 1 (2014) was a very successful podcast. Discussions on social media created **viral** interest in the show and its audience grew over time. As the episodes were available to listen to (or download) online, audiences could access the show immediately and listen to it at their own convenience. This is crucial for programmes such as *Serial*, which is formed around an extended, ongoing narrative. In the past, where access was restricted to broadcast times, an audience member who missed early episodes would be excluded from enjoying the programme.

Television

Like radio, TV became the centre of popular culture and the primary source of media. TV offered information and entertainment across, at first, a limited number of channels. Through the 1960s, 1970s and into the 1980s there were only three UK channels. Channel 4 was launched in 1982 and Channel 5 in 1997. Twentieth-century TV audiences for single programmes could be massive. For example, as many as 27 million people watched *Coronation Street* on Christmas Day in 1987 to see popular character Hilda Ogden get married.

As mass-market television became more mainstream, this created a shared cultural knowledge and experience. In 1980, when the character JR Ewing was shot in the hit US soap opera *Dallas*, it became an important cultural moment. T-shirts were printed and songs were recorded all asking the question: 'Who shot JR?' The identity of the killer became a huge talking point, and the episode that finally closed the case became the most watched TV episode of all time (at that point).

Television is still very popular today, but distribution methods have now changed to such an extent that audiences no longer need a television set to access 'television shows'.

The introduction of domestic video players/recorders in the 1970s revolutionised the distribution and circulation of films and television programmes, and also led to two major changes in audience behaviour:

- Audiences could choose to record TV and watch programmes when they chose rather than at the time determined by the broadcasting institution.
- Audiences could rent films (and later buy them), meaning they had a wide range of film releases available to them outside of the cinema and TV schedules.

In the early days of film rentals, mainly low-budget genre films or films that had had a limited release in cinemas were available to the public. Video rentals also gave these films a second chance to find an audience. For example, the first *Terminator* film had some success on its release to cinema in 1984, but, due to word of mouth and ease of accessibility, it became a huge success on video and went on to become a major Hollywood franchise.

At first, Hollywood feared that videos would impact on its ability to attract audiences to the cinema – the primary source of income for the film industry. Sony was sued for providing technology that could allow people to pirate films and TV shows, but the court ruled that the inventor of a technology could not be held responsible for it being used in a way that broke the law. However, the film industry soon realised it could tap into the audience demand for home video by making more titles available.

At first, audiences rented films; later, a market for the sale of films was established. TV companies found that audiences liked the freedom from TV schedules that home recording provided. They were slower to pick up on the market potential in renting or selling videos but, by the mid-1990s, cult shows such as *The X-Files* and *Star Trek* led the way in the video box set market, which, of course, was superseded by the DVD box set by the end of the decade. By the early 2000s, DVD sales had become a crucial part of the film and TV industry's business model.

△ ***The X-Files:*** **one of the first TV series to be sold as a VHS box set**

By 2012, internet television and the analogue switch-off meant that all television became digital. This was made possible by huge advances in broadband cabling and wi-fi. With this, the floodgates opened to video-on-demand (VOD) services, with content subscription packages challenging the market leaders in cable and satellite television, forcing them to make their own packages more competitive.

While video and DVD box sets made viewing film and TV series much more flexible, VOD services have gone one step further. Netflix led the way in making full seasons of programmes available all at once, giving audiences total freedom to **binge-watch** all episodes in one go, if they so wished. However, recently some streaming services have returned to the 'old' method of distributing series one episode a week. This helps to keep the programme visible in the culture for longer and increases the potential for word-of-mouth recommendations, helping grow the viewing figures over time. Weekly episodes also give space for audiences to discuss and engage with a programme, listen to recap podcasts and share theories about characters and plot developments. This has increased the cultural impact of some drama series, such as HBO's *The Last of Us* (2023–) and HBO's *Succession* (2018–23).

> **Key term**
>
> **binge-watch** to watch multiple episodes one after the other

7.1 The ever-changing nature of the media

Key terms

business model the strategies employed by a company to generate profit

niche audiences audiences with a special interest

Streaming, VOD and digital downloads also allow audiences to watch programmes created for TV on smartphones, computers and tablets, making the programmes more portable, and therefore more accessible than ever before. Streaming services such as Netflix provide programmes over the internet, allow downloads for offline viewing and are making a massive library of film and TV programmes available to subscribers. However, even this **business model** is in the process of changing. Over the last few years there has been an increase in the number of subscription streaming channels – some are for specialised, **niche audiences** (e.g. Shudder, which targets horror fans) while others are services offered by established conglomerates (e.g. Disney+). This means there is more competition for the existing TV content and Netflix has lost the right to stream some popular titles and franchises. For example, all of the Star Wars and Marvel content is freely available to subscribers of Disney+ (see page 207). Without Disney+, viewers need to purchase digital downloads of these products to be able to access them online. Audiences now find themselves having to decide which streaming services they are willing to pay for, meaning Netflix's dominance in VOD services is being challenged.

Music

The phenomenon that is the cultural dominance of late twentieth-century pop music owes its existence to two communication technologies: radio and, at least at first, vinyl records. Records allowed music to be recorded and then distributed to be played at home. Radio played and, therefore, promoted music, allowing audiences to select the music they wanted to buy. Radio could provide musical entertainment based on choices made by radio stations or DJs. Buying a record meant that the audience could play their chosen song whenever they wished.

From the middle of the 20th century, media companies saw the potential for profit in creating and selling music to young people. Beginning in the 1950s, record companies began marketing the new sound of rock and roll to teenagers, the first generation to have a disposable income. Soon, music became a way for young people to express their individual and collective identities. Record companies have attempted to engage and attract new audiences in these ways ever since.

Music was first distributed to audiences through radio, and then through record stores. TV was also part of the marketing and distribution of music, and a music press soon grew around the industry. The music press offered interviews with artists and reviews of singles, albums and live shows. The journalists for publications such as *Melody Maker* and *New Musical Express* became self-appointed experts, offering opinions of what and who was 'in'.

Later, pop music and its stars were covered in *Smash Hits* – a fortnightly magazine that had a circulation of up to 500,000 in its early 1980s heyday and was largely aimed at teenagers. Pop stars were promoted on children's TV and in more general magazines – all of which fed into the distribution and circulation processes.

Apply it

1. In what ways do you think iPlayer is responding to the competition provided by streaming services such as Netflix and Amazon Prime?
2. What advantages does Spotify have over conventional music radio?

As technologies changed, the music industry began offering audiences new experiences to meet their changing behaviours. Cassettes were a hugely popular music format and their popularity rose when audiences began using mobile technologies, such as the Sony Walkman. When CDs were introduced in the late 1980s, audiences were encouraged to update their existing collections by re-purchasing classic and favourite recordings on a new format.

The music industry also invested increasingly large sums of money into music video, using the popularity of MTV and the audience's desire to watch music on television as a new way to market and promote their artists. Music sales rose throughout the 20th century, however, the rise of digital downloads and, later, streaming services such as Napster, YouTube and Spotify, saw changes in audience behaviour that impacted on the music industry's business model. People mostly stopped paying to own recordings of music, so the old models of distribution and circulation of physical products became increasingly irrelevant.

Music sales today are much smaller than in the past so record companies look to other sources of income, such as merchandise sales, live shows, corporate sponsorship and licensing agreements, to generate an income. This has led to changes in the relationship between record companies and their artists. Traditionally, record labels would recoup the expenses accrued from the recording, promoting and distribution of an artist's music from the money made via music sales. Record companies had no claim on money made by their artists in any other way. However, today, new '360-degree contracts' mean that artists are contracted to pay record companies a percentage of their income from *any and all* sources, including performances and merchandise.

Apply it

Create a visual timeline from the 1970s to present day following a specific media production or reception technology. Suitable examples could include television, the computer gaming console or newspaper production methods.

EXAMPLE: Early computer gaming

Computing technologies began to appear as early as the 1960s, but it wasn't until the late 1970s and early 1980s that a small number of enthusiasts began to use computers in the home.

The first gamers used specialist consoles, such as the Atari system and the ZX Spectrum, and players enjoyed simple games with what would now be considered low-quality graphics. Text-based adventure games were also rapidly gaining in popularity among the first PC users, and many of the genres of gaming we know today had their antecedents in these early ventures.

Apply it

Research and write a 500-word case study of a new media form of your choice, tracing it from its beginnings to its present-day form. Suitable case studies might include YouTube, digital comics, online news or event television. Include illustrations where relevant.

Online/Digital media

By the mid-1980s, computers were becoming commonplace in the workplace, and many processes that occurred in the media industry that had been laborious, such as the touching-up of silver photography by hand in art departments and the preparation of newspaper front pages, began to be

7.1 The ever-changing nature of the media

digitised with the introduction of Photoshop and desk-top publishing software. By the 1990s home computing was becoming more common. Connection to the internet at this time was still through slow dial-up modems, meaning much online content was still text- rather than image-heavy. At the same time, the games console market and PC gaming were taking off radically.

Widespread improvements and access to broadband and wireless technologies came with the arrival of **Web 2.0**. Some of the characteristics of Web 2.0 included:

- the advent of social media as a form of leisure activity
- advances in digital image-capture technologies combined with portability, accessibility and affordability, and the ability to embed them into the fabric of the web with ease
- increased human communication and connectivity across the world through collaborative networks and information sharing (wikis and crowdsourcing are also an aspect of this)
- user-generated content due to the decreased necessity for technical knowledge to have a web presence, and ease of content sharing
- the increase in a user's capacity to interact with web content, which might previously have been static sources of information, and user expectation of dynamic properties in the websites they visit.

EXAMPLE: YouTube and Web 2.0

YouTube is often cited as a typical product of Web 2.0. People spend time on it as a leisure activity, and are able to contribute to it using cheap, digital video-capture technologies. It crosses continents and cultures, and, at its more serious, can promote the sharing of information. It requires little technical expertise to submit a video, and other users are free to comment on them, and so it provides social interaction too.

Apply it
Conduct some additional online research into the characteristics of Web 2.0. Create an infographic that shows its properties in an appealing way.

Key terms

technological convergence the gradual combining of separate technological devices into fewer devices or one device with multiple functions

Web 2.0 phase of internet development summed up by increased human connectivity using technology

△ Children following a Joe Wicks fitness video on YouTube

While the development of multiple technologies made Web 2.0 a reality, it would not have been possible without the smartphone: the ultimate **technological convergence** device. Consider all the functions that can now be performed on a smartphone: emailing, traditional work such as creation of documents, basic photo and video editing, graphics, gaming, telecommunications, information access, GPS navigation, personal organisation, health tracking, instant means of communicating with friends and family without the necessity of a phone call – the list goes on.

CHAPTER 7 MEDIA INDUSTRIES

The smartphone has also became a major way for advertisers to gather information about an individual's preferences. In terms of media consumption, tools such as social media algorithms have the capacity to offer personalised media and advertising based on personal interests, harvested from keywords, a person's published information, and their online activity, including searches, 'likes' and posts. This has resulted in an experience that is far more relevant and tailored to a person's personal preferences. For media producers, and advertisers in particular, this is a tool that allows still deeper penetration of a market to the consumers they want to reach.

This personalisation of digital content can already be seen in other new media services and changes in the way we access digital media. Music and podcast purchases, online film rentals, use of streaming services and so on are all likely to lead to us being recommended similarly categorised content, although much is often based at present on simple analysis of what else other viewers watched or downloaded rather than our own personal preferences.

> AQA has created a list of industry ideas that you should be familiar with. You will be asked to apply your knowledge of media industries in Paper 1 Section B and in Paper 2. See Chapter 11 for more details.

7.2 Distribution and circulation: what they are and why they vary across media

The term 'distribution' refers to any way in which a mass media product reaches its target audience. These can be physical, technological or instigated by the media producer or their agents. They may also be audience-driven, as is the case with any carefully managed viral advertising campaign on social media. Distribution in the digital age can be via a mechanism as apparently simple as the uploading of a new game trailer to YouTube – even so, it is likely that a knowledgeable digital marketing specialist is maintaining the channel on which it appears, and observing closely how it performs.

Formal methods of distribution common to **legacy media** such as films, where some studios own their own distribution arms, can co-exist alongside very small specialist distributors, which may focus, for example, on releasing DVD documentaries from non English-speaking countries. Each stage of the distribution process can potentially be handled by a different distributor that has a limited role to play. Each distributor takes a percentage of the profits every time the product is moved on.

In television and radio, distribution refers to the processes involved in broadcasting the programme on a particular channel or station. This might include the selling-on of content to other channels that will pay for it in order to refresh their own schedules. It also involves considering issues of placement in a traditional television schedule, and more recently the featuring and availability of content on TV player, VOD or podcast services.

The Broadcasters' Audience Research Board (Barb) measures ratings for television and TV players in the UK. Established in 1981, BARB is now recognising the challenges of providing accurate up-to-date measures of audience ratings that encompass all types of television viewing including the standard **schedule**. This information can be used by channels or programmers themselves to make decisions about the performance of individual content; crucially, it is also used by advertisers.

Barb measures representative consumption patterns by installing monitoring software in the homes of 5,100 people in the UK from a mixed demographic. Each week it produces a range of reports that show channel share, performance of individual programmes and so on. The most recent of these is the *TV Player Report*, which is based on device usage. The report uses a measure known as

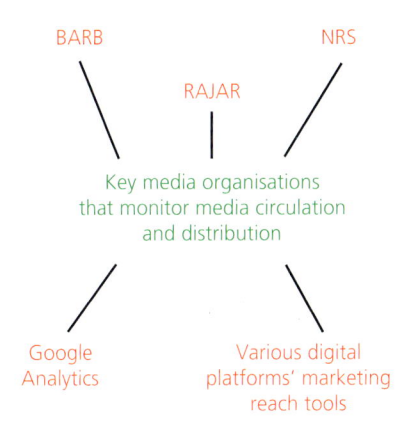

BARB NRS
RAJAR
Key media organisations that monitor media circulation and distribution
Google Analytics   Various digital platforms' marketing reach tools

Key terms

Broadcasters' Audience Research Board (Barb) measures ratings for television and TV players in the UK
schedule traditional way of organising broadcasts in a chronological way to transmit at specific times of day
legacy media a term used to describe pre-digital media forms (e.g. newspapers and television)

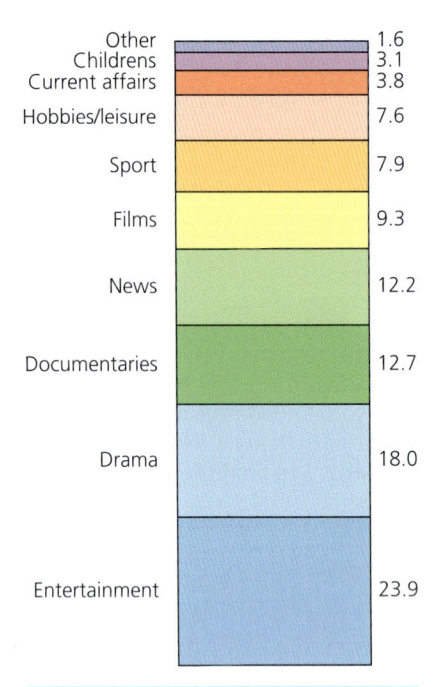

Genre	%
Other	1.6
Childrens	3.1
Current affairs	3.8
Hobbies/leisure	7.6
Sport	7.9
Films	9.3
News	12.2
Documentaries	12.7
Drama	18.0
Entertainment	23.9

△ % share of TV viewing by genre, 2021

Source: Barb, www.barb.co.uk

Key terms

average issue readership (AIR) the number of people who have read or looked at an edition of a newspaper or magazine

average programme stream (APS) measures both live streaming and on-demand viewing, as well as downloads that are watched offline

click-throughs viewing of deeper website content

clicks viewing of the homepage of a website

engagement click-throughs or other interaction with a page or other digital content

Google Analytics market analysis of a website's performance

National Readership Survey (NRS) provides audience research for print advertising trading in the UK

Ofcom the Office of Communications; the government-approved regulatory and competition authority for the broadcasting, telecommunications and postal industries in the UK

on-demand viewing viewing a channel or provider's content outside the traditional schedule

---

average programme stream (APS), which measures both live streaming and **on-demand viewing**, as well as downloads that are watched offline.

In the case of radio, ratings are measured by an organisation known as **Radio Joint Audience Research (RAJAR)**. The methodology of RAJAR involves the use of listening diaries, in which a large number of listeners record their radio listening over a period of a week all year round. RAJAR tells us that radio listening is less varied than television consumption, with most listeners on average listening to a maximum of three radio stations. Interestingly, RAJAR research in 2023 shows that 74 per cent of the population listen to digital radio with 24 per cent of these listeners accessing audio media online. [Source: RAJAR]

Apply it

Keep a diary for one week of your television consumption. If possible, include the viewing of other family members. Count each episode viewed as a separate unit of viewing. At the end of the week, research where each programme originated, and convert the information into a percentage of your household's viewing.

Circulation tends to refer more specifically to print media, and the amount of units sold – or, in the case of free publications, distributed – of a particular print product. Another key measure is **readership**. The **National Readership Survey (NRS)** measures the readership of newspapers and magazines using a currency known as **average issue readership (AIR)**.

This information, indicates rather than counts how large the audience is but is still used by advertisers to inform their decisions about placement of advertisements within publications.

In digital media, circulation can be counted in terms of views or **clicks** and **click-throughs**, and the majority of web hosting services, from blogs to social media business sites, offer detailed breakdowns of the performance of web content. A popular blog can gain over 100,000 clicks per month. Performance can also be measured in terms of:

- **reach** – how many people are aware of the content
- views – how many people click on the content to look at it
- **engagement** – how many people interact in some way with the content.

Google Analytics is another tool used by many digital advertisers to assess how their web content might be performing, and is used to improve targeting of content and rate of click-throughs.

Every year in August, **Ofcom** publishes a very useful document called the *Communications Market Report*. This document provides a statistical examination of what media forms people of all ages are consuming. It offers breakdowns by factors such as age and gender, providing important evidence of evolving consumption patterns, which are invaluable both to industry and media researchers.

Given the hugely profitable nature of media production, it is unsurprising that there are many independent marketing companies regularly commissioning paid-for reports of mass media sectors.

Although the contemporary media landscape sometimes seems to be shifting in its dynamics day by day, many of these changes are subtle, with audiences being reluctant to replace traditional media overnight – they would rather add to it.

CHAPTER 7 MEDIA INDUSTRIES

All media producers try to increase the circulation of their product as this will help maximise their profit. Advertising and marketing is an important part of the process, with some media industries spending vast sums of money on the creation of promotional material. Spending money doesn't guarantee success, but without promotion audiences won't be aware of the product. Attracting the attention of the audience and getting them to discuss and share content about the product is another way to increase circulation.

Apply it

Research the summer blockbuster films of 2023, *Barbie* and *Oppenheimer*.

1 Who funded these productions?
2 Who distributed the films?
3 What type of conventional marketing strategies did they use?
4 How did social media amplify the awareness of the two films?
5 What made the opening weekend of these two films significant in terms of their box-office success?

Apply it

Explore the NRS website (www.nrs.co.uk). Prepare a 1,000-word report on the work of the organisation. This can be sequenced using the website's own subheadings if you wish. Include a section on the readership habits of your own family and/or friends.

Apply it

Research and write a 500-word case study on the journey from commissioning to broadcast of a popular TV programme you enjoy that has a global reach.

a Which aspects of the process do you believe to be common to other products in this media sector?
b What can you find out about the key players in the distribution chain?
c How does it add to your understanding of the way that media producers get products to the right audiences around the world?

■ Globalised patterns of circulation and distribution

Audiences may find accessing products easier in a globalised media market due to more streamlined services and provision of content. One of the most powerful arguments in favour of the communications revolution brought about by the internet is that it leads to increased **democratisation of the mass media**. In theory, more diverse global audiences' opinions are heard more powerfully due to the prevalence of internet forums, fan sites and other unofficial channels of responses to texts. Conversely, they may find there is less diversity of products available to consume, as some products naturally fall by the wayside. However, some media companies may continue to offer riskier or less profitable lines on the basis that failure of one product for a huge parent company can be absorbed by the organisation as a whole with little impact.

Large, Western media company output is often readily available through communications infrastructures around the world. The result is often a sidelining of **indigenous media production**: products that are culturally and linguistically produced by a particular culture or nation. **Domestic markets** without the equivalent economic buoyancy are often hard-hit by US television and film, which tends to have high production values and budgets, making it

Key terms

Radio Joint Audience Research (RAJAR) the organisation that measures radio listening figures in the UK

reach the amount of people who see a link or site, for example in a newsfeed or search engine result

readership the approximate number of consumers estimated to read a print media text

democratisation of the mass media increased ability of the audience to have their voices heard, and to interact with media producers and content

domestic markets the local audience for a media product

indigenous media production media products made by and for a particular culture or nation

7.2 Distribution and circulation: what they are and why they vary across media

185

Key terms

broadcasting licence required for transmission of television or radio services

quota imposing a restriction on certain kinds of foreign media imports

difficult for domestic markets to compete. A good example of this is some of the lengthy US-based television drama series that become popular via VOD services. Some countries may respond to this by restricting the availability of content through a **quota** method. However, the global nature of streaming distributors means that programmes can find an international audience.

△ *Squid Game*, made in South Korea, attracted a massive, international audience

7.3 Issues of ownership and control

Who owns a media production company, the influence they or their advertisers choose to exert on content, and the values held by the organisation can have an enormous impact on the media we consume. Many people are familiar with the political influences that occur in newspapers, and their selection of certain news and angles often based on ownership and bias.

■ Power Without Responsibility

In their 1997 book *Power Without Responsibility*, James Curran and Jean Seaton explored the huge power yielded by owners of the large press groups, such as News International (now News UK). The book has been updated a number of times, and is considered significant in understanding the relationship between who owns the mass media and their output. The authors also discuss public service broadcasting, and who it is really answerable to, as well as web ownership and controls, and considers who will control the future of new media.

Some of the authors' key ideas are as follows:

- The mass media is driven and influenced by political agendas that are difficult to separate from other economic influences, but it often dovetails with them. These are perhaps the most obvious when we look at newspaper reportage, and the relationships between media conglomerates and politicians. However, it is also evident in television news and in competition for **broadcasting licences** as well as infiltrating many other areas, including the influence of politics on themes and subject matter of documentaries and fictional media texts.

- Technological change in the newspaper industry in production methods, where processes are increasingly digitised, has reduced the power of journalists, with stories that displease editors or owners easily pulled and replaced at short notice.
- There had been a loosening of regulations on media industries since the 1980s, reflecting the neo-liberal political values that prioritised individual freedom of choice and the power of the free market.
- Technological optimism in the late 1990s reinforced these attitudes to the **deregulation** of the media, and the process was accelerated. The removal of controls over ownership is an issue because it can lead to concentration of ownership and domination of the market by a few big media organisations.
- The new media market has tended to feature many of the same big brands that dominated old media, which still account for some of the most visited websites. **Globalisation** has simply allowed corporations to become bigger and more powerful.
- Web 2.0 is complicated by the takeover of some initially independently owned companies, with audiences and consumers often unaware that sites and services they use and perhaps believe to be 'independent' are in fact owned by the same few corporations.
- The rise of new media is thought to be associated with a decline in quality across the mass media, which affects every sector, including public service broadcasting.
- The web is a place where dissenting voices can still be heard, but also where big businesses can operate in a less visible way, since most politicians are more focused on national political and business affairs.
- The web is still a **contested space**. Big business could yet be counter-balanced by the strength of web users united in particular activities and with more socially responsible attitudes to the potential of the web.

Key terms

contested space with reference to the internet, the ideological battleground between users and large media conglomerates

deregulation reduction in governmental controls over media ownership

globalisation the breakdown of national boundaries in the distribution and circulation of media products

Leveson Report the report on press behaviour and practices published after the Leveson Inquiry, which was set up after accusations that some newspapers were using illegal methods, including phone hacking, to gather information for stories

EXAMPLE: Journalistic ethics – the Leveson Inquiry

During the phone-hacking scandal, high-profile employees of tabloid newspaper brand News International (now News UK) were summoned to appear at the Leveson Inquiry in 2011–12. The outcome of the inquiry, the **Leveson Report**, made huge criticisms about the way in which some newspapers disregarded journalistic ethics, and it led to the withdrawal of the Press Complaints Commission and its replacement by the Independent Press Standards Organisation (IPSO) in an attempt to more powerfully regulate the industry's activities.

▷ Lord Justice Brian Leveson chaired the inquiry into the culture, practice and ethics of the British press, which became known as the Leveson Inquiry

7.3 Issues of ownership and control

Apply it

OKIDO, a small independent magazine for children, was started in 2007 with just £5,000 of the owners' personal money. It has since gone on to gain a cult following in the UK, including a digitally animated spin-off kids' television programme on CBeebies, *Messy Goes to OKIDO* (2015–23).

Research the magazine. What does it offer compared with more mainstream competitors? How has the magazine managed to survive and grow its brand as an independent in a tough industry?

Include some print media analysis (for example, of the front cover) and your research findings to to help you to draw your own conclusions.

Key terms

conglomerates huge media organisations made up of several companies all with the same ownership

diversification a feature of many media organisations as they try to increase their penetration of wider markets

horizontal integration merger of media companies at a similar stage of development or who offer similar services or products

media concentration where mergers and takeovers of media companies by large corporations leads to a small number of companies controlling a large proportion of the media

vertical integration acquisition of one company in the production chain of another that offers a different service

■ Media conglomerates

As new technologies have emerged in a globalised world, so the number of media **conglomerates** has increased. Large media companies merge with or buy out other media producers to increase their market share and reduce competition. Where companies offer similar services or products, this kind of merger is known as **horizontal integration**. A globalised, conglomerate-run mass media is often viewed negatively by media commentators. Many view them as doing very little to act in the interests of choice and a buoyant, interesting and genuinely competitive market. This is also referred to as **media concentration**.

Vertical integration is another process that describes an alternative model for the merging of companies. In the case of vertical integration, we would usually see a company that owns one stage of media production acquiring others that offer different services within the production chain. This ensures smooth operation over the entire process, from product development through to distribution to audiences. Media companies that merge with one another benefit from the diverse experience they have, and can pool their knowledge to help target audiences in a more effective way. Today, much of this focusing process naturally concerns the improved targeting of advertising in order to increase its effectiveness and drive up revenue for the organisation as a whole.

Diversification is the term used when a media company adds to their core business and branches out into other areas. Diversification can be seen at work in most types of cross-platform marketing and production. It is also a common practice that results from any of the above behaviours in the formation of conglomerates. Profit is maximised and risk minimised by having a presence in more than one area of the market. It is a defining quality of modern, large media organisations.

Media convergence refers to the changes that have taken place in the way in which media industries operate. Media companies use a range of technologies to broaden the way they make and distribute their products. The changing social and cultural uses of the media and the appearance of innovative new products and ways of consuming them is a feature of convergence. Convergence is only possible on the scale we see today because of communications technologies.

■ Alternative and independent media

Not all mass media production is owned by large corporations. Despite the challenges presented by the competition with such huge conglomerates, some **independent** media production companies continue to thrive. This is often because their unique position gives them an insight into the target market, which may be ignored by larger companies far more driven by a profit motive. This allows them to take risks that may not be taken by larger companies, who might view it as a waste of their time to cater to a niche audience. Some of these small media companies remain true to their independent values, whereas others are quickly bought out by larger media companies and continue to exist in name only under the umbrella of the parent company.

Alternative and independent media are not the same thing, although the two terms are sometimes used together. Alternative suggests that the content of the media being offered provides some kind of ideological challenge to the mainstream, adopts a different aesthetic or has cult value. Independent media companies may have output that does this, but they may also simply be smaller companies freed from the constraints of conglomerate ownership and agendas.

It is not surprising that some smaller media producers seek to offer a product that might challenge mainstream ideologies, or content that appeals to a niche audience whose values fail to coincide with much of the mass media content available to them. Doing so can enable stories to be told or perspectives shared that previously would not have been considered commercially viable.

> **Key terms**
>
> **alternative** usually media products that offer some kind of alternative perspective to the mainstream
> **independent** media companies not owned by larger organisations
> **media convergence** bringing different technologies together to make media products available across a range of platforms to provide easy access and extend the user experience

EXAMPLE: The journey of an independently made documentary from production to distribution

O Outro Lado do Cartão-Postal (*The Other Side of the Postcard*) is an independent documentary about human rights in Rio de Janiero, Brazil. The following is an extract from an interview given for this book by the director, David Morris of Script2Screen Media.

We had a budget of about £22,500. With this money we spent about £3,000 on equipment, £5,000 on flights and insurance, £7,000 on music licenses and legal fees, £1,500 on crew fees (only three people received payment, everyone else volunteered), £2,000 on artwork and printing costs and then a final (ongoing) £4,000 on festival submissions and marketing.

With funding (which we were rejected for countless times) we could have done a cinema deal in Brazil with the Odeon. Due to music license fees, classification (where your film is given an age rating – which costs £9/min in the UK by the way) we couldn't take this path. In the end, we took an online distribution deal with TV4E in LA which included an Amazon [Prime] release. As well as this, more money would have meant more time on location and better kit. This may not have made the film any better, but it would have given us the chance to perhaps access the favela more and spend more time with our subjects.

[The documentary was promoted] mostly through social media. Our festival run began in June 2016 and will run for two years. This will also help generate a lot of interest. In Brazil, we have done a lot of private screenings to politicians, professors and human rights organisations. In the UK, it's been a bit more mainstream, looking at radio and news interviews, as well as reviews, articles and print interviews for what feels like a million different publications. We did a live interview on a news channel in Brazil that went out to 12 million people.

△ Rio de Janeiro, Brazil

Apply it

Using the interview with David Morris from the Example box above, sum up the advantages and disadvantages of being a small media producer operating in a global context.

If you have access to it, watch the documentary.

1. Does it have mainstream appeal?
2. Does it challenge dominant thinking about the situation in Rio?
3. Did it educate you about some of the social issues faced by people in the favelas?
4. Do you think that having a lower budget matters when producing this kind of media text?

7.4 How the commercial or not-for-profit nature of media organisations shapes the content they produce

Mass media production can be categorised in different ways. Primarily, the distinction can be drawn between commercial media organisations, which are the vast majority, and those that are not run for profit. The commercial nature of the majority of media organisations should not be forgotten when reading the content they produce, since this can make a significant difference to output.

■ How do we pay for the media we consume?

It's worth considering the number of examples of ways in which we might pay for the media we consume, and how this adds up in terms of the overall cost of media consumption per head (see Table 7.1). Don't forget, technology and wifi/data are hidden costs of media access.

CHAPTER 7 MEDIA INDUSTRIES

▽ Table 7.1 Ways in which we purchase the media we consume

Purchasing methods available	Commercial media product
One-off purchase (physical copies)	Magazines
	Newspapers
	Film (DVD, cinema ticket)
One-off (digital download)	Computer games
	Podcasts
	Music
	Film (download)
Subscriptions (physical media) via: • post • regular order with newsagent	Magazines
	Newspapers
Subscriptions (digital media) • monthly • yearly Subscription service per package	Video-on-demand, such as Netflix, Now TV or Amazon Prime
	Computer games
	Podcast
	Music
	Film
	Magazines
	Newspapers
	Satellite or cable television access to additional channel packages
In-app or in-game purchases	Computer games
	Social media
Licence fee to watch and/or record BBC services on any device, and other channels on TV sets	Freeview television/radio

Apply it

Work out all the paid-for media consumption in your household.

1. How much does your family spend on media entertainment in a year?
2. Which services do you think provide the best value for money?
3. Which other media entertainment do you think you or your family might use in the future?

The advertising contract

Modern app developers have recognised and used to their advantage the simple fact that many consumers will pay *not to have to consume advertising*. They exploit this by offering ad-free services at a premium to compensate the producer for the loss of revenue. Some companies offering subscription services were initially horrified at the thought of ad-skipping technologies, on television in particular, and over the years, a number of legal cases have been brought against the designers of software and hardware that permitted the consumer to skip ads. The arguments have varied, from copyright infringement in the re-broadcasting of material to the suggestion that the consumer entered into a contractual agreement when purchasing the subscription – and part of the agreement was that the advertising was part of the package. It soon became clear, though, that an audience bombarded with advertising in almost every part of their consumption relishes the choice of ad-free services. This also benefits services such as Netflix and Amazon Prime, since the only realistic alternative to advertising revenue to sustain a company is subscription services, or a combination of subscription and paying to eliminate advertising content.

Some cultural commentators argue that the expansion of choice and proliferation of TV channels has led to a degradation in the quality of television programming, and that rather than engaging with the production

Apply it

Keep an advertising diary for a day. List all the advertising you encounter across the entire range of media you consume, in your local environment and during your daily routines such as journeys. Use your findings to write a 350-word first blog entry reflecting on how teens are exposed to advertising.

7.4 How the commercial or not-for-profit nature of media organisations shapes content

of high-quality, original and exciting programme production, many channel owners opt instead to fill their schedules with cheaply produced, imported or repetitive content. Channels may also stick with safe content they know sells in order to attract advertisers to their services.

Print media audiences, particularly for magazines, are used to a large proportion of the item they paid for being taken up by advertising space. Content in magazines is often shaped around that month's advertisers, with linked topics receiving mentions in the **editorial content** itself, and articles known as **advertorials** making a regular appearance in newspaper supplements and magazines. These often promote goods through depiction of an aspirational lifestyle associated with fitness, luxury, beauty routines and so on.

Advertising rapidly becomes the norm on almost any new digital platform that begins advertisement-free. Some user-generated sites and web hosts use models where a percentage of revenue can be made by the individual whose contributions or sites gain the most traffic, and are therefore most valuable to advertisers. This encourages an acceptance of advertising among digital users who also generate content. Many social networking sites now personalise advertising, using data from our **digital footprint** – other sites we visit online as well as content we interact with on their platform – to generate strongly targeted adverts.

Synergy, a term from media marketing that can be used in a number of ways, is often used to describe co-promotional behaviours of companies that work together in economic relationships to maximise the impact of a particular campaign. The result benefits all parties involved. Like convergence, synergy has been enabled by communications and the digital revolution. The idea behind most campaigns that demonstrate synergy is that the message to the consumer is maximised due to increased exposure.

Public service broadcasting

Public service broadcasting (PSB) exists in some form in many parts of the world. It is difficult to define, with slightly different models of funding, purpose, broadcasting model and so on being used in different places, and even within regions in the UK. Public service broadcasters exist in the public rather than commercial sphere – that is, they exist to serve the public interest, not only to generate an income.

The BBC is held in high esteem worldwide for its high-quality programming, but it is not the only public service broadcaster in the UK. In 1982, Channel 4 television first transmitted, having been authorised by the government to offer an alternative channel whose remit was specifically to cater for minority audiences and to offer more niche content, such as from the arts. Unlike the BBC, however, it is self-funding, receiving no public money and generating much of its income via advertising.

Public service broadcasters in the UK have a **remit**, which is a contract they must fulfil for their audience identified by the government, and on which the conditions of its broadcasting licence are dependent. The overall mission statement for the BBC is familiar to many members of the public, and is derived from the founder of the BBC, John Reith's, original vision:

To enrich people's lives with programmes and services that inform, educate and entertain.

> **Key terms**
>
> **advertorial** an advert presented in the style of an article
>
> **digital footprint** the stored information on a person's online activity
>
> **editorial content** original content written for magazines, distinct from advertising
>
> **public service broadcasting (PSB)** broadcasting intended to benefit the public
>
> **remit** the service provided by a public service broadcaster for its viewers
>
> **synergy** mutually beneficial cross-promotional strategies used by media companies

EXAMPLE: The BBC Charter

The BBC Charter, the set of conditions from the government under which it is permitted to broadcast, contains six public purposes:

1. Sustaining citizenship and civil society
2. Promoting education and learning
3. Stimulating creativity and cultural excellence
4. Representing the UK, its nations, regions and communities
5. Bringing the UK to the world and the world to the UK
6. In promoting its other purposes, helping to deliver to the public the benefit of emerging communications technologies and services and, in addition, taking a leading role in the switchover to digital television (www.bbc.co.uk/bbctrust/governance/tools_we_use/public_purposes.html).

Separate remits are then provided for each channel, showing how each contributes to each of the purposes. Governance of the BBC is provided by the BBC Board. The Board has members that include political appointments and its role is to hold the BBC to account over fulfilment of its remits and public purposes.

> **Key terms**
>
> **BBC Charter** the conditions upon which the BBC's licence depends
> **governance** the internal regulation of the BBC
> **Independent Press Standards Organisation (IPSO)** the largest independent regulator of the newspaper and magazine industry in the UK
> **media literacy** the ability to critically analyse and interpret media communications
> **public purposes** the aims of the BBC as an organisation

The media landscape has changed so much since the simpler days of a handful of television channels, among which the defining qualities and purpose of the BBC stood out. It will be a continual struggle for the organisation to redefine its relevance in a climate where similar content can be found across the many commercial channels. Its very existence is becoming an ideological battleground for politicians struggling to agree on what the future of PSB in the UK should look like. Other media industries perceive the public funding received by the BBC as giving it an unfair advantage over those commercial companies that compete for advertising revenue.

> **Apply it**
>
> Choose five contrasting programmes from across the BBC schedules that help fulfil at least three of the six purposes identified in the BBC Charter. Write around 100 words about each programme, explaining how it helps to fulfil the BBC's aims as a PSB. You don't necessarily have to view each one, as long as you are confident about its content.

> **Apply it**
>
> Source three news articles from different online news providers about the BBC, preferably covering different stories. Write a reflective paragraph to accompany each one, outlining the topic and content of the story, what it suggests to the reader about the BBC as an organisation, whether there is any evidence of a bias towards or against the organisation in the way the story has been presented, or whether the story seems neutral. Use at least two quotations from each article to support your points.

7.5 Regulation of media consumption in the UK

Media industries are motivated by profit, but the way they make money has to be within the law, and different media forms have to abide by specific regulations related to the way they produce and distribute their products. Regulation aims to ensure that media producers are accountable for how they create their products and the potential impact they have. While modern audiences have a level of media literacy, regulation protects audiences from misleading or potentially dangerous content.

Media regulators have been set up in each media sector. The main ones in the UK are:

- **Ofcom** – regulates communications including broadcast and online media
- **Independent Press Standards Organisation (IPSO)** and **Impress** – regulate newspaper and other print media

- **Advertising Standards Authority (ASA)** – regulates advertising
- **British Board of Film Censors (BBFC)** and **Pan European Game Information (PEGI)** – not regulators as such but they offer age-limiting certificates for films and games
- **Video Standards Council (VSC)** – responsible for age ratings being applied to computer games.

Media industries are bound by law in the production, content, distribution and marketing of their products. For example, journalists investigating a story are not allowed to break the law to find out information. Representations in media products must not incite violence or break decency laws, as these are criminal acts. If media producers break the law, companies and individuals can be charged and punished within the legal system. However, laws do not always offer audiences full protection from harm that can come from the media and so regulators have been set up to create professional rules that aim to protect the public.

Not all media regulators have a legal power to enforce their codes, instead relying on consensus within the industry to serve the audience in a way that is in keeping with the spirit of regulation. After all, the codes created by most organisations are written with the best interests of the audience in mind, and in the majority of cases there is no vested interest on the part of an individual media producer in breaking the code. Codes are also designed to allow for an element of controversial and ground-breaking publication and broadcasting, and this is often carefully considered by media producers who produce such texts. Since broadcasting licences in the UK for radio and television are issued by Ofcom, in extreme circumstances an organisation could lose its broadcasting privileges if it failed to conform to Ofcom's broadcasting code, although imposition of a large fine is more usual.

Tabloid newspapers, however, have a history of publishing material that contravened the Press Complaints Commission (PCC) Code of Conduct. It was partly for this reason that, in the wake of the phone-hacking scandal that culminated in 2011 in the Leveson Enquiry (see page 187), the PCC was reformed as IPSO, which released a new **Editors' Code of Conduct**, shifting the emphasis to clearly making the editor of a publication legally responsible for the content published.

Consumer opinion about media regulation and **censorship** covers a wide spectrum, as with any public issue. More liberally minded consumers tend to argue that, in a media-saturated world and the age of digital proliferation, it is up to the audience to educate themselves and to **self-censor** content they are likely to find offensive. The difficulty with this argument is that it relies upon everyone being able (or wanting) to decide what constitutes media content that is appropriate for them, being able to see through misleading content and so on.

Heavy censoring of the mass media is deployed in many countries where media content is carefully managed in order not to promulgate material considered to be in some way:

- damaging to the interests of the state
- inconsistent with religious moral standards
- otherwise considered subversive.

Some global media franchises already concede to these countries, with heavily edited versions of their material being shown in some parts of the world to suit local laws and interpretations of taste and decency. Such state control

Key terms

censorship the blocking of certain media material from public consumption

Editors' Code of Conduct IPSO's regulatory framework

self-censor action taken by the individual audience member to select media for consumption that does not offend or otherwise impact on them negatively

Apply it

Produce a visually appealing infographic designed to introduce the work of media regulators in the UK to an audience of 10- to 14-year-olds.

CHAPTER 7 MEDIA INDUSTRIES

takes a high level of investment to maintain and involves not only controlling the point of distribution but also the point of access to mass media. Often, people who attempt to distribute or access forbidden material are dealt with harshly.

■ Regulation in the UK

All regulatory bodies for the mass media in the UK are directly contactable by the public. This process being easy to undertake is really important for issues of fairness and transparency.

Television, radio, Ofcom and the watershed

Established in 2001, Ofcom, the main body responsible for the regulation of broadcast media content in the UK, is an umbrella organisation that regulates all broadcast material in the mass media. This was previously the job of a number of different regulators. In addition to issuing licences to channels based in the UK, it maintains a broadcast code, which all media channels licenced in the UK are expected to adhere to. It is a key stipulation of Ofcom's **Broadcast Code** that content broadcast between the hours of 5.30am and 9pm must be suitable for viewing by children. After 9pm more adult content can be broadcast. This is known as the **watershed**.

In the case of radio, content unsuitable for children cannot be broadcast at times they are most likely to be listening – this refers mainly to the mornings before school starts. The code includes all the areas that have historically been concerns of regulators, which would be familiar to most people – depictions of violence, substance abuse, sexual content and offensive language controls.

Regulation of advertising

The Advertising Standards Authority (ASA) has existed in the UK since 1962, and regulates both print and broadcast advertising across the media. It also offers guidance on pop-up and banner ads on UK websites.

In the case of television and radio, the ASA is supported by its **co-regulator** Ofcom, which is able to enforce judgments on advertising content should the company responsible for any contravention refuse to withdraw the content from publication or broadcast. In this case, Ofcom can impose a fine or, since individual licensed TV channels are responsible for their advertising output, pursue this line. Print advertisers are likely to withdraw any adverts voluntarily that are investigated by the ASA, even if a formal ban is not imposed.

> **Key terms**
>
> **Broadcast Code** Ofcom's regulatory framework for broadcast services
>
> **co-regulator** the sharing of some aspects of regulation by more than one organisation
>
> **watershed** in the UK, the point (9pm) at which content of a more adult nature may be shown in a television schedule

EXAMPLE: 'Are you beach body ready?', Protein World (2015)

Protein World's '*Are you beach body ready?*' billboard advertisement depicted a glamorous woman with model proportions and attracted many complaints by people who felt that it promoted an unrealistic, idealised body image. This complaint was not upheld; the ruling did, however, find that the nutritional benefits of the product being claimed by the company could not be adequately proven, and as a result the advert was banned on the basis that it was misleading.

The ASA is also responsible for advertising content on UK-hosted website pop-ups and banner advertisements. This is proving the hardest area in which to enforce regulation. Because of this, the ASA now includes on its website a list of 'non-compliant' web-based companies – those that have been asked repeatedly to change their advertising content but do not. In the ASA's report in 2016, web advertisements attracted the most individual complaints, although by volume television still had the highest number.

> **Apply it**
>
> Write a 250-word summary of three recent adverse judgements by IPSO, and another 250-word piece on three recent subjects of rulings by the ASA that interest you. These can be readily accessed through the main websites of these organisations. You may use extracts from the actual wording on the websites, but make sure these are presented clearly as quotes, connected by your own wording outlining each case.

Regulation of print and news media

Print media publications in the UK are regulated by a body known as the Independent Press Standards Organisation (IPSO). IPSO was set up in 2014, and is responsible for ensuring that editorial standards outlined in its Editors' Code of Practice are adhered to and that journalism standards are maintained.

Any publication that is subject to an adverse adjudication must correct the facts prominently in a future publication. Complaints about the presentation of news stories in newspapers constitute the vast majority of the adjudications listed online for public inspection. The majority of upheld complaints concern accuracy, where something has been reported in a misleading way.

Contraventions of the code are less likely to occur for magazines. This could either be because their content tends to be less controversial in terms of what is covered by the code, or due to the nature of the monthly, weekly or even quarterly print cycle. Longer periods for legal checking and consideration of the code may result in fewer complaints.

7.6 New technologies and media regulation

Internet-based content is very difficult to regulate. Some householders may choose to install additional controls at the entry point for communications to supplement measures taken by some Internet Service Providers (ISPs). It is not uncommon to use a proxy server or virtual private network (VPN) to bypass many kinds of filter.

Since 2014, the majority of the main fixed line ISPs have responded to a government request to filter potentially harmful content at source, but smaller ISPs have either struggled to implement filtering at source, or seem reluctant to do so. Since legislation does not currently require it, this situation continues.

Ofcom also published a series of recommendations, as far back as 2004, requiring the blocking of unsuitable content to under-18s on smartphones, which are adhered to by most providers. These schemes are not without their critics; among them are some groups who complain of **overblocking**, where sites overly aggressively filter certain search terms and therefore restrict access to sources of information about issues with which people may be seeking help. In November 2023, Ofcom became legally responsible for the regulation of online content. Their approaches to this are still being developed but their role will be to ensure media companies (e.g. Instagram, X) are responding appropriately to user complaints and concerns. Ofcom will not be responding to complaints themselves. The platforms have a legal responsibility to act to keep users safe and Ofcom monitor their systems and approaches to this.

VOD services and subscription packages usually offer different password-protected user IDs and broad preference systems to help ensure that children are only able to select from appropriate material. It is increasingly common for mainstream news websites to preface their video content with warnings where images are graphic or potentially disturbing.

Social media sites are largely expected to regulate their content themselves, and given the huge volume of traffic that passes through the sites, it is unsurprising that unsuitable content is often only brought to the attention of moderators when it is reported by other site members. Asking for the confirmation of the user's age gives site owners a defence – they are offering content suitable for a certain age range because that is who they believe their membership to be.

Some recent arguments surrounding censorship of social media sites have centred on videos playing automatically. Many sites are improving the algorithm to improve the user's ability to self-censor by requesting not to view similar content again. Adults may be capable of doing this, and have the confidence to tailor their experience to one that suits their own sensibilities, but younger users subject to peer pressure or just natural curiosity may lack the skills or inclination to do this.

EXAMPLE: YouTube's community guidelines

YouTube, in common with many sites that consist primarily of user-generated content, publishes **community guidelines**. These emphasise the collective responsibility that users of the site share with the site administrators. Guidelines cover nudity and sexual content, graphic violence, hate speech, misleading material, spam, threats, copyright and harmful or dangerous content.

The challenges are the haphazard nature of relying on users to flag content as inappropriate coupled with the sheer volume of uploads. The threat of removal from the site may be enough to deter some users but not all.

Apply it

Research and write a 1,000-word opinion piece for an online technology and culture website on the problems presented by:

- self-regulation of digital culture
- the measures that already exist to try and protect users of new media against harmful content
- self-censorship strategies useful for users of all new media.

Use at least one source found using Google Scholar, and try to include a good balance of researched facts (which you should credit in the main body of the article) and a clear personal voice.

The **Internet Service Providers' Association (ISPA)** is a trade association, formed in 1995, that represents its members. As such, its methods and purpose differ from what we usually understand by media regulation. Its code does cover some of the standard practice we might expect to see in other regulatory codes.

Apply it

Find out about and collect together the parental controls available on a range of VOD and popular subscription TV packages.

Apply it

Research the community guidelines and reporting procedures for a social media or user-driven site that you use. How effective, in your personal experience, are these guidelines? Do the majority of users abide by them? Write a 500-word case study introducing the site, how it aims to self-regulate, the role of moderation in the running of the site and any other interesting aspects of your findings.

Key terms

community guidelines means by which some websites ask their users to contribute to self-regulation

Internet Service Providers' Association (ISPA) the UK's trade association for providers of internet services

overblocking internet filtering that is considered overly restrictive

7.6 New technologies and media regulation

The ISPA has a sub-committee, which is responsible for internet safety, but this group does not deal directly with complaints from the public, instead supporting other groups. For example, it supported the founding of the **Internet Watch Foundation (IWF)**, a charitable foundation that works to identify online images and videos of sexual abuse and has a national hotline for receiving anonymous reports from the public.

We are left with a situation where ISPs agree in principle through their membership of the ISPA to attempt to regulate certain areas of internet content – and are encouraged to do so both by copyright holders attempting to protect their property and the government. However, they are not penalised for failing to do so. Most of their efforts necessarily surround engagement with controlling public access to more extreme content and preventing copyright infringement.

Computer games in the UK are certificated by the **Video Standards Council (VSC)**. This is a non-profit-making company set up in 1989 at the request of the government to control video and DVD supply, and to make sure retailers and rental outlets understood their responsibilities in the supply of age-rated products. Under the name **Games Rating Authority (GRA)**, this organisation applies the **Pan-European Game Information (PEGI)** age certification, which is an agreed standard across Europe. Importantly, the GRA does not have to agree with a rating awarded to games across Europe, but can veto a game's entry into the country under unusual circumstances, meaning it is not legal to distribute it.

The PEGI system uses a methodology similar to that of film certification, where a game has certain instances of types of violence or behaviour and depictions. The actual certification definitions are necessarily broad, and certificates are issued that offer a fair interpretation.

Key terms

content labels additional information provided by PEGI as part of its rating service

Games Rating Authority (GRA) a division of the VSC that applies the PEGI rating to computer games

Internet Watch Foundation (IWF) a charitable organisation that works to remove images and videos of sexual abuse from the internet

Pan European Game Information (PEGI) the European video game content rating system which helps European consumers make informed decisions when purchasing video games or apps via the use of age recommendations and content descriptors

Video Standards Council (VSC) administrates the PEGI system of age rating for games

Example

The 'We Dare' PEGI controversy

In 2012, *We Dare*, a party game release for the Nintendo Wii and Playstation, was given a PEGI 12 rating. The online advertising for the product, however, was highly sexually suggestive and targeted the adult audience the game was, in fact, intended to reach. The *Sun* newspaper broke the story in the UK, causing its makers Ubisoft to withdraw the adverts due to negative publicity, and also take the decision not to sell the game in the UK or US. PEGI defended the age rating given to the game, since it assessed only the game's content, not how it was advertised.

Some games that could be considered unsuitable for children by some adults would pass a PEGI 12 certificate. To assist parents in making suitability decisions, eight **content labels** are also included, which cover the categories of sex, violence, discrimination, online, drugs, fear, gambling and bad language.

As is the case with films, after the point of sale or access, it is largely up to parental supervision to ensure that age restrictions are adhered to.

Apply it

Using a word cluster generator such as www.wordclouds.com, create a word cloud for each of the PEGI age suitability ratings by inputting key words from at least five ratings summaries for different games.

■ Industry case studies

The following industry case studies exemplify a range of ideas that are included in AQA's enabling ideas and deal with context issues related to each form. This focus on different media producers identifies the effects they have within their industry.

You should consider how these ideas apply to the Close Study Product case studies you prepare for the exams.

CHAPTER 7 MEDIA INDUSTRIES

The case studies focus on:

- the rise of digital producers and distributors
- Netflix: disrupting TV production, distribution and regulation
- Marvel and diversification
- news and social media.

> See Chapter 11: The examinations for more information about the exam requirements.

7.7 The rise of digital producers and distributors

Recent technological changes have offered production opportunities to people from outside the media industries who have developed their own methods of production, distribution and circulation, which rival and sometimes outperform the traditional media industries.

The ability to access production technology that is both cheap and easy to use has radically changed our ways of thinking about who gets to create media products. Anyone with a digital camera and access to the internet can create an Instagram or YouTube account. The rise of affordable and easy to access digital production technologies has removed the initial barrier to production that allowed media industries to maintain their powerful position in the past. Software gives self-taught and self-financed amateurs the ability to record and produce their own music, create 'TV shows', documentaries or fiction films that can be uploaded to video hosting sites, or create online 'magazines' on Wordpress or Instagram.

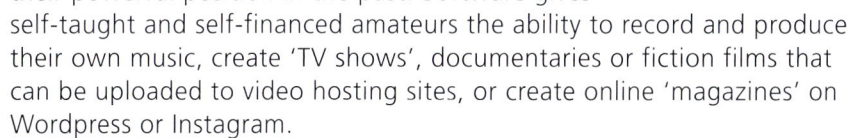

Internet-based distribution platforms are also widely available to amateur producers, allowing them to publish in the **public sphere**. Creating a Tik-Tok, Soundcloud or YouTube account takes very little specialist technical knowledge and once the accounts are populated with images, sound files or videos, the content has a potentially global reach. The internet has made the distribution of media products easier today than it has ever been and, in theory, amateur productions that are hosted online have the same **potential reach** as those hosted by the traditional media industries. These platforms are largely free for the user, as social media platforms rely on the data they receive about users and visitors to the site to create an income. Turow observes that users '*are being quietly peeked at, poked, analysed and tagged as they move through the online world*' (Turow cited in Hesmondhalgh, 2012). This data is sold to advertisers who wish to create specific targeted advertising – as Turow goes on to say; the '*goal is to find out how to activate individuals' buying impulses so they can sell us stuff more efficiently than ever before*'. Amateur media producers can generate an income based on the online browsing and purchasing habits of their audience. A term used for these amateur producers is 'prosumer' (see page 160) – they are both producers and consumers of the media.

Distribution today is the easiest part of the process. Circulation is, however, much harder – especially for amateur producers. Traditional institutions have the benefit of being known by audiences and so are often online destinations for media audiences. The challenge for non-traditional media producers is how to find audiences and attract them to their products. Modern content providers often need 'old media' to help them find wider and broader audiences.

Key terms

potential reach the possible extent of the circulation of a media product

public sphere a location where published work is available to the general public

EXAMPLE: The rise of digital producers – *Lights Out*, David F. Sandberg (2013)

The Swedish filmmaker David F. Sandberg created a short horror film in 2013 called *Lights Out* and uploaded it to Vimeo and YouTube. The film was made with a very low budget and it starred his wife. It was viewed by some people who began to discuss it on social media sites such as Reddit. This word of mouth created wider interest and the film was seen by a Hollywood producer, Lawrence Grey. Grey contacted Sandberg and bought the rights to the film. Grey was able to attract James Wan (the creator of *Saw* and *The Conjuring* series) as a producer for the project and this, plus the viral success of the short film, helped attract studio funding for production, marketing and distribution. Sandberg directed a full-length version of the film that was released in 2016; it cost $5 million to make and generated an income of $22 million in its opening weekend – a clear financial success.

Of course, this is an exception. A search on YouTube for a 'short horror film' brings up nearly eight million videos. The problem for independent producers is not making their products available to audiences, but in making audiences aware of their products. For every Sandberg there are thousands of filmmakers posting online that do not get a job offer from Hollywood.

EXAMPLE: Gleam Futures and online content providers

Gleam Futures is a management company that specialise in representing online content providers. An early client of theirs was Zoella, who became one the biggest YouTube success stories in the 2010s. Having professional management and being part of an organisation that specialises in promoting vloggers helped to maximise the potential for her success. Gleam Futures represents content producers who offer a diverse range of content. In some cases the content is the same as what would traditionally have been found on television, but often Gleam Futures' clients present formats and content that are specific to social media. As the media landscape has changed, the company has expanded into representing authors, speakers for live events and podcast production.

Gleam Futures' clients tend to produce Instagram, podcast and/or YouTube content. Signing to a company such as Gleam Futures not only gives content providers access to more professional technology and production crews, but Gleam Futures also promises relationships with the companies who will pay for advertising and promotion, helping the content providers maximise their income.

Successful social media producers have built their audiences over time and benefit from the viral nature of the spread of information online. Everyone who watches a video on YouTube is part of a social (media or non-media) network. Media producers want to make products that are not only appealing to the individual audience member but also encourage that audience member to share information about the product with their friends. If one viewer has a network of ten people and each of those people has a network of ten people, then one viewer quickly has the potential to link to 100 more and this can soon expand into thousands and millions of views. This can only work if the people watching feel compelled to share with their network though, so social media sites offer detailed analytics that identify who is watching each video and how they arrived on the channel.

Social media **influencers** are the same as **opinion leaders**, as identified by Katz & Lazarsfeld (2005). Influencers have access to a large number of people who follow their recommendations and who are able to create trends and promote products and services. Influencers are valuable to advertisers, as they can be used to help promote consumer products and events. Many social media 'stars' generate income by providing promotional space, becoming **brand ambassadors** and often marketing their own brand of lifestyle-related products (what Hearn calls 'the branded self' (Hearn cited in Hesmondhalgh, 2012)). Influencers are able to promote other media products, whether this is by reviewing games and recording **play-throughs**, or providing film reviews and/or music reviews.

△ A diagram illustrating how content marketing works

Figures from traditional celebrity culture, for example models (e.g. Cara Delevingne), singers (e.g. Selena Gomez), actors (e.g. Dwayne Johnson) and sports personalities (e.g. Ronaldo) have built massive followings on social media. Social media has also created non-traditional celebrities who become '**Instafamous**' or TikTok 'stars' (but do not have a following on other social media or fame in wider society, traditional media or the celebrity scene). They may be unsigned models, health and fitness trainers, comedians or lifestyle bloggers who attract large numbers of followers and whose followers actively engage with their social media posts.

The rise of digital media has had a major impact on audience behaviours and expectations. Traditional media producers are having to adapt to meet this new context to survive. Most media producers, both amateur and professional, rely on advertising revenue for an income. Traditional advertising used audience demographic information to target the placement of adverts. Online advertising is personalised, with the audience member's interests being tracked by cookies as they use the internet or apps. This online **surveillance** information can be sold by online media producers/social media platforms to provide advertising tailored to each audience member's personal interests.

Apply it

Search on the internet to find out which celebrity social media accounts (Instagram, TikTok, YouTube, X (formerly Twitter)) have the most followers.

Access these accounts and analyse the posts.

- How is the celebrity using social media to create a personal brand?
- Is there evidence of the social media account being used to market:
  - products created or endorsed by the celebrity?
  - other consumer products?

Apply it

How has social media and the ease of access to production and distribution technologies impacted on one of the following media industries:

- the music industry
- the gaming industry
- the film industry
- the magazine industry?

Key terms

brand ambassadors celebrities who are paid to represent a specific consumer product or service and its brand values

influencers people who have the power to lead others and sway their opinions and actions. It is now a marketing term that describes individuals who have large numbers of followers on social media, have gained a level of authority and are trusted by their followers. Influencers can communicate with large numbers of people and this means they are able to spread ideas and promote products

Instafamous fame generated by having a successful Instagram profile

opinion leaders people who have the ability to communicate their opinions to others and may influence opinions

personal brand the constructed image created by an individual in order to create an identifiable and specific 'personality' with a view to help promote the individual

play-throughs online videos that show a person playing a game from start to finish

surveillance the use of tracking technologies used by digital media which record audience actions

7.7 The rise of digital producers and distributors

7.8 Netflix: disrupting the TV industry

Netflix is the world's leading VOD subscription service. In 2013, Netflix began to commission production of its own original programming.

Netflix is an American company that was founded in 1998 as a DVD rental service. Its initial unique selling point was that rental DVDs were delivered and returned in the post. The company moved into online streaming of VOD in 2007. DVD sales were in decline and Netflix was able to use developments in broadband and internet infrastructure that made video streaming possible. Netflix stands at the forefront of convergence, as it can be accessed on televisions, smartphones, tablets and computers, with access being available using online software, apps, internet TV systems and games consoles.

Netflix was launched as an online streaming service in the UK in 2012. Since then, it has increased its customer numbers and in 2017 announced that it had reached 100 million global customers (Sweney, 2017). This had increased to 260 million by 2023. It has a global reach but is not available in China, Syria, Russia or North Korea. Despite brief losses in subscribers when prices were increased, this growth is not slowing. Over 9 million new users were added in Q4 of 2023 alone, their largest quarter to date.

Netflix is funded by the monthly fee paid by subscribers. The service provides a range of benefits to the customer including:

- instant availability of content
- portable availability of content (either when online or when downloaded to smartphones, tablets or laptops)
- access to products from a range of producers both domestic and foreign, in English and other languages
- access (often exclusively) to an increasing library of original programming and films
- home screens that are personalised with recommended content based on previous viewing history.

In the UK, audiences were already using VOD services including iPlayer (released 2007), The ITV Hub (released 2008, now called ITVX) and 4OD (launched in 2006 and now called Channel 4).

These on-demand services provided access to content bought or created by the broadcasting institution. The services were branded as 'catch up' services and were seen to be a secondary distribution channel where live broadcast was presumed to be the primary way an audience would access the content. VOD was promoted as a way to watch what may have been missed at the time of broadcast.

Netflix programming is not broadcast live, so streaming video online is used to circulate the material. Hesmondhalgh (2012) calls this **post-network television**.

The monthly cost of a Netflix subscription in 2023 ranged from £6.99 to £15.99, with the increasing cost offering the ability to watch content on multiple screens at the same time and access to **ultra HD** quality images. Netflix's income is mainly generated by subscribers, so its business model is unlike other **commercial television** content providers who look mostly to advertising to generate an income. Netflix seeks to attract and maintain audiences to its service rather than to specific programmes. Of course, the content offered by Netflix motivates audiences to subscribe, but 'success' on Netflix may not be defined by viewing figures for individual programmes in the same way as it is for traditional broadcasters. However, they do use viewing figures to decide whether to renew or cancel existing programming.

△ Singer Selena Gomez

Key terms

commercial television television companies whose primary income source is from advertising

post-network television the culture of television viewing that no longer relies on traditional broadcast methods

ultra HD high-quality digital images

CHAPTER 7 MEDIA INDUSTRIES

Commercial television companies need to sell advertising spots before, after and within their programming. Commercial broadcasters effectively sell the audience to advertisers. Put simply, the bigger the audience for a programme, the more a commercial broadcaster can charge for the advertising space. Similarly, if a programme attracts a specific marketing group in good numbers, advertisers of products for this group will be attracted to buying advertising time. However, as general viewing figures have declined so too has the cost of advertising space, reducing the income for broadcasters but also reducing advertisers' ability to reach their market.

Netflix avoids these economic problems as its primary income is direct from subscribers; however, it is offering its 'Basic with Ads' subscription band which includes adverts during programmes for a lower monthly price.

Key to Netflix's success is the diversity of products it offers. This has the potential to meet the needs of a wide audience range. Programmes cover a host of interests and some are targeting specific audience groups. This can be evidenced in some of the Netflix original programming that ranges from true crime documentary series (*Catching Killers*), animated comedy (*Agent Elvis*), drama (*The Crown*) (right), horror/sci-fi (*Stranger Things*), teen drama (*The Midnight Club*) and sitcom (*That 90s Show*). It funds children's and non-English language programming, comedy specials and takes part in co-productions, such as *Red Rose* with the BBC.

Netflix can also ensure that different audiences are catered for in the programmes it buys from broadcasters such as the BBC (for example, *Peaky Blinders* and *Taboo*). This business model allows it to offer programming that may be for both niche and mainstream audiences.

According to *Variety*, Netflix spent $16.7 billion for content in 2022. In 2011, Netflix outbid other networks for *House of Cards*, produced by David Fincher. Netflix's chief content officer Ted Sarandos anaylsed users' streaming habits and concluded there would be an audience for the programme. Netflix had also identified that the type of people who would be attracted to this TV series would also be likely to want to binge-watch multiple episodes rather than watch one episode per week, prompting the decision to make all episodes of the first series available at the same time.

Netflix has a full commissioning team across each genre of programming, but uses detailed data from users to inform their decisions on what to invest in. However, no method is guaranteed to create popular TV programmes, and some Netflix programmes still received negative reviews.

Both Netflix and traditional TV companies think about creating programmes that will please their local audiences. Much of the programming on Channel 4, BBC and ITV is created specifically to tap into British tastes. Some programmes have success overseas, with ITV's *Downton Abbey* being a notable example and evidence of the increasingly globalised nature of media distribution and circulation. It was broadcast in the USA on PBS and Season 5 was watched by 25.5 million viewers, including more than 12 million views via a streaming service. Other shows such as the BBC's *Doctor Who* and *Sherlock* have found fans in the USA via the BBC America channel. Often, UK programmes are remade for US audiences. The US version of *The Office* ran for nine seasons producing a total of 201 episodes. The show was based on a UK series that produced only 12 episodes and two specials.

Netflix considers different regions in their programming, with local commissioning teams in key regions, which provides a much more globalised service. Some shows appear very British, for example *The Crown*, but the romanticised retelling of the history of the current royal family has global appeal. Since Princess Diana, the younger generation of royals have been treated like celebrities across the world, so the show has a broad appeal in many different countries. *Sense 8* identified itself as a global product in its settings (including the USA, the UK, Mexico, Italy, India and Kenya) and in its diverse cast, representing a wide range of ethnicities and sexual identities. Programmes from Australia (for example, *Superbro*) and Canada (for example, *Kim's Convenience*) can be found on Netflix. Netflix also works with producers from around the world and both purchases and makes non-English-language programmes (for example, the *Money Heist* franchise). One of its most successful TV shows was *Squid Game* from South Korea, released in 2021. However, the success of Netflix has raised several issues that are explored below.

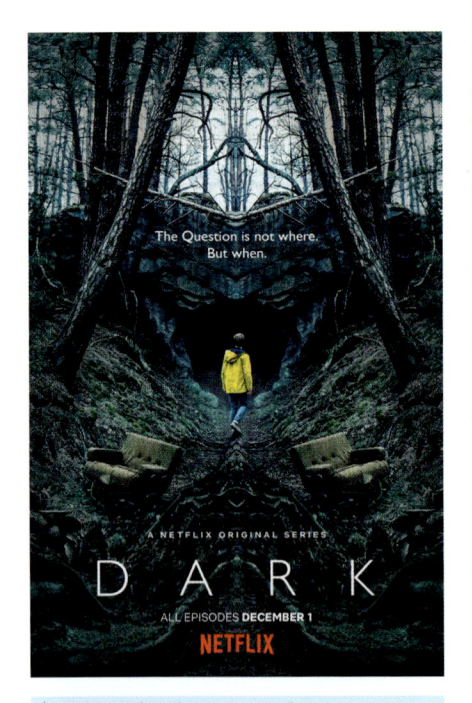

△ Advert for the German language drama *Dark* (2017–20)

CHAPTER 7 MEDIA INDUSTRIES

Broadcasting/narrowcasting

Traditionally, TV has been a **broadcast** medium. This term refers to the idea that a TV programme or radio show is 'cast out' in all directions at one time. That is to say, a broadcast television programme would be transmitted by a TV station at a given time and audience members in a single territory (e.g. the UK) all accessed it at the same time. As previously identified, ever since the rise of the video recorder, this has not been the full story. Video-on-demand and streaming services now mean that TV shows are more accurately described as being **narrowcast**. Audiences now select how, where and when they access the 'TV' content. This makes Netflix more like a library rather than a TV station or channel. Audiences are able to select from a wide range of products that are not geographically or historically limited. The freedom to create their own viewing patterns gives each audience member individual power but can impact negatively on some of the potential gratifications TV shows can provide. The highly personal choices made by people in the way they access media products effectively removes them from general conversation. When a series of *The Crown* is released as a whole season on a given day, audience members may make one of the following choices to:

- binge-watch all episodes immediately
- quickly watch the whole series over a number of days
- watch one episode every now and then
- bookmark the series and come back to it at a later date.

New audiences may find and watch the series several years after its initial release.

Before streaming services, there was the concept of 'watercooler' TV. This referred to the type of shows you could assume most of your acquaintances would be sure to watch. Sitcoms such as *Friends*, soap operas such as *Eastenders* and entertainment shows such as *Gladiators* had mass market appeal and, as they were broadcast programmes, would be watched by millions of people at the same time. These and **event television** such as season finales, sports events and royal weddings could safely be the topic of conversation on buses and at the office 'watercoolers'. Statistically, most people you encounter would have watched these programmes and those who had not had lost the opportunity to do so. There was no concept of a **spoiler** at that time.

Blumler and Katz suggest that one potential gratification provided by media products is that of 'social interaction' (cited in Sullivan, 2012). The narrowcasting nature of TV today means that people are not always connected to others in their immediate social and professional networks by the shared cultural experience of watching a TV show. Social interaction is more likely to be found via the gathering of audience groups online, so the interaction is between strangers who share cultural knowledge. X (formerly Twitter) and other social media platforms provide the social interaction gratification as it is impossible to discuss media experiences with others who have chosen to watch programmes later – or who may not watch the show in question at all.

Key terms

broadcast to transmit information to a mass audience, usually using radio or television technology

event television television shows that attract large audiences and are reported on extensively. They may be one-off events (e.g. a royal wedding), a regularly scheduled event (e.g. the Olympics) or a specific episode of a popular programme

narrowcast to transmit information to a localised, niche or specialised audience and to offer choices regarding the timing of access to this information

spoiler articles and discussions that give away plot developments

△ *Gladiators* (1992–2000) was watched by millions of viewers in the UK when it aired in the primetime Saturday evening slot on ITV

7.8 Netflix: disrupting the TV industry

Competition to other broadcasters

One important content producer is currently notable by their absence from the Netflix listings. HBO has made some of the most critically acclaimed TV of the past 20 years, including *The Wire*, *Boardwalk Empire* and *Game of Thrones*. HBO has a similar business model in the USA to Netflix, where it is a subscription-only cable TV channel or streaming service (HBO Max). HBO often sells its shows to global broadcasters which use a subscription service too, such as the UK's Now TV. This is to ensure that HBO properties are treated like premium products that have to be bought by the audience. Those that do not buy pay-to-view channel subscriptions are given an opportunity to buy their own copies of the show after broadcast as DVD box sets or digital downloads.

Cultural imperialism

Netflix is a **transnational** media organisation. As we have seen, it offers its services to global audiences but most of its content is produced in the USA.

This feeds into debates on **cultural imperialism**, where members of the host culture begin to assume some of the values and ideologies of the media content they are consuming. In contrast to the more positive view of globalisation as a force that can unify cultures, such unification can be viewed as a dilution of national identity. We might also see the suppression of cultural heritage in favour of increasingly bland genre-based content. Where domestic media production survives, often its only option is to reproduce local variations of the big genres to which audience tastes have shifted.

Regulation

Netflix is based in California and its European base is in the Netherlands. For UK viewers this means that content is delivered from outside of the UK and this has an impact on the way the service is regulated. Netflix is regulated by the Dutch media regulator, the Commissariaat voor de Media, rather than Ofcom.

Ofcom is responsible for the regulation of the UK-based delivery of video-on-demand. The way the companies are organised means that Amazon Prime comes under Ofcom's regulations but Netflix does not. Netflix therefore raises a number of issues around the idea of media regulation in the digital era. Traditional ideas about regulation are difficult to apply in the digital and globalised context and it is difficult for local regulators such as Ofcom to enforce its rules. Traditional TV broadcasters can be forced to take responsibility for the way content is accessed.

For example, the watershed controlled the type of content that could be accessed before 9pm. As material was being broadcast into homes, the broadcasters had to take some responsibility for the content of programmes that could be seen by children; 9pm. became a time whereby it was assumed most children would be in bed and the responsibility for controlling their access to adult content was in the hands of the child's guardian. VOD services have removed the relevance of scheduling, as all material is available at any time, so broadcasters cease to have responsibility for keeping children away from adult programming. This is now largely down to the subscriber. Netflix does have a responsibility to provide information on programmes to allow choices to be made and to provide ways to lock children out of certain types of material. Netflix accounts offer parental control and can be locked with a PIN, or profiles can be set up where 'allowed' shows and movies are filtered

> **Key terms**
>
> **cultural imperialism** the influence on language, values etc. that can be exerted by the cultural dominance of another culture via cultural product
>
> **transnational** working across national borders

by predefined maturity levels such as 'little kids only' and 'teens and below'. Netflix programmes also offer an age rating and on-screen content warnings.

The idea of regulation of the media can be very problematic. There are differing opinions on what should be regulated, how and for what purpose. People who see the media as a marketplace and have a commitment to '*free markets, individual rights, personal choice* [and] *small government*' tend to favour '*limited regulation*' (Freedman, cited in Lunt & Livingstone, 2012), although there may be a need to regulate the media industries to control monopolies, generate tax income and to moderate '*anti-competitive behaviour between firms*' (Baldwin & Cave cited in Lunt & Livingstone, 2012). Others hold different values and see the media as both part of and a potential threat to 'civil society' (Habermas cited in Lunt & Livingstone, 2012) and so see the need to ensure the media industries are regulated in order that their need to generate profit does not over-ride their responsibilities to the society they serve.

> **Key term**
>
> **free markets** the neo-liberal economic belief that markets should be deregulated to trade and generate profit without limitations

Regulation makes media industries accountable to the wider society for the choices they make, rather than just their shareholders. Historically, regulation has begun with nation states. The history of a state informs its attitude and approach to regulation, and the rules it imposes on media industries reflect the culture's dominant values. For example, the history of UK media is in public service broadcasting, so the regulation of the media in ways that support British values and to strengthen ideas of national identity and cultural heritage is longstanding. In the USA, the idea of the media as a marketplace has been historically established, so US regulatory bodies tend to refer to business practices where UK regulations often focus on the content of media products. All media has '*become ever more professionalised and market-oriented*' (Habermas cited in Lunt & Livingstone, 2012) and globalisation is said to be '*undermining state control*' (Lunt & Livingstone, 2012). McCheney (cited in Lunt & Livingstone, 2012) noted that the power increasingly lies with '*global media corporations operating across national border and pushing for open markets*'. Netflix can be seen to be a prime example of this type of corporation. In 2007 it provided streaming services to the US market. In 2012 it expanded to Europe and by 2017, by innovating in its use of technology and in its approach to content creation, Netflix had grown across five continents. This global reach not only makes the company immensely powerful but also very difficult to regulate.

7.9 Marvel and diversification

Marvel TV produces superhero TV programmes. It was initially a comic-book publisher that introduced audiences to many superhero related characters such as Spiderman, Captain America, Iron Man and Daredevil. It is now a subsidiary of Disney and Marvel Studios, which produces superhero films. Comic books, merchandise, games and a host of other media all combine to make Marvel one of the great media success stories of the 21st century. Its films are among the most profitable films of all time with several including *Avengers Assemble*, *Iron Man 3* and *Captain America Civil War* all making over a billion dollars.

Marvel TV offers a range of titles to create products for diverse audiences. The company minimises financial risk by producing products that follow conventional genre and narrative conventions (with a few twists here and there). It creates an interconnected universe where characters can mingle and interact, and it bases its stories on characters and situations that have already proven popular with audiences. Marvel has created a reliable brand identity based on recognisable intellectual property (IP). The products feature famous actors and have high production values, using the most up-to-date digital technologies and special effects. Marvel products are fast-paced and exciting. This branding helps minimise the financial risk for the audience. If you know Marvel, you know what to expect, and, if you like what Marvel offers, you'll probably not mind spending money on a cinema ticket, a digital download or a Disney+ subscription.

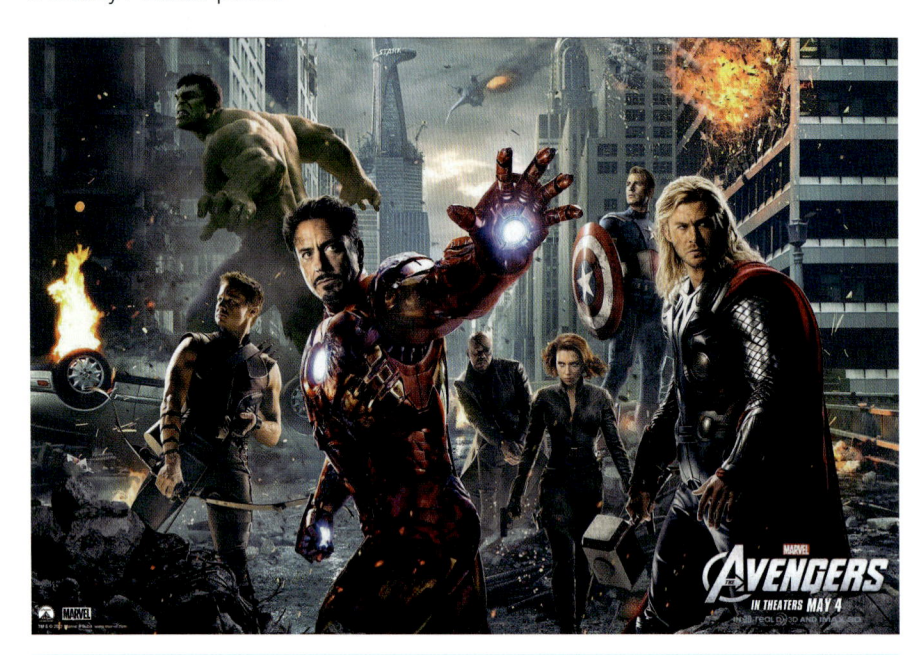

△ **Avengers Assemble**

Although Marvel is a traditional production company, it is not an 'old-fashioned' media institution. As well as still making and promoting traditional media forms, it uses social media extensively. From creating sophisticated online marketing campaigns to exploiting its avid and active audience base, Marvel uses new and digital media to help promote both the primary media products (films, TV programmes and comic books) and the secondary products it generates (merchandise, soundtracks, etc.).

Marvel is a prime example of an institution that produces traditional media forms in a traditional film studio set-up but is still immensely successful despite changes to media production and consumption practices. By using existing intellectual property and revisiting its own, older ideas, Marvel capitalises on audience familiarity with the characters and situations while also maintaining audience interest in the new titles it creates. It uses new distribution and circulation methods (e.g. Disney+) and the internet to market and promote its products.

Even trailers are now an income source rather than just a marketing expense, thanks to platforms such as YouTube. Trailers can attract huge numbers of views online and this explains why a Marvel marketing strategy will include teaser trailers, TV spots, cinematic trailers (often several are released revealing different aspects of the film) and trailers for different audience groups. In addition, these trailers tend to generate response videos, analysis and lots of discussion, further spreading information about the Marvel product.

Disney+ tends to limit the release of new TV programmes to one episode a week. This allows for cultural conversations to develop via social media. TV recap podcasts analyse and discuss each episode and this can help increase the cultural awareness of a product and its circulation. Podcasts such as *Still Watching* or *Decoding TV* often engage with their listening audience and offer critiques, reviews, 'deep dive' analyses and sometimes speculation about future plot developments. Disney+ offers a range of options for audiences – those who come late to a programme can catch up on Disney's streaming service and take part in social media discussions when they catch up. Audiences who prefer to binge-watch can wait and begin watching when all episodes are available.

However, there have been criticisms of Marvel TV's integrated storytelling, with audiences now needing to be knowledgeable about the content of TV programmes to understand films and vice versa. The sheer volume of film and TV content available makes it difficult for audiences to keep on top of the lore created and referenced in these stories. Disney is offering audiences lots of Marvel-branded content but risks oversaturating the market and creating 'Marvel-fatigue'. The need for more and more new content relates to Disney+'s business model. As a streaming service it relies on subscription income; it needs to attract viewers and keep them subscribed to its service. A constant updating of the service with new content is seen to be the best way to attract and maintain its subscribers. However, in recent years the number of subscription services has increased subsequently, and so has the cost to the viewer. Subscription services are in competition with one another.

While Marvel products are still profitable there has been more criticism of the dilution of the brand. The responses to the film *Eternals* (2021) and the TV show *Secret Invasion* (2023) are cited as evidence that the Marvel brand is becoming less popular with audiences. Diversification can oversaturate the market, and audiences who see a brand as being clichéd rather than innovative do not remain loyal.

7.10 News and social media

Traditionally, people got news and information about current affairs from news organisations that distributed the news in print, on television or on the radio. The supply of news to the public was managed by large news organisations such as (in the UK):

- **Broadcast organisations** such as: BBC News, ITN and Sky News. These organisations now create news broadcasts for television and radio as well as video packages for websites and other online platforms.
- **Print organisations** such as: News UK, the Mirror Group and the Mail Group. These organisations have all diversified into the production of online news sites.

Information on the events of the day was traditionally gathered and selected by editors for broadcast or publication.

The information itself tended to come from:

- **news agencies**
- journalists and **correspondents** employed by the news organisation
- public records (for example, the agenda for the day in parliament, a court record, a politician's official diary)
- PR (public relations) sources.

> **Key terms**
>
> **correspondents** journalists who have a specialisation (e.g. war correspondent) or who serve a specific location (e.g. a Westminster correspondent)
>
> **news agencies** organisations that receive and distribute news

Key terms

24-hour rolling news digital TV channels that show only news and that broadcast 24 hours a day

satellite/cable channels television channels that required audiences to buy specialised technologies in order to access them. The term was relevant as a differentiator between 'terrestrial TV' and 'satellite' TV (BBC One and Two, ITV, Channel 4 and Channel 5). Since the digital switchover in 2007, terrestrial TV has been accessible with other 'satellite' channels on services such as Freebox

tabloid newspapers a genre of newspaper that favours entertainment, gossip and human-interest stories. Tabloids tends to use a sensationalist style of reporting. The term is often used when the values of tabloid newspapers are replicated in other media products or forms, e.g. the concept of tabloid TV, tabloid magazines, etc.

News organisations are bound by professional codes of conduct and are regulated by IPSO (print news) and Ofcom (broadcast news). Some methods of sourcing news and information can slip into unethical behaviour. For example, chequebook journalism (the practice of paying sources for stories); door-stepping (waiting outside people's homes to catch them for comment as they arrive or leave); and, as highlighted in the Leveson report, phone hacking.

These sourcing practices are often associated with **tabloid newspapers**, but the competition between news organisations for readers/viewers means that all news organisations are under pressure to gather and present information that will attract as many readers/viewers as possible.

The rise of **satellite/cable channels** and the introduction of dedicated **24-hour rolling news** created pressures on traditional broadcast news organisations. The development of multi-channel TV bought competition to the established broadcasters from international news sources such as *Al Jazeera* and *Russia Today*. Both companies are global institutions and offer UK audiences 24-hour English-language news, giving a non-British perspective on stories and events. Critics of the channels see them as propaganda arms for the Qatari and Russian governments respectively, while others see them as welcome alternatives that present news without being tied politically to the UK government or Western commercial interests.

The introduction of 24-hour rolling news channels offered immediate and continuous access to news stories for audiences but has also created some issues in the way events are sourced and reported. Rolling news is uniquely placed to present ongoing developments in breaking news stories and can respond quickly as events unfold. Traditional news broadcasts – usually scheduled in the morning, in the middle of the day, around 6pm and finally about 10pm – are summaries of events that have already happened. Rolling news created a convention and perhaps an expectation that audiences should be informed as things occur rather than afterwards. However, rolling news broadcasters often don't have much to say – especially as an event is taking place. This has led to the news often being filled with speculation rather than concrete facts and information.

In addition, the competition for viewers often leads news broadcasters to dramatise their reporting style. This is often criticised for turning news into entertainment. Simon Jenkins (a former editor of *The Times*) also warned that '*sensationalising and dramatising a crime*' makes the media '*a megaphone for the act*' (2017). He suggested that the blanket coverage given to events, such as terrorist attacks, could be an 'inspiration' for similar acts.

The main digital challenge to the dominance of the traditional news organisation, however, is not rolling news but online news. Online news offers written stories, video reports and podcasts – everything that used to be accessed via broadcast or print media. In addition, the majority of online news is free. Some news sources do require a subscription to access their content. *The Times*, for example, is behind a paywall and charges from £6.00 to £15.00 per week to subscribe (with introductory prices used to tempt audiences in). Audiences can read online editions of traditional newspapers such as the *Telegraph* or the *Guardian* for free, although both sites offer paid membership benefits as well as subscription to access digital services such as the news apps for smartphones and tablets. Audiences can access the BBC, ITN and Sky News websites, which provide news stories illustrated with images, reports and animations. They can also watch global news broadcasts on YouTube. In addition, the internet offers a host of non-traditional sources for news.

CHAPTER 7 MEDIA INDUSTRIES

For example, **news aggregators** such as *HuffPost UK*, *The Drudge Report* and *The Daily Beast* use **algorithms** to scour the internet for news stories on a specific topic, which are then repackaged and presented on their website. This enables each site to present stories that best support their own **editorial positions** – *HuffPost* collates stories that support a **politically liberal** set of values while *The Drudge Report* offers **politically conservative** viewpoints.

YouTube offers many videos that are part of the communication of news events. Opinion-based **talking heads** offer political opinions and interpretations of current news and events. The *Novara Media* and *Politics Joe* channels offer left-wing analysis and commentary, which counters the largely conservative perspectives of mainstream newspapers such as the *Daily Mail* and the *Daily Express*.

The rise in alternative and independent news sources does offer a range of different perspectives and this means that audiences can get their news from multiple and non-traditional sources. Research undertaken by Natalie Fenton, however, found that, despite the potential for a 'diversity of voices in an on-line context' audiences are not necessarily getting a broad range of ideas and opinions when they access the news. Fenton found that traditional news providers still held most power when it comes to the circulation of news. They still act as **gatekeepers**, selecting what is and isn't newsworthy and most people still got their news from these institutions (source: *The Media Show* BBC Four, 28/10/09).

Most aggregate news sources summarise, reproduce or comment on stories that have been generated by traditional news organisations, but the rise in online news has challenged the economic dominance of these traditional news organisations. To remain competitive, they have had to engage with the changing news environment. In addition to the traditional sources of information, news organisations have looked to use resources found online to help them create interesting and engaging news reports.

■ Clickbait

As clicks on a link or a visit to a page is now a commodified event, attracting readers to a story on a website can be financially very lucrative. Traditional news sites often use **clickbait** – headlines and stories selected or constructed specifically to make audiences want to read more. The technique is also used by organisations that create attention-grabbing headlines that lead to websites that are full of adverts. The most successful types of clickbait are headlines stories that generate emotion in the reader. Shocking, horrifying and outrageous headlines generate clicks and, even better, are likely to be shared between users, generating even more clicks. **Sensationalism** prioritises tabloid approaches to reporting and **hard news** stories are often reduced to their **soft news** elements to attract readers.

Sensationalism drives users to websites and this increases the advertising value of the site, which is one of the reasons why fake news sites have become widespread. These sites generate sensational stories to attract readers but the content of the stories is completely fabricated. The website can then sell data about the visitors to the site to advertisers, making them a valuable commodity.

■ Echo-chambers

Social media platforms analyse a user's interests and behaviours to provide targeted information and so the information received by a user tends to reflect their existing world view, interests or beliefs. A conservative thinker

Key terms

algorithms computer technology that gathers and analyses user data

clickbait stories and headlines that are constructed to encourage audiences to click through to access more information. Clickbait usually attempts to create an emotional response

editorial position the political values that influence the way a media product is constructed

gatekeepers individuals and groups who have the ability to select (and reject) the content of media products

hard news news that is related to politics, economics, science, war, terrorism, etc.

news aggregators refers to (usually) online news sources that use software to gather news from other online sources

politically conservative can be interpreted in different ways but generally refers to a belief system based on the prioritisation of individual social and economic responsibility. Social change is often resisted

politically liberal can be interpreted in different ways but generally refers to a belief system based on the prioritisation of social and economic responsibility. Social change is seen to be both positive and, often, essential

sensationalism a reporting style that seeks to create an emotional response in its readers

soft news news that is related to celebrities, entertainment, sport, gossip, scandal and human interest stories

talking heads the use of a mid-shot of someone speaking, usually with limited mise-en-scène

7.10 News and social media

> **Key terms**
>
> **echo-chamber** the phenomenon caused by audiences limiting their media experiences to products and locations that reinforce their existing beliefs and values
>
> **fake news** fictional or misleading stories that are presented as news
>
> **false consciousness** the belief in ideas that are not based in fact
>
> **naturalisation** the belief that an idea is a natural state rather than a human construction

who reads conservative newspapers and websites and clicks on stories with conservative viewpoints will be offered more and more information that reflects and reinforces their values. It is likely that their social network is made up of other conservative thinkers who share more conservative news and opinions. This creates a digital **echo-chamber** where people experience their own views being reflected back by a range of sources. This can create a **false consciousness** of consensus (Engels, cited in Eagleton, 1992) where ideas go through a process of **naturalisation** as they are repeated (Barthes, 2009) cultivating (Gerbner) specific ideas and values. This can lead to the unquestioning acceptance of information that confirms the reader's views – particularly problematic given the amount of fake news being generated.

■ Fake news

The creation of **fake news** can be motivated simply by the money it generates but it has been shown that fake news stories are used in an attempt to effect people's voting intentions. In 2017, the US Director of National Intelligence accused Russia of interfering with the election by using, among other things, the dissemination of fake news. The echo-chamber effect means that fake news can often be circulated to a wide audience and be very influential. People, including traditional news institutions, have been caught out and become part of the passing on of fake stories. The realisation that fake news exists and can be difficult to identify means that trust in the media is shaken.

Facebook and (fake) news

The spread of fake news was enabled by changes in the way Facebook generated information that finds its way into users' newsfeeds. In 2012, Facebook allowed advertising in newsfeeds via sponsored stories – that is, stories that pay to be placed on selected newsfeeds. The audience for the sponsored story is carefully selected by Facebook's algorithm so there is a high chance the reader will interact with the story in some way. Sponsored stories look almost identical to non-sponsored stories but contain advertising content or content designed to generate clicks. Their appearance in a user's timeline has been paid for. The company pays Facebook to ensure that its message reaches audiences most likely to respond and Facebook uses the data it has gathered on users to provide this service. This allows marketers to create very specific marketing campaigns for very specific types of users. This is used by companies and also by political parties during elections. Facebook has been criticised for having an undue influence on democracy in the way it creates echo-chambers, allows for niche marketing and both allows and benefits from the spread of fake news.

Until 2016, Facebook took no responsibility for the accuracy of the information that was shared on its platform. With over 2 billion users its newsfeed is viewed by more people than any other news provider. In November 2016, responding to criticisms that the social media site had influenced the outcome of the US election, Facebook's CEO Mark Zuckerberg denied it was a media company. In a later interview that year (Constine, 2016) he went on to say that Facebook was not a 'traditional technology company' but a 'new kind of platform' and acknowledged it has an important role in public discourse today.

Facebook's desire to distance itself from being defined as a media company is largely driven by the fact that media companies have to take responsibility for the content they publish and are subject to regulatory rules, whereas technology platforms do not.

techcrunch.com compares Facebook to a newsroom, with the newsfeed algorithm acting as the editor. Facebook has since begun to work with genuine news organisations to help identify when a news story is fake and also to allow users to report fake news. It also intends to scan its web pages to see if sites that are being landed on from Facebook links are ad-based sites, and this data can be used to down-rank some sources of information.

In 2018, Zuckerberg had to respond to revelations about the way Cambridge Analytica used Facebook data to target voters in both the UK's EU referendum and Donald Trump's presidential campaign. Vast amounts of data about Facebook users were analysed in order to send targeted political messages to potential voters in an attempt to influence their voting intentions. Zuckerberg's previous position that sought to distance Facebook from responsibility for the way the platform could be politicised had to be amended and he apologised for his company's inability to protect its customers' data.

Facebook users skew older. According to Herd Digital, the number of users under 24 is decreasing and over 65 is increasing. In contrast, 85 per cent of Snapchat's users are aged between 18 and 35 (Minnesota Libraries Publishing Project). Snapchat is another social media platform that offers its users news stories. This content is from partner companies (newspapers and magazines), and this means that Snapchat has been identified by Bloomberg as being one of the few social media sites that does not have an issue with fake news.

A 2023 research project reported that social media had been identified as being the main source of news for young people (Digital News Report, 2023). Of the people who use the internet, 30 per cent use social media to access their news against 22 % who use news websites and apps. 11% of these use X for news, 14 per cent use Instagram and 28 per cent, Facebook. This project also identified a general lack of trust in news sources, with only 40% of the sample surveyed saying they trust news 'most of the time'.

■ X as a source of news

X (formerly Twitter) offers a way for news institutions to share news stories and it is also a source of **citizen journalism** – that is news and information generated by the public. People who witness an event post (formerly tweet) information, photographs and videos that are shared on the platform and, sometimes, are used as material for reports in professionally produced news stories and news broadcasts. This is a cheap way for news institutions to gather news and information, and it means that information is available much more quickly than in the past. There are issues regarding **copyright** of posts and the images and videos they contain. As they are in the **public domain**, the information can be re-presented in a news article if the source of the information is credited. Some news agencies contact the producers of posts that become popular to offer payment for their use.

X is also used as a source of news itself. It is an immediate source of comments and opinions that can be used by journalists. Comments made by politicians and other public figures are used to show the impact of a news story and the opinions of selected members of the public are used to exemplify public opinion. Analysing the content of X conversations on any given topic allows news institutions to evaluate the responses and gives a snapshot of public opinion, maybe helping them decide on their editorial approach.

> **Key terms**
>
> **citizen journalism** the contributions to news reports made by members of the public
> **copyright** the legal ownership of the content of media products
> **public domain** relates to media products/ideas that are outside the restrictions of copyright law and are freely available to the public

Apply it

1. Access the *Independent* online edition. What features are offered on the website that you think show the influence of online news providers such as Buzzfeed and social media such as Facebook and X?
2. Access X and see what topics are trending. Identify:
   a. stories reported in the news being discussed by X users
   b. stories reported online that are not part of the day's news reports.

→ Summary

- Central to the study of media industries is the consideration of production practices and the way media products are distributed and circulated.
- Huge changes have occurred in media industries in recent decades, driven by advances in digital and communications technologies.
- Distribution and circulation patterns are measured in different ways in the UK. Most are monitored by organisations external to the main industry players, giving them impartiality.
- Patterns of circulation and distribution have changed and, in some cases, expanded due to globalisation of the media market.
- Technologies are impacting on these industry practices.
- Media industries are adapting to try to accommodate changes in audience behaviours and expectations. Digital convergence is seen to be a way to enable traditional media industries to remain competitive in a rapidly changing media environment.
- How the media is controlled and who owns it can impact on the content, as explored fully in the enabling ideas of Curran and Seaton.
- The mass media sector is constantly evolving. Media conglomerates are a key feature of the contemporary media landscape. Business strategies such as convergence and synergy abound.
- Some independent media companies produce products that are considered alternative, as they may cater for a niche audience or run counter to mainstream ideologies in either their product content or business practices.
- Production, distribution and circulation can now be undertaken by independent companies and individuals in ways that offer competition to the dominance of traditional media industries.
- Many media companies make a large proportion of their profit from advertising or subscriptions. Public service broadcasting is still an important feature of the contemporary media landscape in the UK, but has less significance worldwide.
- Media regulation in the UK is controlled by different bodies, each with their own powers as well as limitations. Self-regulation is also an important concept with the growth of the internet and mass global communications.

Chapter 8: Developing media studies skills

What you will learn in this chapter

Chapter 8: Developing media studies skills covers:

- how to analyse and compare the way that media products construct and communicate meaning through the interaction of media language and audience response
- how to use key theories and subject-specialist terminology appropriately
- how to debate key questions relating to the social, cultural, political and economic roles of the media
- how to communicate effectively when answering questions and writing essays.

The media studies specification identifies specific skills that you will need to demonstrate in your non-examined assessment (NEA) and in your examination responses. This chapter will consider the underlying skills that you need to develop when studying the media and make suggestions for the types of activities you can engage with to help you develop these skills further.

8.1 Introduction

Learning about the media can be daunting at first as there is so much to consider. You need to learn about what the media is, you have to engage with a wide range of media forms and products, and you also need to be able to consider media industries, audiences and products in light of the theoretical framework of ideas and concepts outlined in Chapters 1–7. Some media forms are so new that our understanding of them is only now starting to develop, while other forms and genres have been around for a long time and there is a huge and sometimes overwhelming range of theories, interpretations and concepts we can use to help us understand them. The media is constantly changing, so knowledge we have today may be inaccurate or out of date tomorrow.

> **For more on the NEA see Chapter 10, and for the examination, Chapter 11.**

Being an expert in each and every media institution, form or genre is an unrealistic goal. Learning ideas from the theoretical framework is important as they can help you engage with different types of media. Also, more important than just knowing something is knowing how to use that knowledge. You need to apply your knowledge to help you understand and discuss the way the media works, the way media products are constructed, and the way audiences and industries relate to one another. The ability to apply your media knowledge is a skill that needs to be learned and practised. You need to be able to show that you can apply the knowledge to show your understanding of what you have learned. You will be asked to demonstrate this ability to apply ideas in both exam papers (see Chapter 11) and the NEA will ask you to make media products but your research, planning and production choices should be based on the application of your knowledge of the theoretical framework.

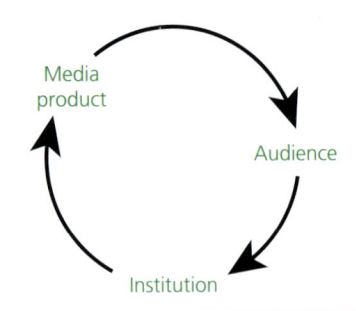

△ The interrelationships between product, audience and institution

At the heart of media studies is the skill of analysis. Analysis is the act of seeking to understand how something works and why it works that way. In media studies, analysis demands a detailed examination of media products, audiences and industries, including the interrelationships between product, audience and institution.

8.2 Analysis of media products and audience response

We have already learned that when media products are being constructed, media producers make careful and deliberate language choices in order to construct meaning. Production decisions are made that attempt to appeal to, attract and please an audience. Knowing this, we can begin to analyse media products by considering the effects that were intended by the media producer as well as the way the choices may have been interpreted by audiences.

Before that, though, it is worth taking a step back to consider what the media product is, and what, in broad terms, it is trying to achieve. You should aim to apply skills of analysis to your Close Study Products as well as your own choice of media products, as this will help you engage with the media theories you will be assessed on in the exams. You will also need to analyse existing media products to help you make your own production decisions for the NEA.

An important part of this communication process is the platform that is being used for distribution (see Chapter 7: Media industries). The platform is always considered very carefully by media producers. It needs to be appropriate for the message itself as well as being the best way to reach the audience; the way information is distributed may vary depending on the target audience (see Chapter 6: Media audiences).

As an example, modern celebrities who target teenage audiences use social media to communicate because this is typically the best way to gain the attention of this demographic. Facebook was the social media of choice of teenagers for some time, but by 2012, only 43 per cent of teens thought Facebook was the most important social media platform, with Instagram, Snapchat, Tumblr and X all showing increases in popularity as Facebook declined. Now, users of Facebook are older than they were in 2008/9 as younger people have moved to alternative social media platforms, such as TikTok.

Each form of media has its own codes and conventions in the way media language is used, and audiences have expectations that vary across forms and genres. The audience's expectation of a news website vary when accessing either a tabloid or a broadsheet website (see Chapter 1: Reading print media). Audiences who watch adult drama, such as *Happy Valley*, have a different expectation from those watching a sitcom, like *Ted Lasso*, and both television programmes (see Chapter 2: Reading audio-visual media) try to meet the specific needs of their audience. Of course, some audience members could choose to read and view many different types of media product in different ways, depending on their mood and needs at the time. People can choose to move from news media forms that provide hard news to light entertainment or music, or indeed vice versa, for example, as their personal requirements change.

Analysing products

The purpose of analysis is to engage with media products to see how they are constructed to make meaning. The theoretical framework can be used to structure your analysis, when you need to:

- identify media language accurately so you can discuss the way a product has been constructed
- discuss the representations and messages conveyed within the product
- identify how the product attempts to appeal to and engage its target audience
- consider the impact of the product's institutional context.

These same ideas need to be applied when you are constructing your own production, when you need to:

- use media language accurately so your product is recognisable
- create representations that are appropriate to the messages you wish to convey
- create a product that will appeal to and engage its target audience
- create a product that engages with the appropriate institutional context.

There are some key questions that you may find useful when it comes to using the theoretical framework to analyse existing media products.

Step-by-step analysis

The following is an example of analysis focusing on the poster for the film *Black Panther: Wakanda Forever* (2022, Coogler, R.) (see right).

> **TIP** ✓
> While you are developing and practising your analysis skills, you may want to follow the process outlined below. You will find that the more you practise analysis, the easier and more natural it becomes.

Step 1

Before you start analysing, it is worth being very clear about what kind of media product you are analysing and what its function is.

What is it?	A promotional poster for the film *Black Panther: Wakanda Forever*.
What is it for?	- This is an advertising and marketing product. - The poster has been created to raise awareness of the film. - The ultimate aim is to encourage people to go to watch the film at the cinema, in the first instance.

Each media language choice has been made with this in mind. It needs to attract the audience's attention, create interest in the film and provide information so audiences can access the product.

8.2 Analysis of media products and audience response

Step 2

Next, you need to make some basic observations as to how the product has been constructed. At this stage, you only need to observe but should try to look for details in the choices made.

What media language choices were made in the construction of the product?	<ul><li>A blue/grey palette has been used for the poster.</li><li>The poster has been divided in two across the middle, with what appears to be land at the top and water below.</li><li>The heads of the characters in the film are used in a montage with familiar characters from the first film in the upper half of the poster, framed by an image of the Black Panther mask and suit.</li><li>New characters are shown in montage below the central line. They are upside down.</li><li>Characters have serious facial expressions.</li><li>A line of warriors is shown moving into the water.</li><li>A cityscape is shown in the distance at the top of the poster.</li><li>There is a reflection of the film's title in the lower half of the poster, also upside down.</li><li>The date of release is given at the centre of the poster, as is the title and the name of the film studio</li></ul>

Step 3

The next step involves thinking carefully about the reasons behind these choices. Everything you have observed has been selected for a reason and often with a clear intended effect.

Why were these choices made? What connotations are created by the media language choices? What effect did the producer wish to achieve?	<ul><li>The colour palette is cool and creates a sombre tone.</li><li>The connotations of the design and the facial expressions of the characters suggest that this is a film that will deal with serious events and situations.</li><li>The poster creates a binary with familiar characters at the top of the poster and new characters below. They are separated by their locations (land and water) and this connotes a conflict between the two groups.</li><li>The conflict is represented symbolically by the image of the warriors with raised spears walking purposefully into the water and the opposition warriors coming out of the water to meet them.</li><li>For those who have seen the first film the lead character is identified as the last Black Panther's sister, Shuri. She is shown posed in a defiant 'Wakanda Forever' salute, which reinforces the serious tone of the film.</li><li>Audiences may be aware that the actor who played him (Chadwick Boseman) died after the release of the last Black Panther film so the image of the superhero behind the characters reinforces (with the title) that the heroic character will be part of this film and a presence within the story.</li><li>The characters at the bottom of the poster are more difficult to see as they are upside down, but this placement and the use of water implies they may somehow be a mirror society to those from Wakanda.</li></ul>

Quick question

If you have seen this film, how successful do you think the poster is in creating the correct expectations of the film for the viewing audience?

Step 4

The choices made are often connected to other ideas from within the media framework. Media language choices create representations, can communicate genre codes and can create narrative information. Some media language choices do all three things at the same time. Making these connections allows you to increase your understanding of the production process.

	Media language choices/Analysis
How does the product create representations of specific people, places, ideas or things?	• The positioning of the characters ensures that the heroic nature of Wakandans, and Shuri specifically, is foregrounded. • The characters all have defiant facial expressions and present the idea that they will defend themselves and fight to protect Wakanda.
How does the product communicate narrative information?	The poster implies a threat to Wakanda that comes from the sea. The antagonist is shown mirroring the protagonist, Shuri, whose position on the poster depicts her as a leader (the hero) who is supported by the other Wakandans and the warriors. The Wakandan characters are shown united behind Shuri's leadership.
How does the product communicate its genre? Does it use genre conventions or subvert them?	• Each Marvel film has its own tone and approach to the superhero genre, so the visibility of the studio's logo helps reinforce the brand identity of the production company. The positioning of the superhero suit behind the characters shows that this is part of the Marvel tradition of superhero films. • Shuri's body language connotes heroic bravery and the idea that the narrative will feature extended conflict and battles to resolve the problems is inherent in the design. • The extravagant costumes and exotic appearance of the villains is typical of the genre.

Step 5

The final step involves thinking about things that may not be present within the poster but that can be inferred through the information presented. Again, using theoretical approaches helps here, as they provide useful questions to support you in taking your analysis further.

Apply it

Complete the table by adding some media language observations and ideas about how the poster has been constructed to attract and appeal to its audience, meet its institutional aims, and create brand identity, values or ideologies.

	Media language choices	Analysis
How does the product attempt to identify and attract its audience?		
How does the product set up audience expectations?		
What relationship does the product have with the producing institution?		
How does the product communicate a brand identity either for itself or the producing institution?		
What values or ideologies are created by the product?		
Is there a connection between the values communicated by the product and its target audience?		

8.2 Analysis of media products and audience response

All the steps taken in this analytical method provide ideas and information that help you answer the most important question:

How has the media product been constructed and how does its construction help it to achieve its aims?

In terms of the example we looked at:

> How does the construction of the film poster for *Black Panther: Wakanda Forever* help it to raise awareness of the film and try to persuade audiences to go and watch the film?

The film poster for Black Panther: Wakanda Forever aims to raise awareness of the release of the film and create anticipation in audiences that will lead to them wanting to go and watch the film. Box office takings are important for a feature film as not only do they create income for the film company, but they also act as a marketing tool later when the film is released for purchase on DVD or as a digital download. In order to try and make it as easy as possible for audiences to access the film, the release date is positioned in the centre of the poster.

The genre of the film is clearly communicated. The film's title refers to an earlier superhero film and the hero's mask and suit dominants the image on the poster. Traditionally, superheroes are either lone figures or members of a unified group. The collection of characters at the top of the poster shows that this is a film that combines the two ideas. The suit shows the importance of the individual hero but the montage of characters depicts them working together as a team. The audience is likely to interpret this representation as a reinforcement of their genre expectations, especially within the Marvel series of superhero films.

The poster offers some narrative information reinforcing genre expectations involving conflict and battles between two opposing forces. Although antagonists are represented in the poster, the nature of the conflict is not made clear, creating an enigma that can only be solved by watching the film.

The general look of the poster, the choice of colours and the stern facial expressions connote a more serious rather than comedic superhero film, so audiences may expect darker themes than usually seen in this genre.

Apply it

The step-by-step method can be used to analyse a wide range of media products.

Find examples of the following media forms and use them to practise analysing the intended meaning of the products:

- **Moving image/audio**
    - television
    - music video
    - radio
- **Print**
    - newspapers
    - magazines
- **E-media**
    - online social and participatory media
    - gaming
- **Moving image/audio/print/e-media**
    - advertising and marketing.

TIP ✓

This type of analysis helps you to understand the thought process that has been followed during production. Thinking about media products in this way will enable you to understand how media producers use media language to help them communicate to their audiences and construct meaning. Identifying the techniques they use could help to inspire you as you start to plan your own production.

■ Considering audience responses

It is always worth considering that, while media producers may wish to create a specific meaning when they create their media products, meaning is actually made by the audiences as much as by the producer. Audiences may accept the intended meaning of a media product and go along with the producer's intent in terms of the way the product is interpreted. *Britain's Got Talent* is constructed to provide light entertainment for a mass audience. A narrative is constructed through the show's competition element that helps audiences engage and become emotionally involved with the programme. The show provides safe and secure mainstream entertainment with talented participants who create a spectacle with their performances. The earlier weeks also include a number of participants whose lack of talent can provide comedic relief or whose development of their skills provides inspirational narratives. Judges are represented as character-types whose responses can be predicted, and the brightness of the mise-en-scène and light musical choices all create an atmosphere of comfort and security for the audience. These are just some of the elements that make *Britain's Got Talent* a mainstream success year after year. Many millions of people accept this meaning and enjoy the programme as a simple but entertaining bit of fun.

However, the idea that people only access media that makes them feel good may be a little simplistic. No doubt this is true a lot of the time, but audiences do choose to access media despite the fact that they negotiate their own meaning (see Chapter 6: Media audiences) and may find the product irritating or annoying. There is evidence that some audience members watch some entertainment programmes 'ironically' – that is, they watch it while rejecting the programme's values, so they can mock and ridicule the programme and/or its contestants. Social media can bring these like-minded people together, who create a community by resisting the producer's intended meanings and sharing their own, alternative interpretations, as in the following reproduction of a post:

Tzemg 1 Oct 2023 21:40
I can't sing a note but am considering entering next year. I'm going to shave my beard off, wear women's clothes and cover myself in glitter. I think I have a decent chance.
Share

Bugella → Tzemg 1 Oct 2023 21:42
What are you waiting for you sound perfect but leave the beard on. Be authentic??
Share

Tzemg → Bugella 1 Oct 2023 21:46
That is a fantastic idea. If it works out I'll forward your commission :D
Share

8.2 Analysis of media products and audience response

Of course, the producers don't really mind what motivates the audience to watch, as the fact that they are watching adds to the viewing figures. Even audiences who don't watch are part of the promotion of the product, as seen in the reproduction of a post below:

> **JCollider3** 7 Oct 2023 11:07
>
> I've never actually watched any episode of it but I am an attentive reader of the live blog because it's always very funny. It shows you don't have to watch a programme to find a write up of it amusing.
>
> I feel if I watched the actual show it would ruin it. Plus the blog takes a few minutes to read the whole thing and you don't have to record it. It's far better than the show in all respects.
>
> Weird outdated tv.
>
> Good live blog.
>
> ⮘ Share

△ *The Fall* (BBC/Netflix)

△ *The Undoing* (HBO)

🔗 See more on Hall's reception theory in Chapter 6: Media audiences.

Some people take pleasure from resisting the intended meaning more directly. Debates and discussions online often provide evidence that various audience members take quite different meanings from media products. For example, there are different and contradictory responses by audiences to the way the media portrays violence against women. Programmes such as *The Fall* (BBC/Netflix) and *The Undoing* (HBO) have storylines that focus on the murder of women. Some see this representation as being misogynistic, focusing on women as objects and victims, while others see them as being about the exploration of real-world events where women can be victims of violence. The producers' intents are not always clear in these types of programmes, so audience engagement with the issues and social media comments and discussions can help them to engage with the debates and consider their own position on the issue. They may engage in a negotiation that considers the many levels of meaning that can be taken from a single media product.

Other, even more resistant audience members may enjoy provoking people by taking a deliberately oppositional position in online debates and discussions. They may be deliberately disrespectful towards a celebrity in order to provoke a response from their fans; they may criticise a TV programme or film with a large and dedicated following; or they may offer oppositional political points of view on a news site that is known to have a specific political allegiance. Deliberately antagonistic comments, often identified as 'trolling', aim to create offence and/or make people angry. These comments seek to provoke arguments, but they often act to strengthen the bond between like-minded audience members by helping them reinforce the more accepted interpretations within their community.

EXAMPLE: Audience response – *Live for Now* Pepsi advert, featuring Kendall Jenner (2017)

In 2017, Pepsi released an advert that was intended to contribute to the brand image of the soft drink manufacturer, create positive associations with the drink and, in doing so, encourage consumers to select Pepsi rather than its competitors. It chose a well-known celebrity who was admired by young people to front the advert (Kendall Jenner) and constructed an advert featuring imagery related to social protest, which, towards the end of the advert, turned into a real-world confrontation between protesters and police.

△ A still from the *Live for Now* Pepsi advert, showing Kendall Jenner handing a can of Pepsi to an actor playing a police officer

Intended reading: Pepsi wanted the advert to create brand and product associations with:

- progressive ideas about individual power and challenging authority (in the context of the protests against the Trump administration and in favour of the Black Lives Matter campaign)
- fashionable youth culture
- elite and beautiful social groups and individuals
- the promotion of peace
- solving conflict.

Many audience members may have made a **negotiated reading** when viewing the advert. Many people would have immediately made no logical connection between a soft drink and the lofty ideas in the advert but would still have had a positive response to the imagery and general message.

The dominant response from commentators on social media, though, was to resist the advert's aims and reject the intended meaning. **Oppositional readings** could be found on Facebook and X as well as in the news reports that followed. Pepsi was accused of being culturally insensitive, reducing Black Lives Matter marches to fashion parades and offering simple solutions to complex social, economic and political issues. Confrontations between protesters and the police in the advert were peaceful and showed tolerance and mutual respect. This was argued to have belittled the situations, where confrontations with US police officers had led to violence and even death.

The pressure created by the oppositional readings led to Pepsi removing the advert from circulation, making a statement that they 'did not intend to make light of any serious issue'.

Meaning is not simply within the text itself. Media producers attempt to create meaning when they construct media products, but audiences construct meaning for themselves and may interpret the product in ways that were not originally intended. The communication between audience members is part of this construction of meaning and some audience members may accept while others reject or negotiate the intended meaning of a product. It is worth keeping this in mind as you analyse media products.

Apply it

Choose a popular media product or personality. Check social media responses to the product/personality and make notes of the different opinions and ideas that are being communicated.

8.2 Analysis of media products and audience response

> **Note for the NEA**
> Your knowledge and understanding of how real media products are constructed and how audiences interpret and interact with media products should influence the way you create your practical production work.

■ Using key theories and subject-specialist terminology

As you learn about media theories it may be tempting to think of them as a body of knowledge that should be learned and then reproduced. Showing you understand the theories is more important than just showing you know them. You can show your understanding by applying the theories and ideas, and this goes beyond simple memory. For example, Todorov stated that narratives follow a three-part structure: an **equilibrium** is first established and then **disrupted** before events **resolve**, creating a **new equilibrium**.

> See Chapter 4: Media language.

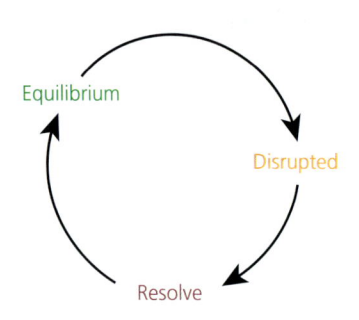

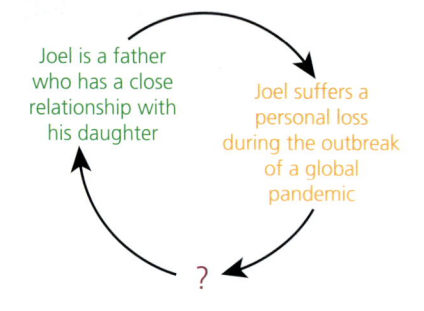

△ (a) Todorov's narrative structure

△ (b) Todorov's narrative structure applied to *The Last of Us* (HBO)

Knowing this is only the starting point in media studies, as the knowledge needs to be applied in order to be of any value. In the exams you may be asked to define some media studies terms (Paper 1) but you could also be asked to apply ideas when analysing media products (Papers 1 and 2). Application of knowledge requires you to be able to use your knowledge to explain **how** a media product creates meaning. When discussing media products you should always provide detailed examples to support the points you are making.

For example:

In *The Last of Us* (HBO) an **equilibrium** is presented in the first episode. The lead character (Sarah) is introduced and through **media language choices** that create narrative markers we learn that she is an ordinary teenage girl who lives with her single father. She is resourceful and is clearly crucial in keeping the household organised. We see her making breakfast for her father.

She has a good relationship with her father, attends the local high school and is thoughtful towards her elderly neighbour. This **equilibrium** is disrupted when a fungal infection outbreak causes infected people to violently attack the non-infected in an attempt to pass the infection along. The stability of Sarah's homelife is **disrupted** and a state of **disequilibrium** is created when the danger from the infected means they have to evacuate their home in an attempt to find safety.

CHAPTER 8 DEVELOPING MEDIA STUDIES SKILLS

△ Joel and Ellie, *The Last of Us* (HBO)

There is no need to explain or describe Todorov's theory to show your understanding of ideas in your analysis. Understanding is demonstrated in the way the ideas are used to explain the meaning being created by a media product. Key to being able to do this is the ability to use the terminology of a theory fluently and with confidence. The key terms provided in each chapter and the Glossary of key terms at the end of this book provide much of the subject-specialist terminology that you should use in your writing. Like analysis, using terminology is a skill that can be practised and the more you do it, the more confident you will become and the more natural it will feel. This is why your teacher sets essays and writing assignments – to help you improve your use of media terminology.

It is important not to forget that when you use a media term you need to provide a detailed product, audience or institutional example as evidence. It is not enough to say that *Britain's Got Talent* aims to entertain its target audience (which it absolutely does). You need to be able to provide concrete examples as to *how* it does this.

Apply it

Select some media terminology – you can use the following examples and then practise using other terms from the Glossary of key terms.

- **Media language** connotations – symbolism – anchorage – myth – signifier – signification
- **Moving image** establishing shot – codes and conventions – diegetic sound – character role – intended meaning – high-key lighting
- **Print** placement – compositional balance – headline – columns – anchorage – crop
- **Narrative** hero – causality – equilibrium – disruption
- **Genre** codes and conventions – familiarity – difference – sub-genre – hybridity
- **Representation** mediation – stereotype – under-representation – self-representation – reinforcing of values – countertypes – constructed reality
- **Audience** demographics – target audience – audience appeal – audience behaviour – gratifications
- **Institution** distribution – ownership – branding – marketing – regulation – income sources

8.2 Analysis of media products and audience response

△ TV presenter Alison Hammond

> Now, using media products/institutions you are familiar with, use the terminology to discuss how products make meaning, how audiences relate to media products and/or institutions, and how institutions attempt to engage with audiences and maximise their profits.
>
> You may start by making simple observations in a bullet point list, then you can develop your skills by building these points into a paragraph of more formal writing. Don't forget, though, that you need to provide examples to support each of the points you are making.

For example:

Noel Fielding and Alison Hammond **appeal** to different **demographics** and create different **audience gratifications** for the audience. This will have been taken into account when selecting Hammond as a replacement for Matt Lucas, who left the The Great British Bake Off after the 2022 series.

Note for the NEA

You will need to submit a Statement of Intent with your production work for the NEA. This statement should demonstrate your knowledge of elements of the theoretical framework as it relates to the brief you have chosen. To demonstrate the extent of your understanding, you should use appropriate terminology when explaining your production plans.

8.3 The social, cultural, political and economic role of the media

Media products are not just standalone artefacts. The media plays an important role in all our lives. It is part of the social, cultural and political context of our culture. The breadth and variety of the contemporary media means that there are many ways to engage with its contextual role. What follows are just some examples.

■ Social

Sometimes a media product can be seen to have a social impact, even becoming part of our society.

For example, social media has become part of people's day-to-day lives in ways traditional media never could be. Social media can be used to access traditional media, providing links to news stories, videos, TV programmes, film trailers and podcasts being shared millions of times each day. Social media also provides audiences with games, and are platforms that give access to and information about all manner of things, including the media itself. Audiences share traditional media content with one another, but they also get to create content themselves – whether this is a simple post or a video uploaded to TikTok or YouTube. Social media has changed the way people communicate, the way they access the media, the way they share the things they create and their own ideas. These are all relatively recent social changes, so the long-term impact of this is still to be seen.

Another social impact can come from changing representations. Historically many minority ethnic groups have been under-represented in mainstream media. In recent years, there have been concerted efforts to increase the diversity of representations in terms of ethnicity, gender identity and sexuality.

The increase in media producers with diverse backgrounds has helped raise the profile of a variety of groups and enabled stories to be told from their own perspectives, rather than someone else's.

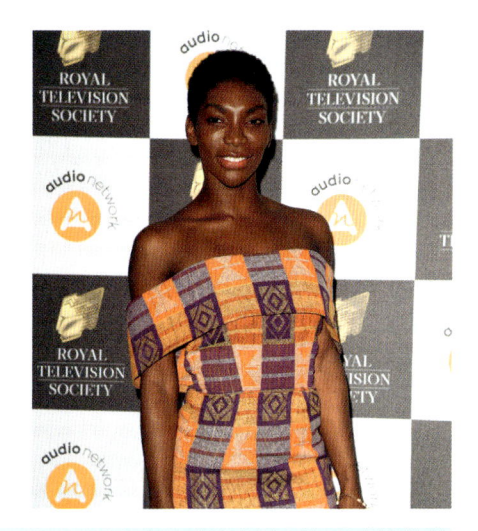

△ Phoebe Waller-Bridge (left) and Michaela Coel (right) bring unique points of view to their writing and performances

■ Cultural

The media is part of our culture. Media products are cultural artefacts and the experiences we share around the media influence the way we think about ourselves and one another.

For example, *The Great British Bake Off* is a programme that grew in popularity, from 2.7 million to over 7 million viewers, over the seven years it was broadcast on BBC Two before moving to BBC One. Its audience grew again for three years, peaking at 14.8 million. In September 2016, it was announced that the show was moving to Channel 4, who outbid the BBC for the rights to broadcast the show. Its cultural impact could be measured by the audience response to this news and the fact that the news media saw this as newsworthy. Audiences took to social media to express their disappointment and, at times, anger and outrage at the news that the show was moving channels, and broadsheet, tabloid, online and broadcast news providers all included this in their reporting over the course of the following week.

The show had a cultural impact as it moved the 'reality-competition' genre away from the back-stabbing (*The Apprentice*), the serious (*Masterchef*) and the back-story led (*Britain's Got Talent*) styles of programming to a gentler, more supportive and collaborative type of competition. Shows such as *The Great British Sewing Bee*, *The Great Pottery Throw Down* and *Handmade* followed suit and used formats that were similar to *The Great British Bake Off* but, perhaps more importantly, kept the more positive, less combative tone of the original show. It was the friendly, positive and supportive nature of the show that audiences feared would be lost in its move to a commercial and more 'edgy' channel. The producers had managed to create a mass market, mainstream hit that created reassurance for the audience and was based on positive values. This was a marked change in the culture of reality competition shows. In addition, the programme was highly influential in terms of its aesthetics, which held connotations of village fetes from a perceived 'simpler time' that plays into a comforting nostalgia for an idea that exists as a cultural myth of an idealised, kind, yet patriotic Britain, where home baking was the norm.

△ Nadiya Hussain, the 2015 winner of *The Great British Bake Off*

■ Political

The nature of most media is that it is political. The media reflects the political climate of the culture that produced it and in some cases can be seen to influence the political culture of the country.

For example, British newspapers are renowned for the fact they each have their own distinct political perspective. Most national British newspapers are on the right politically, with the exceptions being the *Daily Mirror* and the *Guardian* – both of which are ideologically centre-left. Where broadcast news has a responsibility to try to stay impartial, British newspapers are free to promote whatever political perspective and whichever political party the newspaper management decides upon. The majority of the press have supported the Conservative Party since 2010 and their reporting of the Labour Party has been critical, regularly taking a mocking tone; even those 'on the left' may represent relatively centrist views. Newspapers are free to report news stories that protect their own interests and promote their own values – making them an important part of the UK's political landscape. Even though print newspapers are on the decline, the newspapers still set the news agenda that is followed by broadcast news and online media outlets.

Other media also offers political perspectives. Recently, there have been many media products on TV and in cinemas that have focused on the economic inequalities of our time. American programmes such as *The White Lotus* (2021–) and *Succession* (2018–23) and films like *The Menu* and *Triangle of Sadness* (both 2022) show the

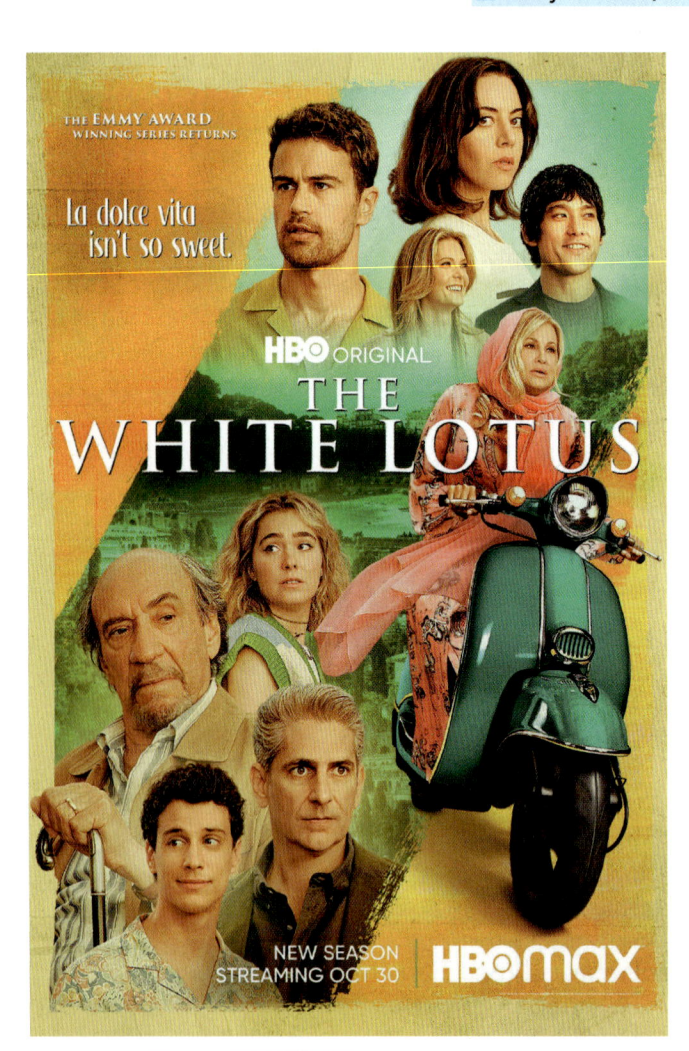

△ A poster for Season 2 of *The White Lotus*

CHAPTER 8 DEVELOPING MEDIA STUDIES SKILLS

inherent hollowness and underlying misery in the lives of the wealthy, while South Korea's *Parasite* (2019) identifies wealth inequality as a global issue with its unique take on the way money (or the lack of it) creates dramatically different life experiences. The Netflix series *You* (2018–) featured the systematic murder of wealthy and entitled people by what was dubbed the 'Eat-the-Rich-Killer'. These products are responding to the political context of an economic system where a small proportion of people have extreme wealth but the majority of the population work hard for increasingly low pay and with reduced rights.

■ Economic

As with all businesses, organisations in the media industry aim to make profit and this leads the decisions made by them in the way they create products. They may make products that attempt to encourage people to pay in order to access or own the product, or they may make products that try to attract large audiences so advertisers can be persuaded to pay more for time or space.

For example, the music industry traditionally made most of its money through sales of music. Audiences would buy singles and albums on vinyl, cassette and, later, CD. The sales of 'hard copies' of music have declined rapidly and when music is purchased it is usually bought as a data file. However, the audience no longer needs to buy the product to access music, since now it can be accessed free via streaming services. Services such as Spotify are funded by advertising, although a monthly subscription often allows the audience to access music 'ad free'. Music can be accessed via YouTube and is often pirated – downloaded from file-sharing sites illegally.

△ Billie Eilish wearing Beats by Dr. Dre headphones on a Tokyo billboard

This economic context has changed the way in which musicians are paid and the music industry makes money. If music is to generate profit, then income has to be generated in other ways rather than just music sales. For example, corporate sponsorship is often provided for tours, and product placement is common within music videos and in the social media of artists who have a large fan-base. Social media has become important in promoting an artist, and the number of followers an artist has can influence the decisions of radio programmers when deciding which artists should go on a show's playlist. This leads to situations where small unknown artists struggle to get radio airplay.

TIP ✓

In order to be able to debate these issues, you will need to keep up to date with what is going on in contemporary culture. This means engaging with the latest news stories that define our social, cultural, political and economic context. You will need to be informed on the general issues of the day but will also need to keep an eye on the developments in the media culture, by learning about the latest institutional issues and the debates that are happening around TV programmes, films, music and celebrities.

Apply it

Do some research:

- Take some time to look through a few newspaper websites – both tabloid and broadsheet.
- Look through the 'media', 'culture', 'TV/radio', 'game' and 'film' sections of the *Guardian* website.
- Have a look through the BBC news website.
- Watch a news bulletin on a non-BBC source.
- Watch some news on an online source.
- Access a review site such as *Den of Geek*.
- Check what's trending on X.
- Read some music news on the *NME* website.

Now try to identify some of the questions and concerns that are helping to define our contemporary culture. Some of these questions may be linked to the media and others may be broader social, cultural, political and/or economic issues.

Note for the NEA

Each NEA brief will ask you to produce a media product within a contemporary media context. When researching and planning for your production you might like to consider how the media product reflects or is influenced by social, cultural and/or political issues. You should also consider the economic context of your production. For example, a music video is an advert for a musician's brand and related media products, and a magazine front cover is constructed to try to persuade audiences to buy the product. Your knowledge of this economic context should be apparent in the production itself.

8.4 Essay writing

Throughout your course you will no doubt complete a number of written pieces of work that aim to help you present your ideas formally. Everyone needs to work on developing a clear writing style and practice will help you improve this crucial skill.

Essay writing is more than presenting a collection of facts or some information; your essays need to present an argument or show the various sides in a debate. You may be asked to evaluate ideas or engage with specific theoretical ideas and concepts. Crucially, though, essay writing gives you an opportunity to show not only what you know, but also how much you understand the media.

When you write an essay, you will usually be responding to a question. This means you have two important initial tasks:

1. Deciding what the question wants you to do.
2. Deciding what the question wants you to focus on.

■ 1 What does the question want you to do?

Working this out should be fairly straightforward. All you need to do is look for the verb in the question. You should also look at *how* the question has been worded. This can give a clear indication of what is expected of you in your response.

The following table shows some of the words and phrasing you could be asked to respond to for an essay, with examples of possible ways to respond.

Key words/phrases	Expectation	For example
Discuss	Present a logical and balanced argument with evidence for the ideas you are using.	A common point of view is that social media is a negative thing in society. There are, however, points of view that propose that social media can be positive.
Evaluate	Present a logical engagement with the issue raised in the question. You will need to discuss how valid your ideas are and show your analysis of strengths and weaknesses of ideas that relate to the issue raised in the question. You should be able to draw conclusions based on your knowledge of media products and theories and not just state the ideas.	Neale says that genres need to offer both familiarity and difference. This idea can be shown to be valid when considering how changes and innovations within the genre have allowed crime dramas to maintain their popularity and appeal to different audience groups. Examples from crime dramas should be used to demonstrate this.
Analyse	To analyse is to engage with a detailed exploration of the elements and/or structure of a media product. Analysis begins with observation (usually based on media language choices) and then goes on to explain why each element was chosen and/or what effect these choices may have. It is often a good idea to use the theoretical framework to support the explanation provided.	See the example of a detailed analysis of a film poster earlier in this chapter.
Explain	To explain is to offer a reason why. Explanations should be supported with examples from media products, and reasons why should not just be an opinion or a personal perspective. Reasons why should be offered that show your knowledge of the theoretical framework or the context of production.	See the example of a detailed analysis of a film poster earlier in this chapter.
Consider	Similar to evaluate. You should discuss ideas related to the question that show you have thought about them rather than simply repeated them. One way you can show you are considering the ideas is to apply the ideas you are considering to media examples/contextual issues. Considered ideas are not simply accepted as 'true' – they are applied, thought about and some may be rejected if they do not fit with the evidence from your analysis.	Although the representation of Stella Gibson in *The Fall* follows some conventions in the way women are usually shown, for example she is often presented as a beautiful and sexualised woman in a way that supports the idea of the male gaze (Mulvey), she also subverts these conventions. Stella is a powerful woman who is shown almost exclusively in a professional environment. She is shown being in control of her career and her romantic relationships. She defines herself and is not defined by her relationship to men.
To what extent ...?	This phrasing is asking you to consider 'how much (is this true/the case)'.	Q: To what extent do mobile devices offer more freedom for audiences? A: Mobile devices offer freedom for audiences in a number of ways. For example, ...

Developing your argument

You should aim to use your perspective to present a reasoned and supported argument. The support for your argument is what will provide the evidence of how much you have studied and your own understanding of the issue raised.

You will need to learn to present an argument but before you can do this you must have one to present. You will learn a range of arguments when you engage with the theoretical framework and hopefully you will hear more in class from your teacher and your fellow students.

What is important is not what other people think but what *you* think. In order to have an opinion on an argument, you will need to engage with other people's ideas and then consider them in light of the media products you are studying.

So if, for example, narrative theory tells us that narratives work on *conflicts driving a narrative forward until resolution is reached,* you may want to consider:

- how soap operas and long-running serials need to manipulate this structure
- how some narratives don't offer conclusive resolutions

8.4 Essay writing

- how (and why) hard and soft news stories offer resolutions that are sometimes shown to be false.

To make the writing process easier, you must be sure where you are going in your essay before you start – you should know what your argument is.

This means that preparation is key. You will need to generate ideas when you:

- practise analysing media products
- practise applying media concepts
- practise using theoretical terminology.

The essay-writing process should start with a detailed, thorough and focused plan – get your ideas together before you begin.

Apply it

Consider this 'why' question. (You can replace the media products for two other successful media products that have similar content if you prefer.)

Q: Explain why programmes such as *You* and *The White Lotus* have been successful?

A: Write down your first thoughts on how you would answer the question, making sure that each response begins with the word 'because' and contains at least one reference to a media concept or theory. For example:

Because:

- they attract *audiences* by offering a range of gratifications
- *audiences* often respond emotionally to these programmes
- *institutions* can target more than one audience group (*ideologically*)
- they encourage the use of *social media* benefiting the *institution* in *generating publicity*
- they encourage the use of *social media*, providing *engagement* and the feeling of being involved for the *audience* members
- they fit in with the current political/media *narratives*.

Some of the ideas in the list above can be connected to or merged with other ideas from the list.

- Once you have a list of ideas you are happy with put them in a rank order starting with your 'best' idea.
- Identify which ideas relate to the theoretical framework you could use to discuss your observation further (you could link to more than one theoretical idea).
- Identify what examples you could use to show how the idea works in the media products.
- Do this for all your ideas. You may find a table like the one on the following page can help you organise your ideas.

Q: Why are programmes such as *You* and *The White Lotus* successful?

Because ... (add your own ideas)	Link to theoretical framework idea (link your idea to an aspect of the theoretical framework)	Example from media product (provide your own examples)
Because they encourage the use of social media, providing engagement and a feeling of being involved. This in turn helps the audience generate publicity for the institution.	*Uses and gratification theory; use of social stereotypes; construction of heroes/villains; viral marketing and marketing techniques; social media and herd mentality.*	*Examples of use of hashtags before ad breaks coinciding with controversial behaviour or comment from characters on the show. Posts from known opinion leaders and other X users to show viral nature of social media.*
Because ...		
Because ...		
Because ...		

From the above table an essay 'structure' can be formed. The reason for the programmes' success can be discussed and ideas can be supported by the **application of concepts** and **theory**, and **textual examples**.

To turn your ideas into an essay response you need to 'write up' three to five 'because' points, giving detailed examples and explanations that show how your idea is related to the programme's success.

■ 2 What does the question want you to focus on?

No question will ask you to discuss everything you know on a specific topic or issue. You will always be asked to focus on a specific, sometimes quite narrow, part of the issue/theory raised.

Consider the following questions – all focusing on representation. You could use the following media forms to answer these questions – choose a form and then use the two CSPs to support your answer.

- **Paper 1**
  - Advertising and marketing
  - Music videos
- **Paper 2**
  - TV
  - Online, social and participatory media
  - Magazines
  - Gaming

1. **Identify and evaluate how ethnicity is represented in the products you have studied.**
2. **Analyse and compare the way the CSPs represent ethnicity.**
3. **How might the representations of ethnicity in your CSPs contribute to an idea of a collective identity (Gauntlett)?**

All three of the questions are on 'representation', but each requires a very different response.

8.4 Essay writing

1 This question needs you to focus on the specific representations of ethnicity in specific media products, and the way media language has been used to construct the representations present. Semiotic analysis could be used to consider the way the media language choices create connotations that add to the possible interpretations that could be made by the audience. Specific examples will need to be given to show that techniques have been *identified* but a discussion on the meaning created by the media language choices and their potential impact would take an answer to this question into *evaluation*.

2 This is a question that is asking for similarities and differences between different products to be engaged with. Observations will be required but *analysis* needs to deal with why the representations are similar and/or different. This may lead to a discussion on genre codes, institutional values, narrative devices, audience expectations and/or the economic context of production, depending on whether you think the representations are the same/different and why.

3 This is a question that needs knowledge and understanding of a specific theoretical idea and how that idea works in media products.

Apply it

Look at the following statements about media products and reword them using media terminology:

1 People really like this programme.
2 This newspaper provides more stories about celebrities than politics, economics and foreign affairs.
3 The drama was very exciting at the start.
4 The decoration in the room looked very posh.
5 The man in charge of investigation got the job done by being violent.
6 The artist was wearing Beats headphones in the music video.

It is crucial that, before starting to write, you have read the question carefully and you are clear on the focus you need to take. There are many ways you could be asked to demonstrate your knowledge and understanding of elements of the theoretical framework, but you will not be asked to simply write down everything you know about representation. You will always be asked to engage with a specific aspect of the element of the framework you are being assessed on and you will be rewarded for providing a focused response that selects theoretical ideas and media examples that are best suited to answering the question.

△ A still from Season 3 of You

■ Writing style

When writing about the media, aim to use media terminology, so practise discussing media text formally and integrating terminology into your writing.

Here are a few things that it is best to avoid when writing an essay:

- **Avoid generalisations, assumptions and guesses:** the idea that 'all women like rom-coms' or that 'older audiences don't understand social media' is simply not true. These are just stereotypes based on the fact that some women may like soaps and not all older people understand social media, but these facts cannot be applied to all people in the group. To avoid generalisations, look for evidence to support your arguments. The producers of rom-coms do assume that their audience will be largely female and that domestic and emotional storylines will appeal to women. Evidence for this can be found in the narrative choices and the representations in the programmes. Your close analysis of media products could support your discussion on the assumptions made by media producers.

- **Avoid absolute statements unless they can be supported by facts:** to say that *Ted Lasso* is a sitcom is to state a fact. This can be supported by looking at the way it uses the codes and conventions of the sitcom. It also uses a range of visual and lexical techniques that attempt to make the audience laugh – the primary function of a sitcom. To say that the programme is funny, however, is an opinion. Given its success, it is clear that some people do find it funny, and so audience numbers can show it is a successful sitcom and analysis of the techniques it uses can show it intends to amuse. Rather than state unprovable opinions it is best to focus on ideas that can be supported and evidenced by using examples from the product itself or facts around its industrial or audience context.

- **Avoid emotive language and value judgements:** when analysing and discussing the media, it is best to avoid language that is based on emotion and judgements that are simply based on your own opinion. Saying that *The Boys* is 'brilliant' or that *Newsnight* is 'boring' shows that your comments are based on your own emotional response rather than analysis. Whether something is good or bad is subjective and there are no clear criteria to enable this kind of judgement. The reason you have your emotional response to a media product is often down to whether or not you are part of its target audience, for example. Many people attempt to write for media studies as if they are writing a review or a blog. Review writers and bloggers don't have to explain the reasons for their feelings about a media product (although good ones do), but media studies students won't be rewarded for personal responses unless they can support their responses by demonstrating a knowledge of the theoretical framework and an analytical approach to their interpretations.

- **Avoid colloquialisms and informal language:** try to keep your writing as formal as you can. It helps you communicate clearly to your readers regardless of how old they are and where they come from. Try to avoid slang terms – TV shows shouldn't be described as 'cheesy'. If you feel they have been cheaply or poorly made then you could analyse the limitations of the mise-en-scène or the clichéd nature of the dialogue (for example) to discuss the way in which they fail to draw the audience into the narrative. Your essay writing should avoid using regional-specific vocabulary and fashionable turns of phrase in which may be related to a specific age group or subculture. Your job is to make your written work clear and understandable for any reader.

- **Avoid cliché and metaphor:** try to avoid using phrases that have either lost their meaning or are metaphorical. TV shows can be described as being a success (evidence can be shown by highlighting viewing figures) but to say they are a 'big hit' is a cliché. For example, 'the protagonist of a drama had an "ace up his sleeve" that was the "final nail in the coffin" for the antagonist' uses two metaphorical clichés. You would be much better saying that 'the protagonist had a final plan/secret weapon/idea that helped put an end to the antagonist's actions and move the narrative towards its resolution'.
- **Avoid too much description:** you will need to provide some description as you have to give examples from media products to support your interpretations. Avoid retelling plot or providing extended descriptions of what you have seen. You should provide enough information on the product you are analysing to demonstrate the point you wish to make.
- **Avoid only stating what you think – instead explain and/or evaluate:** saying that a celebrity's Instagram account includes many marketing posts is probably a good observation. Identifying that Radio 4's *Today* uses an antagonistic technique when conducting interviews shows a real engagement with the radio show. Stating, however, is only the first part of analysis. You need to support your statement in the following ways:
  - Provide examples from the product to show that you haven't made your statement up.
  - Take care not to over-describe (see previous point).
  - Discuss the examples using ideas and terminology from the theoretical framework.
  - Offer an explanation as to *why* what you have observed is significant.
  - Evaluate the impact of your observation.

Note for the NEA

For the NEA you have only 500 words to show your knowledge and understanding in the Statement of Intent, so try to present your ideas as directly as possible and use media terminology to help focus the points you are making.

Stretch and challenge

Practise linking ideas from the framework to show you recognise the interconnected nature of the theories and concepts you study. You could create a spider diagram or a bullet point list to organise your ideas. You could then put your ideas into full sentences and paragraphs to help develop your writing skills.

Using your CSPs, show (for example):

- how media language choices combine to make meaning
- how representations reflect contemporary cultural values and ideas
- how narrative devices create audience gratifications
- how genre codes are used to create audience expectations
- how the industrial context impacts on the way the product has been produced
- how the choice of genre and/or narrative devices related to the industrial context of production.

→ Summary

This chapter has dealt with the skills you will need to develop. You need to:

- develop your analytical skills and your ability to discuss media products in detail to show how they create meaning
- use media terminology and ideas from the theoretical framework confidently and effectively
- be able to relate media products to the social, cultural, political and economic contexts of production
- communicate your ideas clearly. You should aim to be able to produce formal essay-style responses to questions.

Chapter 9: Making media

→ What you will learn in this chapter

Chapter 9: Making media covers:

- an introduction to the practicalities of production
- general information on the basic principles of producing work in print, e-media, audio and with moving and still images, including identifying the type of production equipment and software you will need
- the platforms you will be expected to produce for and the specific issues you may need to consider
- the codes and conventions of some common media forms and genres to help you consider how technology can be used to help replicate them, so you will have more time to create visually appealing and engaging products that succeed in communicating ideas to their audience and creating a product that meets the aims given in the Statement of Intent.

> This information will support your practical production and should be supported by your research and planning, discussed in Chapter 10.

9.1 Producing different types of media

■ Technology requirements

The choices you make when creating your production will be shaped by the technologies you have available.

Media form	Equipment needs	Software needs
Moving image – including television, advertising and music video	**A moving image camera.** There are many specialist cameras for shooting moving image **footage**. You can use the camera on a smartphone but make sure you have your phone in the correct **aspect ratio** (landscape mode) when you shoot your footage. You will need a **tripod** to stabilise your camera. This is especially important if you will be using a smartphone or a tablet to capture images as they can be very difficult to keep stable. Other equipment can be helpful when creating moving image work such as **lighting, green-screen technology**, etc. You may not have access to professional equipment but you can be creative. For example, not many people have access to a **dolly** to create a tracking shot but could you come up with a low-tech way to achieve this effect? You could try moving the camera operator (carefully) on a wheeled chair, or fixing your camera (firmly) on a skateboard that can be pulled along (carefully) by the camera operator.	**Editing software**. It may be possible to use a tablet to edit your work. Editing software (for still and moving images) can be accessed online and is often free (e.g. Filmora Video Editor) and there are many apps that can be downloaded for smartphones and tablets (e.g. iMovie for video; Pixelmator for still images). You may have access to professional software such as Adobe Premier. These software packages are powerful but expensive, so before making any purchase of editing software check that the software/app can do what you need for your production. It is also worth checking that the software/app will allow you to save your moving image files in universally accessible formats, such as MP4 or Avi. If you are going to upload your work to YouTube you should check the list of accepted formats. If you are going to send your work on a **disc or memory stick** you will need to make sure your work can be viewed on any PC or Mac.

Media form	Equipment needs	Software needs
Moving image continued	**Sound recording equipment.** You can capture sound in the camera but this can sometimes lead to problems with **ambient noise,** and **in-camera sound** may not be as loud or clear as you would like. Using separate sound equipment to record sound gives you more control over your sound balance and allows you to add voice-overs, edit your sound recordings and create sound effects. Again, smartphones and tablets can be used to record sound. **A computer or tablet** that enables you to install **post-production editing software.**	
Audio – including radio and podcasts	**Sound recording equipment.** You may have access to professional sound recording equipment but, if not, sound can be recorded on smartphones and tablets. **A computer** that enables you to install **post-production sound editing software** or access the internet.	**Sound editing software.** As with video editing, a range of software is available from professional sound editing packages to be used on a computer to less complex programmes and apps for computers, tablets and smartphones. Free software can be accessed and used online too. You can also use moving image editing software to edit sound. Again, make sure the software you are using allows you to save your files to formats that are easily shared such as wav, MP3, etc.
Print – including newspapers, magazines and advertising	**A computer or tablet** that allows you to install **desktop publishing (DTP)** and **image manipulation software**. **A camera**, **or the camera on a smartphone or tablet** for taking still images.	**A DTP package.** Try to avoid using the templates provided by software packages – you should create your own designs. **An image manipulation software package** to help you edit, enhance and manipulate your still images.
e-media production	As most online, social and participatory media is a multi-media experience you would need access to equipment and software to allow you to **design the pages and the content** for these pages, **create and edit still images** to illustrate your work, and to create and **edit moving images and audio work**.	
Offline production	**A computer or tablet** that allows you to install **desk-top publishing (DTP)** and **image manipulation software**. **A camera, smartphone or tablet** for taking still images and/or moving images. **Specialist equipment, a smartphone or tablet** for recording sound.	There are professional **web design software packages**. Research these before committing to a specific software as some are complex and may need you to learn coding – and this is not a requirement in media studies. **DTP packages** allow you to, for example, design pages for a website. Alternatively, you could design your pages in an image manipulation software package and then import the image files into a DTP or web design package to add hyperlinks and multi-media features. If you use offline software to design your e-media production, you will need to consider how you will submit your work, as the e-media productions will need to be viewable in a browser. This way your work can be viewed as a fully functional product. You may need access to post-production editing software to work on sound recordings, still images and/or moving image footage.

9.1 Producing different types of media

Media form	Equipment needs	Software needs
Online production	**A computer or tablet** that allows you access to the internet. **A camera, smartphone or tablet** for taking still images and/or moving images. **Specialist equipment, a smartphone or tablet** for recording sound.	There are lots of options for online production. **Web design services** such as wix.com allow you to create your website and host it online. These services have lots of features and can be used to create professional-looking websites. You might want to use a **blog site** such as WordPress or create social media pages on sites such as Facebook, Tumblr, X, TikTok and/or Instagram. If you use an online production tool, you will need to show your creative and technical skills in the content you produce for your e-media production. You may need access to post-production editing software to work on sound recordings, still images and/or moving image footage.
Computer games	**A computer or tablet** that allows you access to the internet.	There are lots of online websites that provide users with the opportunity to create games online. Users can create games using game engines provided by resources such as Gamemaker, Unity and Unreal Engine. There are lots of articles online and videos on YouTube that offer ideas and advice for novices with no technical skills who wish to make a game.

Apply it

1. What production equipment do you have easy access to?
2. What production software or apps do you have on your computer, tablet and/or smartphone?
3. What production apps are available for your computer, tablet and/or smartphone?
4. Research online production tools for image manipulation, DTP, web design and game design.

See Chapter 10: The NEA for further information on design in production.

■ Production platforms

The individual tasks within the briefs will focus on one or more of the three platforms. You could be asked to create print, broadcast or e-media products.

9.2 Print production

■ Desktop publishing (DTP) software

When you are creating print production work you need to use **desktop publishing (DTP) software** that gives you as much control over the different elements of a page as possible.

You need to be able to control:

- the typeface: its style, size and positioning
- the page size: different publications use different page sizes
- the presentation of your text: many print productions have quite a lot of text and use columns in the page design
- the presentation of images and illustrations: you need to be able to position images accurately and resize them to fit with your page design
- the presentation of a design house style.

Something you should consider before you begin is printing. What works on screen may not necessarily work in print, so you should make test prints as often as you can to check how your work looks on paper. You will need to use a printer that allows you to print the correct size and weight of paper. If that's not possible, practise printing so that even if your practice run is smaller than the final outcome, it has the correct page proportions.

Basic principles of page layout and design

Regardless of the format of your print production work, there are some basic principles of layout and design you will need to consider before you begin.

Page size and proportion

Before you start creating your layout and design, you will need to set up your paper size, which you should base on the conventions of the form you are making. Most DTPs allow you to do this in centimetres.

So, to ensure your finished work is accurate, you will need to find out what the correct size and **page proportions** are for your publication type. You may be able to search for this information online, but you can also measure an example of the media product you're going to emulate so you know that your page size and proportions will be precise. Most printers use A4 paper and some A3, but not all print products match these sizes. Where your media product is too large to be printed at the correct size, you will need to set up your page for your product to be printed smaller but proportionally correct. If you don't do this, your work may look squashed and the text may appear to be the wrong size.

For example, a large **billboard** advertising poster measures 304.8cm high x 1219.2cm wide. This means that a billboard poster needs to be (roughly) four times wider than it is high. Clearly, you can't create a life-sized billboard poster, but you could use a template on a landscape A4 page that measures 10cm high x 40cm wide and your poster would have roughly the correct proportions.

Newspapers tend to come in two standard sizes:

- tabloids are 28cm x 43cm
- broadsheets are 60cm x 75cm.

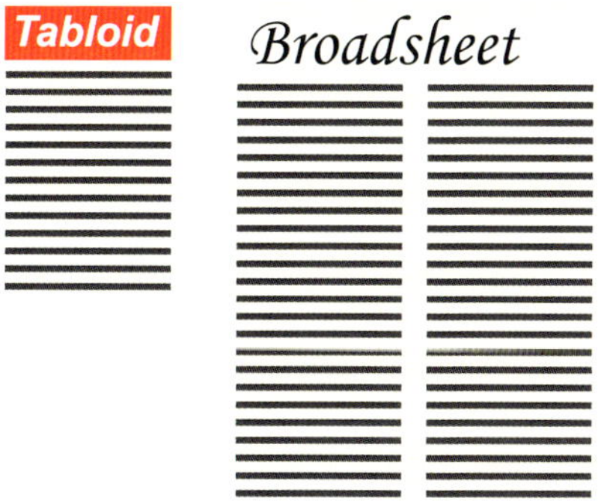

Magazines can vary in size. Smaller magazines use 'digest size', which has much smaller pages than a 'standard-sized' magazine. Digest size pages measure approximately 14cm x 21cm, whereas a standard-sized magazine measures 27.5cm x 21cm, slightly shorter than A4. Most magazines are taller than they are wide but others may be wider than they are tall.

If you are attempting to emulate a specific title for your production work or using a specific magazine as a model, you will need to measure the page size to be sure your finished work is accurate. The page size impacts on the size of the fonts and columns, so if your pages are not the right size you're likely to get the proportions of the **design elements** wrong, and this will limit the effectiveness of your production. If you're creating your own newspaper or magazine title, you should check which page sizes are most often used in the form and genre you are working in.

Magazine and newspaper **adverts** are sized by the percentage of the page covered – so an advert's size is determined by the host publication's size and the page proportions. Identifying where your advert would be published (what type of publication and where on the page) means you can demonstrate that you understand that different publications are different shapes and sizes. You can also show you understand the relationship between your product and the target audience by placing your advert in a publication that shares your target audience.

△ 4 sheet: 101.6cm x 152.4cm

△ 6 sheet: 120cm x 180cm

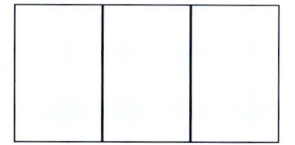

△ 6 sheet: 120cm x 180cm

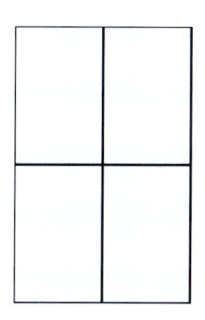

△ 12 sheet: 304.8cm x 152.4cm

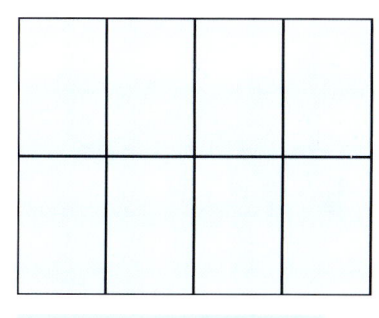

△ 32 sheet: 406.4cm x 304.8cm

You may be asked to create standalone advertising materials such as flyers or posters. The brief may be specific, detailing what type of advertising product or products you must create, or it may allow you to make decisions on what advertising products are suitable for the given task. In either case, an understanding of your target audience should help you decide what forms of advertising product would be the most appropriate to get your message to the right people. As advertising products come in all shapes and sizes, you should decide on the placement of your advert and/or the distribution method so you can set up your DTP page accurately before production begins. Again, the size and proportion you choose influences the way you design your page.

You should use existing media products to investigate the different approaches to print advertising in use today. To get the full effect of magazine or newspaper advertising, and to show your understanding of advertising and marketing, you might want to consider presenting your work within the mocked-up page or pages of the publication it would be found in. With standalone advertising, you could show it in its final location.

Once your page size is set up, you should then start to consider your main design elements.

Proportion in design

You will have a number of design elements you will want to place on your print production page, including images and text and, depending on the form you are creating, you may have design conventions that you need to follow.

As we discovered earlier, a billboard poster is up to four times higher than it is wide. If the billboard poster is to be used to sell a consumer product, for example a perfume, your poster could include:

- the perfume's name/brand name
- an image of an aspirational model
- a background
- an image of the product itself
- a tag line
- a web address and/or social media account name.

Apply it

List the design elements needed on one of the following print products:

- a cover for a PC game
- the front page of a women's fashion magazine
- the back page of a tabloid newspaper
- a flyer promoting a club night.

△ Billboards come in a variety of sizes

CHAPTER 9 MAKING MEDIA

Before you start taking photographs or laying out your page, you should create a design plan to help you work out what you want your finished product to look like. You'll need to consider how you will combine the poster elements on your page, where each element should be placed and also how large or small each element needs to be.

Print layout and design

Whatever size or shape you choose for your page, you should try to apply the following design principles as you lay out your page.

Columns

Column design is one of the first steps in making sure pages look balanced, coherent, aesthetically pleasing and are legible.

As we identified while looking at billboard posters, print productions are designed using a grid, with each page being divided into vertical and horizontal sections. In text-based print publications, these vertical sections are used to divide text into **columns**. Magazines tend to use a three- or five-column layout (see right) depending on the size of the publication. Tabloid newspapers use a five-column layout and broadsheets often use six columns per page. Double-page spreads are often treated as a single page, and designers consider the look of both pages when seen side by side. There are a number of reasons for using columns:

- Page designers use columns to help them create pages that arrange pictures, text, adverts and headings in the most appealing way for the audience.
- Columns also make it easier for audiences to read text, thus making the content easier to follow. Long lines of text are hard to read and make it difficult to find the next line when returning to the left-hand side. There are a number of reasons for using columns:
- Columns also ensure that lines of text are neither too long nor too short for the reader.
- Text can be broken up within columns by using **sub-headings**, pull quotes, etc.
- Columns help designers create pages that are visually balanced and logical for the reader to access. When designing a page it is important that the reader knows which column follows on from the last.

Compositional balance

Compositional **balance** is created when the **weight** of the page is balanced top to bottom and left to right. The placement of your design elements impact on the balance of the page. Large bold and black text is 'heavy', as are dense images. Small or thin fonts, black and white sketches and white space are 'light'. Large, dark, textured and warm-coloured elements tend to appear 'heavier' – they have more visual weight. Elements in the foreground or higher on the page tend to appear heavy on the page, as do regular shapes and vertical (rather than horizontal) objects. A balanced page has similar weight in the top-left and bottom-right sides of the page. This creates the feel of stability on the page and is pleasing to the eye. A well-balanced page guides the reader and makes it clear which images belong to which blocks of text.

Sidebars also help to break up the page. These are small sections of text containing additional information related to the article and often presented in a column or box next to the main text.

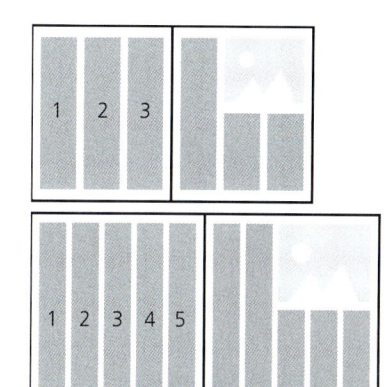

△ **Grids showing three- and five-column layouts image**

△ **An example of a 'heavy' image**

△ **An example of a 'light' image**

9.2 Print production

243

△ An example of a 'light' pages in a magazine spread. Note the amount of white space

Columns also help guide the way the eye travels across the page from left to right and ensure that images don't interrupt the natural flow of reading. Most readers don't take in the fine detail of the page at first. Readers tend to scan the page, or double-page spread, in a Z-shaped eye movement. Page designers need to take this into account.

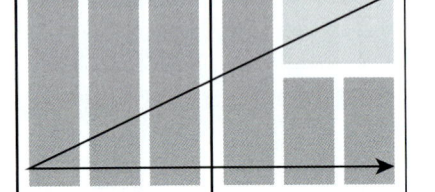

As well as columns, page design considers the balance of the page on the horizontal. The page is usually divided into three and designers use these three spaces in addition to the columns to create **compositional balance** on the page.

△ A Z-shaped design ensures a natural reading flow

Typeface (lettering styles)
Typefaces are split into three basic types:

- **Serif:** styles that have small 'tails' at the ends of the letters:
    for example, Times New Roman or Georgia.
- **Sans serif:** styles that use simple forms for the letters, with no 'tails':
    for example, Arial and Gill Sans.
- **Decorative** or **novelty:** stylised typefaces that can create a very specific look or feel:
    for example, Papyrus or Snell roundhand (they look similar to handwriting and are sometimes called **script** typefaces).

Serif and sans serif typefaces are both very easy to read (though sans serif may be preferred for some forms of accessibility), whereas decorative typefaces can be more difficult for the reader and should never be used in large blocks of text. However, they can be impactful when used for titles, headlines and coverlines.

CHAPTER 9 MAKING MEDIA

When choosing typeface styles for your work, unless you have a specific reason for doing otherwise, consider choosing one typeface for your body text and a second for headings. Tabloid newspapers tend to use a sans serif for headlines and a serif for body text. Use decorative typefaces sparingly and if you do use them, ensure they are large enough so they can be read easily. A page that uses too many different typefaces or that overuses decorative typefaces can look chaotic, **busy** and unappealing to the reader.

Different styles of typeface have the potential to add meaning to your publication. Typefaces create connotations, so make sure you choose typefaces that add to the tone and atmosphere that suits your publication, your message and your audience. Serif typefaces are sometimes thought to look more formal and authoritative, whereas a sans serif typeface feels more friendly and accessible. Experiment with different typefaces and see what kind of tone or feel they create.

You may wish to create a publication that:

- is traditional (Bookman Old Style)
- is modern (Futura)
- is friendly (Comic Sans)
- is quirky (Bauhaus 93)
- looks typed (Courier)
- evokes the 'Wild West' (**Blackoak**)
- is art deco (1920s) (**Braggadocio**)
- looks handwritten (*Mistral*)
- is formal (Times New Roman)
- is casual (Chalkduster).

Font size

Don't forget to use a **font** size that is appropriate to your publication. Posters tend to use small amounts of text and need to use large-sized fonts for visibility. Newspapers and magazines use large-sized fonts in headlines but smaller sized fonts in the body text. Headlines can be as large as 72pt (**pt** = points – the numerical measurement of font size) in some newspapers, whereas the body type can be as small as 8pt or 9pt.

A typical font size for a magazine article is 9pt. Font size choices should also ensure that the content of the product is legible for the intended audience.

EXAMPLE: Different point sizes

- This sentence may be difficult to read because the font is too small.
- This sentence will look clumsy on the page because the font is too big.
- This sentence should look just right as the size of the font has been considered very carefully in relationship to the size and general design of the pages in this book.

You should use existing media products as guides, but have readability at the heart of all your design choices. If you are attempting to recreate an existing publication, these decisions have already been made. You should closely analyse the products to see how they use columns and fonts, so you can emulate their house style and the way they use design elements.

Key terms

balance (page)	a balanced page has been designed to ensure that the heavy objects and lighter ones are positioned to create a harmonious feel
billboard	a large outdoor location for advertising. Traditionally a board for the placement of print adverts but electronic billboards can be found in some locations. Electronic billboards can present all types of video material but they are often used to broadcast adverts
busy	the effect of pages that are created with many design elements, typefaces styles, etc. Busy pages are sometimes difficult for the reader to access and can be confusing and visually off-putting
columns	a way to organise text and images on the page by dividing the page vertically
design elements	the individual parts that combine together to construct a page
desktop publishing (DTP) software	software specifically designed to support the design and publication of print and, in some cases, e-media production
font	the design of the letters used within a specific typeface – its weight and style
page proportions	the size of the page and the relationship between its height and length
pt	points, the numerical measurement of font size
sidebar	a small section of text containing additional information related to the article. It is separate to the article and often presented in a column next to the main text
subheading	a heading for a subsection of an article
typeface	lettering style. All letters and numbers within a typeface are designed to harmonise
weight (visual)	a term used to refer to the effect of the depth, darkness and/or intensity of a design element. Large, dark, textured and warm-coloured elements tend to appear 'heavier' – they have more visual weight. Elements in the foreground or higher on the page tend to appear heavy on the page, as do regular shapes and vertical (rather than horizontal) objects

Key terms

paparazzi professional photographers who seek to capture informal, unstaged and candid images of celebrities or other people identified as being newsworthy

photojournalist professional photographer who uses images to tell a story

9.3 Producing and working with still images

Photography is an important part of media production. Photographs are needed to illustrate print and e-media productions, and they can be used to demonstrate your knowledge of codes and conventions as well as creativity and technical skills.

The style and content of the photographs you use in your production will depend on what you are making, who your product is for and what your product needs to achieve.

If you're making a newspaper product you'll note that tabloids and broadsheets tend to use photographs that give information on the story being reported. Photographs are often simple illustrations of the 'who?', 'what?' and 'where?' of the story being reported. News photographs are often sourced from **photojournalists** or **paparazzi** and can look simple and denotative (see Chapter 4: Media language), as they are taken on the spot as opposed to being set up in a studio.

News photos are selected to help reinforce the specific message a newspaper wishes to communicate, and are carefully constructed and/or edited to create a specific effect.

Construction includes the positioning on the page, the size of the image, the way the image has been **cropped** and the anchorage that is added to the page. The presentation choices are made in an attempt to lead the reader towards a preferred reading of the events being reported. Newspapers also use maps, diagrams and graphs which are helpful to communicate information to the reader. Broadsheet newspapers sometimes use more metaphoric or symbolic images to illustrate a story, while tabloids prefer images that are directly connected to details within the story. Newspaper feature articles use posed portraits taken from stock photography libraries and they too are selected, cropped and possibly edited to reinforce the tone and values within the article itself.

You should take inspiration from products that are similar to the one you are making and/or that are trying to appeal to the same target audience. In particular:

- Does your production need to communicate **genre** through images? How does this work in real media products?
- Will images be part of your creation of **audience** appeal? How does this work in real media products?
- Does your production need to use images to create **representations** that communicate values and **ideologies**? How does this work in real media products?
- Do you need to construct **narrative** information in your images? How is this done in real media products?
- Will the images you use be influenced by the **industrial** context of production? How is this seen in real media products?

Once you have ideas about what you want to achieve with your photographs you should start to plan your photoshoot. In your planning, consider how you intend to use media language to construct the messages you wish to communicate.

Breaking down the media language choices that are used in real media products helps you to create images that are effective and creative.

Your planning should include how you intend to create your **mise-en-scène (m-e-s)** and should include ideas about:

- **Location** – what background do you want to use? Should your images be interior or exterior shots? Do you want to create a specific atmosphere or tone using the location or should your image be set in a certain place? You may wish to check out potential locations, even taking a few snapshots to see how the locations look on camera.
- **Make-up** – do your models need make-up, and if so, what effect are you aiming for? Are you intending to create character with make-up or use it to recreate a specific genre convention? You may wish to design the make-up effects you want in the planning stage. It's also a good idea to practise it before the photoshoot, again taking some snapshots to see how it looks.
- **Wardrobe** – what should your models wear in your photographs? If you have any specific costume needs you may have to source items before your photoshoot.
- **Props** – what objects do you need in the shots? Should your models be holding items? Do you need a specific type of chair for your models to sit on? Are there items that you want to include that you will have to source?
- **Lighting** – will you use natural light or do you want to have other light sources? Will you use the flash on your camera or an external flash? Do you want to try and control the colour, position or strength of the lighting? Perhaps you can use domestic lamps in interior shots? Can you access professional lights to help create tone and shadow in your photographs?

> **Key term**
>
> **mise-en-scène (m-e-s)** everything that can be seen within the scene – set design, props, performance, lighting, costume and make-up, location and lighting

9.3 Producing and working with still images

△ **Does your model need make-up and is special lighting required?**

Apply it

What connotations about characters or situations might you make based on these mise-en-scène choices?

Style of décor	Connotation	Genre
Clean, modern décor with minimalist, modern art objects and functional furniture.		
A mix and match décor with a collection of retro objects in many different styles and colour.		
While clean and tidy, the décor is shabby and in a state of disrepair.		

Mise-en-scène can be used to create a shorthand that communicates ideas and information quickly and efficiently. It can offer the audience clues to a character's background and personality, the historical or geographical setting, the economic status of characters and what they do.

For example, the following **props** give character information:

- a briefcase on the table can indicate that at least one of the characters is a professional
- ensuring that a character's wedding ring is in shot can indicate they are (or have been) married
- lots of pizza boxes lying around can indicate that a character is lazy as they have not tidied up over a period of time.

Certain **settings** are common in specific genres:

- a lonely cabin in the woods is often used as the setting for horror stories
- a British suburban kitchen is often the location for family dramas or sitcom misunderstandings
- a steel and glass skyscraper is often the setting for a corporate thriller.

Costumes can be used to indicate a character's personality, class position or profession, and many genres have costume conventions.

You should also consider the **framing** and **composition** of your shots in your planning to ensure you have the content you want. You should consider how you need to position the people and objects in the frame. Do you want to create close-ups, mid-shots, and/or long-shots on your shoot?

You can plan for framing and composition but it is always a good idea to take a variety of shots from different positions, angles and heights so you can select the ones that work best within your production.

Although we will examine this more closely later in the chapter, you should also consider what **post-production** effects you may want to create after the shoot. You should make sure you plan to take photographs that allow you to achieve what you need. For example, if you plan to insert one of your models into a different background image you must take photographs of your model in front of a white or at least plain background. If you don't do this, you may find you cannot cleanly extract the image of the model from the original photograph when you are using photo-editing software.

There are no rules as to how you should approach planning your photoshoot but you may find using a **storyboard** template, similar to one you would use for moving images, helpful. You can sketch the images you want to create and make notes about specific effects you wish to create while taking your photos.

■ Basic principles of photography

Photography has two stages: **in-camera** and post-production. Most digital photography offers a range of in-camera options, and lenses are usually automatically set up to take the best image possible given the conditions present at the time. This means that, today, many in-camera decisions are in fact made in post-production.

To save you time later in the process, you may try to ensure that the image taken is as close as possible to the one you need for your production. However, as you will see, many issues or problems can be sorted out later by using image manipulation software.

You should have made decisions about mise-en-scène and lighting before you take your pictures. During your photoshoot, but before setting up your shot, you should consider the following:

- **Focus** – relates to the sharpness of the image. What element of your photograph should be clearly in focus? Do you want any elements within your photograph to be out of focus? Smartphones, tablets and most digital cameras make focus decisions as the photograph is being taken. You can alter focus in post-production software, but bear in mind it is easier to blur some aspects of the image than sharpen them. Try to make sure that the most important element in the shot is in focus when you take it.
- **Exposure** – relates to the amount of light that enters the camera when the shot is taken; an under-exposed image is too dark and an over-exposed image is too light. Digital cameras tend to use an automatic exposure calculated on the amount of light that is available at the time the picture is taken. Post-production software can create exposure effects.
- **Framing** – refers to the positioning of elements in the image. If you have a main subject for your image, do you want it to be the only image in the shot? Do you want it to be a small image to the edge of the frame? Do you want it to share the frame with other objects? When you look through the viewfinder you will create a frame for your image – your subject will be 'framed' by the edges of the lens – so you should make sure you have positioned your subject where you want it before you take your photograph.
- **Composition** – also refers to the positioning of elements in the image but in this case it is the way elements are positioned in relation to each other. A well-composed shot has a clear **focal point**, considers the whole frame (often using the rule of thirds) and is well balanced.

△ *Downton Abbey*: costume, performance, props and setting communicate the ideas of class, historical period and genre

Key terms

in-camera decisions made to influence the look of images while shooting with the camera. This includes camera settings as well as external sources such as music, props and lighting to create specific effects

post-production decisions made to influence the look of images after the footage or images have been captured. This is usually done using post-production software

9.3 Producing and working with still images

△ **A well-framed and focused portrait**

△ **A poorly-framed portrait**

As you will be able to crop your image during post-production, you may think that you can create the framing and composition you need after the photoshoot. This is true to an extent, but some framing and composition errors are very difficult to correct. For example, it is difficult to correct an image where the subject does not stand out because the background in the composition creates a complex and muddled view. Similarly, if the head of your subject is outside the frame, this cannot be corrected in post-production.

■ Getting creative (on a shoestring budget)

Not all media studies students have access to professional cameras or equipment. However, the digital camera on your smartphone or tablet can create images that are perfectly suitable for a media studies production. You may also have access to a digital stills camera. This gives you more control over exposure and focus.

You may be able to use the software provided with your camera, smartphone or tablet to create effects as you take your photographs. Internal software can alter the **colour tone** and aspect ratio of the image. You may prefer to take all your images using a standard setting and then make changes in post-production. There may be limitations to the in-camera effects you can create with these types of camera, but there are ways to take creative photographs using a bit of imagination.

The easiest and cheapest way to create effects when taking photographs is to consider and vary camera distances and angles when setting up your shots.

Try taking the same shot from a number of different **distances**:

- Put your subject in context with **long-shots** that include aspects of mise-en-scène that provide information to the viewer.
- Use **mid-shots** to show some aspects of the location but that allow your audience to focus more on your subject. This is a good position to use to communicate character through **non-verbal communication** codes. **Head and shoulders shots** can be used to exclude most elements of mise-en-scène.
- Use **close-ups** to show detail. Take care with focus – make sure that the focal point of the image is in sharp focus.
- Use **extreme close-ups** to exclude all information apart from one small detail.

> **Key terms**
>
> **colour tone** the properties of colour – its shade, hue, warmth, brightness, saturation, etc.
>
> **head and shoulders shot** a shot where the camera is positioned close to a human subject so that the frame excludes all of the body, apart from the head and shoulders
>
> **non-verbal communication** methods of communication that do not include words. Body language and modes of dress are both examples

CHAPTER 9 MAKING MEDIA

△ An extreme close-up

△ A low-angle shot

Try taking the same shot from a number of **angles**:

- Use **low-angle shots** where you shoot your subject from below. This makes your subject loom large in the frame.
- Use **high-angle shots** where you shoot from above to minimise the subject or perhaps create the idea that they are being spied on.

Unless you have the hardware, it can be difficult to get high-angle shots by hand. Take great care if you decide to climb up to create the shot. You may find it easier to use a selfie stick to safely elevate your phone. Do test it first to make sure the selfie stick holds your phone securely.

You could get even more creative by mixing your distances and angles or by experimenting with lighting effects during your photoshoots by:

- using torches or domestic lamps to create spotlights or **low-key lighting** effects
- creating reflectors made of card and tin foil to create soft **light fills** or **high-key lighting** effects
- using objects to create shaped shadows in your image
- using natural light in a number of different ways, for example shoot with the light behind you, shoot with the light to the side or shoot with the light behind your subject. Each position creates a different effect.

During your photoshoot take lots of images using different types of shot and play with light effects, framing and composition as much as you can. Ask your models to try different poses, change the way you use props and alter make-up and costumes during the shoot. You can decide which images work best during post-production. It is always better to have too many photographs than too few.

■ Still-image editing and post-production

The work you undertake in post-production is where you get another opportunity to demonstrate your creative and technical skills. You can use standalone software to edit your photographs or you could use one of the many free editing packages available online, or an app for your smartphone or tablet.

Most post-production software offers similar functions. These are some of the post-production effects you may consider using to enhance your photos:

- **Cropping and slicing:** post-production software allows you to reshape and resize your photographs. You can remove parts of the image that you

> **Key terms**
>
> **high-key lighting** the use of light fills to create a low-contrast lighting effect
>
> **light fills** a light used to reduce the contrast between light and shadow within the frame
>
> **low-key lighting** a style of lighting used to create shadow and areas of bright light within the frame

> **Apply it**
>
> What effects do you think would be created by the following camera shots?
>
> - Low-angle mid-shots
> - High-angle long-shots
> - Eye-level close-ups
> - Low-angle close-ups

9.3 Producing and working with still images

do not want to use by selecting an area of the photo to keep. Cropping usually allows you to keep a rectangular section of the image, but some software allows other shapes to be selected. Cropping also allows you to improve the framing of your shot and, to a certain extent, its composition. Some software packages allow you to select and extract specific elements from the photograph, and add in elements from other photographs. Slicing allows you to select an area of the original image by dividing the image into sections and deleting the parts you don't need.

- **Colour/light editing:** post-production software allows you to alter the overall look of the photo by changing its colour. For example, colour images can be turned into black and white or can be 'aged' by colouring them in a sepia tone. The 'exposure' of the image can be changed, as can the contrast between the dark and light tones. Shadows can be added and specific areas of the image can be brightened.

The ability to edit the colour in images also allows them to be 'retouched' through **photoshopping**, an editing technique that gets its name from Photoshop, one of the most well-known photo editing software packages (however, you don't need Photoshop to edit your images – other software is available). Photoshopping is regularly used to 'perfect' the look of models and celebrities by altering small areas of the image. For example, skin blemishes can be removed and the entire face can be 'brightened' by lifting the corners of the mouth and the eyes, and raising the arches of the eyebrows.

- **Effects filters:** post-production software offers a range of different finishes and textures that can be applied to photographs. Photos can be filtered to look like paintings and drawings, colour filters can create retro effects and leak or enhance the colours, and some filters allow you to alter the depth of field while others can create grainy, glass or crackle effects.

Apply it
1. Go online and search for 'image manipulation effects'.
2. Scroll through some images to get an idea of the types of effect that are possible.
3. Go online and search for 'free online image manipulation'.
4. Access one of the websites and use one of your own photographs to explore the effects that you can create.

9.4 Moving image production

Creating a moving image production is an excellent way of demonstrating your knowledge of media concepts, your understanding of audience and institution, your creativity and technical ability.

Whatever form you are creating you will need to think very carefully about the way you use technology and how you will present your work using **camera**, **sound**, **lighting** and **mise-en-scène**. You will **edit** the different shots you have taken and may also choose to enhance your work by adding special effects during **post-production**.

In order to ensure you get the footage you want and need, planning is key. Like you would in photography, you may create the effects you want in-camera and/or in post-production, but you need to know what footage you will require so you can make sure you have everything needed when you come to edit. Before you begin to film you should research your locations, source your props and costumes, find your actors, and put together a storyboard and script. During the planning process you can consider whether you need to find light sources to help create the effects that you want. One of the challenges in creating moving image productions is that you will inevitably need to work with others in some way – even if it's just with your actors – and this means you need to be able to plan carefully and be prepared to organise other people in order to get the footage you need.

There are many things you need to consider before you start shooting and it is easier to work out how to answer these questions while you are planning rather than during your shoot. Moving image productions need to be 'written' before they are filmed. A script is needed to give your actors dialogue, a **shooting script** adds images and direction to the words on the page, and **shot lists** and storyboards help provide information on how to set up each shot and may also contain information about editing and other post-production elements. In addition to these production issues, there are decisions that need to be made that are dependent on the form and genre you have chosen to make, who your target audience is and what effect you are trying to create. These decisions should have been made during research so now you can think practically about how to achieve what you want in your production. For example:

- What are the conventions of the form you are creating? Which conventions will you follow? Which (if any) will you subvert?
- What are the genre conventions you are working in? Do you wish to subvert the genre conventions and audience expectations? If so, how will you do this?
- How will you approach telling the story? What visual devices will you use to create narrative information for your audience?
- What tone or atmosphere do you wish to create? How will you do this?
- What representations do you wish to create? How will you achieve this?
- How will you create audience appeal?

Key terms

shooting script the written text of a video/film product including details of the use of camera in individual scenes

shot list a descriptive list of the shots required for a moving image production

■ Basic principles of filming

Using the camera

You may have access to professional equipment or you may have to 'make do' with limited resources – either way, there is still plenty of scope to make effective moving image production pieces. You can use smartphone and tablet cameras to capture your footage, but do be aware of the differences between landscape and portrait modes and make sure you have selected the correct one for the form you are making. You may want to record in portrait for social media-related videos or the type of user-generated content sometimes used in news reporting. News broadcasters, however, repackage this footage by adding visuals to the side of the original video to make it more appealing to viewers. Most professional moving-image products are filmed in landscape.

The size and portability of smartphone cameras means you can create shots from perspectives and angles that may be difficult to achieve with larger cameras. If you're using a smartphone or tablet to create a media product that would usually be made using a professional camera, you may want to think about how you can make your work look as professional as possible. For example, using a tripod would help create steady shots and horizontal pans. Tripods are relatively cheap and they can make a big difference in the quality of your work. The comedy-drama film *Tangerine* (2015) was filmed on an adapted iPhone but still makes use of professional framing and filming techniques.

△ A still from the 2015 film *Tangerine*, which was filmed on an iPhone

9.4 Moving image production

Whatever type of camera you are using, you need to familiarise yourself with it and what it can do. The best way to do this is to experiment and make some short videos using some of the built-in settings and effects. Test out any light settings you have in different lighting conditions, both inside and outside. Also, try some of the effects such as slow motion or time-lapse to see if they are effects you would like to use in your video.

Setting up your shots – framing and composition

As with photography, you need to know how to frame your shots. You may wish to consider the composition of your shots by using a 3 x 3 grid to help you design the positioning of people and objects within it. Some cameras come with a grid visible in the viewfinder and this helps you to create balance in the frame. You should think about the **position** of your subject (or subjects) and the relationship between subjects and the background. How you compose your shots will depend on what you want to include in the frame and the effect you want to achieve. When composing the shot, you should consider the objects in the foreground and background and how they look together. You should also consider the balance between the left and right areas of the frame, as well as the top and bottom.

There are many things to think about when considering the position of the camera. The following are just some of the questions you should be addressing when you set up your shot:

- How high or low do you want your camera to be? What point-of-view do you wish to create?
    - Do you wish to create a high-angle or low-angle shot?
    - Do you want your camera to look straight ahead at your subject or look from the left or right?
- How far away should your subjects be?
    - Do you wish to create a long-shot, a mid-shot or a close-up?
    - Do you want to change the distance from your subject within the shot? Will you zoom in or out? Will you track in or out?
- Do you want subjects and/or objects to move within the frame? Will you move the camera during the shot?
    - Do you wish to tilt or pan during the shot?
    - Do you want to track the movement of subjects and/or objects in the shot? If so, how will you achieve a smooth camera movement?
    - Have you **blocked** the actors' movements so that the camera can follow them?

> **Key term**
>
> **blocked** the positioning of people within the frame

There are some basic rules that can be applied when setting up certain shots. Part of your research may be to look at media products and work out what conventions are used in professional productions.

EXAMPLE: Filming a conversation

The conventional way to shoot a conversation between two people is to film the conversation three times from three different positions:

- The **two-shot** – shooting the conversation with two people in the frame together (sometimes two-shots are filmed from different positions or angles).
- **Over-the-shoulder shots** – filming over the shoulder of one actor to capture the other actor's dialogue and their reactions to the first actor's lines.
- **Reverse shot** – a repeat of the over-the-shoulder shot, but taken from behind the second actor.

Shots are then cut and edited together to show the conversation as one continuous event, but presented from a combination of positions and points of view.

CHAPTER 9 MAKING MEDIA

> **Apply it**
>
> 1. Find one of the following scenes (or similar) in a TV programme or film:
>   - a family discussion around the dinner table
>   - a character walking down a city street
>   - a woman getting ready to go out
>   - a man meeting his friends at a sporting event.
> 2. Select one minute from the scene and make a list of the shots used. Consider camera angles, distance and movement.
>   - How many different shots are used in the extract?
>   - How are they edited together?
>   - What effects are being created by these choices?

Lighting

You can use lighting to help with composition by highlighting certain parts of the frame. Lighting can also help to create tone and atmosphere, whether that is the high-key lighting used in hyperreal genres such as reality TV or sitcoms, or the low-key lighting that is a convention in horror. Sitcoms make use of off-screen lighting to create a brightness in the frame, whereas mystery dramas tend to attempt to create a more naturalistic effect by using on-screen light sources such as lamps and candles, which can create contrast and shadow. The horror genre often employs exaggerated low-key lighting to emphasise the contrast between light and dark and to create a mysterious tone. Shadows become as important as light in this genre, as what is hidden is often more frightening for the audience than what is seen.

A **three-point lighting** set-up is often used on professional shoots and altering the position, strength and direction of the lighting can dramatically change the feel of the image being shot. The quality of the light (hard, bright or soft, diffuse light), the colour of the light (natural daylight, yellow-tone interior light, red light for effect) and the position of the light (from above, from the side, from below) all act to alter the feel of the image within the frame. The more you use and control light the more you can control the final look of your moving image footage and its impact. Further lighting changes and effects can be created in post-production.

When setting up your shots, consider whether the light you have is creating the effect you want. You may have to shoot outside at a specific time of day to get the shot you need for exterior shots. When shooting inside you may find using lamps, torches or other light sources helps you create the correct tone for your shot. Always bear in mind that shadows can be useful in a shot but can also be a nuisance. Try to avoid unwanted shadows by making sure you are aware of where the light source is in relation to the subject and the camera. Altering your shooting angle or repositioning the frame can help you too. Don't forget, if your camera is between a bright light and your subject, your camera operator's shadow may appear in the shot.

△ If your camera is between a bright light and your subject, your camera operator's shadow will appear in the shot

Sound

Sound can be recorded in-camera at the same time as the images or separately and then added in post-production. The latter is **foley**, the reproduction of everyday sound effects that are added in post-production to enhance the original sound's audio quality. Voice-overs and soundtracks are recorded separately and added in post-production, but where there is dialogue within a scene, the most common approach is to record at the time of filming. Some cameras have extremely sensitive microphones and others less so. You should create some test

> **Key term**
>
> **foley** recorded sounds to be added as sound effects in the post-production of video and audio productions

9.4 Moving image production

footage with sound to see how well your microphone picks up conversations and the diegetic sounds you plan to include in your work. You should also see how much your microphone picks up the natural ambient sound of your location.

Unwanted ambient sound can be very irritating and you should try to shoot in a location where you can control noises as far as is possible, although this can be difficult when shooting outside. Try to avoid the sound of traffic, distant conversations, washing machines and telephones. Of course, you may need a certain amount of ambient sound in your scene to create a realistic environment. Before shooting, though, you should test the volume of the background noise and ensure that your actors can be heard.

In order to control ambient noise, some moving image producers record required ambient sound separately and then film actors' dialogue in a quiet environment. When you see a nightclub scene in a drama, the extras may be dancing in silence and miming their conversations in the background while the primary action is recorded. The sounds of a nightclub are then added in post-production, keeping the actors audible at the top of the sound mix. Not only does this ensure that the background noise does not become a distraction, but it also means that you avoid the **continuity** issues that come with cutting and editing a scene with music.

Controlling sound is often easier inside, but it is worth checking the **acoustics** of your location before capturing your footage. Some interiors can cause sound to echo, or there may be **dead spots** in certain areas. Where there is dialogue, the most important thing is to ensure the audience can hear everything clearly. Creating test footage is the best way to check if there are likely to be sound issues when recording in-camera.

■ Getting creative (on a shoestring budget)

While using professional equipment can provide you with lots of ways to show your technical skills when producing moving image productions, demonstrating how you have overcome technical and practical limitations to get the effects you want shows great creativity.

Camera

Don't be afraid to experiment and create new and unusual effects. Don't just stick to one type of shot in your moving image production; use a carefully selected variety of shots. When conventions are overused they become clichés, so can you tell your story in a more interesting way by varying angles or shot distances? Without lots of equipment it can be very tempting to use a lot of static shots or create movement with hand-held shots. Often this can look unprofessional and a little dull, so can you think of new ways to create movement in your camera work, maybe by using home-made dollies or low-cost equipment such as selfie sticks in a creative and interesting way?

You may want to experiment with framing and composition. The directors of the 2015 drama series *Mr. Robot* broke lots of framing conventions in order to tell their story. The still image on the right shows how the director positioned actors towards the edge of the frame, while the majority of the background was out of focus. This amplified the unsettling nature of the tone and created an individual media language style.

> **Key terms**
>
> **acoustics** the sound qualities of a specific environment
> **continuity/continuity editing** the creation of logical and/or visual coherence and consistency
> **dead spot** an area created by local acoustics where sound is reduced in volume or flattened in tone

△ Framing and composition were used to unsettling effect in *Mr. Robot* (2015)

CHAPTER 9 MAKING MEDIA

Lighting

Lighting helps you control the tone and feel of your moving image production. You can use it to direct the audience to a specific part of your shot, create emphasis or hide elements of the frame. If you're feeling creative and have access to the equipment, you can use coloured lights or in-camera lighting effects such as strobing. You might use strong lamps to create shadows, halo effects, demonic faces or spotlights. Where professional lighting is not available, try domestic lamps and torches to create specific lighting effects. Create coloured lighting by using coloured transparent plastic, and soft lighting by carefully placing tissue paper over a light source (but not touching the bulb itself, of course), or by using the reflection of light on the subject rather than the light source itself.

You could use light to create shadows for atmosphere, but you could also create shadows to indicate an off-screen object or even a character. A small cardboard cutout of a city skyline could be used to create a city-shaped shadow or a monster could appear only as a shadow or in silhouette using a **back-light**.

Sound/mise-en-scène

If your camera doesn't record sound well you could experiment with creating your production with no recorded dialogue, so all the sound, including voice-over, is sourced and recorded separately. You can then **dub** it in during post-production. When capturing your video footage you should be thinking about how you can tell your story using images rather than sound. Using a visual shorthand reduces the need for dialogue and may help you show how creative you can be with a camera. Early filmmakers told their stories through props, use of camera, setting and performance, and while some of these silent film techniques have become a little clichéd, visual storytelling can be very effective. The passing of time can be shown with a close-up of the hands of a clock moving (either fast or slow, depending on the idea being communicated) or the pages of a calendar peeling away. Narrative information can be provided using newspaper headlines or a montage of social media conversations. For example, newspaper cuttings pinned to a wall can be used to communicate a lot of story information, or it could show us the troubled workings of the mind of a serial killer.

Mise-en-scène

We discussed mise-en-scène in Chapter 1: Reading print media, but it also applies to film, and refers to everything that can be seen within the frame, including the location, set dressing, costumes, props and performance. Lighting is also considered part of the mise-en-scène. Your research should have given you a clear indication of what codes and conventions of mise-en-scène you need to try to emulate for your production. There will inevitably be practical limitations: if you live in a landlocked location, shooting a beach scene may be a little impractical, but you should choose your locations carefully to create the most appropriate backdrop possible for the message you wish to communicate.

A lot of information can be communicated through the mise-en-scène. The location and objects you choose as set dressing and for props can provide lots of narrative information in both denotation and connotation. For example, imagine you are to dress the set of a domestic living room for a broadcast fiction production; the style of décor and the objects in the room will communicate ideas about the characters and their situation to the audience. Perhaps some set dressing choices will also create connotations of a specific genre.

> **Key terms**
>
> **back-light** a light positioned behind the subject
>
> **dub** to add sound elements to recorded images

△ The makers of *Unfriended* (2014) used a range of images from social media platforms to help tell the story

9.4 Moving image production

257

■ Editing and post-production

Post-production in moving image production usually means editing. It can also refer to the addition of visual and audio effects. What effects you are able to achieve will depend on the software you use, but you could consider changing the look of your footage by converting a colour image to black and white or heightening specific colours or textures. You can create titles and add on-screen text or animations to your moving image footage using editing software. Some software allows you to change your footage by adding backgrounds and other objects to your work. You may be able to create special effects such as explosions.

When editing you need to consider the speed and style that will best suit your production.

Speed

- **Fast editing** moves quickly from one shot to the next. An average shot length in a film is approximately eight seconds. In fast editing, each shot is shown briefly before moving to the next. Overly fast editing can be difficult for audiences to engage with, as they may struggle to make sense of the flashes of imagery that are shown. But when done well, fast editing creates a dynamic and exciting scene. Fast editing is often used in music videos, action films and fight scenes.
- A **medium-speed edit** with average shot lengths of between three and six seconds allows the audience to take in more detail from the mise-en-scène and the dialogue. The edit still moves the images along fast enough to be visually engaging, but feels more 'natural'. On average, a human blinks about 12 times a minute, so moving image editing at this speed emulates the 'editing' of images we do ourselves as we look. Soap operas use a naturalistic style that includes medium-speed editing. They are shot on several cameras, so edits usually move from one angle to another with movements such as pans and zooms being created in-camera.
- A **slow edit** allows shots to remain on screen longer between cuts, so the action of a scene can feel slowed down. Long-shots often include camera movements such as tracking, and hand-held and crane/drone shots. Scandi-noir tends to use longer camera shots and slow edits to give a sense of place and atmosphere. The 2006 film *Children of Men* presents three important action scenes as single shots, creating a sense of urgency in each with the dynamic use of camera rather than editing. The use of hand-held cameras in the final battle scene (an apparent single shot of over seven minutes) brings the audience into the action, and the style has connotations of documentary footage or war reportage. This technique was employed to excellent effect in *True Detective* (Season 1, Episode 4) when a drugs raid was presented as a single six-minute take. Director Michel Gondry is famed for using single-shot or slow editing techniques that employ practical, in-camera visual effects in his films and music videos.

Style

A **straight cut** is the most commonly used editing style. It mimics the human eye, creating a blink-like transition between shots. It feels like a natural way to move from one image to the next and often goes unnoticed by the viewer, hence it being part of the technique called **invisible editing**.

There are many ways to move from one shot to the next and different styles have different connotations:

> **Key terms**
>
> **edit (moving image/audio)** the arranging of images or sound to create a coherent visual or audio sequence
>
> **invisible editing** an editing style that appears natural to the viewer, usually exemplified by straight cuts

CHAPTER 9 MAKING MEDIA

- A **fade to black/fade up** transition seems to offer a firm end to the previous scene and allows the following scene to start a new part of the story, or change location or tone without it jarring the audience.
- A **dissolve** allows the first image to slowly dissipate and the new image to come in gradually. Dissolves can connote movement or the passing of time.
- When one image moves across the screen to make way for the next, this is called a **wipe**. Wipes can be simple – a 'barn door wipe' simply slides one image out of the frame and the second one in. Editing software offers a range of shapes for wipes, from the simple iris wipe that uses a circle that grows (or shrinks) in the centre of the frame, to a clock wipe that sweeps across the frame like the hands of a clock, or matrix wipes that use patterned images to change from one shot to the next. Wipes can be obtrusive and tend to be used infrequently, although one of the biggest film franchises of all time, *Star Wars*, famously uses lots of wipes.

Other uses of editing

Editing is often used to move between two different parts of the story. The edit may allow the audience to follow parallel narratives by swapping between the two storylines. These edits are called **cutaways**.

Edits should usually be subtle and unobtrusive. They should be smooth and show the viewer what they need to see, moving them gently between viewpoints or perspectives. It is best not to edit between long-shots and close-ups as this creates a jump for the viewer. Similarly, moving between shots of the same size (one close-up to a second) can also be jarring. Editing should maintain the continuity of the world being presented to the audience, so subjects should not be shown 'leaping' from one side of the screen to the other or changing in size or proportion. Continuity editing maintains the 'reality' of the world presented within the video production.

When capturing your footage you should plan for editing. When you are out filming you may want to consider filming a few extra seconds of 'run-in' and 'run-out' footage to give you space for your edit at the start and end of each shot. You should also shoot 'cover shots' – that is, long-shots of the scene you are filming as well as mid-shots and close-ups. Both these techniques give you more flexibility when you edit. You may also want to shoot images that give geographical or atmospheric information that can be added as **intercuts**.

> **Key term**
>
> **intercuts** alternate scenes or shots from other locations or narrative lines including flashbacks and flashforwards

■ Sound

You can add sound effects, musical soundtracks and voice-overs to your production work using editing software.

You could create your own **foley** (see page 256) by recording sounds using objects around you. For example, the sound of horses running is often created using coconut shells, and helicopter propeller sounds can be made with plastic coathangers. You can also use post-production software to edit sound levels so that dialogue, music, sound effects and/or ambient sound are balanced correctly for the audience.

You can download copyright-free sound effects from the internet to use in your work, so you can create off-screen sounds or enhance and add to the sounds you recorded during filming.

Music is another important part of moving image productions. Again, copyright-free music is available online and, if you select the music carefully and edit it into your work effectively, you can communicate your genre and help steer your audience's emotional responses.

Dialogue that has been recorded separately can be dropped in during post-production. This is a common practice in professional moving image production. The dialogue is first recorded in-camera and then the actors record another version in a controlled environment. They use the moving image footage to ensure the second version is recorded at the same speed as the original and that **lip-sync** is possible. Sometimes sections of in-camera sound are replaced by studio recorded sound – this is not an easy technique as it can be tricky to get a match with the ambient sound and to get the sound to match the lip movement. It is often used in professional media to add dialogue to the scene when the actor who is 'speaking' is not facing the camera.

9.5 Audio production

You can create an audio production quickly and easily using smartphone and tablet technology. If you are lucky enough to have access to sound recording equipment you may have a microphone that provides a better sound quality in your recordings, but mobile technology is perfectly sufficient for your NEA production.

You may want to emulate music programming or create online audio, a radio drama or a documentary. Your initial research into the form you want to make should help you break down the codes and conventions you want to recreate and inspire you to create interesting and engaging content for your audience.

Like moving image production, there are some basic principles you should consider when recording and editing sound, and certain techniques you may wish to experiment with when constructing your audio product.

■ Basic principles of recording

Be aware of your environment

Try to record all parts of your production in a similar environment (the same environment if possible) so that any recording done at different times has a similar audio quality. Make a note of the distance between the speaker and the microphone as this will help you set up the environment again should you need to. If you have access to a soundproof environment, that is ideal. If not, try to remove any exterior noise from your environment so that you are recording in as close to silence as possible.

If you are going to record on location, try to avoid loud, intrusive noises, and record all you need in one location at the same time so that the ambient noise sounds the same. You may even decide to record ambient noise separately and then add it to your 'studio recorded' voices in post-production.

Check your equipment

When you begin your recording, run some tests so you can check the sound levels and any ambient sounds that your microphone picks up. Here are some pre-production tips:

- In a room or studio, record silence and listen to it on full volume. Have other sounds been picked up?
- Check to see if your microphone picks up the page turning of your notes or if your breathing is loud.
- Check the sound of any voices. Do you need to move your microphone a little to avoid it exaggerating 'p' and 'b' sounds?
- On location, record the ambient sound and check how intrusive it is. Can you position your microphone closer to your subject to ensure the sounds you want are not being drowned out?

> **Key term**
>
> **lip-sync** short for lip synchronisation; matching the lip movements of a moving image production to words recorded on a separate soundtrack – or recording the silent lip movements of an actor replicating pre-recorded dialogue or singing

CHAPTER 9 MAKING MEDIA

- If you are able to adjust your recording levels, experiment with them to see which work best for your environment.

You may have identified a number of elements that need recording or sourcing. This may involve going online to download music and/or sound effects, or you might need to record your own.

Depending on what you are creating, you may want to make jingles and **idents**, intros, outros and even audio adverts. If you are creating audio drama you will need to record several voices and include sound effects to help tell the story. Audio documentaries often use incidental music to create tone or help steer the listener's emotional response. Audio products are rarely just one voice, so there is plenty of scope for you to show your creativity and technical ability in the recording stage of production. You will then need to use software to put all the various elements together for your finished production.

■ Editing and post-production

Sound editing, like moving image editing, is the bringing together of the different elements of sound that make up the audio production. Sound editing should move the listener from one sound element to another smoothly, so there should be no jarring movements, for example big changes in volume, as the audio production progresses. Sound can move simply from one sound to the next or transition effects such as fade-outs and fade-ins can be used. Transition sounds, i.e. sounds that can be used with visual transitions, can be downloaded online and may include 'whooshes', 'swishes' or sound effects such as glass breaking or doors closing. Transitions like these should be used for specific sound effects – and then sparingly – or they can become irritating to the listener.

It is worth thinking about sound in layers, as at any given time there may be several sounds playing at the same time, for example a presenter could be speaking over a music **sound bed**. Post-production includes mixing the levels of sound so that some elements (e.g. music) sit below others (e.g. the presenter). In music programming, a DJ often names the next track over its faded introduction and the music may be faded down again towards the end of the track as the DJ begins to speak again.

Serial Season 2, Episode 1 begins like this:

1. A 35-second spoken word advert for Rocket Mortgage, the podcast sponsors, is read out.
2. The presenter introduces the story. This includes audio taken from a video source (audio from video is dropped below the voice and the presenter's voice dominates). The presenter describes the video and occasionally the audio from the video rises in the mix – sometimes it is the sound of voices and sometimes the sound of a helicopter. At the end of the description the audio abruptly cuts to silence.
3. The *Serial* theme tune is played and the presenter announces the name of the podcast and she introduces herself. The sound of a military spokesperson, news reporters and politicians, including Donald Trump and his cheering followers, can be heard as the music continues to play. The voices create a montage of sounds from various sources that provides a range of opinions on the podcast's subject matter. The opening ends with (what is assumed to be) the voice of the subject of the podcast, Private First Class (PFC) Bowe Bergdahl, an American soldier.
4. The presenter proceeds to outline the context of the story, as music plays below the voice track and Bergdahl's voice is heard.

Key terms

idents sounds used to identify the programme, radio station or brand. This could be a jingle or a theme tune

sound bed sounds, sound effects and/or music that plays below the main content of an audio production. Sound beds can communicate narrative information such as location or they can create a tone or atmosphere for the production

Apply it

Listen to the first couple of minutes of a podcast and write down everything you hear.

- What sounds could you source online?
- Make a list of all the recording you would need to do to recreate the start of the podcast.

To create this opening, the following sounds have been recorded or sourced from elsewhere:

Recorded	Sourced
The advert	Podcast theme tune
The script read by the presenter	Audio from a video
An interview with the subject	Incidental music

These six elements will have been edited together in post-production and great care will have been taken in the sound balance of the music and the audio from the video – the latter alters as the extract progresses.

9.6 Approaches to e-media production

E-media is usually a combination of different presentation forms that provide audiences with various ways to access and engage with the information being communicated. Of course, some e-media forms are simply replications of 'offline' formats. A podcast follows similar codes and conventions of radio programming and YouTube videos are very similar to television products that offer similar content. However, as user-generated content has grown it has emulated some professional approaches to production but has also developed its own unique uses of media language.

E-media production employs elements of each of the production areas already outlined in this chapter, and may include the following as part of the presentation of the content:

- print page design, for which you will need to consider basic layout and design conventions but also the codes and conventions of the form being constructed
- photographs as illustrations
- adding moving image and audio productions.

Although you need to show you can use software and equipment when making your productions, you are not required to learn coding or other specific programming skills. You may have ideas that you would like to include in your production but lack the specialist technical skills to create them as fully functional elements. However, this is a great opportunity to show your understanding of contemporary media and your creativity using multimedia and audience participation. E-media products are more engaging when they contain movement and sound, so you could include moving images or audio recordings. Even a simple animation can add the type of visual interest to your e-media work that is not available in print.

E-media allows for greater audience participation and interactivity than other platforms and for audiences to communicate with producers and each other. It has transformed the way in which audiences want to be entertained, so a crucial part of any media production is how it is used to encourage and communicate audience participation. Interactivity can range from asking audiences to click on a simple poll to register their opinion, to providing opportunities for audiences to share ideas and opinions in other ways. Audiences could be persuaded to share media such as photos and videos or they could be encouraged to participate through competitions or getting involved in real-life events and experiences. It may be appropriate for your e-media product to include a comments section or be linked to social media. E-media products can offer choices that allow the audience to feel as if they are able to personalise their experience. For example, it is common practice for audiences to be offered a choice between two or three different versions of an online advert. Audiences can choose the version that looks most interesting or relevant to their needs and advertisers can use different marketing techniques for different parts of the target audience or offer further information, competitions and other ways for the audience to participate.

Apply it

Go online to the following websites and, using the table below, detail how the sites use multimedia to present information and how they try to get audiences involved.

Website	Multimedia	Audience interaction
theguardian.com/uk		
www.bbc.co.uk		
www.mailonline.co.uk		
www.loreal-paris.co.uk		
gillette.co.uk/en-gb		
www.manutd.com		
marvelcinematicuniverse.wikia.com		

■ Offline e-media production

You can also create e-media productions using offline software, such as specialised web design or DTP packages. Consider using software that allows you to design your e-media production and add in multimedia features. If you use offline e-media production software you must ensure that you are able to convert your work to an e-media format that will, in most cases, be accessible via a browser. Some offline software is complex to use and can limit the look and functionality of your finished production, so make sure you choose software that you can use effectively and that can achieve what you want to achieve. Check the specifics of the task instructions in the brief you are working on, as there may be specific guidelines on how you need to present and submit your e-media work.

■ Online production tools (to include websites, social media and computer games)

It is very likely that you will want to use an online production tool to create an e-media production. You might use a blog site, a social media platform or an online game creation tool to create materials for your coursework. These tools offer templates and pre-formed pages but you should try to use as many of your own layout and design decisions as possible in your productions. As you won't be creating everything yourself you should spend time creating content for your online product. This means that you should be using still images, moving images and/or audio within your online production to generate audience engagement and appeal and meet the function of your product.

Most online tools for e-media creation are intended to be simple to use and allow for personalisation. Social media pages are often quite uniform in their layout and design, but the choice of images and written content will set your pages apart from others. You will need to be sure about what you want your social media pages to achieve and how best to appeal to your target audience.

If you're creating gaming material using an online tool, you'll need to make a number of choices before you start. First, you'll need to select the features of the game – its plot and the type of interactivity that are appropriate for the genre of game you wish to produce. Second, you should consider your target audience to ensure that you are making a game they will enjoy. You'll need to think about the style and design of the game, the visual design of the locations, backgrounds and characters, and the sounds and music. You should try to ensure that your gameplay is both suitable and easy for the audience to engage with and that the codes and conventions you use accurately reflect the conventions of the genre and type of game you are replicating.

The NEA: understanding forms

The following are some types of media that you could be asked to make.

■ Television

Non-fiction programming

This could include news bulletins or reports, documentaries, quiz shows, sports programming, talk shows or magazine programming. Lifestyle programming such as cookery, travel and home improvement shows are factual and some reality TV would come under this heading, too. If you are making factual programming you need to know who your target audience are and what type of information you wish to communicate. Having a clear idea about audience will not only help you to decide what the content of the programme should be but, importantly, to decide how to present the information.

> **EXAMPLE: Television documentary styles**
>
> BBC Three offers a range of documentaries fronted by young presenters such as Cara Delevingne, Zara McDermott, Jesy Nelson and Stacey Dooley (left). These documentaries are informative and deal with issues such as sexuality, mental health and racism. BBC Three targets a youth audience and, while the documentaries have a serious tone, the young presenters aim to communicate with the target audience in a way that aims to create identification and avoid the patronising approaches sometimes taken when older adults attempt to discuss issues with young people. Often these presenters are on screen and lead audience responses with their own, often emotional responses to the situations they are reporting on. Information is given to the audience in a very direct way, with the presenter talking to the camera. Interviews are intercut with the presenters being shown immersing themselves in the situations they are reporting on. The effect is immediate, personal and emotional.
>
> Other documentary styles, like some of those seen on BBC Four, for example, and many of the films in the *Storyville* series, employ a cooler, more detached tone, and the documentary-maker is only ever heard from behind the camera, or is often not heard or seen in the film at all. These documentaries attempt to present information with as little editorial input as possible. Audiences are therefore intended to feel free to interpret what they are shown for themselves.
>
> Of course, all documentary-makers are aiming to shape the story they are telling and influence the viewer's perspective, but it is clear that the style of documentary-making seen on BBC Three has the presenter at its heart.

△ Stacey Dooley is sometimes credited with creating a new style of documentary, in which she inserts herself into the action and interacts with her subjects in an empathic way

Fictional programming

Fictional programming is scripted and focused on storytelling. Again, different audiences may have different expectations as to how the story is told and knowing these expectations is important for all media producers. Fictional programming is created for all age groups, whether it's the supernatural storytelling for teens of *Red Rose* (BBC), adult dramas such as *The Last of Us* (HBO) and *Happy Valley* (BBC), or sitcoms such as *Motherland* (BBC) or *Ted Lasso* (Apple TV). Some 'reality' TV is very close to being fiction. Programmes such as *Made in Chelsea* are sometimes called 'scripted reality', 'structured reality' or 'constructed reality' (see Example box on page 85) and, while the characters are not actors and they are being filmed living their own lives, they are often put into situations that the programme-makers have constructed. The participants in these programmes respond to the situations in a way that is similar to the way actors improvise.

Of course, not all television-type programming is accessed on a television. Traditional television programmes are often watched on computers, tablets and smartphones. Some traditional television is accessed on YouTube and Vimeo, and these video hosting services allow TV producers, both professional and amateur, to upload factual and fictional material. The creators of YouTube videos have developed their own forms and genres generating their own visual language codes, with some individuals creating their own visual style. For example, video essayists, such as Abigail Thorn, the host of *Philosophy Tube*, combine costumes and theatrical-style sets with direct address to camera, images and illustrations. These 'YouTube styles' are based on conventional television media language codes but have been adapted to suit the more amateur approach of using webcams and hand-held cameras to create images in non-studio environments. Many of the bigger names in YouTube content creation now have access to high-tech equipment and a studio, but they use it to recreate the 'amateur' look.

△ Abigail Thorn, host of *Philosophy Tube*

■ Radio (audio)

There is as much variety of programming in audio format as there is in television and moving image. Audio programming ranges from news and current affairs, documentaries and magazine programming to dramas, comedy, panel shows, interviews and debates, and, of course, music radio. Local radio programming – as the name implies – is content with a local interest. Some local radio is provided by the BBC and some by commercial broadcasting companies. The latter make money by selling advertising space, meaning local radio content is punctuated by audio advertising.

Podcasts are audio products that can be listened to online or downloaded to computers and/or mobile devices. They are made by professional media companies and can be online versions of radio programmes (such as *Today* – a Radio 4 broadcast made available on BBC Sounds) or they may be made specifically for online distribution. Just like radio, podcasts can cover a wide variety of topics and styles. Successful podcasts include *The Rest is Politics* (political analysis), *The Film Cast* (movie reviews), *The Media Podcast* (media news and analysis), *Where there's a Will there's a Wake* (comedy) and *The Receipts* (described as 'unadulterated girl talk with no filter'). One very successful genre in podcasting is 'true crime'. *Serial* was an early example of the genre and its first season found a large audience.

The NEA: understanding forms

△ The hosts of *The Receipts* podcast, from left to right: Milena Sanchez, Audrey Indome and Tolly Shoneye

■ **Newspapers (print and/or e-media)**

Online news services have impacted on the circulation of print newspapers, but, as we have seen, many of the traditional print titles now have an online version.

Newspapers can be divided into a number of different formats and genres:

- **Free papers** (or free-sheets) have no cover charge and some local editorial content, but are dominated by adverts – the classifieds (text-based listings) and display ads (professionally produced adverts that contain some form of graphic design).
- **Local newspapers** cover a small geographical area such as a town or small city. They contain more editorial content than free-sheets but are mostly based on stories with a local interest. Local newspapers used to be paid for but are now mostly free.
- **Regional newspapers** cover a wider geographical area than local newspapers – a county or a larger city, for example. They report local news but also cover national and international news and, where appropriate, show how larger news stories connect with local interests. Again, regional newspapers were paid for, but now are mostly distributed free and rely on advertising revenue to make a profit.
- **National newspapers** cover the stories that impact on national and international interests. There is a charge for their print issues but online content is usually available for free.

National newspapers can be further divided into two genres: tabloids and broadsheets. The terms originated in the pre-digital era and refer to the size of paper each newspaper was produced on. Since then they have come to identify two different types of newspaper in terms of the papers' news values and reporting style (see Table 9.1).

▽ Table 9.1 Newspaper categories in the UK

	Broadsheets	Tabloids	
		Red-tops	Compacts (sometimes called mid-market or black-top tabloids)
Titles include	The *Daily Telegraph*, the *Guardian*, *The Times*	The *Daily Mirror*, the *Sun*, the *Daily Star*	The *Daily Mail*, the *Daily Express*
News values	Favour hard news over soft news; attempt to be factually accurate and provide information. Try to offer factual detail and provide an analytical overview. Tend to deal with the 'big picture' issues that stem from a news story. Look at wider implications of events and stories.	Favour soft news over hard news; attempt to appeal to the reader's emotions, focus on human interest stories, scandal, gossip, etc. Tend to show how the news story has impacted on individuals or might impact on the reader themselves.	Report hard news but soft news is a dominant feature; appeal to the reader's emotions, focus on human interest stories, scandal and gossip. All tabloids are likely to focus on individuals and personal aspects of a story. Black-top tabloids, like red-tops, often focus on how the news stories would impact on their readership – often in very personalised ways.

CHAPTER 9 MAKING MEDIA

	Broadsheets	Tabloids	
		Red-tops	Compacts (sometimes called mid-market or black-top tabloids)
Reporting style	Attempt to be cool, detached and analytical. This does not, however, mean they avoid bias.	Sensationalised style using lots of hyperbole and word-play to help create an emotional response. Images dominate.	Less exaggerated in their reporting style than red-tops, but still employ emotive language and word-play that deliberately attempts to create an emotional response.
Example front-page headlines	15 February 2023, The *Daily Express*: Defiant Army Chief Says 'We Can Stand Up to Putin' 13 February 2023, The *i*: Hunt urged to boost defence spending – or risk failing to deter Putin	15 February 2023, The *Sun*: Nicola: Stained Glove Found	15 February 2023, The *Metro*: Was it a Hate Crime?

Online, these newspapers tend to follow the same reporting style and news values of their print versions. Online news is important to traditional newspaper companies, as free access to online news in other forms has made it almost impossible for print newspapers to generate a profit. To try and generate web views, broadsheets print lots of opinion editorials that create interest and discussion. Then they use social media to help generate interest in these stories, as having a story go viral is one way that online newspapers can generate income. The *MailOnline* has become one of the most visited news websites in the world – largely because of its celebrity gossip reporting that attracts audiences, and not only those from the UK. The *Independent*, however, no longer has a print edition, as in 2016 it made a decision to focus on online publishing. Remember also that online doesn't just mean websites, as news producers also offer apps for mobile devices.

Online news is provided by other organisations as well as newspaper publishers. Broadcasters such as *BBC News*, *Sky News* and *Channel 4 News* have news websites, as do non-UK broadcasters such as *Russia Today* and *Al Jazeera*. The web allows audiences to access foreign news providers such as *Fox News* and *CNN* from the USA, and there are many independent news organisations that publish online, such as *The Real News Network* and *The Canary*.

■ Magazines (print or e-media)

Magazines tend to fall into two basic categories:

- **Lifestyle magazines** have their roots in shopping catalogues and are guides to the products you may wish to buy to create and enhance your lifestyle. These products may include make-up, fashion, gadgets and holidays, and lifestyles may be defined through decorating, cookery, leisure activities, home improvements and gardening. Lifestyle magazines tend to cover a number of different topics that collectively help create a lifestyle (e.g. *Good Housekeeping*).

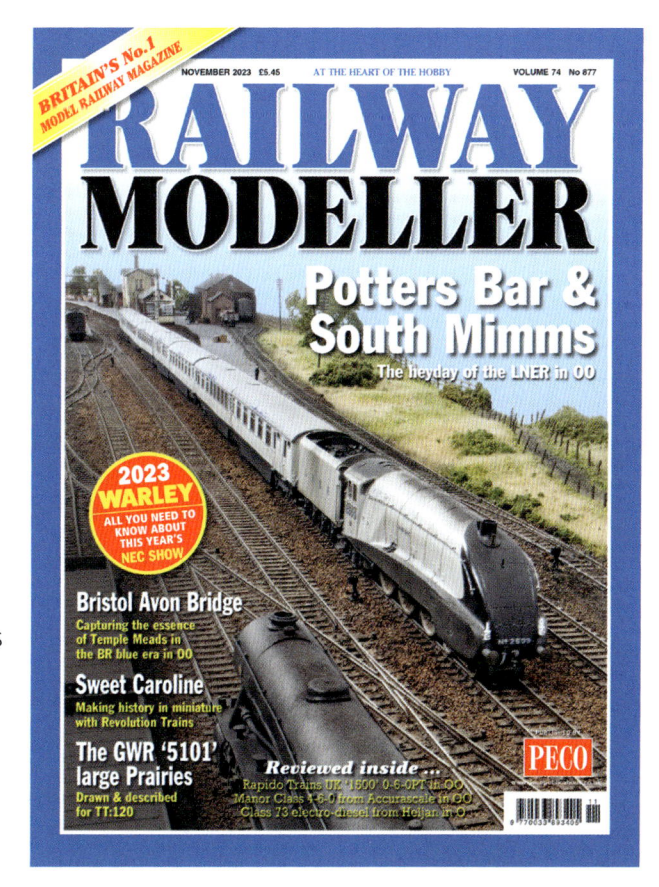

The NEA: understanding forms

267

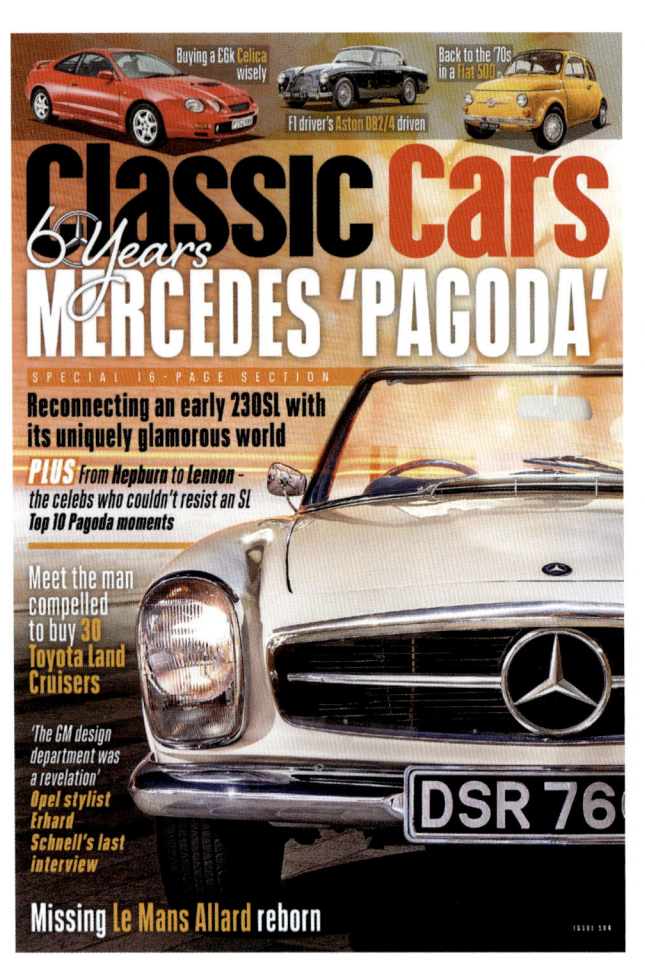

- **Special interest magazines** focus on a very specific topic area – one that may be a niche interest rather than a mainstream one. Special interest magazines offer buying advice but tend to be more focused on offering information (e.g. *Record Collector*, *Railway Modeller*, *Classic Cars*).

Traditional publishers have expanded their magazine brands online and so, for example, fashion magazines (such as *Vogue* and *Elle*), lifestyle magazines (such as *Prima* and *GQ*) exist in print form and online. Print and online versions of magazines share a number of visual codes that create consistency and make the brand recognisable. However, the design and content of the magazine in each platform aims to meet the expectations of the specific audiences of print or e-media respectively.

Print magazines are, however on the decline. Some magazines close down completely if they cannot attract audiences and advertising revenue (for example, *Oh!*). Many other titles have gone online only in recent years (for example, *Boating World* and *Red*). Focusing on online production not only cuts the costs of publishing a magazine but it also allows titles to quickly adapt to audience needs and their changing behaviours.

Creating a clear brand in terms of content as well as attitudes and values is beneficial as this allows audiences to create certain expectations that the magazine can meet. The hope is that this can create audience loyalty so readers will return again and again to a favourite and familiar magazine title.

A more recent form of competition for traditional magazines comes from new online magazines as well as amateur and professional bloggers and vloggers, and Instagram and TikTok content creators. Blogs and social media accounts are often based around a central writer/presenter/content creator, so they have an added advantage in that their own personality and approach becomes their brand.

The style of presentation in both blogging and vlogging has influenced traditional magazines to alter their approaches in print, but most especially online. Magazine publishers now use bloggers as writers and they integrate moving image and audience interaction into their house style. Fashion and beauty bloggers have become increasingly influential, with titles such as *Vogue* and *Cosmopolitan* using conventions that come from blogging in their print and online editions.

■ Advertising and marketing (moving image, audio, print and/or e-media)

Advertising and marketing is not a specific media form as such. Advertising and marketing products can be found in print, moving image, audio and online. Both have the same ultimate aim in that they use the media to create images and messages that attempt to persuade the audience to act in some way. Advertising is easy to spot and identify. There are many forms, including print adverts and billboards, moving image trailers and adverts, and, on e-media, advertising content appears on static text-based web pages, as well as on social media and streaming services. Commercial radio is funded by audio adverts and trailers are adverts for films.

Advertising is content in the media that is paid for. Advertising space is sold in newspapers, magazines, in cinemas, by TV broadcasters and on the radio. Adverts can be created by media industries, for example trailers for BBC programmes. Many are created by a third party (an advertising agency) and the host media has no influence on the content of the adverts (other than to ensure they are meeting their own printing or broadcasting guidelines). Adverts on the internet are sometimes bought and paid for (e.g. the adverts on Channel 4), while others are generated by the data created when you access the internet.

Marketing is often more subtle and is not always easy to identify. Music videos, for example, are media forms in their own right but they are created to promote the artist and market their music.

There are countless methods of marketing and new strategies are continually being created. Marketing aims to build brand awareness, create a buzz around a product launch, insert the product into news and social media discussions, etc. The most successful marketing seeds some interest and then other parts of the media take the message out to the audience. Creating interesting materials that people will discuss and share is difficult, but when it is done well marketing spreads the message about the product across audience groups.

Marketing can occur through, for example, the creation of merchandising that is seen by audiences in shops. The media helps with the marketing of products by responding to marketing strategies. In 2016, with little traditional advertising, *Pokémon Go* became a huge success. The game created a buzz on social media and traditional news media, then picked up on its popularity and within a week of the game's release it had more active users than X or Facebook. The game's success and popularity made it newsworthy in mainstream news media.

Some adverts hope to persuade the audience to buy a product they need (e.g. a shampoo). In this type of advertising, adverts attempt to persuade consumers to choose one specific shampoo over all the others that are available. Some adverts try to create a desire for something the audience didn't know they wanted. When a brand-new product is launched, advertisers need to make it look attractive and turn it into an object of desire. Other adverts attempt to change viewers' behaviour – for example, campaign-based advertising such as road safety adverts use images that shock and induce fear to persuade people to change their behaviour on the roads.

There are many different types of advertising and marketing product, but all act to create a positive response to the product, or message, being advertised.

■ Online, social and participatory media

Much online media developed from the older, traditional forms. A website can be created to advertise a product or provide news and information. Some websites provide the same service as a newspaper and others provide specialist information on a single topic. Some sites offer mixed content in a magazine style, and all types of website can offer moving image and/or audio content as well as the written word. Traditional media institutions provide some of the most visited websites, such as *BBC News* and the *MailOnline*, and these sites have similar functions to their offline counterparts, although they present the information in a different way to the traditional forms. An advertising website, just like a billboard or magazine advert, is made to create a positive response to the product being promoted in order to create desire and persuade the audience to purchase the product.

The NEA: understanding forms

Some websites are created outside the usual institutional context of production, with smaller independent publishers and private individuals being able to publish online and having an opportunity to reach a large audience. Fashion bloggers and influencers have challenged the power of fashion magazines and some individuals have become influential in their own right, such as Victoria Magrath (*In the Frow*) and Ella Catliff (*La Petite Anglaise*).

Participation

What also separates online media from traditional media is the fact that online media can be contributed to or created by 'the audience' as well as by media institutions. Participation encourages audiences to engage more with the material and provides a range of gratifications (see Chapter 6: Media audiences) that traditional media cannot offer. Commenting on news or fan websites, for example, can create connections between people who do not know one another and there can be a sense of community created that reinforces shared values when commentators agree with one another.

Giving people the opportunity to have a say in a public forum is also something that traditional media cannot offer. Participation in this way can take many forms, from user comments and discussions to the ability to upload user-generated content and even participate in the development of a media product by, for example, contributing suggestions for character development in fiction or creating personal experiences within gaming – including creating missions or influencing the way the game's story develops. News providers encourage audience members to send in information, images and videos about developing news stories, as they do not always have journalists in situ when a story breaks and this type of 'citizen journalism' has become important for newspapers and broadcasters that need to keep up to date with events as they unfold. Websites for musicians, bands and other celebrities are designed to ensure that fans feel part of a community, too. As well as providing news and information, celebrity or artist websites often offer some 'personal' communication to create the feeling that the fan is part of an elite group who can access 'insider information' and, importantly, have access to other members of this group – and sometimes, especially through social media, access to the celebrity too.

Muse (www.muse.mu) offer fans the ability to subscribe to a newsletter. Visitors to the website can interact with one another via a forum area and fans can sign up as a 'member' of the fan community, which allows them access to exclusive downloads and advanced access to products sold by the band.

The Katy Perry website (www.katyperry.com) gives fans the opportunity to sign up for a newsletter, but most of the real interaction for this fan group occurs via social media.

Social media

Different social media platforms provide different functions for their users. Facebook gained popularity in the late 2000s as a platform for connecting with friends and sharing information through updates and the posting of images. Over the years, it has developed in order to attempt to offer different functions, as other social media platforms compete for users' time and attention.

Some social media is based around still photography (for example, Pinterest), others on moving images (for example, TikTok), while yet others are based mainly on the written word (X, formerly known as Twitter). The success of TikTok has led all social media platforms to actively encourage the use of short videos, as this is shown to increase audience engagement.

Different social media platforms appeal to different audience groups and some have clearly identifiable demographics. 21.5 per cent of TikTok users are women aged between 18 and 24 (https://nuoptima.com/top-20-tiktok-statistics-2023), while men of the same age made up 17 per cent of users. Almost 70 per cent of Instagram users are under 34 (www.statista.com/statistics/325587/instagram-global-age-group/), whereas Facebook's users tend to be older – the biggest growth for the platform being in the over 65 age group (thesocialshepherd.com/blog/facebook-statistics). Social media content producers, therefore, need to consider the needs of their audience and try to construct ways to use the platform that help encourage the audience to share, communicate and interact with the content they provide.

■ Computer games (e-media)

Computer games cover a range of genres, are accessed using different platforms, use different types of gameplay, and so attempt to appeal to different audiences. Some games are simple, to be played by individuals, while others create complex worlds, where thousands of players can gather online to play together. Some games are produced by large companies that spend enormous amounts of money on their development and distribution, whereas other games are created by lone developers and end up being produced and sometimes distributed through independent companies. Table 9.2 shows examples from all gaming genres:

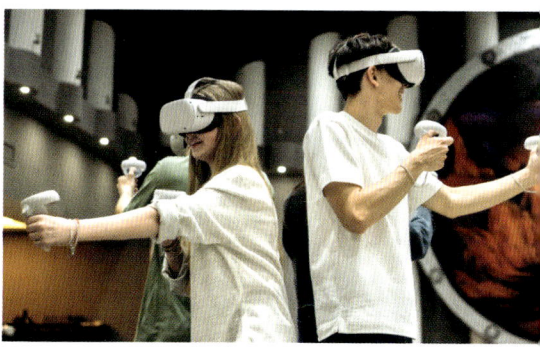

▽ **Table 9.2 Some examples of gaming platforms, genres and distributors**

Platform	Game	Genre	Gameplay	Institutional context
Mobile device, e.g. iOS/Android phones and tablets	Candy Crush	Puzzle	'Match-three' puzzle	Distribution by Activision/Blizzard
Hand-held device, e.g. Nintendo 3DS	The Legend of Zelda: A Link between Worlds	Action adventure	Role-playing game (RPG)	Developed and published by Nintendo
Console, e.g. PS4	Uncharted 4: A Thief's End	Action adventure	Mixed gameplay including puzzle, platforming, third-person shooter	Developed by Naughty Dog and published by Sony Interactive Entertainment
PC	World of Warcraft	Fantasy	Massively multi-player online role-play game (MMORPG)	Distributed by Blizzard Entertainment
PC/console	Call of Duty	War	First-person shooter	Distributed by Activision
VR headset	Eve: Valkyrie	Action sci-fi	Dog-fighting shooter	Developed by CCP Games and published by CCP Games and Oculus VR

■ Music video (moving image)

Music videos developed with the rise of music television in the 1980s. At first, only the biggest artists could afford to have videos made, but today it is necessary for all artists to have a visual way to communicate. The most common way for music to be viewed today is via YouTube and the music video channel Vimeo. Artists and their recording companies receive money from YouTube views but there are many thousands of music videos available to watch, so the biggest issue for artists is how to get audiences to watch *their* videos. Larger artists have a PR team whose job it is to ensure as many people as possible know about the video. Creating a video with interesting or unusual visuals and/or content may encourage audiences to subscribe to share the video and/or subscribe to the artist's channel, so helping with promotion. The more a video is watched, the more likely it is to be placed on YouTube's front page or 'most watched' playlists.

The NEA: understanding forms

Music videos are another form of marketing. In the past, music videos were made to promote the sales of a specific music track that was released as a single. In turn, the single would promote the artist's album. Today, less money is made via the sale of music, so video acts to promote the artist's brand as much as the song itself. For example, having a high profile can offer music artists access to income through sponsorship on social media. Videos themselves can generate an income if they are monetised on, for example, YouTube.

A video is a visual way of reaching an existing audience and attempting to broaden an artist's reach. There are many different approaches to the creation of music videos: some videos offer a brief and relatively simple narrative that is directly related to the lyrics of the song; some offer a metaphorical visual connection to the lyrics; some are performance based; some use intertextual references to other cultural reference points such as specific historical periods, films or TV programmes; and some use apparently unrelated images for visual appeal.

Different genres of music use these techniques in very different ways. The makers of different music genres developed their own video codes and conventions, and sometimes these conventions are used so often that they are instantly recognisable but they become clichés. However, the music genre conventions often reflect the ideologies of the music genre itself as well as the brand image of the artist.

Pop is aimed at younger audiences and is therefore intended to be happy and upbeat. Pop stars therefore tend to make their videos fun, with lots of references to having a good time with friends. They often perform a dance routine in formation in a variety of locations, or sing harmonies, signifying togetherness and friendship.

Hip hop and R&B lyrics often focuses on the ideas of wealth and power, as the genre itself reflects the ideologies of a subculture where wealth equals status and is a sign of power. This is often reflected in hip hop music videos, where signifiers of wealth might include designer clothing and jewellery worn by the artist, or other symbols of wealth such as expensive cars and houses, branded champagne and banknotes. The depiction of women in hip hop, rap and R&B music videos is a way for a male artist to signify his sexual power. In more recent times, female hip hop artists and rappers have reclaimed their identities, both sexually and within the culture, by flipping the script.

One important function of a music video, however, is to successfully reference genre conventions in order to create representations that reflect the values of the genre, and that appeal to the existing audience and may be of interest to potential new audiences. All of this is achieved by the careful consideration of the media language choices made in the video's construction.

△ The Jonas Brothers filming a music video

For further information on media language choices see Chapters 1–3.

→ Summary

This chapter has dealt with a range of different things you need to consider when embarking on your practical production.

You need to:

- research the software and/or equipment needed to create different types of production
- choose which forms you will create as offered in the briefs
- consider the basics of the way the form is usually constructed by researching existing examples of the form

Chapter 10 The NEA

What you will learn in this chapter

Chapter 10: The NEA covers:

- an overview of the A-level Non-Exam Assessment (NEA), which is worth 30 per cent of the A level
- advice on responding to the A-level NEA briefs
- a discussion on some of the types of media you may be asked to create and how this work will be assessed
- demonstrates approaches to each stage of the production process, using a mock-up production brief.

10.1 Introduction to the NEA

For the NEA (non-examined assessment), you will be asked to create two practical pieces that combine to make a cross-media production. To do this, you will be able to choose your project from the six briefs provided by AQA. The NEA brief will ask you to make two media productions, often in two different media forms, that will be linked in some way to the media forms studied for the examination.

For example, you could be asked to create an online magazine and a video production for the same magazine, or a trailer for a TV programme and its accompanying poster campaign.

You could be asked to make products related to:

- television (broadcast: moving image)
- radio (broadcast: audio)
- newspapers (print and/or e-media)
- magazines (print and/or e-media)
- advertising and marketing (broadcast: moving image/audio, print and/or e-media)
- online, social and participatory media (e-media including audio/video video material)
- video games (e-media)
- music video (moving image and/or advertising and marketing).

You will not be asked to make a film product, but it is possible that products related to film promotion could be included in the briefs on offer – for example, film posters, a film website, a magazine article promoting the release of a film, etc.

The nature of the briefs means that you will usually be working across media forms, so your work related to music video could include print productions (e.g. a music magazine), online productions (for example, a fan site) or other types of broadcast media (for example, a radio interview).

Six briefs will be published each year and each brief offers a different combination of media products for you to create. As there are new briefs each year, check that you are choosing from the correct list before you start your research, planning and production work. The year of submission is on the cover of the brief.

Each brief will ask you to create two from the following:

- a video product
- an audio product
- an e-media product
- a print product.

The briefs you should choose from are published on 1 March in your first year of study. Your teacher will give you a deadline for the completion of your work. Typically this is towards the end of the second term in your second year. The two products in each brief will be connected in some way. The connection provided in the brief is what will make your production a cross-media project. You will be given a clear indication of the minimum requirements for each element of the production, including the number of pages required, length of video or audio production, the content of e-media materials, etc.

It is important to read through the briefs carefully, so you are clear what the expectations are. It is also good practice to come back to the brief regularly during the production process, so you don't forget important details.

You should research and plan for your production, but do not submit this material at the end of the project. Your final submission will consist of two elements:

- a 500-word Statement of Intent
- the two finished productions.

You will be given deadlines for submission of each element by your teacher, as they will be marking your work.

■ What will you be assessed on?

Your NEA is assessed on your ability to:

create media products for an intended audience, by applying knowledge and understanding of the theoretical framework of media to communicate meaning.

(Assessment Objective 3, page 28 of the A-Level Media Studies specification v1.2)

You will receive a certain number of marks for your Statement of Intent and another number for your productions.

Statement of Intent

The Statement of Intent should be no longer than 500 words and is worth a maximum of 10 marks, or one-sixth of the NEA marks. AQA provides a template that you can use to present your Statement of Intent. You'll find it in the Student Booklet for the NEA, published each year by AQA, along with the briefs.

You should write your Statement of Intent after choosing the brief and conducting research based on its requirements, and before you create your media products. In it, you should discuss the way you intend to respond to your chosen brief. The Statement of Intent should be specific and refer directly to what you plan to do in your production work and why.

CHAPTER 10 THE NEA

In your Statement of Intent, identify how you will be responding to the specific requirements of the brief you have chosen, especially how you will address your target audience and how your products will fit in with the industrial context provided in the brief. You should also show that you have considered the relationship between the products and how they work in light of the digitally convergent nature of modern media. Your plans should include some of the specific media language choices you intend to use and explain how they will attract and appeal to the target audience for your productions. Don't forget to use media terminology as you write your Statement of Intent; check you are using them accurately and the ideas you discuss are relevant to the plans you are discussing.

> **Chapters 4 to 7 provide detailed information on the theoretical framework.**

Productions

The mark you receive will be based on how effectively you apply your ideas from the theoretical framework in a practical context.

The marks for the productions are allocated between the following areas:

- media language
- media representation
- media industry and audience

The evidence you offer for your knowledge and understanding of the theoretical framework will be in the practical work you produce.

What follows are suggestions as to how you can show evidence of your knowledge in your practical work.

Media language

You need to use media language effectively in your productions to communicate meaning to the audience identified in the brief. Your language choices should be appropriate for the form and genre you are creating. Media language should be selected carefully and could include:

- identifiable denotations and connotations to help create your message
- techniques such as symbolism and/or anchorage to help create meaning
- using (or subverting) genre codes as appropriate
- constructing narrative codes and markers to help communicate your ideas
- using postmodern techniques such as bricolage or intertextuality where appropriate.

Media representation

You need to combine media language elements effectively to create representations that communicate meaning. This could include:

- creating images that offer more meaning than simple illustration
- using or subverting stereotypes as appropriate
- using representations to reinforce or challenge dominant values
- using representations to construct an idea of identity if appropriate
- using representations to highlight specific gender or race issues if appropriate.

Audience and industry

You need to demonstrate an understanding of who the target audience is and how best to attract them, address them and meet their expectations.

10.1 Introduction to the NEA

You should also consider the industrial context of production. This could include:

- considering the products' distribution
- seeking to increase circulation
- issues around finances such as funding, commodification, generating an income, etc.
- relevant issues around regulation
- issues related to globalisation, diversification, convergence as appropriate to the brief.

Of course, how you approach demonstrating your knowledge and understanding will depend on the requirements on the brief and the decisions you make in your response to it.

10.2 Working on the NEA

The production process should work as follows.

■ Brief selection

Your first task is to choose which brief you wish to complete. You may wish to make your decision based on your media interests, so, for example, a brief based on the music industry may interest you more than any other. Being interested in the topic will certainly help as it is often easier to research and engage with topics that spark your enthusiasm, and you will be working on your NEA for a significant amount of time. Your level of interest will inevitably come across in your work, too.

Another consideration is the type of productions you want to create. You may have found you enjoyed some types of practical production over others, so you may decide to pick a brief that helps you play to your strengths. You may be specifically interested in creating moving image products or working with layout and design on desktop publishing software. You may be limited in your choices because you lack access to certain types of equipment and/or software. However, what you create is more important than how you create it.

> **See Chapter 9: Making media** for more practical production advice.

Apply it

1. Based on your studies of the Close Study Products (CSPs), give each form a mark out of 10 to indicate which areas of the media you are most interested in (closest to 10) or least interested in (closest to 1).

Media form	Level of interest
TV	
Radio	
Newspapers	
Magazines	
Advertising and marketing	
Online, social and participatory media	
Computer games	
Music video	

2. Give each of the following production areas a mark out of 4 (where 0 is the lowest and 4 is the highest) to put them in rank order based on the criteria given.

Production area	Your own experience	Level of expertise	Level of enjoyment
Print			
E-media			
Video			
Audio			

The briefs cover different media forms and ask for different types of productions each year, but knowing your own interests and strengths will help you decide which brief you should select for your NEA.

◼ Working with the brief

Each brief provides two distinct types of information:

- the brief's instructions
- the minimum requirements.

The brief's instructions

This is where the specifics of what you must produce are provided. You will be told what you need to produce and who it is for. You will also be given some information about the contexts of the production in the given media industry and/or the convergent (see Chapter 7: Media industries) nature of the project that you should keep in mind when making your products.

The brief will leave you to make some key decisions, too. You may be told what to make (e.g. adverts as part of an alcohol-aware campaign) but you will need to decide on what techniques to use (e.g. which persuasive techniques for your campaign advert). All decisions you make should take the information provided in the brief into account. So, if the brief identifies you are targeting older adults with your public service advertising campaign you should choose persuasive techniques that are likely to be more effective for this age group.

The minimum requirements

This section of the brief gives you a clear indication of what you need to include in each of your productions. You will be told how many pages and/or minutes you need to produce. Each production area has its own requirements and you will be given a clear indication as to what specific features you should include within the production you have chosen, such as the number of images, how much written content, etc.

It is expected that you will create all the images and footage you submit for your NEA, in other words, all photos, illustrations and moving images must be your original work. The only exception to this is if you include existing company logos (for example, TikTok, Instagram, etc.). You can download these images from the internet. If you are using fictional company logos as part of your production, you should create these yourself.

It's worth noting that these are the minimum requirements. You could do more than is asked, but it's a good idea to focus on creating the best work possible that meets the minimum expectations of the tasks.

Research

Once you have chosen which brief to work on, you can begin your research. It's important to undertake different types of research in preparation for your planning and production, as the production decisions you make should be based on your knowledge and understanding of how media products are constructed, how they attempt to appeal to their target audiences and the impact of the industrial context.

It would be a good idea to:

- research real media products to find out how media professionals construct media products
- research your target audience. You can do this through the study of existing media products to find out how media producers attempt to appeal to the target audience. You can look at a range of media products and this will help you work out what media producers assume your audience will respond to
- apply ideas from the theoretical framework to your product research and this may involve further theoretical research.

For example, if you're intending to make a series of public service adverts for magazines and for billboards, you could investigate:

- the codes and conventions of magazine advertising
- the codes and conventions of billboard advertising
- the codes and conventions of public service adverts
- the codes and conventions of the genre of public service adverts you are making
- the codes and conventions of adverts aimed towards your target audience
- the way your target audience is usually addressed
- the needs, desires and interests of your target audience that are assumed in other media products
- the narrative codes that are conventionally used in public service adverts
- the representations that are conventionally used in public service adverts
- the industrial context of advertising and, specifically, public service advertising
- the regulations that should be considered when making public service advertising.

The knowledge gained in this type of research will help you plan your approach to the productions and can be discussed in your Statement of Intent.

Researching for the NEA

Whichever brief you choose and whichever form you are working in, you must be very clear before you start as to what the brief is instructing you to do and what choices you have to make:

- Is the form defined by the brief or can you choose?
- Is the genre defined by the brief or can you choose?
- Is the target audience defined by the brief or can you choose?
- Is the function of the product defined by the brief or can you choose?
- Is the content of the product defined by the brief or can you choose?
- Is the institutional context of the product defined by the brief or can you choose?

Once you have identified what you are being asked to do and the choices you need to make, you are ready to start the first stage of the production process – research.

Practical tips for undertaking research

There are two main types of research you need to undertake:

- practical research into existing media products similar to the one you are making
- research into the theoretical framework and how it relates to the instructions in the brief and the product you are making.

Both types of research are closely related and need to be undertaken at the same time – hence, using the theoretical framework as a structure for your research (see table) may save you a lot of time. This research is crucial as you need to start to plan and then produce your product from a position of knowledge and understanding of media practices and of the theoretical ideas related to them.

	Existing media products	**The theoretical framework**
Media language	How is media language used in the production of this form?	How can ideas from semiotics (connotation, denotation, myth, etc.) be seen in action in these media products?
	What are the codes and conventions of the form and the genres within it?	How are narrative codes constructed?
	How is media language use influenced by the products' target audiences?	Are genre conventions adhered to or subverted?
	How is media language used to create narratives?	
Representations	How are representations used to appeal to the target audience?	What stereotypes or countertypes are common in the media products?
	What ideas are generated about specific locations, social groups, etc.	What evidence is there of selective representation?
		How might the representations contribute to hegemonic values?
		Do the representations contribute to ideas about identity?
Audience	How can the target audience be identified?	How do audiences use the product?
	How do the products attempt to reach and appeal to their audience?	What gratifications does the product offer?
		What would the conditions of consumption be?
	How do the products engage with the audience? Do they encourage interaction/action?	How might audiences interpret the meaning of the product?
Industry	How do the products contribute to their circulation and/or distribution?	How do the products fit in with the notion of a free market?
	How has modern technology influenced the production of the products?	Do the products raise issues regarding globalisation, surveillance, privacy, etc.?
	What are the economic factors evident within the products?	

Using the theoretical framework in research

The purpose of your research is to gather the knowledge and develop the understanding that will enable you to create an appropriate and recognisable media product in your chosen form. You need to be able to:

- use media language accurately so your product is recognisable
- create representations that are appropriate to the messages you wish to convey

10.2 Working on the NEA

- create a product that will appeal to and engage its target audience
- create a product that engages with the appropriate institutional context.

To enable yourself to do this, you need to be familiar with the way real media products are constructed. The theoretical framework can be used to analyse existing media products and will help you engage with ideas that will enable you to create a more realistic and effective product.

While you are not expected to simply copy the styles and techniques you find, real media products should inspire you when you make your own production choices. You may decide that you wish to mix and match ideas from different media products or bring in ideas of your own so you take a more creative approach to production. You need to research the codes and conventions of the form and genre you wish to create.

You cannot make an effective production if you do not have clear ideas about your target audience – who they are, what they expect and what might appeal to them. Your media language decisions will be shaped by your understanding of your audience. All media producers have a target audience in mind for their product when they're creating it, so you can learn a lot by looking at products similar to the one you wish to make or those targeted at the group you have chosen.

EXAMPLE: Game shows targeting different audiences

The game shows *Only Connect* (BBC) and *The Big Fib* (Disney+) clearly target different age groups. The presentation of the two shows is quite different. *Only Connect* is for adults and is a knowledge quiz. Its theme tune is in the style of classical music and the set is based around two teams of three sitting at a desk, while the host (Victoria Coren Mitchell) sits in the centre at her own desk. It is a low-stakes game as the teams compete against each other to move forward in the competition; there is no prize other than the winning team being declared champions. The show is deliberately difficult; contestants are asked to make connections and identify sequences between items from any topic, rather than relying on general knowledge alone.

The Big Fib is a children's game show. The mise-en-scène is dressed as a stylised 'library' with the contestant sitting on a 'gold throne' with a 'robot' co-host. The programme is punctuated with animations and comedy moments, but it also offers some educational content. The hosts are used to create comedy and ramp up enthusiasm in the contestants, studio audience and viewers. There is no real jeopardy for the young contestants – they simply need to work out which of two 'experts' is lying. The first round is deliberately easy, with one of the experts being obviously fake, but the second round provides a real challenge for the contestant. The contestant plays for a trophy and the 'fibber' is doused in foam.

△ Victoria Coren Mitchell, host of quiz show *Only Connect*

Age and gender are two ways an audience can be defined but many products consider their audience less by how old they are and more by what type of person they are – what they like and what makes them happy. For example, if you were going to try to launch a new music magazine website you could define your target audience as pre-teens, teenagers, young people under 30 or adults 30 and above. You could define your target audience by gender or by ethnicity. These approaches would influence the creative decisions you make. You could also define the audience by their musical taste and their relationship with musical culture.

See Chapter 6: Media audiences for more information on audience.

Apply it

How would you approach creating a music website for the following audiences? Consider how the audience would influence various choices you would need to make when you create your media product.

	The general tone of the website	The style and design of the site	The techniques you would use to try and encourage audience interaction	The subject matter you will include – including musical artists and other features
Casual pop fans				
Serious fans of classic rock music				
Avid dance music fans				
Fans who are also musicians				

It is not just age that defines how an audience reacts. A fan of classic rock may be 60 or 16 and any gender, but regardless of these characteristics they will want to see articles about rock musicians of the past – perhaps with a focus on guitar heroes – and will expect a magazine website aimed at their interest. They will expect you to take rock seriously and promote the idea that it has a value beyond simple entertainment.

Key to creating a successful product is knowing who the audience is and what they are likely to respond positively to. Media producers find out about their audience using a range of techniques, from focus groups to analysing social media. You will need to research your target audience so you can shape your creative decisions to meet their needs. The best way to work out what your audience responds to is to engage with products it uses.

△ Classic rock fans want to read articles about rock musicians of the past

10.2 Working on the NEA

Once you have a clear idea of your target audience you can focus on creating representations that communicate your message clearly and effectively to your chosen group. By accessing real media products you can see what type of representations are common in the area you are working in and what type of representations are used to communicate and appeal to your target audience. While analysing existing media products, don't forget to think about the industrial context:

- How would your product be distributed and circulated?
- Can you include any strategies that might make your product more successful and increase its circulation?
- What regulation issues would you need to be aware of when creating your product?
- What economic factors may impact on the way you construct your product?

When you have a good understanding of the form and its context of production you can start to plan your own practical work.

Apply it

View the following Drinkaware poster here: https://tinyurl.com/yhd7snnh. What can you learn about advertising techniques, public service adverts, the way the audience is addressed and how the adverts have to conform to advertising regulations?

Complete the table below by making observations about the advert and then linking your observations to the media language choices. You can then extend your analysis by considering why these choices have been made.

What does the advert do?	How does it do it?	Why does it do it?
Shows a young woman having fun on a night out		
Attempts to show the negative side of drinking to excess		To help persuade the audience to regulate their alcohol intake

■ Planning

Once you have clear ideas as to how real media products work, you can decide what ideas and techniques you will replicate in your own productions. You may, of course, decide you want to do something original, and subvert conventions and/or expectations. You should judge which conventions you wish to follow and which you want to challenge, but remember to always keep your target audience in mind and make sure that you are considering any issues in the industry – for example, regulatory concerns that may impact on the content of your production. Take care that you don't subvert conventions so much that the meaning becomes unclear.

Base your planning on the research you have undertaken, which will vary depending on the product you are making.

CHAPTER 10 THE NEA

For example:

Planning for audio production	Planning for e-media production	Planning for print production
Locations for recording	Layout and design of pages	
Casting	Planning for photographic shoots – location, lighting, props, casting, make-up, costume, etc.	
Script	Written content	
Plans for music, sound effects, etc.	Illustrations	
Editing/post-production plan	Plans for post-production image editing	
	Plans for audience interaction	
	Multimedia content plans: audio and/or video	
	Planning for the integration of social media	

■ The Statement of Intent

It is at this point that you should write your Statement of Intent. Try to have a clear idea as to how you will approach the practical productions and, most importantly, why you will approach the tasks in the way you have selected. This should be based on what you learned in the research stage. The Statement of Intent should be carefully constructed to enable you to outline your plans for both production pieces.

- Discuss each task separately, but also make sure that you explain how the two artefacts are linked as a cross-media production.
- Make it clear how you intend to target your audience, and how you will use media language to create appropriate representations to communicate the intended message.
- Be clear about the industry context of your production.
- Also show your knowledge from the theoretical framework and demonstrate your understanding of ideas by using media terminology.

It is important to show that you have engaged with the brief when you write your Statement of Intent, so make sure you explain what you intend to do in your productions and how your intentions relate back to the brief's instructions.

■ Production

Once you have finished your pre-production research and planning you should have a clear idea as to how you will meet the brief's requirements in your production work.

Let's follow this process using a sample NEA brief.

10.3 A sample NEA brief

The brief	Minimum requirements
Create a front page, a contents page and a double-page spread for the print version of a new independent cross-platform youth magazine aimed at young people aged between 15 and 25. The magazine offers some lifestyle content but its main unique selling point is that it offers comments and opinions on current affairs for its youth audience. You should create four pages in total, including at least eight original images. This magazine would be published by an independent publisher.	**Front cover to include:** - title for a new magazine and masthead - selling line - cover price - dateline - main cover image (this image should not be used on the other pages created for this brief) - at least five cover lines. **Contents page to include:** - full list of contents for the magazine - reference to the magazine's website and social media - at least three images related to different articles (these images must not be the same as those used on the front cover or in the double-page spread). **Double-page spread to include:** - headline, standfirst and subheadings - original copy for double-page feature (approx. 400 words) that links to one of the cover lines on the front cover - main image plus at least three smaller images - representations of a social group, event or place that is relevant to the magazine - pull quotes and/or sidebar. **All pages to include:** - clear brand and house style for the magazine, including use of images, colour palette and fonts.

Create a new functioning website as an e-media version of the magazine
 	
The website should include:
- a homepage featuring information on the website's sections and content including a link to:
  - a feature article on a topic appropriate to the magazine/website's brand
  - a third page based on audience interaction and/or user-generated content.
 	
The site will incorporate one minute of audio material and you can choose where this should feature on the website.
 	
Like the magazine, the website is aimed at young people aged between 15 and 35.
	The website to include:
	- at least six additional original images across the three pages that communicate the magazine/website's branding message
	- use of appropriate language and register for the target audience.
	
	The homepage should include:
	- original title and logo for the website
	- clear navigation and working links to the rest of the site
	- one main image plus at least two other images that are appropriate for the website's brand and style.
	
	Pages 2 and 3 should include:
	- at least 100 words of copy on each page
	- one minute of audio including two different voices and other sound sources such as music, sound effects, etc. on at least one of the pages
	- at least three further original images
	- working links to the other pages
	- the ability for users to interact, e.g. by adding comments or liking other comments on the page, submitting images, video or audio for publication or any other interaction that is appropriate for the website.

■ Research

Having selected the brief, the first part of the process is to undertake some research based on the brief's requirements. There are several 'clues' in the brief itself that indicate the type of knowledge required to complete the brief effectively.

Codes and conventions of the form

The first stage is to be clear about the codes and conventions of the products identified in the brief – in this case magazine front covers, contents pages and feature articles, and website homepages, articles and user-generated content/interaction pages.

Magazines

You will be studying two magazine CSPs and both offer examples of the layout and design of their front covers and examples of inner pages. These magazines have different target audiences and are published by very different institutions; however, the way the front covers and articles are presented follow similar conventions. By looking at these, and other non-CSP magazines, the general codes and conventions for each part of the magazine can be identified. At this stage, the content of the magazine is not important as the codes and conventions are the shared characteristics of the form, which will then be used in ways that suit individual magazines' contents and target audiences.

Front covers	Contents pages	Feature articles
Magazine title using recognisable font at the top of the page	Heading used to identify the contents page	One large image and two or three smaller images used to illustrate the story
One main picture of a model or celebrity – sometimes someone featured in the magazine	Contents sometimes broken up into sections	Large, short, punchy headline – often crossing two pages
Limited colour palette used – magazine title's colour sometimes changed to reflect this	Page numbers indicate the location of specific articles	Smaller but longer subheading
Dateline and cover price sometimes included	Titles of articles provided	Text laid out in columns
Cover lines provide information about the magazine's content and often use a punchy phrase followed by a brief explanation of the content	A brief summary of the contents also provided	Text broken up with short subheadings, pull quotes or other visual devices
A small selection of fonts used to create visual interest (but always legible)	Images used to illustrate the contents of the magazine that are connected to some or all of the articles	Text often broken up with small illustrations
Advertising language used to 'sell' the magazine		Text laid out for easy legibility/readability
Numbers often used to indicate that there is a lot of information/content in the magazine		Sidebar often used to offer additional, related information
		Pages are often designed using a limited colour palette
		Fonts and other design elements are used to illustrate the page

Apply it

1. This sample brief requires materials to be made for a lifestyle/current affairs magazine. Look at some examples from these magazine genres to see if they have their own codes and conventions in the way they present front covers, contents pages and feature articles.
2. You are asked to produce an independently produced magazine. Look at other independent magazines to find out whether they use codes and conventions in similar or different ways from those magazines produced by large publishers.
3. The target audience for your production is young people. Look at other magazines for young people to see what design elements they use and how they address their audience.

Once this research has been undertaken and you are familiar with the conventions of the forms you are making, you may want to look a little more closely at three other types of magazines to help you make your own examples:
- magazines from the genre(s) you are working in
- magazines with a similar institutional background
- magazines for your target audience.

10.3 A sample NEA brief

Each A-level NEA brief has two tasks, asking you to make two productions in total, so you should research both productions in terms of codes and conventions, industrial context and the way the audience is appealed to and addressed.

In this sample brief the second production is a website. Website design has changed over the years as web designers adapt to new digital technologies and audience behaviours. For example, the placement of menus has changed to give audiences accessing websites on tablets and smartphones a better visual experience.

Your website research should look at a range of websites to identify their codes and conventions:

- a range of different homepages
- a range of different online articles
- a range of pages featuring user-generated content
- a range of pages that encourage and use audience interaction
- lifestyle magazine sites
- current affairs sites
- sites for young people
- sites for independent magazines.

This level of research will give you knowledge of contemporary web design and it is from this position that you are able to engage with the requirements of the brief. You can then use this knowledge to create your production plans, your Statement of Intent and, finally, the productions themselves.

You should use the knowledge you gain while analysing existing media products to make production decisions. Your production decisions should always be based on creating a recognisable product that will be appealing to your target audience and meet the brief's requirements. You may decide that the best way to achieve all of this is to create a media product that subverts conventions and offers the audience something different. This is a valid choice as long as your approach enhances audience appeal and effectively communicates your messages.

■ Planning

Once you have researched existing media products you can create your own plans for production. As indicated earlier, the plans you create will depend on what you are making. Planning is an important part of the process. You should consider the layout and design of print and e-media work; you are advised to script audio and video work and consider what arrangements you should make to ensure you have the correct actors, props, lighting and other equipment available. Photography should be carefully planned, and not only are you likely to want to find models, but you should also make decisions about shooting locations, props, costume and make-up before you start taking photographs. Use your plans to explore what equipment, resources and software you will need. If your plans include using a dozen different models on one photoshoot, you should consider if it is possible to get all your models in one place at the same time. It is better to find out what you can and cannot do at this stage so you can alter your plans rather than discover a problem later that means you have to start again. A lot of time can be saved by planning effectively.

■ The Statement of Intent

Your teacher will set a deadline for the submission of your Statement of Intent and you should write it after you have completed your research for the productions but before the productions are completed. It should show the outcome of your research, not by describing what you found, but by discussing how the research has influenced your approach to the production tasks.

> **TIP** ✓
> Be explicit in how you are using your knowledge of the theoretical framework in your approach to the tasks set in the brief.

■ The production

Your teacher will provide you with a deadline so you should make sure you give the NEA enough time. After the pre-production planning, you will want to shoot footage, record audio and/or take photographs, and give yourself time to edit and enhance your work in post-production. You are also advised to give enough time to the design of print and e-media products and the addition of any multimedia elements you require.

> **TIP** ✓
> Most students find the production part of the project fun but time-consuming, so make sure you schedule in enough time.

You should also leave some time to review your finished productions so you can make improvements to your work. You are being assessed on how your practical work demonstrates your understanding of the theoretical framework, so when reviewing your work you should ask the following questions:

Media language
- Are the media language choices appropriate for the form and genre of the production?
- Are the products recognisable and easy to follow/understand?
- Do the media language choices effectively communicate the intended message?

Representations
- Have representations been created in a way that is appropriate to the:
  - form
  - genre
  - audience
  - industry
  - brand image
  - function of the product
  - effective communication of the product's messages?

Audience
- Has the target audience been identified?
- Is the audience addressed appropriately?
- Does the product create audience appeal?
- Does the product encourage audience interactivity (where appropriate)?

Industry
- Has the product been created in a way that is appropriate for the distribution method?
- Does the product have a recognisable brand image?
- Does the product act to attract its audience?
- Does the product demonstrate an attempt to increase circulation?
- Does the product reflect its industrial context?
- Are the products convergent?
- Does the product meet any regulations that impact on this form?

10.3 A sample NEA brief

Finally, check your finished work against the brief and the minimum requirements:

- Have you created work that responds to the tasks set in the brief?
- Does your work contain all the minimum requirements identified in the brief?

■ Presentation of work

After all your hard work, you need to make sure that your NEA is presented in the best possible way, so it can be seen as you intended. You may have used specific software to make/edit your work, but as it could be sent off to the exam board you should make sure it is easily accessible.

Always check for the current advice about submission of work; this advice will be provided by the exam board.

Test your production work before submission

- Test prints of your print and online e-media work before you submit it – first, in black and white, so you can check your print margins and the proportions of your pages, and then in colour to make sure your images, fonts and text are as you want them.
- Make sure you have tested to see if your audio/video files play properly, including any e-media walkthroughs.
- If you are submitting an offline e-media production, check that all your pages and links work properly. Does everything look the way it should? Do any multimedia elements play correctly? Do links work?

Audio/video: data files

- You should convert any video/audio files to a universally accessible format. MP3s and MP4s are usually playable on a range of devices, but .mov, .avi and .mkv are often better quality for video work.

e-media: offline submission

- You should send your work in a format that means it can be accessed via a browser and not as the working file you have used in your software package. Convert your finished work to an .html file that can be sent to the exam board on an encrypted flash drive or other storage device (AQA may begin to allow different methods in future, so for the most recent guidance, see their website).
- Check your offline e-media work through different browsers to make sure it looks the way you want. It's also a really good idea to send some screen grabs of your e-media work with your folder just in case there are any technical difficulties accessing it.

e-media: created online

- Work that is created or hosted online should be submitted as a working url. The best way to do this is create a hyperlink to your product on a word processor document, so there are no problems transcribing long urls.
- An alternative way to submit online work would be to record a 'walkthrough' using screen recording software.

> **TIP**
> It's a good idea to check e-media productions work using several different browsers before submission.

> **TIP**
> Always check the most recent submission guidelines from the exam board.

Final production checklist

What have I created and who is it for?	
What did I need to achieve in terms of the instructions in the brief?	
What is the institutional context of my production?	
How have I made my product appealing for the audience?	
How effectively does the product follow the conventions of the form?	
How successful have I been in replicating or subverting the conventions of the genre I am working in?	
What representations have I created and why?	
Is the content clear?	
Have I created meaning in a clear and understandable way?	
What ideas and values are being created by my production and why?	
Does my production meet all the minimum requirements stated in each task of my chosen brief?	

> **TIP**
>
> Analysing your practical work in this way may give you some ideas as to how to improve your production work before it is submitted and marked.

Summary

The NEA is an important part of the assessment of the A-level. You should give enough time to planning and producing your products.

This chapter has offered advice and guidance on:

- selecting your brief and making sure you meet the brief's requirements
- researching and planning your practical productions
- writing your Statement of Intent
- making appropriate choices in the production of your media products
- submitting your work for assessment.

Chapter 11: The examinations

→ What you will learn in this chapter

Chapter 11: The examinations covers:

- an overview of the of the two A-level examination papers
- the structure of the papers and the types of questions you can expect
- sample questions which you can use to practise your responses and test your knowledge and understanding as you prepare for the examinations
- information about the examiner's expectations in the way you respond to exam questions and suggestions for helping you respond to the different types of questions.

11.1 Introduction to the A-level examinations

The A-level qualification requires you to complete three formal assessments:

- The **Non-Exam Assessment (NEA)**: based on the completion of a cross-media production. This is worth 30 per cent of the A-level qualification (see Chapter 10: The NEA for further information).
- **Paper 1: Media One**: a two-hour written examination that is worth 35 per cent of the A-level qualification.
- **Paper 2: Media Two**: a second two-hour written examination worth a further 35 per cent of the A-level qualification.

Each paper will ask questions designed to check your knowledge of the theoretical framework. The exams are structured so you can be sure which media forms and Close Study Products (CSPs) you need to use in each paper:

- Both papers will include a non-CSP media product.
- **Paper 1: Media One** questions require a focus on the targeted CSPs.
- **Paper 2: Media Two** questions require a focus on the in-depth CSPs.

You will sit both papers at the end of your second year of study.

The table below shows the structure of each paper and provides an overview of the expectations in terms of the framework and the CSPs.

Paper 1: Media One		Paper 2: Media Two
Section A	Section B	THEORETICAL FRAMEWORK
THEORETICAL FRAMEWORK	THEORETICAL FRAMEWORK	All areas of the framework
Media language and representation	Audience and industries	FORMS
FORMS	FORMS	(In-depth CSPs)
(Targeted CSPs)	(Targeted CSPs)	Magazines
Advertising and marketing	Radio	Television
Music video	Newspapers	Online, social and participatory media
UNSEEN/NON-CSP PRODUCT	Film (industries only)	Gaming
		UNSEEN/NON-CSP PRODUCT
The exams may not ask questions related to all the media forms studied.		

290

CHAPTER 11 THE EXAMINATIONS

Each paper will provide a different **non-CSP media product** – that is, a media product that you will not have worked on before the examination. The non-CSP product will relate specifically to the focus of the paper and, where appropriate, the section of the paper. For example, the non-CSP product in Media One will be related to advertising and marketing or music video, and the question will test the application of knowledge of media language and/or representation.

Both examinations will test your knowledge and understanding of:

- the **theoretical framework** (see Chapters 1 to 6)
- **media contexts** and their **influence on media products and processes**.

You will also be assessed on your ability to apply the theoretical framework to:

- analyse media products (considering context and using theory)
- evaluate theories
- make judgements and draw conclusions.

The content of the examinations will always be based on the detailed information provided in the specification as to the content of the theoretical framework and the CSP guidance document provided by the awarding body.

The key areas for revision are:

- the **theoretical framework** – specifically, the enabling ideas for each area of the framework
- the application of ideas from the theoretical framework to **non-CSP** media products
- the application of the theoretical framework to the eight **in-depth CSPs** and the **nine targeted CSPs** from the **nine media forms**.

Each paper will include a non-CSP product, often called the 'unseen'.

■ Non-Close Study Products

The non-CSP text in Paper 1

Question 1 (8 marks) – the unseen is printed and presented in Section A of the paper and so the question will relate to ideas from the media language or representation parts of the theoretical framework. The product will relate to advertising and marketing or music video in some way.

Question 2 (12 marks) – this is a comparison of the unseen and one of the CSPs, focusing on an aspect of representation.

The non-CSP text in Paper 2

Question 1 (9 marks) – you will be given a printed media product and will be asked to discuss it using specific ideas from the media language area of the framework.

■ Close Study Products

It is possible that some of the CSPs may change from year to year, so you must make sure that you are studying the right CSPs for your examination.

11.2 Paper 1: Media One

Paper 1 will ask you to answer questions that demonstrate your knowledge and understanding of the theoretical framework using targeted CSPs and a non-CSP media product that will be provided for you in the examination.

This is a two-hour paper and it is split into two sections. It is expected that you would spend one hour on each section.

Section A – Four compulsory questions:

- theoretical focus: media language and representations
- using CSPs from the following media forms – advertising and marketing and music video
- one non-CSP media product (unseen).

Section B – Three compulsory questions:

- theoretical focus: audience and industries
- using CSPs from the following media forms – radio, newspapers and film (industries only).

Different questions will offer different amounts of marks. This should be your guide when you work out your timings in the examination.

As a guide, you should try to spend:

- approximately 10 minutes on questions that offer up to 10 marks
- approximately 15 minutes on questions that offer between 10 and 20 marks
- approximately 30 minutes on questions that offer 20 marks.

There are several different types of questions that you could be asked in Paper 1. Some may be multiple-choice, some short-answer questions and some may ask you to provide an extended answer.

- You could be asked to demonstrate your knowledge by providing definitions or explanations.
- You could be asked to apply a specific idea or theory from the framework to one or two media products.
- You could be asked to evaluate a media theory or an idea from the theoretical framework.

In this paper, you will be assessed on your knowledge and understanding of media language and representation as applied to advertising and marketing and music video (Section A), and industry as applied to film and industry and audience as applied to newspapers and radio (Section B).

As long as you have a general understanding of the theoretical framework and have prepared your CSPs thoroughly (using the appropriate theoretical ideas), you will be prepared for the exam. The specification offers more detail on the specific knowledge required for each area of the theoretical framework and the CSP guides offer lots of different ideas that you can consider when studying the CSPs.

Plan your timings in detail before you start and then stick to your plan. Spending too much time on individual questions may mean that you run out of time and lose marks. The number of marks offered for each question indicates the relative depth that is expected in your response and the final question in each section carries almost half the marks for the paper. You must spend more time on these questions than the others.

> **TIP**
> You should spend most time on the questions that offer the most marks.

> **You learned about the theoretical framework in Chapters 1–6.**

CHAPTER 11 THE EXAMINATIONS

■ Section A: media language and representations

You must answer **all** questions in Section A. One of the questions in this section offers 20 marks.

You can answer the questions in any order; you might decide to deal with the shorter questions first. However you decide, make sure that you divide your time equally between Sections A and B.

This section of the examination will assess your knowledge and understanding of two areas of the theoretical framework – media language and representations – which means that you will need to refer to the unseen product where instructed. The CSPs you need to refer to in this section will come from advertising and marketing. Each question will make it clear which CSPs you should use in your response.

You should make sure you understand the ideas and theories from the media language and representations chapters and are able to discuss how they apply to media products using media terminology.

Too much listing or description will reduce the number of marks you can achieve for this type of question. You need to select three or four key observations and ideas that you can cover in some detail in your written response rather than try to force in lots of observations that will end up being a descriptive list rather than an answer to the question.

> **Find examples of analysis and the application of theoretical ideas throughout this book, but specifically in Chapter 8.**

■ Section A: types of questions

Non-CSP question

One of the questions on this exam paper will ask you to look at a non-CSP media product. There will be questions which require a relatively short answer that will be directly related to the use of media language and/or the construction of the representations in the unseen product. It is likely that the non-CSP specific question will be a short-answer question, which means you will need to spend about 10 minutes writing your response.

This question could ask you to discuss any aspect of these two areas of the theoretical framework.

As the product will be related to either advertising and marketing or music video in some way, the question may ask you to discuss the nature of the form of the product. This question will test your knowledge and your ability to apply that knowledge by quickly analysing the media language choices made and the way they combine to create meaning. For this non-CSP focused question, you should only refer to the product provided in the exam when constructing your response.

Take a look at the Dove advert on the left. It's designers have used a number of media language choices in its layout and design, the selection of images and in the way it uses words to address the target audience. As an advert, its primary functions are to:

- reinforce the Dove brand
- create positive associations with the brand and the product
- attempt to create desire for the product that will lead to its purchase.

11.2 Paper 1: Media One

There are many shampoos on the market, so the advert needs to give the consumer a reason to choose Dove over the others. Every media language choice is made with a view to help the target audience (adult women) make Dove a product they want to buy.

Over many years, Dove has invested heavily in advertising and marketing campaigns, which have helped construct the brand image and USP that Dove celebrates diverse female beauty. This idea is in reaction to criticism that beauty brands often set narrow and unrealistic ideals that are difficult for most women to achieve.

With an unseen media product such as this, you could be asked to focus on any aspect of the use of media language and/or the representations constructed within this advertising and marketing product.

> How do the representations in the advert help create audience appeal?
>
> or
>
> How do the images and words in this advert combine to construct a positive brand image for Dove?

Apply it

Using the Dove advert on the previous page, answer the following questions.

1. How does the design of the advert help create audience appeal?
2. How do the images and words in this advert combine to construct a positive brand image for Dove?
3. How do the representations of the women in the advert help to sell Dove shampoo?

In your answers to questions such as these, you should make sure that you provide a detailed analysis of aspects of the product provided. When discussing the design of the product you may want to include the **rule of three**, the use of **direct address** or the **placement** of the product in the bottom right-hand corner of the design. Your answer should include some detail and use relevant terminology as much as possible. So, if you identify that the colour palette is largely white and pale blue, you should also be able to indicate what **connotations** these colour choices might create. Also crucial is that you link your observations to the question – how do the colour palette choices help create audience appeal? How do they construct a positive brand image for Dove, or help sell Dove shampoo? There are many ways to answer these questions and the ideas given here are not the only ones you could use. The examiner is always going to be interested to read what you think, even where it differs from other people's responses.

■ Compare/contrast the non-CSP to a CSP question

You will need to answer a question that asks you to discuss both the non-CSP product **and** one of the targeted CSPs. This question will again be based on representations, but you may be asked to compare or contrast the media products in some way and to demonstrate a knowledge of the impact of context on the construction of media products. This question is most likely worth 12 marks. Make sure you spend an appropriate amount of time on your response.

One of the current (at the time of writing) advertising and marketing CSPs is an online advert for the beauty retailer Sephora. You could use adverts for any beauty/make-up products to practise comparing and contrasting two adverts.

The example given here, Maybelline Indonesia's *That Boss Life Part 1* advert for a new mascara, is available to watch on YouTube at:

www.youtube.com/watch?v=UkdA0J2BeEE&ab channel=MaybellineIndonesia.tugas

CHAPTER 11 THE EXAMINATIONS

The advert features social media celebrities and is set in a high-rise Manhattan hotel. It is promoting a new mascara from the Maybelline make-up range.

Some ways you could consider the advert:

- the use of media language choices made in the advert's construction
- the construction of narrative within the advert
- the use of representations of ethnicity, age, gender and lifestyle
- the use or subversion of stereotypes
- the values and ideologies communicated in the advert
- the use of media language and representations to create desire for the product
- the way the advert addresses the target audience.

A number of context issues could also be considered when looking at this advert, including:

- the fluidity of gender identity
- the aspirational, consumerist lifestyle
- diversity of representations
- the importance of social media 'influencers'
- the use of non-traditional advertising methods.

In these example questions you would be asked to demonstrate your detailed knowledge and understanding of the Maybelline advert in relation to the unseen media product – in this case, the Dove advert on page 4.

> How are representations of women used differently to promote these beauty products? Your answer should refer to the Dove advert and your CSP, the Maybelline mascara advert.
>
> or
>
> How are the representations of racial diversity shaped by the context of production? Your answer should refer to the Dove advert and your CSP, the Maybelline mascara advert.
>
> or
>
> How do the brand identities created in the adverts relate to the target audiences? Your answer should refer to the Dove advert and your CSP, the Maybelline mascara advert.

For questions like this, you need to provide detailed references to both products in your responses. Choose examples from the products that help you make the point you wish to raise. In addition to details from the Dove advert you could discuss the mise-en-scène of the Maybelline advert, as well as the advert's use of camera, editing and sound. You should use terminology as much as possible.

You should not simply describe the advert in the exam but should use your detailed knowledge to apply ideas from the theoretical framework. You could consider the way media language choices create meaning, issues around representation and the construction of ideologies.

> **See Chapter 8: Developing media studies skills** for further advice on analysing and writing about media products.

> **Apply it**
>
> Answer the following questions. You could spend time researching, analysing and planning your responses, but work towards writing each of your answers in about 15 minutes. Your answers should refer to the Dove advert and your CSP, the Maybelline mascara advert.
>
> 1 How are representations of women used differently to promote these beauty products?
> 2 How are the representations of racial diversity shaped by the context of production?
> 3 How do the brand identities created in the adverts relate to the target audiences?

Although this example compares two advertising products, the exam may ask you to compare an advertising product to one of the music video CSPs.

■ Analyse media products using a specific aspect of the theoretical framework (media language or representation)

Another type of question you may encounter in Section A is one in which you are asked to analyse one or two named CSPs using a specific theory or idea. You may be asked to discuss the advertising and marketing CSPs or the music videos you have studied in this way. In Section A, this type of question focuses on a specific idea or theory related to media language or representation.

As this type of question will ask you to focus on one or two named CSPs, it requires that you discuss the product or products in detail, providing examples from the CSPs to support the ideas you wish to raise.

For example, here are some of the ideas you should have covered when studying the music video CSPs:

- How is media language used to create the music videos?
- How do media language choices construct meaning in the videos?
- How have technologies influenced media language choices in the two videos?
- How is narrative created within the music videos?
- How do the videos create audience appeal?
- What relationship do the videos have with the codes and conventions of:
  - music videos (as a form)
  - the genre of music video
  - the genre of music?
- How is intertextuality/hybridity created or used within the videos?
- What type of representations are created in the music videos, including:
  - ethnicity
  - gender
  - other?

Again, you should prepare for the exam by applying theories to the music videos and considering how the videos relate to ideas including:

- Neale's ideas about genre
- Todorov's ideas about narrative

- Butler's ideas about gender
- Hall's ideas on representation
- Postmodern theory (including Baudrillard)
- theories around race and ethnicity (including Gilroy).

You should also have considered the music videos in their cultural context.

If you've prepared for the exam by studying the two videos using media language and representation ideas, you should be able to discuss the theoretical ideas when discussing either or both of the music videos.

Your answers to these questions should:

- address the question directly
- use specific examples from the music videos to support your ideas
- use media terminology and ideas from the theoretical framework in your discussion.

A previous music video CSP was 'Letter to the Free' by Common.

You can watch it at www.youtube.com/watch?v=KO7tVuPHOxA

How does Common's 'Letter to the Free' use media language to represent the experiences of African-Americans?

How	For example	Terms/theory
Setting parts of the video in a prison location	See 0:24, 1:20, 1:41, 3:00 through the video.	Stereotype mise-en-scène Reinforcing dominant values Cultural expectations Cultural positioning
Lyrics: *Southern leaves, southern trees we hung from …* *Forgive them father they know this knot is undone,* *Tied with the rope that my grandmother died*	Reference to the song 'Strange Fruit' about lynching of black men in the US southern states in the 1930s. *Southern trees bear strange fruit* *Blood on the leaves and blood at the root* *Black bodies swinging in the southern breeze* *Strange fruit hanging from the poplar trees*	Intertextuality Historical reference Historical, situational identity
Use of tracking shot through the prison to the light (and an exit sign)	See the first 35 seconds of the video.	Symbolic encoding Visual metaphor Camera movement Positioning audience Construction of narrative Low-key lighting Binary opposition of light/dark; incarceration/freedom

11.2 Paper 1: Media One

> ## Apply it
>
> Consider the following questions and plan your response before spending approximately 10 minutes each writing your answer. You can practise using these questions to discuss both of your current music video CSPs.
>
> > How do your music video CSPs use media language to create audience appeal?
> >
> > How do your music video CSPs use media language to represent the experiences of different social/cultural groups?
> >
> > How do your music video CSPs use and/or challenge subvert stereotypes?
>
> Now use your knowledge to answer these, more specific questions.
>
> > Hall argues that black culture is often shown from a white person's perspective, the 'white eye'. How valid is this idea? You should refer to your music video CSPs in your response.
> >
> > Mulvey argues that women are often shown from a male perspective, the 'male gaze'. How valid is this idea? You should refer to your music video CSPs in your response.

These examples focus on music videos, but you may be asked about advertising and marketing in the extended response question.

■ Extended response questions

The extended response question in Section A offers 20 marks. You should spend more time answering this question than the others in Section A. The question will ask you to use named CSPs in response to the question. This question will be based on a specific theory or idea from the theoretical framework, and it will ask you to engage with and evaluate the idea, and use the CSPs to demonstrate your perspective. You will be marked on your knowledge and understanding of the theory as well as the way in which you make judgements and come to conclusions.

> Neale discusses the idea that genres have to change to maintain audience interest. To what extent does an analysis of your music video CSPs support this idea?
>
> or
>
> Gilroy argues that music by black artists can express 'diasporic experiences of resistance to white capitalist culture'. How valid is this argument when looking at the representations in music videos? In your response you should refer to your music video CSPs.
>
> or
>
> Narratives are based on conflicts between binary oppositions. How valid is this idea when looking at narratives in music videos? In your response you should refer to your music video CSPs.

This type of question offers more marks than others in this section because you have more work to do in your response. Not only do you need to apply the idea provided in the question to the media products and analyse specific examples to show how the idea can be applied, but you also have to consider the validity of the idea in light of the evidence from the CSPs. You need to evaluate the theory as well as apply it.

When writing a response based on these kinds of ideas, as with all other questions, it is important to provide detailed examples from the products to support your observations and to use media terminology.

Before starting to write your answer to this type of question, be clear about what you think about the issue or theory you are being asked to evaluate. You may want to write notes before starting your answer.

> **Narratives are based on conflicts between binary oppositions. How valid is this idea when looking at narratives in music videos? In your response you should refer to your music video CSPs.**
>
> *Initial idea/notes (using 'Letter to the Free'):*
>
> *Using the conflicts created by binary oppositions is a useful way to explore the ideas created in these music videos.*
>
> *Supporting evidence:*
>
> *'Letter to the Free' uses the binary between freedom and imprisonment in its visual imagery and its lyrics. The overall narrative is one of hope - hope that there is a way out of the current situation of extreme incarceration of black men and criminalisation. Religion is offered as a solution and is in opposition to the experiences of black people in the USA at the moment where violence, racism and political oppression are still present.*

Of course, in the exam there isn't a lot of time to think and make such detailed notes. This is why preparation for the exam is so important.

■ Section B – Industries and audience

As with Section A, one question in Section B is worth 20 marks and you should make sure you spend more time on this question than the others. You should allow approximately one hour for Section B.

This section of the examination tests your knowledge and understanding of media industries and audiences. In your responses, you will need to use the relevant targeted CSPs for this area, taken from the following media forms:

- radio
- newspapers
- film (assessed via questions on media industries only).

This paper requires you to discuss **two** of these three media forms. One question will ask you to use one of the forms and the other two questions will focus on a second form. Each question will be focused on ideas about audience and/or industries. It won't be possible to predict which forms will appear on the paper, so you will need to make sure you have studied all three.

In preparation for this section, you should have engaged with all the ideas from the Media industry and Media audiences sections of the theoretical framework (see Chapters 6 and 7). You should be able to define media terms and the main theoretical ideas. You should also have considered these ideas when studying the CSPs and in preparation for the exam, and you should be confident about the industrial and audience issues related to each of the CSPs.

Section B: Types of questions

Short-answer questions

You will find that one of the questions in section B requires shorter responses than the others. This question is split into two (a and b). One will be a multiple-choice question and the other a standalone question. Both focus on testing your knowledge of an aspect of the theoretical framework. You may be asked to recall terminology, provide definitions or show you understand a specific aspect of the industry and/or audience areas of the theoretical framework.

Multiple-choice question:

> Which three of the following relate to the fan behaviours?
>
> a) Textual poaching
> b) Socialisation
> c) Cultivation
> d) Participation
> e) Mainstreaming
> f) Collective identity

You will be given instructions on the exam paper as to how you should identify the correct answers in a multiple-choice question.

Standalone question:

> What is a prosumer? Give an example from the media.

You may be asked to provide a brief example or explanation in your response to the standalone question, but you should not spend too much time providing lots of detail.

Typically these two questions offer 3 marks each.

Mid-length questions

Mid-length questions typically offer 9 marks. You may be asked a question that will ask you to demonstrate your knowledge and understanding of an area of the framework and/or the way context influences media products and their production. As with all questions in this section, you could be asked to consider industry or audience and be asked to focus on radio, newspaper or film CSPs.

> Explain the influence of economic factors on the production and distribution of films. In your response you should refer to the industrial context of your film CSP.
>
> or
>
> How does the context of attempting to appeal to an audience impact on the presentation of news? In your answer you should refer to your newspaper CSPs.
>
> or
>
> Using your radio CSPs, demonstrate how social/cultural context issues impact on the production and/or distribution of radio programmes.

These questions need you to consider various aspects of the context of production of your CSPs. There are many ways that these questions could be answered and you should consider a number of contextual issues when you study each CSP in preparation for the exam.

Here are just some of the context issues you could use in your answers to these questions. They are not the only ideas you could cover, but, in the time allowed, it will not be possible to deal with all potential context issues. You should select two or three ideas that you think will be most useful to you when addressing the question and you should offer examples and explanations for these ideas. Don't try to cram in 'everything you know' when answering the question; this will lead to an unfocused response that lacks detail.

Film (industrial context)	Newspapers (audience appeal)	Radio (social/cultural context)
Economic issues related to filmmaking, including: • production budget impacting on production choices and techniques • distribution techniques • marketing strategies • responses to audience behaviour patterns, etc.	Responses to the decline in sales of print newspapers: • the paper's attempts to reach its target audience shaping its presentation style • the paper's attempts to offer broadsheet and/or tabloid gratifications • the way the reporting style is influenced by online news conventions • attempts to provide ways for the audience to interact with the publication.	Historical issues could include: • radio as competition to newspapers and cinema newsreels • narrowness of choice for audience in terms of media technology • innovations in the use of the form. Contemporary issues could include: • focus on niche audiences • impact of competition from digital and social media • attempt to encourage audience participation.

Examples here refer to audience and institution CSPs but you should also engage with context when studying all of your CSPs.

Apply it

Research and plan your answers to the questions on the previous page. You should aim to be able to write a written response to these questions in approximately 15 minutes. This means you cannot cover everything, so select two or three key ideas.

Extended-response question

The extended response question requires you to offer a longer, more detailed response than the other questions in this Section. As shown earlier in this chapter, there is an extended response question at the end of Section A and another at the end of Section B. This question typically offers 20 marks, so make sure you give yourself time to provide a more detailed answer. Aim to spend 30 minutes on each extended response question.

This question aims to test your knowledge and understanding of audience and industry, and will ask you to use your newspaper, radio or film (industries only) CSPs. You will also have to show that you can make judgements and draw conclusions that show you can critically evaluate the ideas and theories you are using to answer the question.

Questions will focus on a specific aspect of the theoretical framework and ask you to use your CSPs to provide evidence for your analysis of the ideas you are discussing. As with all the questions on this paper, the specific ideas that could come up in this question are taken from the detailed list of ideas and enabling ideas published in the AQA specification. Your preparations should have included the application of lots of different audience and industry ideas that you can use to help you answer the question.

> **Apply it**
>
> Research and plan for your responses to the following questions. When you have considered the issues and feel ready to write, spend approximately 30 minutes writing your response for each question.
>
> Don't forget to use media terminology and specific and detailed examples from your CSPs to support your response.
>
> How important is convergence in the success of British newspapers? In your answer you should refer to your newspaper CSPs.
>
> Hall argues that audiences understand media products according to their own cultural upbringing. How useful is this idea when considering audience responses to radio programming? In your answer you should refer to your radio CSPs.
>
> How important is it for contemporary media industries to consider changing patterns in the way audiences access and consume media products? In your answer you should refer to your film CSP.

11.3 Paper 2: Media Two

Paper 2 asks you to demonstrate your knowledge and understanding of the entire theoretical framework as applied to the in-depth CSPs. It is a two-hour paper and you will need to complete four compulsory questions. One question is based on an unseen, non-CSP media product. The other three questions require you to discuss CSPs from three of the in-depth media forms – magazines, television, online, social and participatory media and/or gaming.

You may be asked questions on any aspect of the theoretical framework. You could be asked to evaluate and apply ideas, so it is important that you have a thorough knowledge of the framework and can apply it confidently to media products.

Typically, Paper 2 begins with a question based on the non-CSP product requiring a medium-length response based on the media language section of the framework.

The questions are typically:

- Q1 – the unseen (9 marks)
- Q2 – evaluation of theory (25 marks)
- Q3 – application of context (25 marks)
- Q4 – application of theory from across the framework (synoptic) (25 marks).

One of the 25-mark questions requires an extended response, in which you need to develop a line of reasoning, while another of the longer-response questions is synoptic.

Q1 – the unseen, non-CSP-based question

For the non-CSP-based question you need to show your knowledge and understanding of some aspect of the media language and/or representation areas of the framework. The question will make it clear which ideas you need to discuss. This is often presented as bullet points, and you should make sure you cover each bullet point in your response.

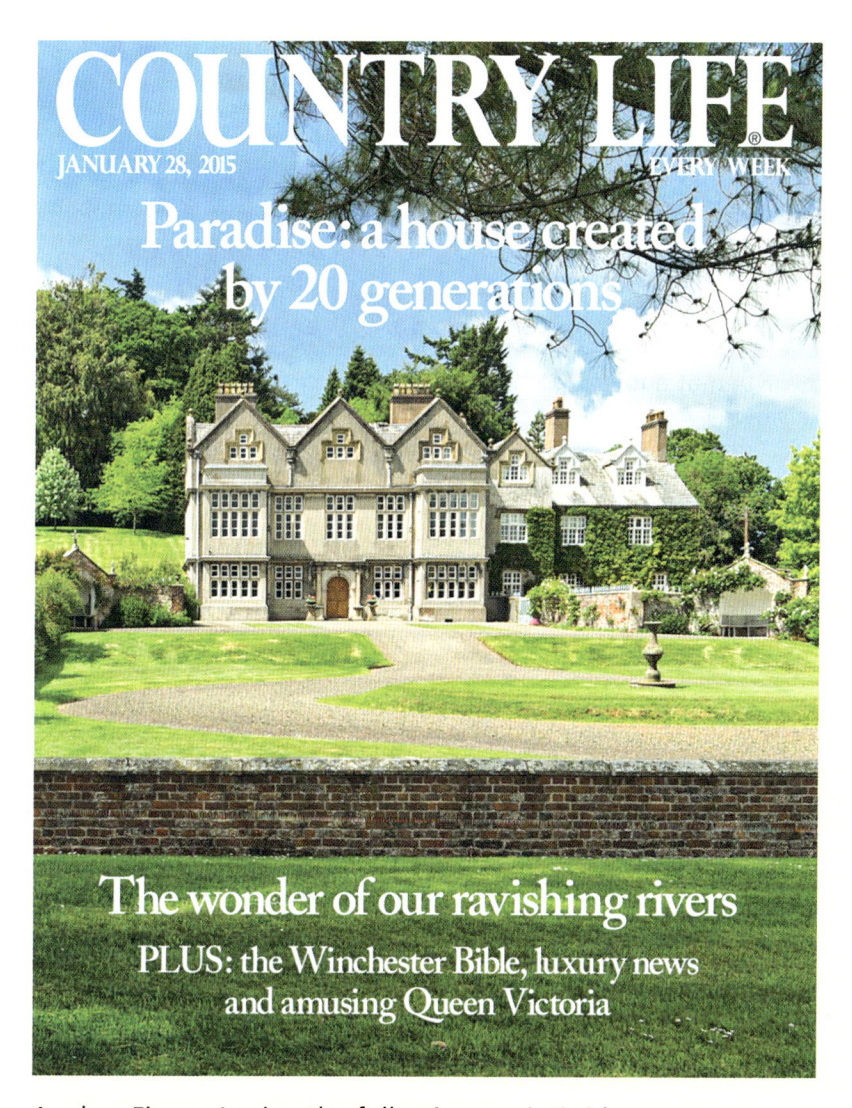

COUNTRY LIFE
JANUARY 28, 2015 — EVERY WEEK
Paradise: a house created by 20 generations
The wonder of our ravishing rivers
PLUS: the Winchester Bible, luxury news and amusing Queen Victoria

Analyse Figure 1 using the following semiotic ideas:

- denotation
- connotation
- myth.

The unseen, non-CSP product will be provided in the examination and will be print based. The non-CSP product could relate to any of the in-depth media forms.

Look at the *Country Life* magazine cover above:

- What denotations are used in its construction?
- What connotations are created by the combined media language selections?
- How does the cover tap into/reinforce/challenge cultural myths?

11.3 Paper 2: Media Two

You can prepare for this type of question by considering the ideas you are learning using the theoretical framework when you access the media. You can do this every day – as you are looking at magazines or scrolling past adverts on Instagram.

For example, here are some notes on the media language choices made in the construction of the front cover of *Country Life* magazine and how the denotations and connotations relate to cultural myths.

> *The cover of the magazine **denotes** a large country house set in a rural location. The house is presented in long-shot, ensuring that its location is clear. The magazine title, dateline and coverlines are all placed over the image but the house itself remains the central focus of the cover. The blue sky, the dominance of the green of the grass and leaves combine with the choice of the word 'paradise' to **connote** an idealised **myth** of the countryside. Anchorage is created with the phrase 'a house created by 20 generations', **reinforcing the values** that it is longstanding traditions that support the idea of a utopian vision of the countryside. The cover creates **connotations** of a nostalgia for a **mythic** 'golden age' of the past. The traditional values of the magazine are further **reinforced** in the mentioning of the royal family (specifically Queen Victoria) and its idealisation of the countryside in the promise of a feature on 'ravishing rivers'.*

Apply it

Provide a written response to the following question. Aim to complete your answer to each question in 15 minutes.

Analyse a media product using the following semiotic ideas:
- denotation
- connotation
- myth.

1. Answer this question using one of the pages from your magazine CSPs.
2. Answer this question using one of the pages/posts from your online, social and participatory media CSPs.
3. Answer this question using a cover from one of your gaming CSPs.

Even though you are using your CSPs, this activity is an excellent preparation for the unseen question as you are practising applying specific ideas from the framework to different media products.

■ Longer-response questions

The other questions on this paper require a detailed and extended engagement from you as you consider the issue raised in the question and then explain your response using ideas from the framework and examples from your CSPs. These questions are worth 25 marks each. You cannot predict which CSP products you will need to discuss using which ideas, so you must make sure that you have prepared all CSPs, thoroughly. As in-depth CSPs you will need to have some background knowledge on the industrial context of the products, as well as a detailed knowledge of the way media language is used in each product's construction and the specific representation and audience issues raised by each product. You should also have considered any relevant social, political or historical context related to each CSP.

TIP
When preparing for the examination ensure you have covered all areas of the theoretical framework in your analysis of each in-depth CSP.

CSP name	Main industrial issues	Audience	Use of media language (including genre and narrative)	Representation (including ideology)
Television CSPs				
Online, social and participatory media and CSPs				
Magazine CSPs				
Gaming CSPs				

There are several different types of longer-response questions that could come up in the examination.

Q2 – evaluation of theories

You may be asked to show your knowledge and understanding by evaluating a specific idea or theory. In this type of question, the idea or theory will be detailed in the question, and you will be asked to discuss how valid or useful you feel the ideas are. This type of question needs you to show that you can engage with ideas and understand them. In this type of question you don't necessarily have to agree with the theory. If you feel a specific idea is limited or even just not valid, you are able to challenge the ideas in your response. However, don't simply agree or disagree. You need to be prepared to explain your thoughts on the theory and provide support for your evaluation from your CSPs. The question will specify which CSPs you should provide examples from.

> Social learning theory speculates that audiences can be influenced by media representations. How valid is this idea? Refer to your online, social and participatory media CSPs in your answer.
>
> or
>
> Binary oppositions create conflicts that drive narratives forwards. Is this a valid idea when considering the appeal of television drama? You should refer to your television CSPs in your answer.
>
> or
>
> Mulvey said that 'the determining male gaze projects its phantasy on to the female form which is styled accordingly'. Is the male gaze a useful idea when considering the representations in magazines? You should refer to your magazine CSPs in your answer.

These questions direct you to think about a very specific idea and CSPs from one media form to help support your ideas. What follows are notes showing how the question about Mulvey's ideas (third question in the box above) can be approached using a previous CSP, *Oh Comely*. View the cover here: https://tinyurl.com/4sdzh7mk

11.3 Paper 2: Media Two

305

'Oh Comely' is an example of how some contemporary media products act to reject the male gaze and the male 'phantasy' of how women should be. The model on the front cover of the CSP is presented as androgynous and, although she is wearing some make-up, has not been styled in a stereotypical way. She controls the gaze by looking directly into the camera and, even though she is wearing earrings, the rest of the styling subverts the conventions of how women usually look on magazine front covers. Her body is covered and the image is anchored with words that are not stereotypically associated with the feminine: 'power', 'wisdom' and 'strong'. The model is not sexualised in any way and, although this challenges Mulvey's assertion, we can perhaps argue that the idea of the male gaze is a useful tool to help us engage with the ideologies created by media representations of women. Mulvey's ideas are still valid in other contexts (conventional lifestyle and fashion magazines) but 'Oh Comely' is an independent media product which wishes to appeal to an audience that does not identify with the femininity often represented in mainstream products. The representations chosen here are in response to the conventional ways women are usually presented to be gazed upon.

Apply it

Make notes and plan responses to the questions on the previous page where you refer to several examples from the relevant CSPs to help you evaluate the theories. You could attempt to write responses in approximately 30 minutes.

Q3 – application of context questions

You could be asked to show the impact of context on media products using your CSPs as examples. You will be told which CSPs you should use to help you answer the question but you may have to select a context issue to discuss.

To consider context is to consider the circumstances specific to the production and reception of a media product. Context can be considered in the following ways.

- The **cultural context** refers to the relationship the production of and/or reception of a media product may have with the other things created at the time (technological developments, other media products, art, literature, etc.).
- The **economic** context can refer to the industrial context of production as well as the broader economic context, including the impact of capitalist, consumerist and materialist values.
- The **political context** refers to the impact that dominant ideological ideas may have on media products and their reception.
- The **historical context** refers to the circumstances specific to the era of production.

These ideas of context often overlap. The most important thing is to recognise that media products are influenced by the context of production and some media products can have an impact on the context that surrounds it.

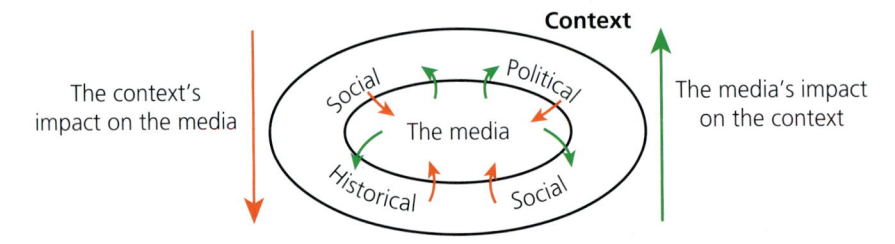

Context

The context's impact on the media → Social, Political, Historical, Social / The media ← The media's impact on the context

Take one aspect of the contemporary cultural context – the development of microblogging technology (for example, X). This technology has had a major impact on politics, the way the news is reported, celebrity culture, advertising, the way people communicate, the creation of fan communities, etc.

CHAPTER 11 THE EXAMINATIONS

Apply it

How has X changed our cultural, political and social context?

Complete the following table by making notes on the way X has impacted on a range of different aspects of contemporary culture.

The impact of X on ...	
Politics	
The reporting of news	
Celebrity culture	
Advertising	
Communication between strangers	
The creation of fan communities	
Other changes?	

No examiner will expect you to know everything there is to know about the contemporary context, but they will expect that you have looked at specific context issues related to the CSPs. As with the other questions on this paper, you could be asked to focus on any of the theoretical framework areas and any of the media forms you have studied in depth.

Media products can challenge the social attitudes and values of the context of their production. To what extent do your magazine CSPs support this idea?

or

Media producers need to respond to changes in audience behaviour to be successful. Discuss this claim, making reference to your TV CSPs.

or

Contemporary media needs to offer more choice and variety if it is to be competitive. How far does an analysis of your online, social and participatory media CSPs support this idea/

or

Media products are often shaped by economic concerns. To what extent does your study of the gaming CSPs support this idea?

11.3 Paper 2: Media Two

There will always be a number of ways you could answer a context question. You should ensure that you give plenty of evidence for your ideas. Evidence largely comes from the media products themselves and ideas from the theoretical framework.

Here are some ideas that you could use when answering the questions above.

Magazines: contemporary attitudes and values	Television: impact of audience behaviour	Online media: choice and variety	Gaming: economics
Cultural values around gender and sexuality in the content and representations within the magazines Representation theory: methods of encoding, cultural decoding; fluidity of identity; stereotypes and countertypes Gender theory: feminism, post-feminism; gender fluidity; gender as performance; male/female gaze	Social context of technology leading audience behaviour – mobile technology, streaming, etc. Development of long-form narrative; genres reflecting adult interests (literary influences); subversive binary oppositions; extended narratives using online products; rise in subscription services changing economic models of production Audience fragmentation; importance of niche groups; rise of social interaction via social media Audience choice and freedom from schedules, the television, mainstream broadcasters	Democratisation of production (to an extent): easy access to production technologies for individuals and smaller media companies Audience fragmentation and the importance of niche groups; media products as community hubs; convergence offering alternative experiences Economic factors: changes in funding models, data mining; selling an audience to advertisers Audience interaction, influence of amateurisation	Competitions within the form – need to attract and appeal to audiences Different selling points: high tech gaming engines, social media interactions Income streams – direct purchase vs free-to-play (sponsorship and in-game purchases) Traditional marketing vs encouraging participation and viral marketing

Apply it

Make notes and plan responses to the following questions on the previous page where you refer to several examples from the relevant CSPs to demonstrate your application of contextual ideas. You could attempt to write each response in approximately 30 minutes.

Q4 – application of theory from across the framework (synoptic)

One of the questions on this paper will be a synoptic question. This is a question about any aspect of the theoretical framework and you may be asked to show your knowledge and understanding of more than one theoretical area and/or context. You could be asked to show connections and relationships between theoretical ideas and you will be assessed on your ability to draw on different areas of study. The synoptic question focuses on one of the in-depth areas of study, but you will not be able to predict which one before the examination. It will most likely be the last question on the paper, so you must make sure that you leave enough time at the end of the examination to complete the question in full – you should leave at least 30 minutes for this question. If you produce a limited response in the synoptic question, it can have a negative impact on your mark.

CHAPTER 11 THE EXAMINATIONS

Providing a synoptic response relies on your having made connections between the ideas you have been studying. For example:

- When looking at **media language**, you will have engaged with the idea that choices in the production of media products create meaning.
- **Media producers** create the products and **audiences** interpret them, and through the creative choices made, **representations** are constructed.
- **Media language** choices are selected to appeal to **audiences** and some **media producers** have access to more **economic/industrial** support, which influences the production choices they make.
- Limited budgets may make some **genres** inaccessible and could mean that productions have to be creative in the way they use cheaper technologies.
- Production choices and audience responses are influenced by the social, historical, political, cultural and economic **contexts of production** and **reception**.

The separate aspects of the theoretical framework are, of course, not really separate at all. The synoptic question will ask you to demonstrate your understanding of this.

> Magazines are struggling to appeal to contemporary audiences and therefore remain economically successful. To what extent does your study of the magazine CSPs support this statement?

or

> Narratives offer a range of audience gratifications. Demonstrate this using examples from your television CSPs.

or

> Multiculturalism and ethnic identity can be commodified by media industries. To what extent do your online social and participatory media CSPs support or challenge this idea?

or

> The genre of a game influences the representations used and the ideological meaning created. Discuss this idea, making reference to your gaming CSPs.

Each of these questions requires you to refer to ideas from different parts of the theoretical framework if you are to answer them fully.

Let's take the final question and explore how to answer it.

> The genre of a game influences the representations used and the ideological meaning created. Discuss this idea making reference to your gaming CSPs.

This question needs you to connect the construction of meaning (**media language**), genre theory (**media language**) and ideas about representation (**representation**).

11.3 Paper 2: Media Two

In your answer you could refer to ideas such as **genres of order and integration**, **encoding and decoding**, **cultural codes** and **cultural myths**. You could link different genres to different **audiences** and the **gratifications** they seek. You could consider the use (or not) of **quest narratives** and **character roles** within specific genres and the way **binary oppositions** lead to **ideological meaning**. You might be interested in the way genres use ideas related to gender and/or race (**identity**, **feminist**, **post-feminist** and/ or **postcolonial theories**) and the relationship genres have with **dominant ideologies** and **hegemonic values**.

> ### Apply it
> Make notes and plan responses to the following questions on the previous page where you refer to several examples from the relevant CSPs and ideas from different parts of the theoretical framework. You could attempt to write responses in approximately 30 minutes.

As we have identified, three of the four questions on Paper 2 are longer-response questions. These offer higher marks and you will need to provide more detail than the answers to shorter-response questions.

You will also need to do more than simply show what you know. You should demonstrate that you are able to assess, evaluate, make judgements and draw conclusions. You need to be able to engage with ideas and develop an argument. For example, remembering what intersectionality is is very important, but what is its significance? Does this idea help us understand the impact of representations and the experiences of some segments of the audience? How does it relate to cultural discussions about race, gender and sexuality?

> ### TIP ✓
> When responding to a longer-response question, you will not only be asked to show what you know, but also that you have engaged with the ideas you are discussing and have considered them carefully. You should evaluate their validity as ideas and use examples from your CSPs to support your points of view.

→ Summary

Preparation for the A-level examinations can be broken down into the following elements:

- detailed knowledge of the theoretical framework
- thoughtful engagement with the ideas from the theoretical framework
- detailed knowledge of the CSPs – to include relevant contextual issues
- application of the theoretical framework to CSP and non-CSP products.

So, remember:

- Read the questions carefully.
- Consider time management based on the marks offered for each question.
- Make sure you use the correct theoretical framework ideas and CSPs as identified in each question.
- Use specific examples from CSPs to demonstrate your ideas in action.
- Paper One: Targeted studies
  - Section A: Media language and representation
    - advertising and marketing and music video
  - Section B: Industries and audience
    - newspapers, radio and film (industry only)
- Paper Two: In-depth studies
  - all areas of the theoretical framework
  - magazines, television, online, social and participatory media and gaming

Glossary of key terms

180-degree rule	one of the rules that constructs space in visual language – the camera must stay one side of an imaginary line when filming a scene, unless a cutaway or visible movement leads the audience to another perspective
	The rupture of the 180-degree rule has an unnerving effect.
24-hour rolling news	digital TV channels that show only news and that broadcast 24 hours a day
30-degree rule	one of the rules that constructs space in visual language – the camera must move more than 30 degrees in order to avoid an ugly cut
	The sequence breaks the 30-degree rule.
accelerated motion	the speeding up of footage during editing
	This scene uses accelerated motion for comic effect.
acoustics	the sound qualities of a specific environment
advertorial	an extended print advertisement that may resemble editorial in its use of codes, but will be clearly labelled 'advertisement' under UK media law
	The magazine includes a number of paid partnerships in the form of advertorials for health products.
aerial shot	from in the air, often shot from an aircraft
	'The use of an aerial shot gives a sense of magnificence to the landscape.'
agenda setting	theory relating mainly to news media that views the media as actively selecting certain issues and shaping public opinion of these by reporting on them more frequently
	British newspapers play a role in agenda-setting as the majority select similar news stories.
AIR	average issue readership
algorithms	computer technology that gathers and analyses user data
alterity	in a Media Studies context, the state of being 'other' in representations from dominant representations of in-groups
	The alterity of the women is signified by their dress code.
alternative	usually media products that offer some kind of alternative perspective to the mainstream
analepsis	commonly known as a flashback
	The use of analepsis here is poignant because ...

apparatus	term used for the equipment and methods used in media production
	The apparatus of production is seen, which is unusual.
APS	average programme stream
arbitrary relationship	a relationship between signifier and signified that is not obvious (e.g. the word 'cat' written using the Roman alphabet and our mental image of the animal)
	The shaka is an arbitrary sign unless the cultural meaning of its association with surf culture and friendly intent is understood.
archetypes	basic, rather simple character types who appear over and over in narratives
	The protagonist's rival is a 'black knight' archetype, whose strength is considerable but whose morals are questionable.
architecture	the structure and navigation of a website
	The website's architecture is complex, meaning the audience needs to spend some time exploring its content.
atmosphere/ soundscape	background sound, especially in fiction media texts, which is constructed to contribute to verisimilitude
	The soundscape evoked is gentle and relaxing.
attempt to repair	in Todorov's theory of narrative, attempts made by the protagonist or other characters to bring about a new equilibrium
	The couple entering marriage guidance counselling is clearly sequenced following recognition as an attempt to repair the broken relationship which is ultimately unsuccessful, leading to the new equilibrium of their divorce.
aural code	term used to describe all the techniques relating to sound
	The sequence uses aural codes to signify danger.
back-light	a light positioned behind the subject
backstories/lore (in computer games)	contextual narrative information, often fed in through cut scenes and used by fans to embellish the narrative and increase immersion through fan behaviours
	The backstory may be analysed structurally through conventional theoretical approaches.
balance (page)	a balanced page has been designed to ensure that the heavy objects and lighter ones are positioned to create a harmonious feel

banner	commonly used term for any block of information at the top of a website; can also refer to the site's 'masthead', its identity
	The banner signifies boldness through use of strong typographic codes.
BARB	British Audience Research Board. It measures ratings for television and TV players in the UK
bardic function	the modern role of television in our lives as an aggregator of many different ideas and cultural influences
	Crime dramas have a bardic function in our processing of moral issues facing society.
BBC Charter	the conditions upon which the BBC's licence depends
billboard	a large outdoor location for advertising. Traditionally a board for the placement of print adverts but electronic billboards can be found in some locations. Electronic billboards can present all types of video material but they are often used to broadcast adverts
binge-watch	to watch multiple episodes one after the other
bird's-eye shot	extreme high angle or directly from the sky downwards
	The choice of a bird's eye shot is effective because ...
body text	the majority of article text, usually at the smallest size, appearing in a magazine or newspaper
	There is a high proportion of body text to image in the article, signifying the audience is prepared to read to acquire the specialist knowledge it provides.
brand ambassadors	celebrities who are paid to represent a specific consumer product or service and its brand values
brand recognition	when an audience becomes familiar with a brand
	The pack shot contributes to brand recognition.
brand value	the image a company intends to convey of its product or service
	The centring of the advert on the home and family leisure time promotes its brand values as wholesome.
bricolage	a product that is made from other media texts, or borrows signs from them
	The fan videos produced on the channel are a form of bricolage.
British Film Institute (BFI)	organisation that promotes the work of British cinema and studies cinema as a pastime among British people
broadcast	to transmit information to a mass audience, usually using radio or television technology
Broadcast Code	Ofcom's regulatory framework for broadcast services
broadcasting licences	required for transmission of television or radio services
business model	the strategies employed by a company to generate profit
busy	the effect of pages that are created with many design elements, typefaces styles, etc. Busy pages are sometimes difficult for the reader to access and can be confusing and visually off putting
camera proxemics	sometimes known as para-proxemics, this is the distance/relationship between subject and audience
	Distance is implied in the relationship using para-proxemics.
canted angle	sometimes known as a 'Dutch' angle – a shot that leans over to the side
	The angle is canted and feels disorientating.
caption	written anchorage accompanying an image and fixing its meaning
	The caption for the image constructs him as a victim.
captioning	the adding of subtitles to a video, sometimes used as another term for titling
	The video is captioned, making it readily shareable on social media.
card-based design	trend in web design that prioritises visual rectangular clickable links – 'cards' that often have a picture and captioning
	The use of card-based design promotes a fashionable and vibrant visual aesthetic.
causality	the way in which the events, usually driven by the desires and motivations of characters and the events that impact on them, drive the logic of a narrative forwards
	The behaviour of the model referred to in the magazine article constructs narrative causality as an explanation for her declining health.
celebrity endorsement	the process by which a celebrity is paid to become the face of a brand. This might include appearing in advertisements, using the brand in high-profile places, being a spokesperson for the brand
	In the campaign, the trainers are endorsed by a number of prominent sportspeople.
censorship	the blocking of certain media material from public consumption
chronology	this is the time order of narrative events
	The narrative chronology is disturbed to show that the product could have helped the bride avert disaster in the final shot.
circuit of communication	Hall's model of communication which identifies experience of a textual product as a series of 'moments' in the communication process
	The circuit of culture is a more flexible way of interpreting how meaning is produced, as well as the relationship between producers and audiences.

Glossary of key terms

circulation	amount of copies of a print media publication sold (paid circulation) or distributed (free publications funded entirely by advertising)
citizen journalism	the passing of footage or photographs taken by witnesses as events to either mainstream or alternative news distributors
Citizen journalism can foreground the stories of minority groups in the news agenda.
citizen journalism	the contributions to news reports made by members of the public
clawback	the way in which television can give a sense of recognition of the self and cultural identity, our experience of our culture
For an LGBTQ+ audience, the programme has a clawback function in terms of constructing meaningful representations.
click-throughs	viewing of deeper website content
clickbait	stories and headlines that are constructed to encourage audiences to click through to access more information. Clickbait usually attempts to create an emotional response
clicks	viewing of the homepage of a website
close-up	often just face and shoulders
A close-up effectively constructs him as a sympathetic character.
co-regulator	the sharing of some aspects of regulation by more than one organisation
cognitive surplus	the way in which people globally now use their free time to develop collaborative online projects
The fan wiki has been developed using the cognitive surplus of fans.
collective identity	aspects of our identity we share with others
The advertisement reinforces our sense of collective identity.
collective identity	sense of ownership of media representations and fandoms or the sense of belonging to a sector of a media audience
colour tone	the properties of colour – its shade, hue, warmth, brightness, saturation, etc.
colourisation	the way in which the saturation or other elements of how we perceive colour may be altered post-production, either to harmonise footage from different shoots or locations, or to achieve a particular aesthetic
The colourisation is desaturated slightly.
columns	a way to organise text and images on the page by dividing the page vertically
combining	using elements of more than one aspect of media language and form to achieve a desired representation
The muted décor of the room combines with the sombre dress code to signify mourning.
commercial revenue	profit generated by a media organisation
commercial television	television companies whose primary income source is from advertising
commercialisation	the practice of running an institution or creating media products specifically with an aim to generate financial gain
commodification	to turn something into a product that can be sold
community guidelines	means by which some websites ask their users to contribute to self-regulation
compassion fatigue	the process by which the media audience lose empathy for victims of crime, disaster or war zones due to repeated exposure (especially to news)
Audiences exposed to a saturation of charity campaign advertising could develop compassion fatigue.
composite image	presentation of images using a montage effect
The poster uses a composite image to signify character hierarchies.
compression of screen time	the way in which media texts, through editing, reduce the real time in which events would unfold
Screen time is compressed considerably by the montage sequence.
conceptual map	the reference point for people in interpreting media texts according to their individual world view
Younger women may read the advert differently from the older generations because of differences in their conceptual maps.
conditions of consumption	a wide range of factors that can affect how a media text is interpreted by the audience, both in terms of ideological reception and physical consumption practices
Our viewpoint on the issue may differ from another's resulting in different conditions of consumption.
conglomerates	huge media organisations made up of several companies all with the same ownership
constructed identity	the view that the mass media constructs identities in the representations it offers us
constructionist approach	approach that suggests readers of a text or its producers can wholly fix meaning
By adopting a constructionist approach, we can see that meanings are made as a result of both the intentions of the producer and the audiences. Their interpretations may differ.
consumer culture	a model of culture where the audience receives texts but does not 'interact' with them
Magazines are a form of consumer culture.
content labels	additional information provided by PEGI as part of its rating service
content providers	individuals, groups or organisation who create the content of media products; they may or may not be media producers
contested space	with reference to the internet, the ideological battleground between users and large media conglomerates

Glossary of key terms

continuity editing	dominant mode of editing that does not draw attention to itself, allowing the audience to focus on the subject-matter
	The sequence begins by disrupting standard continuity editing ...
contrapuntal sound	sound that does not seem to match the action, often deliberately used to unnerve the audience or even create a blackly comic effect
	The contrapuntal sound of the child laughing creates an eerie effect.
convergence	the use of different technologies and/or platforms to produce and distribute media products
copy	the term used for body text in a newspaper, print advertisement or magazine
	The copy is situated in the left side third, drawing the eye.
copyright	the legal ownership of the content of media products
corpus	group of texts identified as belonging to the same genre
	The film contributes to the corpus of coming-of-age stories.
correspondents	journalists who have a specialisation (e.g. war correspondent) or who serve a specific location (e.g. a Westminster correspondent)
counter-representation/ countertyped	a representation that offers an alternative to stereotypes
	The protagonist is countertyped when contrasted with more common stereotypes of teen girls.
coverline	feature and secondary articles promoted on the front of a magazine
	The coverlines all connote positive messages about the audience's capacity for self-improvement.
crab	a short tracking shot
	The camera crabs to one side, revealing...
crane shot	any footage taken using a crane – highly mobile and versatile in terms of movement
	This crane shot allows us a privileged view over the action.
critical theory	an approach to the study of culture that considers how various forces are at work in its production
	Critical theorists focused on gender have tended to focus on representations of women in popular culture.
cropping	the removal of sections of an image to emphasise its subject or remove clutter or unwanted signs
	The image of the politician on stage has been cropped to show them alone.
cross-dissolve	the gradual fading of one shot into another
	The cross-dissolve connotes tenderness.
cultivation differential	the extent to which someone's world view and perception of their social reality is shaped by the volume of television they consume
	Understanding the cultivation differential is vital when weighing up the likely size of a potential media effect.
cultivation theory	branch of effects theory that looks at the effect of media saturation (particularly television) on the audience
	Cultivation theory prioritises the time spent consuming a particular type of media.
cultural absolutism/racial essentialism	the linking of a person's cultural and racial heritage to a place of national or ethnic origin
	The text avoids cultural absolutism by careful selection of a range of news about people from different communities and backgrounds.
cultural capital	the ability to mix in higher levels of society because education has given the individual qualifications, ownership of cultural products or access to works of culture
	The broadcast assumes high levels of cultural capital on the part of its listeners.
cultural categories	a way of understanding genre labels as products of both industry and audience
	Genre identification helps us to navigate cultural categories in our media experience.
cultural hegemony	the process of indoctrination through cultural products of the dominant ideologies in a society
	The magazine reinforces cultural hegemony through the mode of address used in the headline of the article.
cultural identity	aspects of our identity that are derived from cultural influences such as region, religion or family
	Aspects of the main character's cultural identity are used to define them in the opening sequence.
cultural imperialism	the domination of mostly English-language, well-funded products of the global media market
	Popular genres can play a role in cultural imperialism by saturating indigenous markets.
cultural industries	the industries that are involved in the production, distribution and circulation of cultural artefacts, including media products
cultural regime of verisimilitude	our connecting of a genre text with our wider cultural knowledge
	The representation of the court case requires us to draw on our knowledge of the cultural regime of verisimilitude.
cultural relativism	judging of other cultures against white European values
	Failure to represent both sides of this news story is an example of cultural relativism.

Glossary of key terms

cultural shorthand	a way of understanding how stereotypes communicate ideas quickly to the audience *It's thought that this use of cultural shorthand communicates meaning faster and more effectively.*	**democratisation of the mass media**	increased ability of the audience to have their voices heard, and to interact with media producers and content
cultural syncretism	the blending of different influences to form a new means of expression.	**demographics**	studying how populations may consume the media in different ways according to where they live
cultural tropes	plot elements, themes or figures of speech that are used repeatedly in literature or popular culture *The image of a woman meditating is used as a cultural trope signifying a focus on wellbeing.*	**deregulation**	reduction in governmental controls over media ownership
		desensitisation	the process by which media audiences can become used to seeing violent content and are better able to tolerate it *There is concern that some computer games may desensitise players to real-world violence.*
cultural/ referential code	one of Barthes' five narrative codes; the frame of reference that is human knowledge *The shadow shape of the wolf uses northern European fairytales as a cultural/referential code to signify danger to the children from their online activities.*	**design elements**	the individual parts that combine together to construct a page
		diaspora	a scattering or spread of people *The text is mindful to appeal to a broad section of communities descended from the African diaspora.*
cumulation	collective term for audience theories that consider longer-term exposure to media texts *Games consumption should also be considered in light of cumulation, with wide variation in hours of gameplay across the audience.*	**diegesis**	the world of the media text, the story world especially in fiction-based media *The score contributes to our sense of immersion in the diegesis.*
		diegetic sound	refers to sound supposedly generated within the diegesis *The diegetic sound of the car engine.*
cut scenes	non-interactive animated sections of games that contexualise an element of play *The game uses cut scenes to generate new hermeneutic codes that engage the player.*	**digital immigrants**	the older generation who have had to acquire the skills to participate in the digital world more consciously *Digital immigrants will feature less in the demographic of TikTok.*
cutaway shot	footage that shows another subject before returning to the original *The use of a cutaway functions as product demonstration.*	**digital locker**	system whereby a television show or film is purchased (sometimes as a physical copy) but also exists for that buyer to watch on other devices *Digital lockers have largely replaced DVD purchases of films.*
cutting rate	the way in which pace is controlled in editing – many shots of short duration lend a fast cutting rate; longer duration results in a slower rate *The fast cutting rate emphasises the frenetic action.*	**digital native**	community of media users who have grown up with the internet *Digital natives are more familiar with celebrity influencers.*
cutting rhythm	the length of shots, particularly when edited to a soundtrack or score, when these appear to have rhythmic qualities *The cutting rhythm matches the track.*	**digital revolution**	sweeping changes brought about by the internet and advances in digital technology *The digital revolution had a wide-ranging impact on television consumption.*
dead spot	an area created by local acoustics where sound is reduced in volume or flattened in tone	**digital subscription platform**	content provided digitally for a monthly or annual payment
decelerated motion	the slowing down of footage during editing *The use of decelerated motion combined with a close-up shot makes the product seem more desirable.*	**direct/indirect address**	the way in which a text addresses its audience; for example, where a subject is gazing into the lens of the camera, this could be said to be a direct mode of address *The actor's mode of address is direct, using an eye-level shot so we feel they are knowable.*
deconstruction	accessing the meanings of a media product about society using the tools of structuralist analysis *Deconstruction of the advert reveals a society fascinated by celebrity culture.*		
décor	selection of the appearance of interior locations *The décor is shabby, signifying poverty.*		

Glossary of key terms

discourse	an academic discussion or debate about a subject embodying a range of perspectives around a similar subject
	Exploring feminist discourse around music videos is a productive form of analysis.
disruption	in Todorov's theory of narrative, an event that disturbs the equilibrium
	The equilibrium is disrupted by the arrival of the athlete's new coach who has new training methods.
distortion	the phenomenon by which the way the media usually represents women's lives does not reflect the reality of many real women
	The all-female investigative team in the drama can be seen as an example of distortion.
distribution	methods used to make media products available to audiences
diversification	media companies' move into the production of a range of different types of media product
dolly	a fixing for a camera that allows it to be moved smoothly over a set floor or on a track
	The use of a dolly shot creates a smooth, hypermobile effect.
domestic markets	the local audience for a media product
double consciousness	two aspects of black experience; living within a predominantly white culture and having an aspect of identity rooted somewhere else
	The text could construct a sense of double consciousness given the reductive use of racial stereotypes.
drop cap	an enlarged first letter – an attention-grabbing aesthetic device
	The use of a drop cap adds prominence to the opening section of body text and adds to its visual appeal as an entry point to the article.
DTP	a commonly used abbreviation for desktop publishing that refers to software specifically designed to support the design and publication of print and, in some cases, e-media production
dub	to add sound elements to recorded images
dynamic content	content that is regularly updated
	The use of dynamic content makes the homepage appealing to repeat visitors.
early adopters	individuals who take advantage of technological developments before they become mainstream
echo-chamber	the phenomenon caused by audiences limiting their media experiences to products and locations that reinforce their existing beliefs and values
edit (moving image/audio)	the arranging of images or sound to create a coherent visual or audio sequence
editorial content	original content written for magazines distinct from advertising
editorial position	the political values that influence the way a media product is constructed
Editors' Code of Conduct	the IPSO's regulatory framework
effects theory	the collective term for media theories that explore the correlation between media consumption and audience behaviours or interpretations of the real world
	Effects theories suggest that media consumption can influence people in the real world.
emasculate	to remove masculinity
	The antagonist is represented as being angered and emasculated by his female boss.
embodied cultural capital	the acquired knowledge of culture experienced and outwardly presented by a person
	The article uses representations of embodied cultural capital as part of a narrative of success in theatre prior to film.
encoding and decoding	the process whereby a producer of a text generates a meaning and the audience interprets it.
	The sign of the wolf encoded in the opening titles may be decoded by the audience as signifying threat.
enculturation	the adjustment of people's values to mesh with the culture and society they inhabit
	Enculturation is a form of socialisaton through the media.
end of audience theory	changes in the way in which we conceptualise audiences and understand how we should even define audience
	End of audience theory helps to account for changes in audience dynamics between producer and consumer.
engagement	click-throughs or other interaction with a page or other digital content
entry point	a visually appealing and prominent spread in a magazine
	There is a use of aesthetically-pleasing and dramatic landscape photography at the entry point.
enunciative productivity	sharing the meanings and ways of talking about the text – 'fan-speak' and wearing clothing, or styling hair or make-up in a particular way
	Integrating character sayings into everyday conversation can be seen as form of enunciative productivity.
equilibrium	in Todorov's theory of narrative, the stable situation or balance at the beginning of a narrative, and the new state achieved by the end
	An equilibrium where the runner is training hard but not winning competitions is established in the slug.

Glossary of key terms

ergodic narrative	a digital narrative that has different outcomes according to the interaction between the 'user' of the text and the 'rules' of the game
	The narrative is ergodic, with many different potential endings to the game.
establishing shot	often exterior locations, but can be interiors – used to set a scene
	The establishing shot shows a huge, barren fen.
ethnocentrism	seeing an issue from the perspective of a specific cultural heritage – usually refers to a white European perspective
	In neglecting diversity, the producers leave themselves open to accusations of ethnocentrism.
event television	television shows that attract large audiences and are reported on extensively. They may be one-off events (e.g. a royal wedding), a regularly scheduled event (e.g. the Olympics) or a specific episode of a popular programme
expectations and hypotheses	requirements to be fulfilled, and narrative and other predictions made by an audience based on their prior experience of a genre
	The audience anticipates events in terms of expectations and hypotheses.
extra-diegetic narration	voice-over provided by an unseen person from outside the diegesis
	The extra-diegetic narration distances us from the events.
eye-line match	usually means the pairing of a shot of a person with the object of their attention in the next frame
	The eye-line match signifies equality between the two characters.
fade-in/fade-out	the gradual dissolution of a shot
	The fade-in follows the titles.
fade-through-black	technique that allows the audience a moment to reflect, by placing a short breathing space over black between scenes
	The transition between the scenes is slowed using a fade-through-black.
fake news	fictional or misleading stories that are presented as news
false consciousness	the belief in ideas that are not based in fact
female gaze	the subversion of the male gaze in which men become the subject to be looked at by women
	The band are photographed in such a way as to appeal to the female gaze.
first order of signification	the recognition of the agreed meaning of a sign
	Using the first order of signification, the uniform tells us he is a military man.
fish-eye shot	a shot, usually using a specific lens for the purpose, which brings in a range of angles of view
	The fish-eye shot distorts the view and distances us from the events.
fluidity of identity	the concept that people do not have a fixed identity that is wholly and permanently a part of them
focusing	building of a representation through techniques such as repetition or elimination of comparisons
	The advert uses focusing on female uses of technology as a strategy, as no men appear.
foley	recorded sounds to be added as sound effects in the post-production of video and audio productions
following pan	movement where the camera remains in one position but is turned on its axis to follow an action
	A following pan is used to draw our eye to where the ball lands.
font	the design of the letters used within a specific typeface – its weight and style
framing	careful selection of what will appear in a final shot
	The paparazzi shot is framed to emphasise her reaction to the encounter above others.
framing (news)	a news story's bias and the way in which it is read by the audience according to their own interests and situation
	The audience tends to frame their understanding of the story in light of their political viewpoint.
free market	trading based on unrestricted competition between private companies
gatekeepers	individuals and groups who have the ability to select (and reject) the content of media products
gender performativity	the idea that men and women 'perform' gendered behaviours and roles dues to acquired cultural expectations
	The main characters all demonstrate to some extent gender performativity.
generic regime of verisimilitude	the norms and laws of a genre; what is probable or likely in a genre text
	The flamboyant setting is in keeping with the generic regime of verisimilitude.
genres of order and integration	systems of genre categorisation that foreground the social and cultural uses of genre and classes them as essentially 'male' or 'female'
	Soap operas are primarily genres of integration.
gestural codes	the way in which we read expression through movement
	His gestural codes are expansive, signifying confidence.
global village	term coined by Marshall McLuhan in the 1960s to describe the impact of media technologies on global culture
	Instagram content related to the brand contributes to the global village effect on audiences, where national boundaries feel insignificant.

Glossary of key terms

globalisation	the increased interconnectivity of businesses and cultures worldwide
	Globalisation has changed the face of the media landscape in the UK in recent decades.
Google Analytics	market analysis of a website's performance
governance	the internal regulation of the BBC
GRA	Games Rating Authority (a division of the VSC)
graphical elements	any graphics generated that do not consist of pure typography or photography
	The graphical elements include oceanic elements of illustration to signify his connection with the sea.
habitus	the way in which a person has been socialised into and interacts with the world according to their education, social class, etc.
	Reading the supplements in public spaces might contribute to a person's display of habitus.
hand-held shot	footage taken using a camera held and operated by a person
	The hand-held shot feels unstable to us.
hard news	news that focuses exclusively on serious issues relating to domestic or world events
	Hard news is often seen as having less appeal to the target age range of the audience.
head and shoulders shot	a shot where the camera is positioned close to a human subject so that the frame excludes all of the body, apart from the head and shoulders
hermeneutic code	one of Barthes' five narrative codes; enigmas or puzzles in a narrative
	Hermeneutic codes are established by the use of the slogan as well as the image which sets up the problem to be solved by the product.
hero image	use of a large, dominating image that fills the majority of the viewable homepage before scrolling occurs
	The hero image connotes authenticity through use of a natural landscape as background for the product.
heteronormative	using the perspective of heterosexuals (and therefore omitting alternative perspectives)
	Marriage is represented in a heteronormative way as being between men and women.
high angle	a shot positioned slightly higher than the subject that diminishes it
	The high angle shot makes the child seem vulnerable.
high-key lighting	the use of light fills to create a low-contrast lighting effect
hook	any technique used to draw the audience into a narrative
	The pre-title sequence uses a hook to ensure continued viewing.
horizontal integration	merger of media companies at a similar stage of development or who offer similar services or products
house style	the way in which codes combine in print media to produce a familiar and recognisable brand
	The typographical codes and graphical features throughout the magazine form a consistent house style.
hybridisation	the mixing of one genre with another
	Both products show signs of hybridisation with other genres.
hyperlinks	links within a web page to other parts of the site or external content
	Hyperlinks take the reader if desired to connected news stories on similar issues.
hyperreality	merging of the real and media worlds to the point where it is difficult to distinguish between them
	The actor's social media posts contribute to the hyperreal presence of the star in the digital landscape.
hypertextuality	web 'intertextuality' – the linking from site to site of other content
	Fan sites are rich in hypertextuality.
hypodermic needle model	simple effects model that assumes the audience to be passive recipients of media content
	The hypodermic needle model is often seen as a very simple example of effects modelling.
iconography	repetition of certain visual images or symbols, usually associated in media with particular genres
	The scene borrows iconography from expressionist cinema.
idents	sounds used to identify the programme, radio station or brand. This could be a jingle or a theme tune
ideological reading	a conclusion that aims to expose how power relationships between social groups operate and manifest themselves in cultural production
	An ideological reading of the homepage would take into account the lack of ethnic diversity.
ideology	in the context of A-level study, dominant ways of thinking in a society shared by many people within it
	The text communicates through shared ideologies about childhood.
imagined communities	the way in which a nation is imagined by the people who live within its national boundaries
	The front page coverage of the Queen's funeral addresses an imagined community of pro-Monarchy patriots.
implosion	the media's constant recycling of itself and its signs
	The phenomenon of the reality contest show can be seen as an example of implosion.

Glossary of key terms

in-camera	decisions made to influence the look of images while shooting with the camera. This includes using camera settings as well as using external sources such as music, props and lighting to create specific effects
in-groups	members of a dominant culture
	Men are often seen as an in-group despite making up approximately half of the population.
independent	media companies not owned by larger organisations
indigenous media production	media products made by and for a particular culture or nation
individuality paradox	a known philosophical quandary in studying identity, that most people wish to simultaneously be seen as an individual while experiencing commonality and social belonging
influencers	people who have the power to lead others and sway their opinions and actions. It is now a marketing term that describes individuals who have large numbers of followers on social media, have gained a level of authority and are trusted by their followers. Influencers can communicate with large numbers of people and this means they are able to spread ideas and promote products
institutionalised cultural capital	recognised qualifications that symbolise someone's worth in terms of cultural capital
	The magazine is a niche product that appeals to those who have institutionalised cultural capital.
intellectual property	the ownership of ideas, creative productions, artistic works, etc.
intentional approach	approach that suggests meaning is imposed by the producer of the text
	This would suggest an intentionalist, fixed meaning to representations but does not allow for differences in audience interpretation.
intercuts	alternate scenes or shots from other locations or narrative lines including flashbacks and flashforwards
interpellation	the normalisation in media texts of certain ways of thinking, attitudes and values so powerfully that they become part of a person's identity
	Consumers are interpellated by these kinds of advertisements into a belief in the role of make-up and beauty regimes in perceived attractiveness.
intersectionality	the acknowledgement that issues of power relating to gender, race and social class all intersect
	The focus on black working-class women's lives acknowledges the issue of intersectionality.
intertextuality	the process by which one media text consciously references another text or genre, therefore deriving further layers of meaning for a reader who has experienced both texts
	The red cape worn by the influencer in the article intertextually references Superman.
intra-diegetic narration	voice-over provided by a person or character from within the diegesis
	As an intra-diegetic narrator, we trust her account of events when in fact she is unreliable.
invisible editing	an editing style that appears natural to the viewer, usually exemplified by straight cuts
IPSO	the Independent Press Standards Organisation
ISPA	Internet Service Providers' Association
IWF	Internet Watch Foundation
jib shot	any footage taken using a camera, remotely controlled, on a metal arm
	The film uses a jib shot which suspends our view close to the flowing river.
jump cut	where the camera moves less than 30 degrees, creating an ugly and dissonant effect – sometimes used deliberately, but is not part of continuity editing style
	The use of jump cuts feels jarring and causes anxiety in the audience.
laudatory stereotypes	stereotypes that contribute positively to views of social groups
	The refugees are represented in a laudatory way, focusing on their bravery and humanity.
left side third	area of a magazine cover where key content is usually positioned
	The majority of the coverlines are positioned in the left side third to emphasise value for money.
legacy media	a term used to describe pre-digital media forms (e.g. newspapers and television)
Leveson report	the report on press behaviour and practices published after the Leveson Inquiry, which was set up after accusations that some newspapers were using illegal methods to gather information for stories
lexical codes	words selected to generate specific effect
	The choice of 'adventurous' and 'death-defying' in the lexical coding of the headline for the article emphasise his masculinity.
liberal pluralism	a centre-right approach to reading the media that is pro-consumer choice and lessens emphasis on the identification of ideologies in the media
	A liberal pluralist perspective would suggest that consumer choice is already prevalent in the range of online lifestyle magazines available to consumers.
light fills	a light used to reduce the contrast between light and shadow within the frame

Glossary of key terms

lighting temperature	the feel lent to a scene according to how it is lit – warm or cool, for example	mass amateurisation	state of the media today, where professionally made media that was consumed by audiences in a fairly simple model no longer predominates
	The cooler lighting temperatures in this scene emphasise the distance between the characters.		*The tablet computer has become a facilitator of mass amateurisation.*
linguistics	the study of structural aspects of language, with many sub-specialisms	masterplot	an overarching group of bare narrative elements that are meaningful to a particular culture
	A linguistic analysis of the lexical codes allows us to read the headline as being in favour of the government's move.		*'Revenge narratives can be considered to be masterplots, since they have universal qualities to them which are understood globally.'*
lipstick feminism	a brand of third wave feminism that allows women to portray themselves as equal to men in terms of their sexuality by expressing it in any way they choose	masthead	the name of a magazine
			The masthead has a distinctive typographical style connoting technology.
	The celebrity's statement defending the photoshoot could be interpreted as an example of lipstick feminism.	matched cut	pairs of shots that have a logical connection
			The door opens in one scene and cuts abruptly to the closure of the pool door in the next, using a matched cut.
location	choice of place for an exterior shoot		
	The choice of location of a farmyard signifies that he is at home in any environment and has a highly adaptable personality.	mean world index	in cultivation theory, a way of measuring the belief that the world is a more dangerous place than it actually is due to viewing of violent acts on television
logo	a design, sometimes consisting of typography and a symbol, that identifies a brand		*The programme could contribute to the mean world index through repetition of fictionalised acts of violence against women.*
	The logo is an arbitrary sign but highly recognisable to a youth audience and is therefore prominently positioned.	media concentration	where mergers and takeovers of media companies by large corporations leads to a small number of companies controlling a large proportion of the media
long shot	full body at any distance		
	Introducing the character in long shot makes him harder for us to relate to.	media convergence	the coming together of many aspects of media businesses, including commercial, technological and cultural
low angle	a shot positioned slightly lower than the subject, which elevates it		*Convergence culture has resulted in an increase in leisure time consuming a range of media.*
	We understand him to be the dominant figure in the room because of the use of a low angle shot.	media literacy	the level of awareness of the audience about factors affecting the production of meaning in media texts
low-key lighting	a style of lighting used to create shadow and areas of bright light within the frame		
mainstreaming	in cultivation theory, the process of ideological alignment between media audiences and content		*Level of media literacy is a crucial factor when considering a historical media product's likely reception.*
	Mainstreaming may play in important role in the run-up to a general election.	mediation	the process by which the mass media represents aspect of reality
male gaze	describes the way we all are conventionally positioned to look at women in film in an inferior, and often sexualised way		*Stereotypes are often heavily mediated versions of real-world representatives of social groups.*
		medium shot	mid-body shot
	The young women are all represented submissively to appeal to the male gaze.		*The group are filmed in medium shot, allowing us to see them in the context of the classroom.*
manufacture consent	the process, as identified by Noam Chomsky (see Chapter 4), that media institutions use to persuade audiences of the validity of national policies	mise-en-scène	term in audio-visual analysis that refers to individual codes and signs that contribute to meaning
			The dress code makes a significant contribution to the mise-en-scène.
	Chomsky would argue that the newspaper helps to manufacture consent on the issue of funding the NHS.	mise-en-scène (m-e-s)	everything that can be seen within the scene – set design, props, performance, lighting, costume and make-up, location and lighting
Maslow's hierarchy of needs	pyramid-based model offering a hierarchical visualisation of human needs		
	Maslow's hierarchy of needs was influential in sociological research into the mass media.		

Glossary of key terms

mode of address	how the text 'speaks' to the audience – can be formal or informal – created by use of codes	narrowcast	to transmit information to a localised, niche or specialised audience and to offer choices regarding the timing of access to this information
	The mode of address is personal and the lexical coding addresses the reader directly as 'you'.	naturalisation	the belief that an idea is a natural state rather than a human construction
monopoly	when one corporation dominates the provision of a specific product or service so there is no choice for the consumer	negotiated identity	ways in which we negotiate the various influences on our composite identities – how we perceive ourselves in relation to others
montage editing	an editing style where the audience is given a snapshot of different clips	neo-liberalism	political values that prioritise individual freedom of choice and the power of the free market
	The trailer uses conventional montage editing.	neo-Marxist	critiques of culture and the media that have a left-wing bias
moral panics	term coined by Stanley Cohen to describe the press reaction to a negative event in the real world		*A neo-Marxist reading of the text would critique the representation of the working-class characters as petty criminals.*
	The spate of recent dog attacks is presented as a moral panic over irresponsible dog ownership.	news agencies	organisations that receive and distribute news
multi-take	non-continuity technique, where a dramatic event may be filmed from several angles and the moment duplicated for effect	news agenda	the priority given to particular news items by a news organisation
	The smashing of the cup is filmed as a multi-take to make the moment have more impact.		*The issue has featured prominently on news agendas.*
multiculturalism	a politically inclusive policy towards ethnically mixed nations/communities that welcomes diversity and respects cultural differences	news aggregators	refers to (usually) online news sources that use software to gather news from other online sources
	The broadcast represents multicultural Britain by choosing vox populi from a range of people from minority ethnic groups.	niche audiences	audiences with a special interest
		niche publications	print media publications serving a special interest or with a small circulation
mytheme	small unit of myths that Lévi-Strauss identified in the traditional stories of the tribal groups he studied	non-diegetic narration	voice-over created by an unseen person from outside the diegesis
	The advert uses a recurring mytheme of transformation to signify the effectiveness of the product and its effect on those around the protagonist as part of its narrative construction.		*The non-diegetic voice holds warmth and sounds affectionate towards the characters.*
		non-verbal codes	in human subjects, this is facial expression, posture, body language and some aspects of appearance and personal expression such as tattoos and hair
narrative arc	the journey of an individual character		
	This contributes to the character's narrative arc by …		
narrative codes	a collective term for Barthes' breakdown of the features of storytelling involved in the construction of narrative		*'The portrait of the singer with an angry expression and close-up photography that emphasises his body modifications combine to signify the metal genre.'*
	Barthes' narrative codes help us to see the complexity of the ways in which this single-page advert communicates.	non-verbal communication	methods of communication that do not include words. Body language and modes of dress are both examples
narrative image	the expectations of a genre text based on its label, often passed by word of mouth	NRS	National Readership Survey. It provides audience research for print advertising trading in the UK
	The narrative image signified by the trailer strongly suggests the crime drama genre.	objectified cultural capital	a cultural artefact that confers status on the person who owns it
narrative strands	different 'storylines' or sub-plots that usually contribute something to the main narrative subject		*The villain's art collection is a signifier of objectified cultural capital.*
	The episode has several narrative strands.	Ofcom	Office of Communications
narratology	the structuralist study of narrative	omniscient narration	style of narration where the audience is privy to most contextual narrative information even where this is withheld from characters in the diegesis
	Narratology can be used to explore how the text sequences ideas for the audience in order to engage them.		
			The use of omniscient narration effectively juxtaposes the action of the two scenes.

Glossary of key terms

on-demand viewing	viewing a channel or provider's content outside the traditional schedule
opinion leaders	people who have the ability to communicate their opinions to others and may influence opinions
otherness	the state of being defined as 'different'– views of an out-group held by an in-group
	The earthquake victims in the report are defined by their otherness, signified for example by multi-generational accommodation and the destruction of the food market.
out-groups	minorities living within a dominant culture
	Ethnically-Chinese British people are represented in the article as an out-group.
outro	the concluding piece of a recording
over-the-shoulder shot	a shot in which the back of someone's head and shoulder is partially in view – often used to shoot dialogue – and makes the audience feel they are sharing in the exchange
	The over-the-shoulder-shot feels intimate, as though we are part of the moment.
overblocking	internet filtering that is considered overly restrictive
page proportions	the size of the page and the relationship between its height and length
paparazzi	professional photographers who seek to capture informal, unstaged and candid images of celebrities or other people identified as being newsworthy
para-proxemics	the perceived 'distance' between the audience and a character on screen that contributes to their meaning to the viewer
	In terms of para-proxemics we feel closer to this character because of the use of a close-up shot.
paradigm	the choices of related signifiers and signifieds available in producing meaning
	The jacket is selected from the paradigm of alternative dress codes.
parallel development	the apparently simultaneous presentation of another narrative strand in a text, which is actually achieved by alternating between the two spheres of action
	The action cuts between the two scenes as the tension builds using parallel development.
participatory media	digital media that the audience interacts with, helps construct and distribute
	Online videos encourage responses and interaction from the audience, which can be seen as a form of participatory media.
passive ideological state apparatus (ISA)	according to Althusser, the function of the mass media in maintaining the status quo
	In this sense, the media can be seen as a passive ISA that reinforces the positive handling of the crisis by the government.
pastiche	the making of a new media text from components of another
	The series title sequence makes such strong use of intertextual references and genre codes it may be considered a pastiche.
patriarchy	a system where men predominate in power structures
	The magazine represents a challenge to patriarchy by focusing on powerful women and avoiding sexualisation.
PEGI	Pan-European Game Information
pejorative stereotypes	stereotypes that demean their subject
	Pejorative stereotypes of young Asian men are sometimes used in the tabloid press.
personal brand	the constructed image created by an individual in order to create an identifiable and specific 'personality' with a view to help promote the individual
personal identity	identity made up of individual preferences and views
	Young women may engage with the broadcast to differing extents according to their personal identity.
photojournalist	professional photographer who uses images to tell a story
plugins	additional features such as social media buttons or embedded players, for example for YouTube, that encourage sharing and connectivity
	The website's use of plugins makes it a good example of a technologically converged product.
point-of-view shot	shot that allows us to share someone's perspective
	The use of point-of-view shot allows use to share her perspective more profoundly.
politically conservative	can be interpreted in different ways but generally refers to a belief system based on the prioritisation of individual social and economic responsibility. Social change is often resisted
politically liberal	can be interpreted in different ways but generally refers to a belief system based on the prioritisation of social and economic responsibility. Social change is seen to be both positive and, often, essential
polysemic signs	possible multiple meanings of a sign
	The figure of the woman is polysemic.
post-broadcast era	term sometimes used to define the shift away from scheduled media consumption
	Audiences are freer to select content and time of viewing in the post-broadcast era.
post-network television	the culture of television viewing that no longer relies on traditional broadcast methods

Glossary of key terms

post-structuralism	later work on structuralism that both extends its ideas and critiques its approach
	This emphasis on the multiple meanings of the car as a sign is post-structuralist.
postcolonialism	the study of the many ways in which the legacy of colonialism affects race representations
	Postcolonialism is a vital tool in decoding representations of race and ethnicity.
postmodern theory	a school of thinking that questions the idea of 'reality' as anything other than a collection of constructs apparent in any culture – the mass media is seen as playing an important role since it helps shape and reflect our understanding of our culture. The movement resists solid definitions and answers in many disciplines within the arts, humanities and even sciences
	Postmodern theory can be used to explore our attitudes to celebrity culture.
potential reach	the possible extent of the circulation of a media product
precession of the simulacra	the series of stages between simulacrum and simulation
	Development of the genre may be seen as an example of the precession of the simulacra.
press packs	information released by a company to promote its work, often to prospective investors or advertisers
	The magazine's press pack contains its mission statement and a clear definition of its target audience.
primary image	the image that predominates visually where more than one has been used
	The primary image has been selected to send a powerful message about the environment.
proairetic code	one of Barthes' five narrative codes; units of resolved action through cause and effect
	The first paragraph constructs a sequence of narrative chronology through proairetic codes describing the events leading up to the search.
product placement	the paid inclusion of branded products on screen
production	the manufacture of media products
profiling techniques	ways by which media producers discern their target audience
	Profiling techniques are used to focus on a youth demographic.
prolepsis	commonly known as a flashforward
	The use of prolepsis at the start establishes the genre as science fiction.
propaganda model of communication	the sustaining in media profile of a genuinely threatening event for political purposes
	News coverage of the war on terror following 911 fulfils Chomsky's definition of the propaganda model of communication.
proprietary fonts	fonts that are developed exclusively for a particular publication
	The magazine uses a proprietary font for its headlines which is a distinctive part of its branding and house style.
props	items that are consciously added to a shoot because they contribute to meaning
	Eighteenth-century furniture is used to lend a nostalgic, whimsical feel to the photoshoot.
proxemics	power relationships signified by relative positioning within the frame
	The positioning of mother slightly in front of daughter signifies her protective role.
public domain	relates to media products/ideas that are outside the restrictions of copyright law and are freely available to the public
public purposes	the aims of the BBC as an organisation
public service broadcasting (PSB)	broadcasting intended to benefit the public
public sphere	a location where published work is available to the general public
puff	a call-out feature, often circular in shape, that draws attention to a price or promotion on a front cover
	The puff bleeds over the masthead to draw attention to the publication's supposed value for money.
pull quote	excerpt from interview enlarged as a device to hook the reader in and for visual contrast with body text
	Pull quotes are used to construct an emphasis on the emotional response of the celebrity to the event.
qualitative representation	using techniques such as semiotic analysis to draw conclusions about the nature of media representations
	Qualitatively the representations in the series are complex.
quantitative representation	using techniques such as content analysis to draw conclusions about representations in media texts
	The advert has limited diversity and features only one person from a minority group.
queer theory	critical approach that explores LGBTQ+ perspectives on culture and the media
	Queer theory is sometimes neglected in approaches to the study of gender and the media, but is a useful tool.
quest narrative	an established narrative convention which comprises journey and maturation of a main character or characters
	'The storyline of the episode establishes a classic quest narrative.'
quota	imposing a restriction on certain kinds of foreign media imports

Glossary of key terms

RAJAR	Radio Joint Audience Research
raunch culture	specifically associated with music video but with cultural resonance seen elsewhere – the overt sexualisation of female artists
The shots of the artist performing are highly sexualised and in keeping with raunch culture.
reach	the amount of people who see a link or site, for example in a newsfeed or search engine result
reaction shot	demonstrates a response to an event or person
The use of multiple reaction shots signifies shame among the group.
readership	the approximate number of consumers estimated to read a print media text
reception theory	considers that different audience members may interpret a single text in varying ways
Reception theory gives us differing possible audience response to the product.
recognition	in Todorov's theory of narrative, the realisation that a disruption to the equilibrium has occurred
Recognition occurs when the girl in the advertisement realises she has hair breakage.
reflective approach	approach that suggests meaning is inherent in what is being represented
We would not consider a reflective approach to be valid since it suggests that meanings cannot be subject to change by the process of representation or the medium it appears in.
remit	the service provided by a public service broadcaster for its viewers
repertoire of elements	identifiable aspects of texts belonging to the corpus in genre theory
The audience will recognise the locations because of their familiarity with the repertoire of elements.
repetition and sameness	the tendency of genre texts to repeat aspects of successful formulas – always in tension with variation and change
Genres retain familiarity due to use of repetition and sameness.
representation	the way in which people, places, abstract concepts and events are mediated in a particular way in media texts
Representations are significant because they communicate ideas about our culture and society.
resonance	in cultivation theory, the reinforcement of ideologies or experiences by mass media content
restricted narration	style of narration where information is withheld from the audience
The use of restricted narration is conventional in the crime drama.
Sabido method	named after its creator, Miguel Sabido, who has acted as a writer and advisor on television serials in many parts of the world, and created a method for embedding educational messages successfully into the series
The narrative has been strongly influenced by the Sabido method.
satellite/cable channels	television channels that required audiences to buy specialised technologies in order to access them. The term was relevant as a differentiator between 'terrestrial TV' and 'satellite' TV (BBC One and Two, ITV, Channel 4 and Channel 5). Since the digital switchover in 2007, 'terrestrial TV has been accessible with other 'satellite' channels on services such as Freebox
schedule	traditional way of organising broadcasts in a chronological way to transmit at specific times of day
scheduling	in traditional television viewing, choosing the optimal time of broadcast to reach the highest potential target audience
The viewing of scheduled television is in decline.
screen time	the amount of real time a character is present on screen for, e.g. two minutes
Screen time is manipulated to make the dive scene feel as though it's happening in real time compared with the moments leading up to it.
second order of signification	a layered and more subtle interpretation of a complex sign
The non-verbal codes of the soldier and debris and dirt on his uniform suggest compassion but also battle-weariness.
secondary image	an image that appears to be hierarchically less important when more than one is used
The secondary image focuses on the social aspects of the activity.
selection	choosing to represent one thing over another
The rural lifestyle is represented only through idyllic landscape shots and large houses.
selective focus	use of the lens where a particular section of the frame is in focus
The use of selective focus draws attention to the snail on the leaf.
self-censor	action taken by the individual audience member to select media for consumption that does not offend or otherwise impact on them negatively
semantic code	one of Barthes' five narrative codes; connotations in a narrative
Semantic codes are used such as the close positioning of images of the two protagonists to suggest a relationship between them.

Glossary of key terms

semiology	Saussure's term for the study of signs, which he regarded as a science
	A semiological reading can be determined by breaking down the complex sign into its component signifers + signifieds.
semiotic productivity	the meanings made from the source texts by the fan
	A fan's emotional affiliation for the celebrity could be seen as a form of semiotic productivity.
sensationalism	a reporting style that seeks to create an emotional response in its readers
shareholders	groups or individuals who are part owners of a company, as they have invested money by buying shares
shooting script	the written text of a video/film product including details of the use of camera in individual scenes
shot list	a descriptive list of the shots required for a moving image production.
sidebar	a small section of text containing additional information related to the article. It is separate to the article and often presented in a column next to the main text
signifying practices	techniques used to construct representations
	Television producers may use a range of signifying practices to construct meaning.
simulacrum	state of semiotics where a sign no longer refers to any original meaning, but to other signs, like a hall of mirrors
	The narrative of the video has lost its original reference points and is understood by the audience as part of the simulacrum where original meanings have been diluted and disappeared.
simulation	end product of the precession of the simulacra. In the simulation we no longer perceive any difference between representation and reality
	The audience find themselves in a simulation, inhabiting a digital world encoded with the signs of social media content and gameplay that dominate their social interactions in the real world.
skyscraper	object positioned to run up the side of a website – sometimes a narrow advertisement
	The skyscraper signifies the connection between real and hyperreal by promoting a festival featuring the act.
slug	a line in larger print introducing a feature that acts as a hook
	The slug draws in the reader by using a quote from the celebrity.
SMCR/ transmission model of communication	simplistic early approach to communication study
	The SMCR model is considered linear because the message travels very simply and in one direction from sender to receiver.
social learning theory	branch of effects theory that considers vicarious learning to be a highly significant factor in how people respond to media content
	Effects theories cover a range of approaches that seek to explore our relationship with the media.
soft news	news that can be seen as focusing mainly on entertainment or celebrity-focused stories
	Soft news stories are given prominence to increase entertainment value.
soft news	news that is related to celebrities, entertainment, sport, gossip, scandal and human interest stories
sound mix	the combination of sound into a soundtrack, and the differing emphasis placed on certain sounds for effect
	The sound mix prioritises the noise of the machinery.
sound-bed	sounds, sound effects and/or music that plays below the main content of an audio production. Sound beds can communicate narrative information such as location or they can create a tone or atmosphere for the production
split screen	simultaneous depiction of two events on screen by physical splitting of the frame
	Split screen is used to show that the two people use the same product in different ways.
spoiler	articles and discussions that give away plot developments
standardisation	in cultivation theory, the proposal that norms and behaviours of people in the real world are modelled through repetition in televisual media
	Standardisation of male and female roles in society is potentially influenced by traits of masculinity and femininity represented in television drama.
stereotypes	reduction of a social group to a limited set of characteristics
	The artist himself conforms strongly to stereotypes in his dress code.
strapline	sometimes accompanies the masthead on a magazine – a promotional slogan
	The strapline states that the magazine is the most 'original' of its genre.
structuralism	a way of analysing culture that prioritises its form/structure over function according to codified systems
	A structuralist reading of the text would highlight the repetition of the conventions of adverts for grooming products.
studio shoot	a highly contrived photographic set-up, usually in an interior location
	The use of a studio shoot projects an image of perfection and highlights the importance of personality in the article.

Glossary of key terms

sub-genres	The formulation of a new sub-group within a genre which shares some of the qualities of the parent group but also has defining qualities of its own.
	Within the magazine, action sci-film is marketed as a sub-genre appealing to a predominantly male audience.
subheading	a heading for a subsection of an article
supplements	extra inserts to newspapers that tend to have a specific focus; issued particularly at weekends or on a certain day of the week. May be themed by finance, business, arts or other categories
surveillance	the use of tracking technologies used by digital media that record audience actions
surveying pan	slow pan on the camera's axis, often to establish either exterior or interior environment
	A surveying pan conveys effectively the size of the quarry.
suspension of disbelief	allowing oneself to be immersed in a fictional world
	The sequence rapidly encourages suspension of disbelief through immersive effects.
sweet spot	position to the centre left of a single page of print media, where the eye naturally falls
	The coverline is positioned in the sweet spot to draw attention to the feature article.
symbolic code	one of Barthes' five narrative codes; deeper meanings and binary oppositions
	Symbolic codes in the lexical coding of the magazine article reference the tension between the couple's troubled homelife and their public displays of unity.
syntagm	'chains' of meaning constructed by the grouping and association of signifiers and signifieds
	The sequence of codes at the end, including the appearance of the slogan and pack shot, creates a conventional syntagm which encourages action from the audience.
systems of representation	identified by Hall – our conceptual map, and the language we use to navigate it
	Hall's systems of representation describe both the way we make sense of communications and the signs we use to construct them.
tabloid newspapers	a genre of newspaper that favours entertainment, gossip and human-interest stories. Tabloids tends to use a sensationalist style of reporting. The term is often used when the values of tabloid newspapers are replicated in other media products or forms, e.g. the concept of tabloid TV, tabloid magazines, etc.
talking heads	the use of a mid-shot of someone speaking, usually with limited mise-en-scène
teaser (newspapers/magazines)	a brief indication of the content within the publication. Used to encourage the reader to purchase the publication to be able to read further
technological convergence	the gradual combining of separate technological devices into fewer devices or one device with multiple functions
textual poaching	the act of reappropriating a cultural product which may result in new meanings
	The re-cutting of the series titles on YouTube may be seen as an act of textual poaching.
textual productivity	fan-made texts as sense of ownership of the source text
	The game has stimulated textual productivity in the form of fan art and even fan fiction based on its characters and narratives.
the other	the state of being defined as 'different' due to cultural differences
	The women in the camp are defined as an 'other', potentially narrowing the range of possible readings of their situation.
third order of signification	the relationship between the first and second orders of signification and myths and ideology
	The positioning of the soldier in the aftermath of the attack signifies an ideological reading about the role of British forces in the conflict as peacekeepers.
tilt down	movement where the camera is angled down on its axis
	The rapid tilt down makes the audience experience vertigo.
tilt up	movement where the camera is raised up on its axis
	The tilt up makes the building feel grand in scale.
titling	the use of lexical coding over black or over image – has become very common in digital media texts
	The titling uses discreet typographical codes.
tracking shot/following shot	follows action by travelling alongside or behind it
	The tracking shot keeps pace with the car.
transactional model of communication	used to describe models of communication such as Hall's which build more subtlety and feedback into the stages in a communication chain
	Hall's circuit of culture is a transactional model of communication.
transition	the way in which movement from shot to shot is managed in editing, most often a straight cut
	Shot transitions are unusual because they use many dissolves, meaning one image is superimposed over the previous.

transnationality	in the case of text, having a presence or value that crosses cultural and geographical divides
	The series has transnationality in its appeal to audiences due to use of widely recognisable genre codes.
two-shot	two people in the same shot, often implying a relationship between them
	The friends are shown in two-shot.
two-step flow	communications-based model that highlights the significance of opinion leaders in the transmission of messages in the mass media
	Influencers are a contemporary example of the two-step flow model in action.
typeface	lettering style. All letters and numbers within a typeface will be designed to harmonise
typographical codes	selection of font and graphical choices
	The typographical codes signify on the brand values of the magazine and its arthouse aesthetic.
ultra HD	high-quality digital images
universal themes	themes to which many people across cultures can relate
	The film review emphasises the universal theme of coming-of age and it is this which makes it a truly internationalised product.
variation and change	the tendency of genre texts to reformulate with new qualities to prevent audiences from becoming tired of a formula
	Genres are subject to variation and change, preventing staleness.
vertical integration	acquisition of one company in the production chain of another that offers a different service
viral	the organic sharing of information by word-of-mouth and sharing on social media
virtual communities	groups of people who come together in cyberspace through a shared interest without geographical barriers
	Fans of the show have formed a virtual community.
visibility	how high profile a particular issue, group or event is in media analysis
	People with disabilities have limited visibility in the media.
VoD (video on demand)	any service where users can choose what they want to view and when
	Many streaming services work on the principle of video on demand.
vox populi	soundbites and/or visual clips of different respondents discussing a topic or answering a question intended to reflect a range of opinions
	The use of vox populi suggests this attitude is widely shared.
VSC	Video Standards Council
watershed	in the UK, the point (9.00pm) at which content of a more adult nature may be shown in a television schedule
Web 2.0	phase of internet development summed up by increased human connectivity using technology
weight (visual)	a term used to refer to the effect of the depth, darkness and/or intensity of a design element. Large, dark, textured and warm-coloured elements tend to appear 'heavier' – they have more visual weight. Elements in the foreground or higher on the page tend to appear heavy on the page as do regular shapes and vertical (rather than horizontal) objects
whip pan	rapid following pan, widely used in action sequences
	The use of whip pan lends energy and frenetic pace to the scene.
wide-angle shot	a shot, usually using a specific lens for the purpose, which shows a wide field of view
	The wide-angle shot allows us the see all of the hall in the frame.
worm's-eye shot	extreme low angle or directly from the ground upwards
	The worm's eye shot allows us to absorb the sight of the small bomber plane coming into view.
zoom	movement of the camera lens to bring a subject closer or to distance it
	The slow zoom in intensifies the predicament the man is in.

Glossary of key terms

Index

A

accelerated motion 32
acoustics 256
address, mode of 10, 14, 26
advertising 268–9
   'Are you beach body ready?' Protein World advert (2015) 195–6
   Bisto advert (2021) 33
   as business model 191–2
   codes and features 9, 14–15
   and culture 4
   digital media 50
   Dove brand 293–4
   Green & Black's chocolate advert (2017) 71–2, 79
   'Kenzo: World' perfume advert (2016) 25–6
   layouts and sizes 242
   Live for Now Pepsi advert (2017) 223
   male grooming products 46
   Man on the Moon John Lewis advert (2015) 38
   and myth 6
   print advertising 14–16, 20
   regulation 195–6
   VIM 1950s advert 116
   see also trailers
Advertising Standards Authority (ASA) 195
advertorials 14, 192
aerial shot 29
age
   of audiences 136–7, 280
   representations of 104
algorithms 211
alternative media 189
Althusser, Louis 80, 110, 120
American Gods (2017) 40–1
analepsis 35
analysis, step-by-step 217–19
anchorage 7
Anderson, Benedict 126
Andrew, Dudley 20
Angels (2015) 30
apparatus 31
arbitrary relationships 4
arbitrary signs 7
archetypes 38–9
'Are you beach body ready?' Protein World advert (2015) 195–6
Art of Manliness website 51
A Series of Unfortunate Events (2017) 69
atmosphere 34

Attitude magazine 107
audiences
   constructing 135–6
   demographics and profiling 135–42, 226, 271, 280
   end of audience theory 167–71
   expectations of 43–4, 135, 143
   fan culture 84, 159–67
   nature of 112
   participatory culture 163–7, 169–71, 270
   responses of 220–3, 281
   role of 100–1
   theories of impacts and effects 145–58
audio production 260
audio-visual media
   editing 31–3
   genre 41–5, 72–4, 76
   intertextuality 46–7
   moving image production 252–60
   narratives 35–41
   recording equipment 238–9
   semiotic analysis 26, 43
   technical codes 24–6
   see also camerawork
augmented reality (AR) 75, 85, 86, 144
aural codes 33, 60, 70
average programme stream (APS) 184

B

background sound 34
backstories 61–2
Bandura, Albert 147, 149
banner 49, 50
bardic function 147
Barthes, Roland 5–6, 16–18, 38, 55, 61–2, 71–2, 78
Baudrillard, Jean 84–7
BBC (British Broadcasting Corporation)
   Charter 193
   children's television 137
   cultural capital 141
   public service broadcasting (PSB) 114, 192–3
   trustworthiness 157
bias 77, 94, 157, 211
binary oppositions 79–81, 106, 299
bird's eye shot 28, 29
Bisto advert (2021) 33
Black Mirror (2011) 87
Black Panther: Wakanda Forever (2022) 217–20

Blumler, Jay G. 152, 205
Bobo doll 147, 152
body language 10, 25
body text 14
Bourdieu, Pierre 140–1
Bowling for Columbine (2000) 154
Boyd, Danah 166
brand ambassadors 201
brand recognition 11, 207–8
brand values 15
bricolage 84
Britain's Got Talent 220–1
British Film Institute (BFI) 137
Broadcasters' Audience Research Board (Barb) 183
broadcasting licences 186
Butler, Judith 123

C

Cahoone, Lawrence 82
camera positioning 10, 11
   see also proxemics
cameras 238
camerawork
   analysing 69
   angles 28–9
   computer games 60
   movements 29–30
   principles of filming 253–6
   shot types 27–8
canted angle 28, 29
captioning (video) 54
captions (print) 11
catchphrases 22
celebrities, and social media 57, 58, 201
celebrity endorsement 46
censorship 194, 197
centrist politics 78
Chandler, Daniel 4, 5
Channel 4 192
character types 38–40
children's television 137
Chomsky, Noam 111
Chuck (2007–12) 160
circuit of communication 101
circulation 174
citizen journalism 52, 169, 213
Citizen Khan (2012) 129
clawback 147
clickbait 211
close-up 27, 251
clothing 9, 146, 272
codes, creating meaning 7

see also technical codes
Cohen, Stanley 150
collective identity 112, 113
colour codes 9, 21, 25
colourisation 33
comedy 42
commercialisation 175
communication, models of 100–1
community guidelines 197
compassion fatigue 155
composite images 14, 15
compression of time 32
computer games 59–66, 75, 94, 144, 151, 159, 181, 198, 240, 271
   see also audio-visual media; gamers
conglomerates 188
connotations 5, 7, 38, 51, 218
constructionist approach 99
consumerism 6, 160, 163
consumption 84–5
content providers 174
contrapuntal sound 34
copy 11
copyright 213
copywriting 15
Cornwall 106
corpus 43
cosplay 162–3
counter-representations 92, 106–7, 109
countertypes 109
Country Life magazine 303–4
coverlines 12, 13
crab 29, 30
crane shot 29
critical theory 3
cropping 9, 10, 251–2
cultivation theory 153–5
cultural absolutism 130
cultural capital 140–2, 162–3
cultural categories 43, 58, 64
cultural change 76
cultural code 17, 18, 38, 62, 72
cultural hegemony 110–11
cultural impacts 227
cultural imperialism 114, 206
cultural myths 6, 81
cultural relativism 114
cultural shorthand 91
cultural tropes 35
Curran, James 186
cutaway shot 27, 33
cutting 33, 258–9

D

Daily Telegraph 143
Das, Ranjana 168–9
decelerated motion 32
decoding 7, 100
   see also print media: decoding
deconstruction 79
décor 9, 10, 25–6
Delwiche, Aaron 163

denotation 5, 7
deregulation 187
desensitisation 155
design principles 243
   see also print production
desktop publishing (DTP) 240–6
diaspora 130
diegesis 34, 35
diegetic sound 34, 70
digital immigrants 167
digital locker systems 143
digital media
   circulation 184
   codes and conventions 49–50
   computer games 59–66
   digital revolution 143–5, 167–8
   genre 58, 63–5, 75
   historical contexts 181–3
   intertextuality 65–6
   narratives 54–7
   online video content 52–4
   and participatory culture 164
   personalisation 145, 183
   regulation 196–9
   websites 49–51, 75
disability, representations of 105
Disneyland 87
disruption 16
distortion 120
distribution 174
diversification 174, 188, 207
documentaries 72–3, 85, 109, 264
dolly 29, 31, 238
dominant ideology 6, 7, 39, 110–11
double consciousness 129
Dove brand 293–4
dress code 9, 22, 24–6
drop cap 14
dub 257
Dyer, Richard 92
dynamic content 50

E

early adopters 173
echo-chambers 211–12
editing
   audio-visual media 31–3, 258
   computer games 60
   software 238
   sound 259–62
   still images 251–2
effects theories 145–52
encoding 7, 100
enculturation 153
enigma 8
entry points 14
equilibrium 16
ergodic narrative 62
essay writing 230–6
establishing shot 27
ethics, in photo-journalism 9
ethnicity 139

   see also race representation
Exodus: Our Journey to Europe (2016) 109
extra diegetic narrator 34

F

Facebook 212–13, 216, 223, 270
fade-through-black 32
fake news 212–13
false consciousness 212
fan culture 84, 159–67
female gaze 116
feminism 114–23
film magazines 19
film posters 15, 17
first order of signification 5
fish-eye shot 27
Fiske, John 147, 161–3
flashback 35
flashforward 35, 36
focus 29, 30
foley 255, 259
folk devils 150–1
following shot 29
font styles 11, 21, 246
framing 9, 10, 25, 249
free markets 174, 207

G

gamers 108
gaming *see* computer games
Gauntlett, David 112–13, 151–2
gender
   and audiences 137, 280
   media representations of 101–3, 114–21, 124
   performativity 123
   and tropes 39
genre 17
   audience expectations 43–4, 135
   in audio-visual media 41–5, 72–4, 76
   codes and conventions 45, 74
   in computer games 63–5
   and cultural change 75–6
   in digital media 58, 63–5, 75
   hybridisation 43, 74
   in print media 18–22, 75
   sub-genres 43, 44, 74
Gerbner, George 153–4
gestural codes 25
Gillmor, Dan 169
Gilroy, Paul 129–31
globalisation 142–3, 185, 187
global village 143
Goode, Erich 150
Google Analytics 184
Gramsci, Antonio 110, 120
Grand Theft Auto V (2013) 60
graphical elements 11, 12
grassroots journalism 169
Great British Bake Off 227–8

Great British Social Class Survey (2013) 140–1
Green & Black's chocolate advert (2017) 71–2, 79
gross constituent units 81
Guardian 143

H

Hall, Stuart 91, 99–101, 158
hand-held shot 29
hard news 138, 211
hegemony 110–11, 123, 126
Hello! magazine 110–11
Henderson, Jennifer J. 163
hermeneutic code 16–17, 18, 38, 62, 71
hero 39
hero image 49, 50
heteronormativity 110
high angle 28, 29, 32, 251
Hollow Knight (2017) 62–3
hooks 35, 36
hooks, bell 121–2
house style 11, 12
hybridisation 43, 74
hyperlinks 50
hyperreality 86–7
hypertextuality 50
hypodermic needle model 146, 149

I

iconic signs 5, 8
iconography 21, 22, 26
identity 6, 57, 111–13
idents 261
ideological reading 77–8, 80
ideologies 6, 45, 77–8, 80, 110–11
implosion 84
independent media production 189–90
Independent Press Standards Organisation (IPSO) 193
indexical signs 5, 8
individuality paradox 112
influencers 201
in-groups 106
Inspire Her Mind Verizon advert (2016) 120–1
Instagram 143, 199, 200, 213, 236, 271
intentional approach 99
Internet Service Providers' Association (ISPA) 197–8
Internet Watch Foundation (IWF) 198
interpellation 80–1
intersectionality 119, 121–2
intertextuality 83–7
   audio-visual media 46–7
   digital media 65–6
   print media 21–2
   see also media language
intra-diegetic narrator 34
Ito, Mimi 166
Iuzzolino, Walter 143

J

Jason Bourne (2016) 103
Jenkins, Henry 142, 160, 164–7
jib shot 29, 31
Jonze, Spike 25
journalism
   citizen journalism 52, 169, 213
   grassroots 169
   narrative theory 55
   photo-journalism 9, 246
   see also news
jump cut 31

K

Katz, Elihu 152, 205
Keepers, The (2017) 72–3
'Kenzo: World' perfume advert (2016) 25–6
Kowert, Rachel 108

L

languages 4–5
   see also media language
left side third 12, 13
left-wing politics 78
legacy media 183
lettering systems 4
Letter to the Free (2016) 80, 297
Leveson Report 2012 187
Lévi-Strauss, Claude 61, 78, 79–81
Levy, Ariel 117
lexical codes 11, 12, 15, 22, 33, 51
Life is Strange (2015) 66
lighting 25–6, 247, 251, 255, 257
Lights Out (2013) 200
linguistics 2–3
lipstick feminism 117
Live for Now Pepsi advert (2017) 223
Livingstone, Sonia 168–9
location 10, 25–6, 247
logos 15
long shot 27, 28
lore 61–2
low angle 28, 29, 32, 251

M

magazines 267–8
   analysing 285
   design elements 12–14
   film magazines 19
   front covers 6, 12–13
   genre 18–22, 75
   historical contexts 176–7
   layouts and sizes 241
   online 52
   true crime magazines 21
   see also print media
mainstreaming 154
male gaze 116
male grooming products 46
Man on the Moon John Lewis advert (2015) 38

marginalised communities 103
Marvel 207–9, 217–19
Marxist theories 110, 126
masculinity 102–3, 125
mass media 3
masterplot 40
masthead 12, 13
McLuhan, Marshall 143
mean world index 154
media industries
   business models 190–3
   circulation 174, 184–6, 199
   distribution 174, 183–6, 199
   historical contexts 173–83
   impacts of 226–9
   ownership and control 186–90
   regulation 193–9, 206–7
   technological changes 175
   see also individual industries by name
media language 68, 218–19
   postmodernism 21, 45, 82–7
   post-structuralism 2–3, 79, 82
   structuralism 2–3, 78–81, 109
   values and ideologies 77–8
   see also intertextuality
media literacy 148–9, 193
media representations
   abstract concepts 94
   of age 104
   analysing 93–4, 96–7
   constructing reality 98–110
   counter-representations 92, 106–7, 109
   cultural contexts 132
   as cultural hegemony 110–11
   of disability 105
   of ethnicity, race and religion 103–4, 125–31
   forms and techniques used 95–7
   of gender and sexuality 101–3, 107, 114–21, 124
   historical contexts 131
   and ideology 110–11
   industry contexts 114
   of men 102–3, 125
   misrepresentation 95, 107–8
   of place 106
   of social class 104
   social contexts 131
   social impacts 226–7
   stereotypes 42, 92, 94, 101–10, 120, 127
   theories of identity 111–13
   theories of representation 91–7
   of women 102, 115–22
mediation 94
medium shot 27, 28
Meet the Superhumans (2012) 105
menu strips 12
#MeToo 116–17
Metroidvania games 64–5
Miele 15

mirrors 26
mise-en-scène 24–5, 47, 59–60, 69–70, 247–8, 257
misrepresentation 95, 107–8
mock documentaries 85
mode of address 10, 14, 26
Molchanov, Alexey 58
monarchy 110–11
monopolies 174
montage editing 31
moral panics 146, 150–1, 154
moving image production 252–60
multiculturalism 125–31
multi-take 32
Mulvey, Laura 116
music industry 180–1
music score 34
music videos 29, 30, 271–2, 298
mythemes 81
myths 6, 8, 79, 81, 102

N

narration styles 35
narrative arc 35
narrative closure 35
narrative codes 16–18, 38
narrative enigma 8, 16–17
narrative theory 16–18, 55, 70–2, 79–81, 224–5, 299
   audio-visual media 35–41
   binary oppositions 79–81
   computer games 61–3
   digital media 54–7
   print media 15–18
narratology 2, 35, 78
narrators 34
narrowcast 205
National Readership Survey (NRS) 184
Neale, Stephen 41, 43, 45, 64, 74, 298
Nehuda, Ben 150
neo-liberalism 174, 207
neo-Marxist theories 140
Netflix 202–7
news
   clickbait 211
   as conversation 169
   fake news 212–13
   online 55–6, 75, 209–11, 269
   personalisation 145
   political agendas 77, 138, 211, 228
   regulation 210
   and social class 138
   and social media 209–13
   trustworthiness 157
   see also journalism
newspapers 77, 92, 138–9, 143, 175–6, 194, 209–10, 228, 241, 266–7
   see also print media
No Man's Sky (2016) 65
non-diegetic sound 34
non-verbal codes 10, 25–6

O

OA, The (2016) 124
Ofcom 184, 193, 195–7
Olatunji, Olajide 53
Oldmeadow, Julian 108
omniscient narration 35, 36
Omo soap powder 6
online magazines 52
online video content 52–4, 144, 199–200
   see also YouTube
On Our Radar website 55–6
order of signification 5–6
otherness 107, 127
out-groups 106
Outlander (2014) 44
over-the-shoulder shot 27, 28, 32, 254

P

panning 29, 30
paparazzi 246
paradigm 26
parallel development 32
parallel sound 34
Paralympics 105
para-proxemics 10, 24–5, 29
Paris Match 6
parody 45, 76, 83, 85
participatory culture 163–7, 169–71, 270
participatory gap 142
participatory media 56–7
passive ideological state apparatus 110
pastiche 83
patriarchy 102, 114, 125
Peirce, Charles 5
Perkins, Tessa 108–9
personalisation 145, 183
photography 9, 10, 246–52
photo-journalism 9, 246
plot 40
plugins 50
podcasting 74–5, 177–8, 265
point-of-view shot 27, 28
Pokémon Go (2016) 144
Poldark (2015–19) 106
Polite Society (2023) 17
political bias 77, 138, 211, 228–9
polysemic signs 91
post-broadcast era 52
postcolonialism 125–8, 130–1
post-feminism 117–18
postmodernism 21, 45, 82–7
post-production 249, 258
post-structuralism 2–3, 79, 82
press packs 139
primary images 12, 13
print advertising 14–16, 20
print media
   circulation 184
   decoding 2–15
   digital revolution 143
   and genre 18–22
   intertextuality 21–2
   reading narratives 15–18
   regulation 196
   semiotic analysis 2–23
   technical codes 9–15
   see also magazines; newspapers
print production 240–6
Prisoners (Temporary Discharge for Ill-Health) Act 1913 115
proairetic code 17, 18, 38, 62, 71
profiling 135–6
prolepsis 35, 36
propaganda 22, 111
proprietary fonts 11, 12
props 9, 10, 25–6, 247
prosumers 160–1
proxemics 10, 11, 12, 24–5
public domain 213
public service broadcasting (PSB) 114, 192–3
puff 12, 13
pull quotes 14

Q

qualitative representational analysis 93
Qualley, Margaret 26
quantitative representational analysis 93
queer theory 114, 123
quest narrative 40, 62

R

race representations 103–4, 125–31
racial essentialism 130
radio 74–5, 94, 144, 159, 177, 184, 195, 265
Radio Joint Audience Research (RAJAR) 184
raunch culture 117–18
reaction shot 27, 28, 32
reality TV 76, 85, 97, 105, 135
reception theory 156–8
referential code 17, 18, 38, 62, 72
reflective approach 99
Reith, John 192
representation
   definition 92
   systems of 99
   see also media representations
right-wing politics 78
role-playing games (RPGs) 61, 64
rolling news 210

S

Said, Edward 127
Saussure, Ferdinand de 3, 7, 78–9
Schatz, Thomas 45
scheduling 137, 183
score 34
screen time 32
Seaton, Jean 186

secondary images   12, 13
second order of signification   5
selective focus   29
self-referentiality   86
semantic code   17, 18, 38, 62, 71
semiology   3, 78–9
semiotic analysis   68
   audio-visual media   24–6, 43
   print media   2–23
semiotic productivity   162
semiotics   2, 91
sensationalism   211
Serial (2014)   178, 261, 265
sexuality, media representations of   101–3, 107
shadow cultural economy   161, 166
shareholders   174
Sherlock Holmes   166
She's Always A Woman John Lewis advert (2010)   120–1
Shirky, Clay   169–71, 174
shooting script   253
shot list   253
shot types   27
sidebars   243
signification   3–6, 8, 26, 79, 119
signifying practices   91
signs
   decoding   4–6
   and signifiers   3–6, 8, 26, 79–80
   and simulacra   85–6
   systems of representation   99
Simpsons, The   47
simulacrum   84–6
simulation   59, 86
situation comedy   42
skyscraper   49, 50
slogans   22
slug   14, 50
SMCR (Source/Message/Channel/Receiver) model   100
soap operas   76
social class   104, 138, 140–2
social learning theory   147–8, 149
social media   87, 109, 216, 270–1
   audience responses   221–2
   Facebook   212–13, 216, 223, 270
   impacts of   226
   influencers   200–1
   Instagram   143, 199, 200, 213, 236, 271
   and news   209–13
   regulation   197
   TikTok   52, 201, 270–1
   usage   56–8
   X (formerly Twitter)   213, 270
soft news   138, 211
sound

atmosphere   34
   computer games   60
   diegetic   34
   editing   259–62
   editing software   239
   foley   255, 259
   recording   239, 255–6
sound mix   33
soundscapes   34, 60
split screen   32
sport   58, 105, 184
Star Trek: Discovery (2017)   122
stereotypes   42, 91–2, 94, 101–10, 120, 127
stock characters   39
Stranger Things (2016)   37
straplines   12, 13
structuralism   2–3, 78–81, 109
studio shoots   14
sub-genres   43, 44, 74
sub-plots   36
suffragette poster (1913)   115
sweet spot   12, 13
symbolic code   17, 18, 26, 38, 62, 72
symbolic signs   5, 7
syntagm   26

T

talking heads   211
technical codes   69–70, 92, 94
   audio-visual media   24–6
   digital media   49–54
   print media   9–15
television
   digital revolution   143
   documentaries   72–3, 85, 109, 264
   fictional programming   265
   historical contexts   178–80
   Marvel   207–9
   Netflix   202–7
   non-fiction programming   264
   reality TV   76, 85, 97, 105, 135
   regulation   195, 206–7
   video-on-demand (VOD)   74, 143, 179–80
   see also audio-visual media
textual poaching   164–5
third order of signification   6
TikTok   52, 201, 270
tilting   29, 30, 33
time, passage of   32
titling   33
Tobias, Ronald   40
Todorov, Tzvetan   16, 36, 55, 61–2, 71, 224
Toffler, Alvin   160
tracking shot   29, 30
trailers   73, 95, 105, 208, 268–9

transactional model of communication   100
transitions   32
transmission models   100
transnationality   127
tripod   238
tropes   35, 39
true crime magazines   21
trust, of news sources   157
Twitter   213
two-shot   27, 28, 254
two-step flow model   146
typeface   244–5
typographical codes   11, 12, 21, 33

U

Undateables, The (2016)   105
universal themes   35
urbanisation   84
uses and gratifications theory   152–3

V

van Zoonen, Liesbet   119–20
video-on-demand (VOD)   74, 143, 179–80
Video Standards Council (VSC)   198
VIM 1950s advert   116
violence on screen   147, 149, 153–5
viral video   52
virtual communities   56
virtual reality (VR)   75, 144
vlogs   53–4, 161
vox pops   94

W

watershed   195, 206
Web 2.0   182, 187
web-page design   50
websites   75, 269–70
   card-based design   51
   codes and features   49–50
   web design software   239–40
Weinstein, Harvey   116–17
wide-angle shot   27, 28
worm's-eye shot   28, 29

X

X (formerly Twitter)   213, 270

Y

Yeoh, Michelle   57
YouTube   52–3, 75, 142, 161, 182, 197, 200, 211

Z

zooms   29, 30
Zuckerberg, Mark   212–13

Acknowledgements

Photo credits

Photos reproduced by permission of: **p.3** *r* © pio3/stock.adobe.com, *br* © Suraphol/stock.adobe.com; **p.4** © NYgraphic/stock.adobe.com; **p.5** *c* © Stefan Mokrzecki/stock.adobe.com, *r* © mumindurmaz35/stock.adobe.com; **p.6** Neil Baylis/Alamy Stock Photo; **p.7** © Anthony/stock.adobe.com; **p.8** *tl* © Hedgehog/stock.adobe.com, *l* © Laura Pashkevich/stock.adobe.com; **p.10** © DimaBerlin/stock.adobe.com; **p.13** *bl* © Anthem Publishing/www.womensrunning.co.uk, *br* © The English Garden/Clive Nichols; **p.15** © 20th Century Fox Film Corp./Everett Collection Inc/Alamy Stock Photo; **p.17** © FlixPix/Alamy Stock Photo; **p.19** © Antiques & Collectables/Alamy Stock Photo; **p.20** © Chris Jobs/Alamy Stock Photo; **p.22** © World History Archive/Alamy Stock Photo; **p.25** *t* © IxMaster/Shutterstock.com, *b* © s_bukley/Shutterstock.com; **p.27** *l* © jakubstepan/stock.adobe.com, *r* © NDABCREATIVITY/stock.adobe.com; **p.28** *l* © fesenko/stock.adobe.com, *r* © NMest/stock.adobe.com; **p.30** © Pitroviz/Shutterstock.com; **p.33** © rocketclips/stock.adobe.com; **p.37** © Netflix/Everett Collection Inc/Alamy Stock Photo; **p.39** © Ivy Close Images/Alamy Stock Photo; **p.41** © STARZ/Album/Alamy Stock Photo; **p.42** © Moviestore Collection Ltd/Alamy Stock Photo; **p.43** © Tim P. Whitby/Getty Images for Sky; **p.44** © Starz!/Everett Collection Inc/Alamy Stock Photo; **p.45** © BFA/Alamy Stock Photo; **p.47** © 20th Century Fox Film Corp./Everett Collection Inc/Alamy Stock Photo; **p.49** © peshkova/stock.adobe.com; **p.51** © The Art of Manliness; **p.53** © Andrey Popov/stock.adobe.com; **p.54** © Fred Duval/Shutterstock.com; **p.56** © On Our Radar; **p.58** © YANN COATSALIOU/AFP via Getty Images; **p.59** © smile35/stock.adobe.com; **p.60** © Rokas Tenys/Alamy Stock Photo; **p.63** © Team Cherry via Wikipedia/Fair use; **p.65** © Daniel Krasoń/Alamy Stock Photo; **p.66** © flowgraph/Shutterstock.com; **p.68** © PureSolution/stock.adobe.com; **p.69** © Netflix/Everett Collection Inc/Alamy Stock Photo; **p.70** © Netflix/Everett Collection Inc/Alamy Stock Photo; **p.71** © Cheryl Ann Studio/Shutterstock.com; **p.72** © FILM 45/TRIPOD MEDIA/Album/Alamy Stock Photo; **p.74** © Starz!/Everett Collection Inc/Alamy Stock Photo; **p.75** © kite_rin/stock.adobe.com; **p.77** © The Sunday Times Magazine/News Licensing; **p.78** © alexmillos/Shutterstock.com; **p.79** © UNESCO/Michel Ravassard via Wikipedia/Creative Commons Attribution 3.0 Unported license; **p.81** © Ian/stock.adobe.com; **p.83** © droopy76/Shutterstock.com; **p.85** © Feel good studio/stock.adobe.com; **p.87** © TCD/Prod.DB/Alamy Stock Photo; **p.88** © ZOO.BY/Shutterstock.com; **p.92** *c* © Giannis Papanikos/Shutterstock.com, *b* © Monkey Business/stock.adobe.com; **p.93** © Faraways/Shutterstock.com; **p.98** *t* © Jordan Strauss/Invision/Associated Press/Alamy Stock Photo, *l* reproduced with kind permission of Emma Harper, *r* © WALT DISNEY PICTURES/Album/Alamy Stock Photo; **p.100** © ARaihanDOTcom/Shutterstock.com; **p.102** © Go My Media/Shutterstock.com; **p.103** © Universal Pictures/Everett Collection Inc/Alamy Stock Photo; **p.104** © David Grossman/Alamy Stock Photo; **p.105** © Howard Davies/Alamy Stock Photo; **p.107** *l* Reproduced by permission of Emerald Life, *r* © Strand Releasing/Everett Collection Inc/Alamy Stock Photo; **p.109** © Craig Stennett/Alamy Stock Photo; **p.111** *t* © Kathy deWitt/Alamy Stock Photo, *r* © Mirko Kuzmanovic/Shutterstock.com; **p.112** Reproduced with kind permission of David Gauntlett; **p.114** © PA Images/Alamy Stock Photo; **p.115** © GRANGER - Historical Picture Archive/Alamy Stock Photo; **p.116** *l* © Neil Baylis/Alamy Stock Photo, *r* © Photo 12/Alamy Stock Photo; **p.117** © Masarik/stock.adobe.com; **p.118** © Yaacov Dagan/Alamy Stock Photo; **p.119** Reproduced with kind permission of Liesbet van Zoonen; **p.121** © Anthony Barboza/Getty Images; **p.122** © Pictorial Press Ltd/Alamy Stock Photo; **p.123** © Wirestock Creators/Shutterstock.com; **p.124** © JoJo Whilden/Netflix/Everett Collection Inc/Alamy Stock Photo; **p.128** © Asian Express; **p.129** *c* © WENN Rights Ltd/Alamy Stock Photo, *b* © Lewis Patrick/Shutterstock.com; **p.135** © Anton Gvozdikov/stock.adobe.com; **p.137** *tl* © Ludo Studio/Album/Alamy Stock Photo, *tr* © BBC Studios - British Broadcasting Corporation (BBC) /TCD/ Prod.DB/Alamy Stock Photo; **p.139** © Eastern Eye; **p.141** © Wikimedia Commons/Public Domain; **p.142** © vectorfusionart/stock.adobe.com; **p.143** © Tabatha Fireman/Getty Images; **p.144** © Friedrich Stark/Alamy Stock Photo; **p.146** © HARTSWOOD FILMS/BBC WALES/Album/Alamy Stock Photo; **p.147** © ZZTop1958/Shutterstock.com; **p.150** © epa european pressphoto agency b.v./Alamy Stock Photo; **p.151** © The Sun/News Licensing; **p.153** © Moviestore Collection Ltd/Alamy Stock Photo; **p.154** © Cinematic/Alamy Stock Photo; **p.156** © leungchopan/stock.adobe.com; **p.158** © Eamonn McCabe/Popperfoto via Getty Images; **p.160** © Cinematic/Alamy Stock Photo; **p.161** © Xavier Collin/Image Press Agency/Alamy Stock Photo; **p.162** © Mauro Rodrigues/Shutterstock.com; **p.163** © VM.Shpilka/Shutterstock.com; **p.164** © Odua Images/stock.adobe.com; **p.165** © Chris Harvey/Shutterstock/com; **p.166** © OnTheRoad/Alamy Stock Photo; **p.169** © James Duncan Davidson via Wikimedia/CC BY 2.0; **p.174** © Stuart Miles/Shutterstock.com; **p.175** © Richard Levine/Alamy

Stock Photo; **p.176** © borabajk/stock.adobe.com; **p.177** *t* © Alan Wilson/Alamy Stock Photo, *b* © Everett Collection/Shutterstock; **p.179** © Alan Wilson/Alamy Stock Photo; **p.180** © True Images/Alamy Stock Photo; **p.181** © Sergey/stock.adobe.com; **p.182** © Ian West/PA Images/Alamy Stock Photo; **p.185** © rblfmr/Shutterstock.com; **p.186** © Hit Stop Media/Shutterstock.com; **p.187** © NEIL SPENCE/Alamy Stock Photo; **p.188** © OKIDO Magazine; **p.190** © mauritius images GmbH/Alamy Stock Photo; **p.196** © Richard Levine/Alamy Stock Photo; **p.199** © highwaystarz/stock.adobe.com; **p.200** © TCD/Prod.DB/Alamy Stock Photo (© Warner Bros. - New Line Cinema - Atomic Monster - Grey Matter Productions); **p.201** © Song_about_summer/Shutterstock.com; **p.202** © Tinseltown/Shutterstock.com; **p.203** © ArtMediaWorx/Shutterstock.com; **p.204** *tl* © Erman Gunes/ Shutterstock.com, *tr* © CBS TELEVISION/Album/Alamy Stock Photo; *b* © NETFLIX/Album/Alamy Stock Photo ; **p.205** © Trinity Mirror/Mirrorpix/Alamy Stock Photo; **p.208** © FlixPix/Disney/Alamy Stock Photo; **p.210** © Dedi Grigoroiu/Shutterstock.com; **p.215** © Irina Popova/stock.adobe.com; **p.217** © FlixPix/Alamy Stock Photo; **p.221** © Ploppy/Alamy Stock Photo; **p.222** *l* © Artists Studio/Collection Christophel/Alamy Stock Photo, *bl* © Niko Tavernise/HBO Max/ WarnerMedia Entertainment/The Hollywood Archive; **p.223** © Retro AdArchives/Alamy Stock Photo; **p.225** © PlayStation Productions/Sony Pictures Television/Album/Alamy Stock Photo; **p.226** © Featureflash Photo Agency/Shutterstock.com; **p.227** *r* © Featureflash Photo Agency/Shutterstock.com, *l* © Scottish Government via Wikimedia Commons/CC BY 2.0; **p.228** *t* © North West News/Alamy Stock Photo, *b* © HBO/PictureLux/The Hollywood Archive/Alamy Stock Photo; **p.229** © Ned Snowman/Shutterstock.com; **p.230** © lovelyday12/stock.adobe.com; **p.234** © FlixPix/Alamy Stock Photo; **p.239** *t* © nisara/stock.adobe.com, *c* © dobrorez/stock.adobe.com; **p.240** © themorningglory/stock.adobe.com; **p.242** *l* © I-Wei Huang/stock.adobe.com, *r* © Rawpixel.com/stock.adobe.com; **p.243** *r* © Paul Marriott/Alamy Stock Photo, *br* © aluna1/stock.adobe.com; **p.244** © Paul Buceta/Strong Magazine ; **p.246** © Robert Daly/KOTO/stock.adobe.com; **p.248** *tl* © andrii kobryn/stock.adobe.com, *tr* © amixstudio/stock.adobe.com; **p.249** © Photo 12/Alamy Stock Photo; **p.250** *tl* © Mix and Match Studio/stock.adobe.com, *tr* © boyloso/stock.adobe.com, *l* © DmitryDolgikh/stock.adobe.com; **p.251** *tl* © Firefighter Montreal/stock.adobe.com, *tr* © stone36/stock.adobe.com; **p.252** © Davide Angelini/stock.adobe.com; **p.253** © Cinematic/Alamy Stock Photo; **p.255** © Eugene Kalenkovich/stock.adobe.com; **p.256** *l* © peopleimages.com/stock.adobe.com, *bl* © UNIVERSAL CABLE PRODUCTIONS/Album/ Alamy Stock Photo; **p.257** © Photo 12/Alamy Stock Photo; **p.258** © yaroslav1986/stock.adobe.com; **p.260** *tl* © Rawpixel.com/stock.adobe.com, *l* © zhu difeng/stock.adobe.com, *bl* © smolaw11/stock.adobe.com; **p.262** © MclittleStock/stock.adobe.com; **p.264** © WENN Rights Ltd/Alamy Stock Photo; **p.265** *t* © SOPA Images Limited/Alamy Stock Photo, *c* © Nick Beer/stock.adobe.com; **p.266** *t* © Alan D West/Alamy Stock Photo, *b* © Maurice Savage/Alamy Stock Photo; **p.267** © Railway Modeller; **p.268** © Classic Cars; **p.271** *tr* © CoCo Jones/Alamy Stock Photo, *r* © frimufilms/stock.adobe.com; **p.272** *tl* © Everett Collection Inc/Alamy Stock Photo, *l* © Mihail/stock.adobe.com; **p.273** © Monkey Business/stock.adobe.com; **p.274** © Jahanzaib Naiyyer/stock.adobe.com; **p.275** © M-Production/stock.adobe.com; **p.278** © Sentavio/stock.adobe.com; **p.280** © Featureflash Photo Agency/Shutterstock.com; **p.281** © Ganna Tokolova/Shutterstock.com; **p.290** © Gorodenkoff/stock.adobe.com; **p.293** © Retro AdArchives/Alamy Stock Photo; **p.301** © fergregory/stock.adobe.com; **p.303** © Country Life Magazine; **p.307** © Thx4Stock team/Shutterstock.com; **p.308** © Faiz/stock.adobe.com.